The Long Crisis

The Long Crisis

*New York City and
the Path to Neoliberalism*

BENJAMIN HOLTZMAN

OXFORD
UNIVERSITY PRESS

OXFORD
UNIVERSITY PRESS

Oxford University Press is a department of the University of Oxford. It furthers
the University's objective of excellence in research, scholarship, and education
by publishing worldwide. Oxford is a registered trade mark of Oxford University
Press in the UK and certain other countries.

Published in the United States of America by Oxford University Press
198 Madison Avenue, New York, NY 10016, United States of America.

Library of Congress Cataloging-in-Publication Data
Names: Holtzman, Benjamin, author.
Title: The long crisis : New York City and the path to neoliberalism /
Benjamin Holtzman.
Description: New York, NY : Oxford University Press, [2021] |
Includes bibliographical references and index.
Identifiers: LCCN 2020025576 (print) | LCCN 2020025577 (ebook) |
ISBN 9780190843700 (hardback) | ISBN 9780190843724 (epub) |
ISBN 9780190843731
Subjects: LCSH: Urban renewal—New York (State)—New York—History—
20th century. | Urban policy—New York (State)—New York—History—
20th century. | Capitalism—New York (State)—New York—History—
20th century. | Neoliberalism—New York (State)—New York—History—
20th century. | New York (N.Y.)—Economic policy. | New York (N.Y.)—History—1951–
Classification: LCC HT177.N5 H55 2021 (print) |
LCC HT177.N5 (ebook) | DDC 307.3/4160974710904—dc23
LC record available at https://lccn.loc.gov/2020025576
LC ebook record available at https://lccn.loc.gov/2020025577

1 3 5 7 9 8 6 4 2
Printed by Sheridan Books, Inc., United States of America

For Ari and Ruby

Contents

Acknowledgments   ix

Introduction   1

1. Low-Income Housing in Crisis   20

2. From Renters to Owners   58

3. Remaking Public Parks   95

4. Patrolling City Streets   133

5. The Trouble with Development   167

6. The Governance of Homelessness and Public Space   200

Conclusion   235

Notes   243

Index   313

Acknowledgments

I AM TRULY grateful to have the opportunity to thank the many people who made undertaking and completing this book possible.

This project began at Brown University under the direction of Robert Self. Robert has been an extraordinary mentor. He has been unfailingly sage with his feedback, encouraging with his guidance, and generous with his time. I will, in short, forever be grateful for the support he has given to this project and to me. Sandy Zipp has been an excellent mentor and friend since our first conversation, which spanned from the state of metropolitan history to DC punk. His critical feedback, spirited encouragement, and genuine intellectual curiosity have greatly enhanced this project's development.

I am truly grateful to Kim Phillips-Fein, who years ago met with me to discuss 1970s New York and then graciously agreed to be on my committee, for the guidance, time, and support she has given to me and this project. Suleiman Osman generously served as my faculty mentor as part of my Miller Center fellowship and he has remained a consistently insightful and kind colleague in the years since.

Several fellowships not only provided generous and necessary financial support, but also fostered intellectual and collegial environments that proved critical to researching and writing this book: the Postdoctoral Visiting Scholar fellowship at the American Academy of Arts & Sciences; the National Fellowship at the Miller Center at the University of Virginia; and the Mellon Fellowship for Dissertation Research in Original Sources at the Council on Library and Information Resources. I also benefited from a number of grants that underwrote critical research trips: the Thompson Writing Program Research Grant and the Professional Development Award at Duke University; the New York State Library Anna K. and Mary E. Cunningham Research Residency; the New York State Archives Larry J. Hackman Research Residency Award; the University of Texas-Austin

Dolph Briscoe Center for American History William and Madeline Welder Smith Research Travel Award; the Vassar College James Ryland and Georgia A. Kendrick Fellowship; and the William G. McLoughlin Travel Fund, A. Molho Graduate Travel Fund, and the Graduate Research Travel Grant, all from Brown University.

Archivists were, of course, indispensable to undertaking the research at the heart of this book. I would particularly like to thank Douglas Dicarlo at the La Guardia and Wagner Archives; Dwight Johnson and the late Leonora Gidlund at the New York City Municipal Archives; Jim Folts at the New York State Archives; Kaitilin Griffin at the New York City Department of Parks & Recreation; and Erin Butler at the Greenacre Reference Library of the Municipal Art Society of New York. I am also grateful to the entire staff at these archives as well as the archivists and librarians at the Tamiment Library/Robert F. Wagner Labor Archives at New York University; Dolph Briscoe Center for American History at the University of Texas-Austin; City Hall Library of New York; Bryant Park Corporation Archive; Rare Book & Manuscript Library and the Avery Architectural and Fine Arts Library at Columbia University; Brooklyn College Library Archives and Special Collections; New York State Library; Association for a Better New York; Citizens Committee for New York City; Council of New York City Cooperatives; Brooklyn Public Library's Brooklyn Collection; Queens Public Library's Archival Collections; and the New York Public Library's Manuscripts and Archives Division.

I owe a tremendous debt to the interlibrary staff at Duke University, Harvard University, and, especially, Brown University, who patiently dealt with my seemingly endless requests for documents, books, and articles. That the Brown ILL staff only chastised me once for requesting such an extraordinary amount of materials is truly a testament to their patience.

I am very grateful to the staff at organizations that welcomed me into their workspaces to rummage through their file cabinets, storage units, and basements. I am especially thankful to Andy Reicher at the Urban Homesteading Assistance Board; Sara Cedar Miller at the Central Park Conservancy; Patrick Markee and Mary Brosnahan of the Coalition for the Homeless; and Doug Lasdon of the Urban Justice Center, who all took precious time away from their busy schedules and important work so that I could access materials related to the early years of these organizations.

Several kind individuals were willing to share relevant materials from their personal collections. I am especially grateful to Kim Hopper, who transported boxes and boxes of materials from his home to Columbia

University and set me up in his office to go through them. I also thank Ellen Baxter, Vicki Chesler, Matt Kovner, Charles Laven, and Ronald Shiffman, who all also shared materials from their personal papers. Tremendous thanks also to everyone who invited me into their homes and offices for oral history interviews: Winifred Armstrong, Roberta Axelrod, Ellen Baxter, William Beinecke, Vicki Chesler, David Clurman, Gordon Davis, David Goldstick, Francis J. Greenburger, Robert Hayes, Ann Henderson, Matt Kovner, Henry Lanier, Doug Lasden, Charles Laven, Marc Luxemburg, Carol Ott, Ruth Nazario, Andy Reicher, Betsy Barlow Rogers, N. Anthony Rolfe, and Daniel Rose.

This book has been greatly enriched by colleagues and friends who volunteered their time to read parts of this project at various stages of its development: Sara Matthiesen, Dan Platt, Matt Lassiter, Anne Gray Fischer, Jonathan Soffer, Themis Chronopolis, Matt Lasner, Liz Searcy, Lindsay Schakenbach Regele, Jennifer Klein, Jeannette Estruth, Palmer Rampell, Gabe Winant, and Bryan Winston. I am also grateful to the audience members and the many astute commentators who provided insightful feedback at conferences. I've also gained a great deal from the conversations and camaraderie I've shared with Dan Berger, Chris Dixon, Claire Dunning, Jon Free, Lily Geismer, Paige Glotzer, Brian Goldstein, Emily Hainze, Hannah Marcus, and Lauren Tilton. Two friends, Brent Cebul and Rebecca Marchiel—who lucky for me are among the best American historians of our generation—read the manuscript in its late stages and offered insightful and enthusiastic comments that helped improve the book and sustain my spirits in the final stretch.

At Oxford, I have been absolutely thrilled to work with Susan Ferber, who has been consistently helpful and supportive and whose judicious editing trimmed (at least some!) of my verbosity. The reviewers at Oxford University Press exemplified peer review at its best, providing engaged and thorough comments on the entire manuscript. Thanks also to Jeremy Toynbee for guiding a smooth production process and Anna Sanow for her shrewd copyedits.

Some of the material in this book has been published in earlier iterations, and I am grateful to the editors and peer reviewers whose comments helped improve my work when it initially appeared. A small portion of the first chapter was published in *Affordable Housing in New York: The People, Places, and Policies That Transformed a City* (Princeton University Press, 2015), edited by Nicholas Dagen Bloom and Matthew Lasner, and parts of chapter 2 were published in "'I Am Not Co-Op!': The Struggle over Middle-Class Housing in 1970s New York City," *Journal of Urban History* 43, no. 6 (November

2017). Portions of chapter 5 initially appeared in "Expanding the Thin Blue Line: Resident Patrols and Private Security in Late Twentieth-Century New York," *Modern American History* 3, no. 1 (March 2020).

While in Providence, I received a second education away from College Hill on the city's south side, where I worked for years with No One Leaves and the Tenant and Homeowner Association at Direct Action for Rights and Equality. The members of the Tenant and Homeowner Association in particular welcomed me into the group and humbled, inspired, and educated me in the day to day realities of racism, poverty, and the ongoing struggle for justice. I am also proud to have worked alongside colleagues and friends in Stand Up for Graduate Student Employees, who made time on top of their demanding schedules to organize together to better the collective rights of graduate student employees. Thanks as well to my more recent conspirators in Black and Pink–Boston for bringing all of their beautiful queer ferociousness to the struggle against incarceration and for queer and trans justice.

My colleagues in the Thompson Writing Program at Duke were terrific. I am especially grateful to Alison Klein, Seth LeJacq, and Mandy Wetsel, as well as to all of the members of the Duke Faculty Union who work to improve conditions for non–tenure-track faculty. I am also appreciative of the mentorship of Denise Comer and Marcia Rego and the administrative support of Vanessa Turnier.

As I was finishing this book, I had the terrific fortune of joining the History Department at Lehman College. I have been made to feel at home by my fantastic colleagues. I especially thank Tim Alborn, Martin Burke, Rhiannon Dowling, Jose Rénique, Robyn Spencer, Robert Valentine, William Wooldridge, and Amanda Wunder, as well as our extremely supportive chair, Marie Marianetti, talented and kind administrator, Laura Guerrero, and exemplary dean, James Mahon. Thanks also to the ambitious, curious, and enthusiastic students at Lehman, Duke, and Brown from whom I have learned as we've thought together about historical change and the inequities of the American past and present.

I've been blessed with amazing friends who have inspired and sustained me over the course of working on this book. There are many, many to thank, but my heart is especially full because of Mara Branch, Lindsay Branch, Chris Carrera, Joe Carroll, Jimmy Choi, J. Clapp, Grace Cleary, Jeff Cunningham, Stephanie Curry, Claire Dailey, Audrey Danielle, Alex Dean, Al Fair, Andy Farrell, Anne Gray Fischer, Sam Franklin, Peter Hahn, Craig Hughes, Brooke Lamperd, Kathleen McIntyre, Mike Maccarrone, Jim McAsey, Jess McDonald, Brendan O'Neill, J. Oberman, Dan Platt, John Rosenberg, Tyler Schauer,

Robyn Schroeder, Elizabeth Searcy, Maritza Silva-Farrell, Christopher Samih-Rotondo, Nada Samih-Rotondo, Tom Thomson, Matt Trower, Kevin Van Meter, Bryan Winston, and Liz Wolfson. No person had as significant a mark on my life over the last decade as Sara Matthiesen. I am grateful for all the ways I have benefited from her dazzling intellect and extraordinary heart.

I am truly blessed to have the family that I do. All my love and gratitude to mom, dad, and Ray. Thank you for everything.

The Long Crisis

Introduction

JOURNALIST BARRY GOTTEHRER looked around New York City in 1965 and took little comfort in what he saw. New York had become "a terrible place to live" in Gottehrer's view, "a nightmare" for most residents.[1] The prior year, Gottehrer had led a team of New York *Herald Tribune* reporters in conducting a "full-scale investigation" into New York life, producing a four-month series on "New York City in Crisis." "New York is the greatest city in the world," the series opened, "and everything is wrong with it." Articles depicted a city overcome by poverty and crime, substandard schools, unmanageable bureaucracy, ballooning budget deficits, deserting businesses, and a vanishing middle class. Surrounded by such depressing conditions, even the jokes New Yorkers could once make about lighter matters like traffic congestion "no longer are amusing."[2] "Problem has piled upon problem," Gottehrer believed, "and crisis has followed crisis."[3]

"Crisis" was frequently used to describe New York City during the late 1960s and 1970s. "The truth of [New York's] deep and worsening crisis," opined *Fortune* associate editor Richard Whalen, "is widely accepted as self-evident."[4] While the term "crisis" can easily be deployed as hyperbole, the regularity with which New Yorkers invoked it suggests a not insignificant degree of concern. The term "urban crisis" especially was used in the late 1960s to encapsulate a range of tangible—and, to many, disconcerting—conditions: aging housing, unstable municipal budgets, a declining industrial economic base, rising welfare rolls, dilapidated parks.[5] These circumstances signaled to Gottehrer and others that the city was facing an uncertain and troubling future.[6]

Despite years of hand-wringing over New York's urban crisis, dispiriting conditions seemed to many only to worsen as each year passed. By the mid-1970s, the situation was exacerbated when the city could no longer pay its bills. New York's debt accelerated beginning in the mid-1960s as officials relied on short-term notes to fill budget gaps.[7] The city's troubled financial position reached its nadir during the mid-1970s when financial institutions refused to underwrite additional municipal bonds, restricting the city's access to private capital, and ushering in a period known as the fiscal crisis.[8] New York tumbled toward bankruptcy, which was prevented only by intervention of state and federal officials who, along with financial and business elites, enacted strict cutbacks to city budgets.

The Long Crisis examines how New Yorkers at different scales of power launched imaginative remedies and policy prescriptions to address local crises during this tumultuous period.[9] These initiatives forged the path toward a greater dependence on the private sector and market to address urban problems. Market-based initiatives were not merely imposed from above by conservative ideologues; neither were they the handiwork of a single elected official, such as Mayor Rudolph Giuliani (1994–2001), who is often credited with ushering in privatization policies and reorienting the city toward the "free market."[10] Rather, the economic and political circumstances from the 1960s onward led to re-evaluations of existing municipal practices by local elected officials as well as a variety of residents, from block associations to grassroots organizations to foundations to professional associations. As economic conditions seemed to undermine the ability of municipal government to maintain basic services—at first only temporarily and then, as the 1970s went on, perhaps permanently—city-dwellers increasingly took action to improve conditions themselves.

These projects arose from nearly every pocket of the city. In the late 1960s and early 1970s, for example, residents of poor neighborhoods of color like the South Bronx launched a "self-help" initiative in which they took over the buildings that landlords had recently abandoned, emphasizing personal ingenuity over state resources. At the same time, in moderate and middle-income areas like Manhattan's Yorkville and St. Albans, Queens, neighbors came together in newly formed groups dedicated to harnessing volunteerism and private sector donations to improve the rapidly deteriorating conditions in municipal parks. These projects were linked, even if the diverse residents involved would hardly have identified with one another at the time. In the face of dwindling municipal resources, residents and policymakers grappled with difficult—sometimes desperate—choices. Overwhelmingly, they experimented. They tested new ideas and sometimes reimagined older ones to alleviate these circumstances and sustain key areas of urban life, particularly as officials proclaimed that municipal resources could do little.

Collectively, these experiments facilitated a process of marketization—a term that refers to the city's greater reliance on the private sector and market—rather than on traditional mid-century institutions of urban liberal governance. In some cases, the subjects of this book consciously sought just such an outcome, but in many others, they did not. They retained a certain confidence in mid-century liberalism, but their loss of faith in city government ironically led them to embrace experiments that helped facilitate New York's market turn—even when such a sweeping transformation was not their intention.

The Long Crisis traces how New Yorkers pushed for new solutions to address alarming conditions affecting the city's livable environments: the home and public space. These areas touched all New Yorkers. They were central to city-dwellers' lives, as spaces where they lived, where they spent leisure time, where they interacted with loved ones, and where they sought comfort. They were realms for which residents were especially incited to act as they began to suffer in ways municipal government alone seemed no longer able to fix. The process of marketization became embedded throughout New York's lived environments, shaping even the spaces residents experienced most intimately.

This book examines six of these areas: abandonment of low-income buildings; middle-class housing; dilapidated parks; rising crime; stagnant economic development; and public homelessness. These cases demonstrate how a city heralded as a national apex of postwar liberalism took a leading role in the ascent of marketization in the late twentieth century. They reveal a process that percolated up through local contestations, often in ways unintended, rather than one that was simply imposed by conservative elites. Instead of explicitly pro-market ideologies coming first in the ascent of market-based policies in the late twentieth century, *The Long Crisis* illustrates how for many New Yorkers *experiments* came first, ideology second.

THE LONG CRISIS moves away from the conventional narratives about the ascent of marketization during the final decades of the twentieth century that have focused overwhelmingly on conservatives and free-market proponents. Historians have commonly depicted the imposition of market-based logics as being a product of the dogged influence of the business sector, economists, libertarians, or conservative activists.[11] In doing so, they have created a rich portrait of how actors and institutions at the federal level and in major sections of the country worked to deconstruct key tenets of New Deal Liberalism and expand the role of the market and private sector in American life.

This book, however, argues that local actors, struggling in the face of shifting political and economic circumstances to improve distressing conditions, steered these processes.[12] They influenced city life in ways that went beyond their own imaginations.[13] The neoliberal turn, rather than simply being imposed by a narrow set of elites, took form through a process of *popular marketization* that involved a wide range of urbanites who transformed the political economy from the ground up. Tracing this progression allows us to understand how the reliance on the private sector and market intensified in ways that became so penetrating in scope, extensive in impact, and durable over time.[14]

Three groups of New Yorkers played different roles in this process. The first are city-dwellers from a variety of social positions who professed little ideological allegiance to the superiority of market solutions but whose actions nonetheless helped orient the city in that direction. For example, there were community members who, grappling with rising crime and municipal cutbacks, formed neighborhood patrols or hired private guards to surveil city streets. There were also rent-regulated tenants who came over time to embrace owning their apartments even if doing so chipped away at state regulations and provisions. These actors sought new ways to solve problems they associated with their neighborhoods, livelihoods, and even the city as a whole during a period in which it increasingly seemed that municipal government had limited capacity to do so. These individuals and groups pushed for creative solutions to troubling situations that unintentionally helped to further processes of marketization. Though they were not driven by an ideological adherence to free-market principles, their messaging and actions promoted the notions that the city itself was no longer able to solve the crises affecting its livable spaces and that new initiatives from those outside of government were needed. In so doing, they forged pathways for private actors and the private sector to become key players in major domains of urban life.

Local officials, most importantly New York's mayors, further expanded the role in governance for private actors; they comprise the second category of actors. These mayors include not just Democrat Ed Koch (1978–1989), whose unabashed pursuit of private enterprise and reluctance toward social welfare provisions pioneered "the Democratic Party version of neoliberalism," as historian Jonathan Soffer has noted, but also his predecessors John Lindsay (1966–1973) and Abraham Beame (1974–1977).[15] Koch's embrace of the market no doubt exceeded that of Lindsay and Beame. Both liberal Republican Lindsay and Democrat Beame were on the left side of the political spectrum and were not market ideologues who believed that private sector solutions were necessarily superior to those that relied on the state. Yet they anticipated transformations in the Democratic Party and liberalism that would become increasingly common in subsequent decades by supporting and also developing a variety of initiatives that looked to private actors and the market to respond to city problems as they navigated the difficult, changing economic conditions of the period.[16] Even Lindsay—who historians have depicted as exemplifying 1960s liberalism—by his second term was eager to augment the role of the market and the private sector in governance.[17]

Indeed, far from bit players during an era often portrayed by historians as one of conservative dominance, Democrats and liberals were fundamental to the market turn. In some cases, actions by these officials—particularly under the Lindsay administration—were undertaken with the hope of maintaining robust municipal services, but nonetheless contributed to the subsequent dismantling of liberal policies and to the simultaneous materialization of neoliberal conditions. This was less a case of a fervent drive for marketization than an instance of unintended consequences. In other cases—especially under the Koch administration—Democrats willingly embraced the shift away from robust liberalism toward market-based solutions as simply reflecting the new realities of fiscal governance in the late 1970s and 1980s.

This remaking of liberalism occurred both through the actions of officials and residents. For decades, liberal municipal leaders had developed a set of expectations for what government could deliver. But by the late 1960s, many New Yorkers felt these expectations were no longer being met. Residents believed they were entitled to conditions like decent homes, clean parks, and low crime, and they launched new means to achieve them that relied more on private actors and the private sector. They primarily did so not as an explicit rejection of liberalism, but rather to secure what officials (it was hoped, temporarily) could no longer provide.[18] Only as these initiatives expanded and seemed to achieve some success and as municipal resources declined further in the 1970s did they come to be seen increasingly as potential replacements for—rather than supplements to—municipal government. Marketization emerged not simply from a hostile rejection of liberalism, but rather from a process by which residents attempted to assist officials in securing the conditions that liberalism had long promised to maintain.

Marketization's growth was also facilitated by a third category of actors: New Yorkers who had a greater proclivity for private sector and market-based solutions. These actors ranged from real estate professionals who wanted to strip what they believed was the unfair burden of market regulations on their industry to the few outliers who first proposed that the private sector could better care for public parks than city government in the early 1970s. To these groups and individuals, the lessons of economic turmoil were clear: New York must embrace market and private sector–based solutions. These actors—who disproportionately came from realms like real estate and business—commonly held economic resources and political influence; their significance belies any simplistic depiction of marketization emerging solely from the grassroots. But while tracing the important role these actors had, this book argues that their actions should be understood as complementing the path forged by far less ideologically committed New Yorkers rather than dictating its direction. As experiences with the limitations of municipal government became widespread beginning in the late 1960s, everyday residents began to step in for the state, creating the crevasses that enabled the private sector and market initiatives of this third group to gain ground in these domains as well.

Ultimately, *The Long Crisis* illustrates how political and economic developments beginning in the late 1960s affected people on the ground, in their homes, public spaces, and neighborhoods, and shaped their sense of political possibilities. New Yorkers were no doubt influenced by larger political and economic currents—including stagflation, the fiscal crisis, declining federal support of cities, and national electoral victories of conservative candidates—that helped narrow their conception of what government could deliver. These currents did not, however, diminish urbanites' sense of what their living conditions should be. Nor did they cause New Yorkers to retreat from public life. Local actors remained powerful forces in shaping city life through the diverse projects they initiated to improve New York.

The effects of the imaginative and influential enterprises launched by disparate actors such as neighborhood residents, nonprofit foundations, community and professional organizations, and cultural institutions proved critical to the escalation of market logics and market-based policies. This process reveals how market rationales took root across New York in ways that were often subtler than large swaths of voters backing pro-market candidates. In shifting focus to actors typically at the periphery of scholarship on the ascent of market policies, this book highlights a route to neoliberalism that was remarkably local, experimental, and shepherded by New Yorkers who were driven to maintain or improve the conditions of their neighborhoods and city.

IF IN THE late twentieth century many New Yorkers ceased to see local government as the ideal provider of civic services, when did they begin in earnest to believe that it could be? And how did this faith begin to come undone? A brief overview of the expanding role of the state in New York life is instructive.

A hundred years before *The Long Crisis* begins, as the United States emerged from the Civil War, most Americans had minimal expectations for how much government—even local government—could improve their everyday lives. Historians commonly point to the Populist and Progressive Eras as when many Americans began to fundamentally rethink their relationship to government. Local urban governments in the late nineteenth century began to take on expanded and new regulatory or service-providing functions, such as installing and maintaining streetlamps, developing and enforcing robust health and building codes, and enlarging the park system. During the early twentieth century, reformers pushed the state's presence even further. New York City's progressive reformers "believed that government might properly become a powerful regulatory force and a public service provider," as historian John Louis Recchiuti has described, leading to legislation like the Tenement House Act (1901) that prevented the building of particularly egregious and dangerous forms of low-income housing.[19]

The notion that government could be the dominant force in municipal life gained greater strength during the Depression and World War II when federal funding and programs for urban areas rapidly accelerated. New York's Mayor Fiorello La Guardia and President Franklin Roosevelt (a former Governor of New York) maintained a close relationship and shared the view that government resources could draw the nation out of the Depression and improve the quality of life and well-being of residents. The federal resources that flowed into New York during this period were staggering; the results were metamorphic.[20] The influx of federal and municipal resources, as historian Mason Williams has richly documented, "built highways, tunnels, bridges, subway extensions, and a major world airport" as well as schoolhouses, public housing, higher education campuses, and neighborhood health clinics.[21]

The New Deal ultimately did more than enlarge municipal infrastructure and services. It furthered the sentiment that local government could have an expansive and beneficial role in everyday life. The New Deal made New Yorkers "more cognizant of their governments."[22] To be sure, local government was hardly a positive force for all urbanites at all times. A resident's relationship to local government was highly influenced by one's race, gender, class, politics, legal status, sexuality, and religion. Local government could be as destructive as it was munificent, and those most socially marginalized in the postwar decades—particularly low-income African American residents—were most likely to feel its violence, whether via a police baton or an urban renewal bulldozer.[23] But the New Deal and World War II period also meant that wide swaths of New Yorkers saw local government as a critical provider and protector of fundamental services, whether as the caretaker of a new local park, a supporter of rent-regulated housing, or the supplier of a free college education. This vigorous presence, as Williams argues, encouraged many postwar New Yorkers to "reach instinctively for state-driven solutions to social problems."[24]

Even as federal support declined in the years after World War II, the vestiges of the New Deal helped propel robust government programs into the postwar period, such as through the continued creation of public housing and expanding social welfare programs. The combination of the New Deal, a powerful unionized workforce and long standing left-wing institutions and groups provided the supporting structure for a "homegrown version of social democracy that made life in New York unlike anyplace else in the United States," as historian Joshua Freeman put it.[25] This included being the "national center" of public housing and rent regulations to having an unprecedented twenty-two municipal hospitals.[26]

The extent of the city's socially democratic characteristics may have made it exceptional, but its relationships to the private sector and market were in line with other metropolitan areas in mid-century America. Government programs may have intervened in some of the detrimental byproducts of capitalism, such as by preventing runaway rents or providing affordable public housing. But overwhelmingly, city policies aimed to bolster market capitalism and New York remained dependent on the private sector as its principal economic engine. What's more, both local and federal officials relied on the private sector as a partner in many of its projects. The private sector, for example, was fundamental to carrying out urban renewal (launched by the US Housing Act of 1949), the most important federal urban policy following World War II, which sought to attract white, middle-class suburbanites back to central cities as residents and shoppers.[27] To do so, it relied on what scholar Hilary Ballon describes as "the first wide-scale use" of the public–private partnership "mode of development."[28] Ultimately, local officials saw no contradiction in supporting market capitalism—and in partnering with the private sector to facilitate its growth—and believing government to be the provider of a hearty civic life.[29]

As far-reaching as New York's social democratic measures were, they were also precarious. The system was destabilized by a large exodus of middle-class residents to the suburbs, fears of the growing populations of color, and a declining industrial and manufacturing economy that not only diminished municipal revenues but also the unionized workforce that supported many left-leaning institutions. By the 1960s the waning economic base, alongside concerns about crime, refuse-infested public spaces, and visible racial tensions, signaled to many that New York had been infected by the urban crisis that was plaguing northern and Midwestern cities.

Nonetheless, New Yorkers retained faith in local government's ability to steer the city out of its troubles. Even the *Herald Tribune* screed, for example, sought to expose not just what was wrong with the city, but "what can be done to make New York the city it should be."[30] Changes in municipal government were foremost. The newspaper series aimed to dissuade three-term Mayor Robert Wagner from running again in 1965 and to encourage young New York Congressman John Lindsay's campaign for mayor.[31] Running as a Republican during a time when political parties did not map neatly onto "liberal" and "conservative" lines, Lindsay presented himself as a progressive to voters of the heavily Democratic city.[32] Lambasting the inefficiencies and entrenched bureaucracies of Wagner's tenure, Lindsay proposed to modernize government, infuse it with new and bright minds, bring it closer to the people, and, ultimately, harness its robust powers to reinvigorate civic life.

Despite the optimism many felt about Lindsay's election, near the end of his first term, a growing number of New Yorkers began to believe that government was failing in its duties as a provider and protector of civic services. To be sure, there were important events outside of the city that caused Americans to develop a more cynical and even hostile view toward government during this period. Vietnam and Watergate in particular engendered a much more distrustful attitude toward elected officials during the early 1970s.[33] Similarly, rampant inflation undermined many Americans' confidence in the federal government's ability to manage the economy.[34] But ultimately it was tangible developments and experiences in the city that led New Yorkers to seek solutions beyond what they felt local elected officials were capable of providing.

FOUR CATALYSTS BETWEEN the late 1960s and late 1970s hastened the turn toward the market and private sector: worsening economic conditions, evolving federal urban policy agendas, shifting race relations, and the tenure of Mayor Ed Koch. None of these can easily be reduced to a single moment, as their development and effects played out over a number of years. These overlapping experiences reinforced the fledgling belief that solutions beyond government were needed. Each helped spur or otherwise help proliferate new experiments to improve the lives and well being of New Yorkers in ways that looked to the market or private sector.

The first catalyst was New York's prolonged economic difficulties. Though for decades there had been clear signals of economic decline, New York entered a protracted period of fiscal trouble after the 1969 national recession. Job loss, particularly because of deindustrialization, became especially acute. Between 1970 and 1974 alone, the city lost 219,000 jobs in manufacturing, 83,000 in sales, and 10,500 in the FIRE (finance, insurance, and real estate) sectors, further dissipating key footholds of the tax base.[35] This followed a loss of 180,600 manufacturing jobs between 1960 and 1970.[36] Officials attempted to raise revenues through a variety of new taxes and other schemes such as off-track betting and strident ticketing in order to offset these losses.[37] But many fell short of expectations.

As the economy struggled, Lindsay administration officials strained to maintain resources and match city expenditures. Lindsay had direct control over a relatively small percentage of city spending: parks, police, fire, and sanitation services and general government expenses.[38] While municipal spending did rise in the early 1970s, increases overwhelmingly went to Medicaid, welfare, salaries, and debt service.[39] Instead, the city significantly slowed or stopped hiring, with many departments experiencing declines in the overall number of workers through retirement. Departments' meager budget increases often did not outpace inflation.

This meant that for years before the city nearly went bankrupt, New Yorkers heard officials proclaim that they were limited in terms of what they could do to address the problems of urban life. As, for example, in the 1960s residents across the city encountered parks filled with "broken benches, deteriorated pavement, uncut grass, unpruned trees, and uncleanliness"—as one major user survey reported—they were told by officials that limited financial resources tied their hands.[40] And as landlords walked away from thousands of buildings in low-income areas—leaving residents like Carmen Rodriguez and her children at 29 West 104th Street in the winter of 1969 without water and shivering because the only heat emanated from the flame of the kitchen stove—officials offered no program to effectively stem the abandonment crisis.[41] By 1972, as these and other problems mounted and municipal resources grew more constrained, only one in ten New Yorkers rated the quality of city government as "good" (no residents believed it excellent).[42] The perceived inability of government to address New Yorkers' alarm over their homes, neighborhoods, and livelihoods during this period increasingly spurred residents to seek new solutions, ones that would—often inadvertently—expand the presence of the market and private sector in the workings of city life.

Concerns about the limits of government worsened with the fiscal crisis. The causes of the fiscal troubles were numerous. Most directly, the crisis stemmed from the city's growing debt. By the end of fiscal year 1974, a year in which the city's general revenues amounted to $10.5 billion, its gross outstanding debt stood at over $13.5 billion.[43] Over $3.7 billion of this was short-term debt. Throughout 1974 and early 1975, the city's largest creditor banks grew fretful about its finances. Soon after a state authority, the Urban Development Corporation, defaulted on its debt, the banks froze New York out of the private capital market, leaving the city with insufficient capital for its ongoing expenses.[44]

Backed by federal and state officials, New York's business, finance, and banking leaders exerted relentless pressure on local policymakers to radically alter hallmarks of the city's social democracy.[45] The result of the state and federal supported retrenchment that began in 1975 was an end to free tuition in the city's college system, increased subway and bus fares, reduced services to hospitals, roads, schools, parks, streets, libraries, subways, and fire services, and a public workforce that decreased by nearly 70,000 over the next few years.[46] Cuts meant that many public-sector institutions that had once been "attractive to all sorts of New Yorkers became subnormal institutions of last resort."[47] Even New Yorkers who had remained stalwart through years of declining municipal services were forced to confront the fact that in the eyes of state and federal officials, along with private lenders, New York was fiscally and politically insolvent.

Although there were several competing explanations for the source of fiscal troubles, one version emerged victorious in the press and popular imagination: the crisis was principally due to an overgenerous city government. Republican President Gerald Ford voiced this position repeatedly. Ford blamed New York's problems on its employee salaries and pensions, municipal hospital system, free higher education, and its "welfare burden."[48] The belief that New York's robust liberal policies were at fault echoed in city and national media. These explanations dramatically and often intentionally simplified the fiscal crisis and justified austerity as the only reasonable solution, even as other explanations and resolutions were possible. For example, no city paid as high a percentage (25 percent) of all assistance and administrative costs of federal welfare as New York. Stepped up enforcement of payment of uncollected taxes, fees, and fines of the hundreds of millions of dollars that the city was owed each year may also very well have prevented the crisis.[49]

The fiscal crisis nonetheless helped reinforce in the public mind the notion that local government could not be counted on as before. Critically, this idea had been developing since the city encountered financial difficulty in the late 1960s; residents had already begun to act in earnest to address concerns over their homes, public spaces, and livelihoods. But the fiscal crisis intensified and helped proliferate this view as forced cutbacks decimated municipal resources. "New York can longer afford its parks," one park advocate described in *New York* magazine at mid-decade amidst ongoing fiscal turbulence, but turning to private volunteerism and philanthropy offered hope that parks "might yet be saved in spite of . . . this age of austerity."[50]

The second major catalyst in New York's market turn derived from the city's experience with federal policies and occurred in two phases. The first began during the New Deal in the 1930s, when the federal government vigorously began promoting homeownership and suburbanization as national policy. Housing policies administered through the Federal Housing Administration and the Veterans Administration underwrote home loans, making homeownership far more economically feasible for whites than ever before (while remaining exceedingly difficult for African Americans). Suburbanization was further buttressed by the 1956 Interstate Highway Act that saw the federal government pay for 90 percent of the construction costs of roadways, helping to make suburban areas even more accessible.[51] These policies helped drain the city of its tax base. New York City lost a half-million white residents in the 1940s, 1.2 million in the 1950s, and another half-million in the 1960s, with most going to nearby suburbs.[52]

Businesses and corporations quickly followed homeowners. This was particularly painful for New York, which had long been a national center of corporate headquarters. Between 1967 and 1974, the number of Fortune 500 companies headquartered in New York City declined by 30 percent. Most relocated to nearby suburbs, which saw their share of headquarters increase by over 50 percent during the same period, while others went to the Sunbelt, another area that had benefited for years from federal investment.[53]

Ultimately, although financial leaders and federal officials framed the fiscal crisis as a failure of progressive governance, its root causes more accurately lay in the numerous federal policies that fueled disinvestment in northern cities like New York.[54] The contradictions of postwar liberalism—in which a federal government pushed pro-suburban, pro-Sunbelt policies, while liberal municipal leaders tried to sustain a comparatively robust social welfare program—underpinned the crisis. Prominent narratives about the fiscal crisis reduced this contradiction of urban liberal policy into being a lesson about the failures of progressive governance.

In the second phase, which followed President Lyndon Johnson's Great Society initiatives, federal policies designed to bolster older cities like New York evaporated and the national government retreated in the face of the urban crisis. During Johnson's presidency (1963–1969), federal officials professed a commitment to a shared responsibility for solving urban problems.[55] From the War on Poverty to the creation of the Department of Housing and Urban Development, "the federal government's commitment to America's cities in the post–World War II era reached its apotheosis," as historian Roger Biles has observed.[56] But this shared responsibility diminished after the Johnson administration, just as New York encountered significant economic troubles. Johnson's successor, Richard Nixon, eviscerated programs that targeted the traditional inner cities of northern and Midwestern cities and boosted ones that favored the growth of metropolitan areas in rival regions such as the Sunbelt—a direction that continued under Presidents Gerald Ford and Jimmy Carter.[57] Federal retrenchment was less severe in New York than in many other northern cities, but officials nonetheless faced significant cutbacks in areas such as programs for the poor and housing.[58] Even when overall federal funding remained stable, local officials were constantly concerned that federal cutbacks could be imminent, given the rhetoric of federal administrators in the 1970s and 1980s.

The federal retreat from urban areas had significant ramifications. More robust federal support may have alleviated the worst of the city's economic difficulties and therefore prevented the decimation of municipal budgets in the 1970s. Instead, the open hostility of federal officials encouraged the view that New York needed new means to preserve its livable spaces. In the years ahead, intergovernmental aid would comprise a diminishing percentage of the city's expense budget, falling from about 50 percent of revenues in the early 1970s to close to 30 percent by the end of the 1980s.[59] This shifting terrain underscored for many officials and residents that they needed to look beyond government solutions.

The third catalyst was racial politics, which made an indelible mark on American cities in the postwar decades. The ascent of marketization in New York cannot be separated from those politics. On one hand, the growing African American and Latinx populations moving into New York contributed to the fretful white middle-class base moving out, one important cause of the city's economic destabilization. For the white population that remained, racial politics increasingly dissuaded them from supporting liberal officials.

This was particularly the case in ethnic outer borough neighborhoods, where many whites came to associate liberalism with fueling—rather than protecting them against—black militancy, encroaching populations of color into "white" neighborhoods and simultaneous declining property values, and accelerating rates of welfare and crime.[60] In the 1960s and 1970s in the mostly middle-income Italian and Jewish Brooklyn community of Canarsie, for example, the belief that liberals were at fault for a growing black population supposedly destabilizing the community's social, economic, and cultural fabric led whites to associate liberalism with "profligacy . . . irresponsibility, and sanctimoniousness."[61] Though racial politics did not transform New York into a conservative stronghold or directly push these white residents toward developing political and economic initiatives that relied less on government, white ethnic concerns about race dampened the electoral success of candidates associated with liberalism and a more activist state.[62]

This shift was brought to bear in the election of Ed Koch in 1978, the beginning of the fourth major moment in New York's market turn. In his campaign, Koch eschewed the support of working-class people of color and distanced himself from the city's liberal past, while successfully winning favor among outer borough white ethnics.[63] Once elected, Koch and his appointees took lessons not just from the city's recent history with racial politics, but also its fiscal crisis and its upended relationship with the federal government.

Koch brought into local government a steadfast vision for expanding the role of the private sector and market. To Koch, the lessons of the fiscal crisis were clear. Koch administration officials believed that the bloated spending and irresponsible fiscal management of prior administrations had driven the city into economic catastrophe.[64] The fiscal crisis, along with federal retrenchment, offered them overwhelming evidence that older ways of municipal government simply would no longer work. "Under Lindsay and Beame," Koch explained, "the thrust of city policy was to make this a town where business and economy were of less importance than the welfare syndrome."[65] Koch administration officials believed the city needed to reverse this equation. It could only survive by turning to the private sector not just to lead economic development, but even to take on areas that had previously been the domain of government.

Ultimately, these four catalysts—economic crisis, shifts in federal policy, racial politics, and the tenure of the Koch administration—helped to facilitate New York's market turn. Economic troubles helped engender the idea that residents would need to look beyond government to solve city problems, which was further reinforced by the curtailing of big federal urban projects and the federal-municipal partnerships of the Johnson administration. In response, beginning in the late 1960s residents, officials, organizations, and businesses experimented with an array of creative solutions to the twin crises of government and economy. These initiatives forged a path away from government even before the crisis, but as the fiscal crisis then further cut away at municipal resources, the seeming viability of truly public policies narrowed.

The result was an even more vigorous pursuit of solutions for urban problems that looked beyond government. As difficult as city-dwellers' experiments were to initiate, they seemed more viable—and to some, more desirable—than attempting to find ways to increase government resources. These efforts did not simply quicken the pace of marketization, but also launched the process in a wide swath of areas that may never otherwise have experienced an expanded presence of the market and private sector. What's more, these experiments had a compounding effect, as they became models for new initiatives in other areas. Once, for instance, New Yorkers showed that it was possible to have the private sector raise money for and even manage cherished parks, this idea was cited as an example for other public parks and additional areas of civic life.

The election of Ed Koch made the vision for expanding the market and private sector in governance into a defining feature of municipal policy. The success of the Koch administration in doing so, however, derived in large part from the ongoing work of a variety of city-dwellers who had since the beginnings of the economic crisis developed private solutions. Koch administration officials expanded, transformed, and officially adopted long established efforts designed by residents, grassroots organizations, cultural institutions, professional organizations, and philanthropists to address perceived lapses of government. Koch used his power to build on the momentum of these prior initiatives, to attempt to shape them in the direction he desired and, in some cases, to hasten their market-orientation. The result at the end of the 1980s was that the private sector and market had gained a dominant presence in the political and economic governance of New York.

EACH OF THE chapters that follows traces how New Yorkers responded to disconcerting conditions affecting the home or public space. Though organized chronologically, several of the chapters run parallel in the time period they cover. The first four chapters of *The Long Crisis* explore events that principally traverse the late 1960s into the early 1980s, whereas the final two examine events that span the mid-1970s into the early 1990s.

The first two chapters center on the home. Chapter 1 examines how poor and low-income residents confronted widespread building abandonment that began in the late 1960s. During this period, extensive disinvestment and an eviscerated real estate market led landlords of low-income housing to walk away from their real estate holdings, leaving thousands of buildings unoccupied and often city-owned due to nonpayment of taxes. In response, Latinx, African American, and some white residents protested the blight these buildings brought to their neighborhoods by directly occupying and seeking ownership of abandoned buildings through a process they called urban homesteading. Activists framed homesteading as a "self-help" initiative, often emphasizing their own ingenuity over state resources as the key to solving the problems of low-income urban neighborhoods. Such framing was understandable given the unstable economic terrain of the 1970s, and won activists support not just from the political left but also the right. But it also positioned homesteading as demonstrating the superiority of private-citizen and sector-led revitalization in ways that left homesteading projects vulnerable as it became clear how necessary government resources would be to their success.

The second chapter turns to the struggle over moderate and middle-income housing. After numerous failed state-led initiatives to stem the exodus of middle and moderate-income residents, landlords, alongside major real estate associations and many housing experts, proposed their own solution for creating greater opportunities for homeownership: converting middle-income rental housing into cooperatives, a process that would also enable the owners of rental housing to profit handsomely. Tenants initially widely rejected apartment ownership, preferring the security of rent-regulated housing, which set off a decade-long battle over the control and nature of moderate and middle-income housing. Over the 1970s, however, the growing acceptance of conversions by tenants would begin to tilt the housing stock toward market-rate cooperatives and condominiums.

The next two chapters concern public space. Chapter 3 examines the decline and subsequent "revitalization" of major parks through their control by public–private partnerships by the 1980s. The extensive private sector involvement in parks, however, was far from the elite-initiated takeover that has been depicted.[66] This shift dates back to community residents' organization to revive degenerating local spaces that had suffered municipal neglect. What first began as community park revitalization efforts in neighborhoods throughout the city spread to initiatives that involved broader elements of the public and private sectors. Indeed, the subsequent involvement of businesses and corporations in the care and management of parks was spurred by years of campaigns by concerned residents, nonprofits, cultural institutions, and officials who had lost faith in the ability of local government to maintain parks.

Chapter 4 traces how in the late 1960s and 1970s New York became engulfed in rising rates of crime and fostered the belief among residents that navigating city streets was no longer safe. In reaction to the perceived inadequacies of governmental responses to crime, city-dwellers formed citizen patrols, in which neighbors joined together to surveil their residential streets. Businesses and institutions also began to forge their own initiative to deter street crime by hiring private guards to patrol the public streets of their neighborhoods. These efforts grew alongside one another and reinforced a similar logic about the need for private action against crime. Both helped to perpetuate and ultimately normalize the patrolling of forces beyond the police. By the early 1980s resident patrols slowly began to fade from city streets, whereas the presence and role of private guards expanded and soon became an established part of policing the streets.

Chapters 5 and 6 principally examine the city as it emerged from its urban crisis and began to experience the hallmarks of economic revitalization: rising real estate values, a growing middle- and upper-class population, and capital investment in private and public spaces. Chapter 5 focuses on how, with limited federal and city funds at their disposal, Democratic and liberal officials came to embrace generous tax and incentive policies to directly spur sagging development and rehabilitation. Though municipal officials had for decades used tax exemptions, these new incentives empowered the private sector to take the dominant role in economic development with little state oversight. As these policies began to face criticism for unnecessarily subsidizing development in gentrifying neighborhoods, officials turned to a new strategy: binding subsidies to developers' commitments to make local improvements (e.g., street repairs and infrastructure enhancements). Doing so at once continued to diminish tax coffers and helped shift neighborhood improvement projects from the public to the private sector.

The final chapter brings together home and public space by examining the extraordinary growth of people experiencing homelessness who resided in public spaces during the 1980s. Public homelessness emerged at a time of rising value of public spaces, which finally began to receive infusions of public and private capital after years of neglect—a development homeless bodies seemed to threaten. The city's seeming inability to stem public homelessness led private sector actors and the quasi-public officials who oversaw the subways and major Manhattan transportation centers where the homeless resided in the greatest numbers to implement more punitive policies as a "solution" to public homelessness. Buttressed by new legal measures that expanded the private sector's governance of public space, these tactics ultimately influenced officials' implementation of similarly aggressive measures toward public homelessness to protect the enhanced value of public space.

BY THE BEGINNING of the twenty-first century, New York City had been transformed. To be sure, it did not become a city in which all municipal authority had been replaced by the market and private sector. Local government retained an extraordinary size and scope. The number of municipal employees grew by over 18 percent between 1978 and 1989, reaching a higher level than in 1961.[67] In constant dollars, expenditures doubled between 1964 and 1990.[68] Municipal government endured as a dominant force in city life.

But while governmental power and resources remained enormous, they were increasingly deployed to facilitate the role of the private sector and market in urban life. Government shaped the reach of the market and private sector in ways that were both subtle and explicit, from creating incentives to fuel private development to empowering private organizations to run and even own public spaces.

Indeed, the substantial scale of government should not obscure the profound changes that occurred over the previous four decades. For one, the market and private sector had expanded into or within critical areas of life, even if residents were not always aware of such changes. Unlike decades before, a New Yorker on a Sunday stroll at the turn of this century may very well have found herself walking out of a condominium that was formerly a rent-regulated apartment, accessing the subway through a privately owned "public" atrium, walking down a street policed by private security guards and managed by local businesses, and playing basketball in a privately run "public" park.

Residents and officials were more likely to turn to private sector–driven solutions in areas in which they would have previously looked to the state. Businesses in a commercial area concerned about refuse and litter might form a Business Improvement District that could hire private sanitation workers and security guards rather than continue to demand greater services from government. Concerns about conditions in a local park might spur residents and local businesses to form a Friend of the Park group to supplement municipal services, or even a nonprofit organization that aimed to take over management of the space. While New Yorkers had reached "instinctively for state-driven solutions to social problems" decades early, that impulse had become supplemented by one premised on the viability of turning to the market and private sector.[69]

The nature of the relationship between government and the private sector had also changed. Public–private partnerships, for example, which proliferated in the later decades of the twentieth century, were distinct from the kinds that existed in the postwar period. Under urban renewal, federal and local officials wrote the checks and the rules, even as they relied on the private sector. Although state authorities partnered with and were influenced by business in carrying out urban renewal, these authorities ultimately were "genuine expansions of state capacity" in which state actors played leading or at least equal roles in their relations with the private sector.[70] Decades later, this equation was often reversed. Take, for example, two of the most common partnerships—the private groups that began to manage parks and Business Improvement Districts. These kinds of public–private partnerships were ultimately designed to bolster the power and resources of the private sector and market in their relationship with the state as well as the public.

Additionally, officials in the 1980s and 1990s began to explicitly advocate for privatization, which further empowered the market and private sector in governance. Whereas municipal officials often looked to expand the scope of government in the decades after World War II, their successors commonly sought out the private sector and market to shed sectors of government. This was especially true during the tenure of Mayor Rudolph Giuliani, who made privatization a central component of his campaign. Even before Giuliani took office, his aides began drafting proposals to transfer control over several municipal hospitals to private, nonprofit corporations and to sell the city's Off-track Betting Corporation.[71] By the end of his two terms, Giuliani administration officials had realized sixty-six of their privatization initiatives.[72]

The Long Crisis shows how New York reached this moment. It traces how this logic came to shape life and governance over the last four decades of the twentieth century. It reveals how New Yorkers struggled to resolve alarming conditions affecting the city's livable spaces, ultimately helping capitalism to emerge from economic calamity stronger and more entrenched in urban life.

I

Low-Income Housing in Crisis

POLITICIANS DID NOT travel to the South Bronx in the 1970s for inspiration. Like many poorer sections of New York City, the area had suffered for years from the extensive building abandonment and arson that had given the city the reputation of having the most severe urban blight in the nation. But in the fall of 1977, after passing through blocks of vacant and fire-ravaged buildings, President Jimmy Carter came upon a site that gave him hope for the area's—and city's—future: a six-story, formerly abandoned tenement on Washington Avenue that had been revitalized by dozens of community members and now featured rooftop solar panels and freshly painted, oak-floored apartments.[1]

The Latinx and black community members responsible for the building referred to themselves as the People's Development Corporation. The name called attention to years of government neglect of poverty-stricken areas of color like the South Bronx, as well as the potential of community residents to lead the revitalization of their neighborhoods. The People's Development Corporation described their rehabilitation of a vacant, decaying building into an affordable housing cooperative as "urban homesteading."

Urban homesteading—taking over landlord-abandoned buildings and turning them into owner-occupied cooperatives—grew beginning in the late 1960s out of the crisis low-income residents faced in securing a stable home. In addition to a paucity of decent, affordable housing, low-income areas of color began at this time to be ravaged by building abandonment. Between 1966 and 1968 alone, landlords abandoned 100,000 rental apartments—a total greater than the number of units demolished through so-called slum clearance over the previous twenty years.[2] What began with a handful of buildings in pockets of low-income neighborhoods in the mid-1960s spread to encompass entire blocks by the early 1970s, resulting in "small sections of the City" becoming "ghost towns," in the words of a 1972 report commissioned by the city.[3] Vacant tenements lining the streets of low-income neighborhoods of color served as reminders of the depths of the city's worsening economic condition and its punishing effects on the poor.

Homesteading emerged as a local response to the emergency of abandonment that officials seemed to be doing little to stem. Fed up with municipal government's inability to prevent abandonment or alleviate its pernicious effects, low-income residents of color took action themselves. The group on Washington Avenue was just one of hundreds engaged in homesteading initiatives as the abandonment crisis took hold. In 1973, a Columbia University researcher found 136 landlord-abandoned or -neglected buildings in which low-income tenants were attempting to become resident-owners.[4] "Many low-income families who might once have awaited housing action by their landlords or the City, State, or Federal governments," one group of homesteading advocates proclaimed, "now realize that the only viable alternative left to save their homes, blocks and communities will be their own initiative, determination and sweat."[5] Though homesteading emerged initially as a

FIGURE 1.1   In the late 1960s and 1970s, building abandonment ravaged New York's low-income neighborhoods.

Courtesy of the NYC Municipal Archives.

survival strategy, proponents communicated a greater political message: low-income people could themselves solve the problems of disinvestment and a negligent government by turning abandoned buildings into owner-occupied cooperatives.

These actions were aided by the flurry of grassroots, low-income housing organizations that formed in the late 1960s and early 1970s. What brought these groups together was the desire to improve conditions of—and hasten tenant and community control over—local housing. The movement, which grew to over fifty groups by mid-decade, organized to prevent landlord abandonment, fought for greater community influence in housing policies, won employment opportunities for low-income residents in housing renovations, and helped transfer ownership away from reticent landlords to tenants and neighborhood housing organizations. Despite the variety of these tactics, none of these initiatives captured the attention of the city and even the nation as did homesteading.

This chapter traces how homesteaders navigated the city's shifting economic and political terrain as they responded to the crises of building abandonment and low-income housing. Homesteaders charted a path that aimed to distinguish their efforts from decades of unsuccessful public and private initiatives to improve low-income areas. Calling attention to the failures both of government and the private market around low-income housing, they emphasized their own resourcefulness as the lynchpin to solving the problems of these urban neighborhoods.

Homesteading advocates articulated a politics that seemed to bring together positions from the left and the right. On the one hand, proponents echoed recent civil rights and Black Power groups that emphasized the need of low-income people of color to have power and control over community resources and the decisions that shaped their lives. Homesteaders also recognized the importance of government support and fought to gain sufficient resources to make their efforts successful. Given their focus largely on housing that the private sector had failed, they were deeply critical of the market's ability to meet the needs of poor communities.

On the other hand, advocates promoted homesteading as a "self-help" initiative that emphasized individual responsibility, entrepreneurship, and private ownership—notions popular on the right. While they lambasted the recent history of urban liberal governance for seesawing between destructive policies like urban renewal and outright neglect, they also acknowledged the limitations on available governmental resources amidst the economic turbulence of the decade.

In part as a result of this framing, homesteading was hailed as among the most viable solutions not just to abandonment but to the larger urban crisis affecting low-income neighborhoods. Homesteading garnered support from across the political spectrum. Liberals saw in it the social and political possibilities of grassroots organization among the poor, while conservatives saw in it a self-help ethos unattached to state support. Homesteading advocates helped to produce and reinforce these sentiments, from emphasizing how homesteading facilitated community self-sufficiency to contrasting it from government programs that provided "handouts." The idea that low-income residents themselves were leading the response to a housing and economic crisis with their own sweat and labor gave homesteading broad political currency.[6]

As municipal and federal resources tightened in the 1970s, political officials increasingly pointed to particular tenets of homesteading, such as individual enterprise, while diminishing others, like the need for adequate governmental resources. Political officials from the mayor's office to the Oval Office championed homesteading as a fruitful example of policymakers relying more on private enterprise and less on government resources. For certain rhetorical appeals—like homesteading's emphasis on self-help—there was shared agreement about meaning between homesteaders and political supporters. But other points—like the emphasis on community empowerment—could be more selectively interpreted to stress limiting government resources and encouraging private-citizen responsibility in their place. In a way homesteaders and advocates encouraged but did not fully intend, homesteading became heralded for demonstrating the importance of private-citizen and sector-led paths toward urban rejuvenation. It was a particularly powerful example because it emanated not from business or the elite, but from the poorest communities.

Homesteading and the Urban Crisis

Though a problem nationwide, the number of buildings deserted in New York in the late 1960s was nearly half of the total abandoned across the country.[7] While experts debated the causes of abandonment, many agreed that rents in poorer neighborhoods were often simply too low to result in sufficient— if any—profit for landlords. Real estate industry spokespersons repeatedly blamed rent regulations for producing too little capital to maintain buildings. But defenders of these policies pointed out that the problem of abandonment extended to cities with no such laws. A more likely explanation was the combination of years of housing disinvestment in lower income areas of color, a declining real estate market, and a sharp increase in landlords' expenses as a result of inflation and rising taxes and oil prices.[8] The result was the same whatever the causes: landlords walked away in droves from the buildings they owned.

For low-income renters, landlord abandonment underscored the private market's seeming inability to provide decent, affordable rental housing. Little new housing for low-income—or even moderate-income—residents was built in the 1960s. The city's vacancy rate in 1968 was only 1.2 percent, the lowest in the nation.[9] This made finding a home an exceedingly difficult task for those on the economic margins, especially for residents of color who had long borne the brunt of a discriminatory housing market.

Homesteading thus first emerged as an emergency response among the poor as they became increasingly closed off from meaningful housing choices. In most cases, when a landlord abandoned a building, the tenants soon followed. But in dozens of buildings throughout the city tenants stayed, attempting to run the building themselves rather than face potential homelessness. These residents formed what one observer called "de facto cooperatives" in which the largely poor tenants organized to provide their own basic services and repairs.[10] In the second form of homesteading, tenants organized to transfer ownership away from their reticent landlords before abandonment. In both cases, homesteaders were mostly African American and Latinx and poor; they included women and men, the young and elderly, and those with families and without.

Attempting to run a landlord-abandoned or -neglected building required extraordinary courage and resilience. The experience of the residents of Phoenix Cooperative in Central Harlem is instructive. For over twenty years, a tenant's organization had sporadically tried to get the landlord to make necessary repairs. He rarely did. By the time the landlord finally abandoned the seven-story, forty-seven-unit property in 1971, there was no lock on the front door (which had opened the building to unwanted drug selling and sex work), most of the mailboxes were destroyed, the roof was in disrepair, several apartments had been damaged by fire and were open to the elements, and there was no heat or hot water. The tenants reached out to a sympathetic lawyer who had represented tenants of a Bronx building in similar circumstances. Working with the attorney and a leader from the Bronx homesteading project, the tenants learned the process of self-management. They agreed to a common rental charge of $65 a month, with which they began to manage the building's finances and slowly fund necessary repairs.

They confronted those engaged in illicit activities, fixed the locks repeatedly before local vandals finally stopped breaking them, and stomached "free-loader" residents who refused to pay the communally assessed rent once there was no landlord to legally evict them. After two years of successfully running the building themselves, the tenants gained legal control of the building from the city, which had taken ownership through tax foreclosure.[11]

As astonishing as efforts like the Phoenix Cooperative were, the third type of low-income cooperative that began to form in the early 1970s required even bolder actions: taking over and renovating abandoned buildings. This strategy tended to be the province of younger people—not surprising given the amount of physical labor involved—who were vocal in bringing attention to their actions.

One such group was the Renigades of East Harlem. Along with the South Bronx and Central Brooklyn, Harlem had the greatest number of abandoned buildings in New York.[12] The Renigades described themselves as a local street gang and were composed largely of formerly incarcerated Puerto Rican and African American young men. With the city doing little to reverse Harlem's deterioration, the Renigades proposed their own solution. They took over and began renovating a six-story building that had come under city ownership after its prior owner defaulted on municipal tax payments. On the ground floor, the group planned to open a construction job training office and food cooperative. "Instead of destroying the neighborhood or watching it come down all around us," one Renigade described, "we're learning construction skills and building ourselves our own home."[13]

The Renigades recognized the deteriorating housing stock not simply as blight but as a potential opportunity to arrest the effects of years of disinvestment, negligent landlords, inadequate community capital, and municipal austerity. "What do you do," the Renigades asked the community, "when the landlord . . . has abandoned your building and cannot be located to make repairs? What do you do when the City, which has the moral responsibility to assist tenants when landlords walk out, claims it cannot help?? Do we all surrender our homes, and our lives to the advance of abandonment, the plague or rats, and the final demolition of our community into vacant lifeless parking lots??" No, the Renigades answered: "We can rebuild our community ourselves!!!"[14]

The group proposed that fellow East Harlem residents follow their initiative. They offered their knowledge and resources to facilitate subsequent takeovers so that Harlemites could own their own homes and "finally be rid of the rats, the landlords, the leaks, and the City."[15] The proposal that

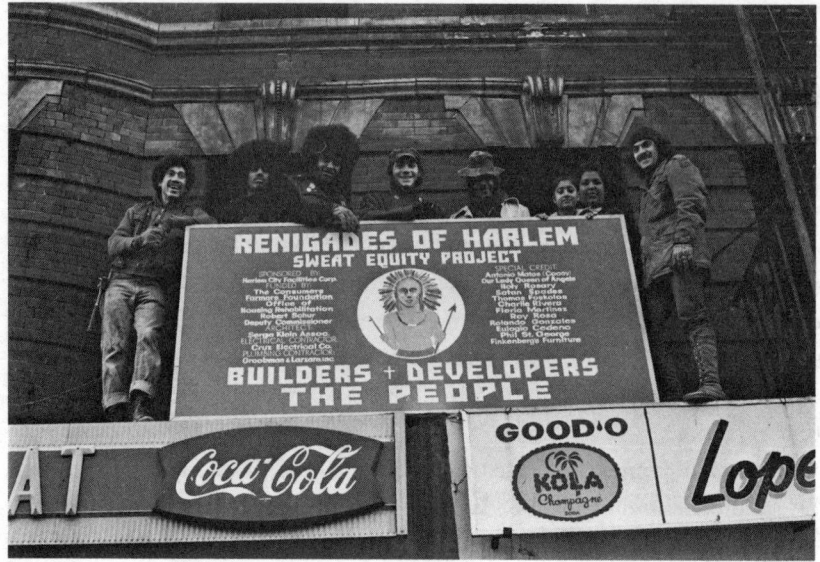

FIGURE 1.2 Members of the Renigades pose in front of an abandoned Harlem building the group was rehabilitating. The Renigades reflected homesteading's promise of low-income community members themselves becoming the "builders + developers" who rebuilt their neighborhoods.
Courtesy of the NYC Municipal Archives.

Harlem residents eschew both government and private capital and rebuild their community themselves was ambitious, but the Renigades had successfully renovated one formerly abandoned building and were at work on their second.

By the early 1970s, homesteading looked increasingly like a fruitful strategy. Officials admitted that city policy, which focused on sealing or demolishing unsafe buildings and selling tax foreclosed properties back to landlords, regardless of their willingness to further invest in low-income neighborhoods, had done little to stem abandonment.[16] By contrast, homesteading was spreading across all five boroughs, though it was especially prominent in Manhattan's Harlem and the Lower East Side, the South Bronx, and Brooklyn's Williamsburg and Crown Heights neighborhoods.[17] Mayor John Lindsay (1966–1973) began to express support for the concept of low-income cooperatives by his second term, but officials also believed the city's increasing financial precariousness precluded a full-scale homesteading initiative.[18] Housing officials also worried about caliber of work and dependability of untrained homesteaders. Philip St. Georges, who in 1972 was an enthusiastic Housing Department intern working on homesteading projects, wrote of his colleagues: "To a man, the other 'housing professionals' had images of boiler explosions, building collapses, shoddy workmanship, and inept or lazy tenant self-helpers."[19]

Although homesteaders like the Renigades expressed concern about relying on government and although municipal officials had some apprehension about homesteaders, the process often necessarily brought the two groups together. For one, many buildings abandoned by their owners came into city ownership as landlords stopped paying local taxes (often well before they completely walked away from the property). Homesteaders taking over these city-owned buildings (which were called "in rem") forced municipal officials to respond. Second, after years—and sometimes decades—of landlord disinvestment, most buildings were in desperate need of repair. With private banks typically refusing to loan money in low-income communities of color, the city was a surprising source of potential financing. Its Municipal Loan Program offered owners of low-income housing who otherwise could not attain conventional financing long-term, low-interest rehabilitation loans. Lindsay grew the program's available funds exponentially, from $8 million in his first year in office to $141 million by the end of 1970.[20] Even as homesteaders positioned themselves as the key antidotes to urban decline, they quickly recognized the loan program and related municipal resources as critical sources to facilitate rehabilitating decayed housing.

Financing would only matter if homesteaders could take legal possession of buildings; the city created new pathways for them to do just that in the early 1970s. Most of these programs originated in the Office of Special Improvement (OSI), which was directed by Robert Schur, a leftist supporter of low-income cooperatives. The OSI helped create a small Sweat Equity Program in 1972, which offered technical assistance and below market-rate financing for homesteading projects.[21] This support hardly came with no strings attached. Loans needed to be paid back with interest and tenant "sweat equity" would be required "to reduce the costs of housing rehabilitation and maintenance."[22] For Lindsay administration officials, these programs offered an escape from unwanted ownership of in rem properties, a means to return these buildings to the tax rolls, and a potential path toward arresting abandonment through greater reliance on the initiative of low-income residents.[23] Additionally, as Mayor Lindsay approvingly noted, homesteading's focus on private ownership gave "each tenant a stake in his building and his apartment."[24] Homesteading thus seemed to offer a path that satisfied both residents of low-income areas plagued by abandonment and officials looking for a low-cost means to curtail the crisis.

New York was not the only city in the early 1970s that looked to this solution to the desertion and decay afflicting urban areas. Cities such as Baltimore and Philadelphia instituted programs through which they gave away or sold for a nominal fee abandoned properties to those promising to move in and undertake repairs.[25] Most cities, however, oriented their homesteading initiatives toward providing cheap homeownership opportunities to those who had left for the suburbs or were contemplating doing so. Faced with building abandonment and declining middle-class populations, many cities were content to offer properties to potential homesteaders—typically the young and economically mobile—who were willing to invest both their time and capital into a vacant and decaying stock of single-family homes. The federal government similarly encouraged homesteading. By 1973, the Department of Housing and Urban Development (HUD) owned or held mortgages on upward of 200,000 housing units, which it offered to sell to cities for $1 to implement homesteading projects.[26]

The idea of intrepid residents responding to the crisis of abandonment with a roll-up-your-sleeves self-help mentality captured media attention in many areas. Boston's Mayor Kevin White declared homesteading the "sexiest political idea of the year" in 1973. News stories commonly depicted urban centers as the modern day American frontier—recalling older, racialized tropes about nineteenth-century homesteading in which white "pioneers" and "settlers" were offered plots of land to tame "wild" or supposedly people-less areas. "The urban frontier—the decaying center of our cities," one positive television report described, "needs a new kind of pioneer"—the homesteader.[27]

Despite such enthusiasm, many municipal homesteading programs faced significant problems. Properties often required substantial rehabilitation, which could cost more than homes were worth. When restoration was economically viable, homesteaders typically needed loans, even if the homes themselves were free. Given property locations in often racially diverse and economically struggling neighborhoods, bank loans were not easily forthcoming. On the public side, cash strapped cities usually were reluctant to devote financing or other resources to homesteading, despite their professed enthusiasm for programs.[28]

Homesteading had greater success in New York, though it faced unique difficulties there. Participants were often poor and rarely had their own investment capital. The housing stock also consisted primarily of multiunit buildings rather than single-family houses, meaning that homesteading projects needed to be coordinated across several—if not dozens of—individuals and families to be successful.

But unlike in other cities, homesteaders were buttressed by the city's fledgling neighborhood housing movement. A few of these groups could be traced back to Lyndon Johnson's anti-poverty programs, though the vast majority were new grassroots initiatives that formed in the early 1970s by low-income residents who came together to address what they believed to be the most pressing need for their communities: housing. These groups formed in lower-income areas throughout the city, particularly in heavily African American and Latinx areas of Brooklyn, the Bronx, and Manhattan. They were most often led by residents of these communities, though they commonly included some young white leftists from outside of these neighborhoods. These grassroots efforts organized tenant associations, intervened with negligent landlords, managed apartments under the city's receivership program, and facilitated building rehabilitation projects.[29]

In addition to shared strategies and resources, these groups were tied together by a common ideology: they believed in the transformative power of tenants improving and gaining greater control over housing. Neighborhood housing organizations knew that housing was just one facet of the struggles within low-income communities, but it marked a powerful starting point. As Henry Lanier, the founding executive director of Los Sures, in heavily Latinx south Williamsburg, recalled:

> Our theory at Los Sures was educate and organize around housing. Get people to take control of their own buildings. Assist them in that, but let them take the lead . . . And if you get them organized around their immediate housing needs—fixing the roof, fixing the refrigerator, getting the lock on the front door to work . . . they will understand the power of community organizing, of banding together. . . . Then they'll know how best to advocate for better police, for better health care work, for better school teachers and educations . . . Housing [was] the hook to get people to understand how powerful they can be at the street level.[30]

Housing activism was not just a means to improve dire living conditions, but also a potential lynchpin for individual and community transformation. Many activists saw housing as connected to larger structural barriers—the lack of political power, racism, underfunded community institutions—that perpetuated inequalities in the neighborhoods in which they organized. They worked with residents on alleviating emergency housing conditions and gaining greater control over their housing through cooperatives and tenant associations. These collective bodies could not only challenge exploitative landlords and inattentive officials, but also had the potential to spur greater organizing around a range of oppressive structures affecting low-income people and people of color.

Though not all community housing groups were involved in home-steading, low-income homeownership became especially alluring to many housing advocates. Renting meant one's housing and money were entrusted to a potentially derelict landlord, while in a "coop people can feel more se-cure and they know where their money is going," as homesteader Edgardo Caraballo described.[31] The goal was not profit—which seemed highly un-likely at this time—but rather to transfer control of housing to low-income urbanites of color, a group for whom proprietorship was typically out of reach, especially due to long-standing discrimination by both the real estate industry and government policies.[32] Homeownership was thus a means to achieve the movement's larger goals of not only improving living conditions, but empowering community members. "The process of trying to turn a building into a co-op is one of the people reclaiming the right to make their own decisions about their own needs," explained another homesteader. "Most of us are not used to having any power in the place where we live."[33]

In some cases, housing groups embraced homeownership as a goal after recognizing the limitations of other tactics. Many groups found that what had long been seen as the most effective tactic of tenants against landlords—the rent strike—only hastened abandonment in low-income areas. Other approaches produced similarly inadequate results. Mobilization for Youth Legal Services, for example, a legal aid organization in the mostly poor and Latinx Lower East Side, sued unresponsive landlords and the city for failing to enforce dangerous housing codes violations. After years of litigation and few concrete results to show for it, by the early 1970s the group began to work with tenants on taking control of their buildings themselves.[34]

Many housing groups also participated in the Community Management program, which the city created in 1972 in response to pressure from grassroots housing organizations. The program was similar to homesteading but carved out a greater initial role for a neighborhood housing organization. The group would take over a city-owned, landlord-abandoned property and work to create a strong tenant association, with the ultimate goal of tenant self-management and, eventually, ownership.

With their focus on private ownership, these projects were distinctive from New Deal–birthed public housing. The emphasis on private ownership as the ideal means to engender individual empowerment and community control would help win homesteading support from the political right, but also invited criticism from New York's far left. Cooperative ownership, as one socialist group charged, "shifts the responsibility for providing low-income housing on the poor themselves"; a better strategy would be to force "the government to take over, own and maintain more housing, under tenant control."[35]

But homesteaders eschewed the kind of mammoth, modernist government-led projects like public housing and, especially, urban renewal, which had been dominant in prior decades. Critiques that urban renewal destroyed neighborhoods and perpetuated racial segregation had largely dislodged renewal as the leading urban development strategy by the late 1960s.[36] Acutely aware of the racist legacies of many liberal urban development projects, homesteaders emphasized that local low-income residents and grassroots housing organizations should instead take the lead. The result was a rhetoric that shunned government-led development in favor of self-help projects initiated from within communities that were reliant on the active leadership of the poor. As a banner outside a Renigades homesteading building proudly proclaimed, the structure was a "sweat equity project" in which "the people" had become the "builders + developers."[37] The Renigades, as one account put it, represented "poor people taking control of their own housing, their own problems, their own community, their own destiny."[38]

Despite the formidable obstacles of transforming New York's declining low-income, multifamily buildings into tenant-owned cooperatives, initial successes revealed the viability of homesteading. One early project, for example, involved a building in the Bronx that was without adequate heat or hot water and in which the plumbing, wiring, windows, and roof all needed immediate replacement. The bank that held the mortgage had no interest in the property. The landlord, an elderly Chinese American immigrant, was substantially behind in municipal tax payments. Though his tenants surely suffered, he was no traditional slumlord attempting to milk the building of its remaining resources while residing outside the neighborhood. Indeed, he too lived in the building. Nevertheless, despite effectively living without a landlord under catastrophic conditions, many tenants remained and began to organize together with the goal of improving circumstances themselves and securing cooperative ownership. Working with a neighborhood housing group, they began to help run the building, secure repairs, and pressure the city to take control and resell the building to tenants with municipal financing.[39]

Although homesteaders faced an uphill battle, their activities received a major boost from the formation of the Urban Homesteading Assistance Board

(UHAB) in 1974. A few years earlier James P. Morton, a well-known left-wing priest who was newly appointed Dean of The Cathedral of St. John the Divine, invited Donald Terner, an urban studies professor at the Massachusetts Institute of Technology, to discuss New York's abandonment crisis and the low-income cooperatives already forming. Terner had spent years researching grassroots self-help housing initiatives among poor people throughout the world and believed homesteading to be an inspiring example domestically. Morton and Terner's discussions prompted them to found UHAB, along with a few housing activists: Charles Laven, a recent graduate of MIT, and Philip St. Georges, a recent Yale graduate and former Housing Department intern.

UHAB quickly became homesteading's most influential proponent. The group benefited not only from its founders being highly educated and white, but also from its association with the prominent St. John the Divine, the cathedral of the Episcopal Diocese of New York. This helped the group gain media attention and meetings with officials. UHAB aimed to provide citywide technical assistance to individual homesteaders and their sponsoring neighborhood-based groups and expand existing municipal programs and resources with the goal of increasing homesteading tenfold, from twenty to two hundred buildings, within two years.[40]

To do so, UHAB worked to convince officials and potential funders that homesteading was not only a more viable solution than prior policies but also especially feasible amidst constraining municipal resources. "Twenty years of public and private efforts have failed to adequately improve housing in the poorest neighborhoods," UHAB proclaimed. Amidst the continued crises of building abandonment, housing affordability, and municipal cutbacks, only homesteading avoided "the long-term maintenance problems of public housing," "the strains and tensions of private landlord/tenant relationships," and cost-prohibitive new construction that would only be possible with "massive subsidy programs which are not now available."[41] Homesteading, as UHAB and many other homesteading groups argued, did not demand much from the economically flailing city, and the support it did require would be short-term. Homesteading principally relied on participants using their own labor; municipal loans, which would be paid back with interest to the city; and tax abatements, which represented "no loss, since abandoned buildings pay no taxes to begin with."[42] It was "categorically the lowest cost way to add an additional dwelling unit to the City's housing stock." The process also trained participants in construction trades, creating a path toward desperately needed, decently paying jobs. These were precisely the characteristics that had helped homesteading to win early support from the Lindsay administration.

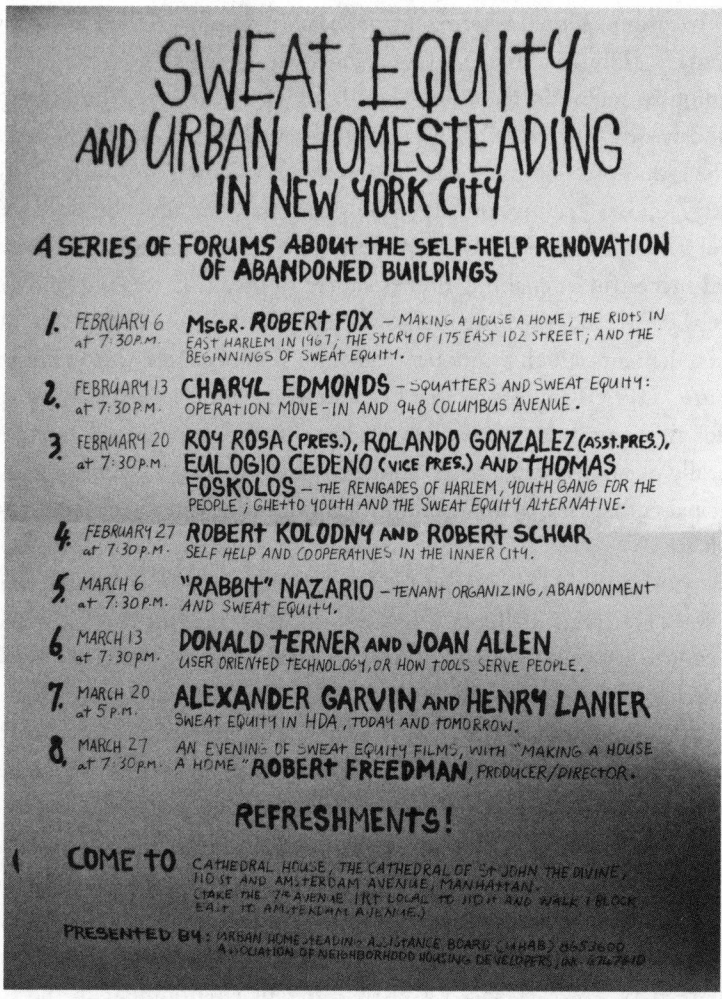

FIGURE 1.3 The Urban Homesteading Assistance Board (UHAB) became the city's most prominent homesteading advocates. The group provided technical assistance to homesteaders and aggressively promoted homesteading to officials and residents, such as through this eight part series on homesteading.

Courtesy of the Urban Homesteading Assistance Board.

UHAB also emphasized the bootstrap, self-help nature of homesteading. UHAB was hardly the only group to utilize this rhetoric; homesteaders and neighborhood housing groups consistently spoke of the promise of self-help that relied on the "sweat equity" of the poor. But more so than groups like the Renigades, whose rhetoric tend to be less filtered, UHAB crafted a message that aimed to make homesteading politically palatable to range of politicians' ears. The group, Donald Terner made clear to funders, "does not provide handouts."[43] Homesteaders, though "often the City's most oppressed— struggling to maintain lives, jobs, and families in the worst buildings and neighborhoods"—were self-helpers who sweated out building renovations and the arduous co-oping process to improve their own conditions.[44] These activities replace "feelings of helplessness with new-found feelings of energy, control, and self-respect."[45] UHAB stressed how these initiatives had already proved successful in enabling homesteaders to take "matters into their own hands by converting the once useless and dangerous hulks of the many aban- doned tenements which litter our streets into safe, decent, low-cost homes."[46] Of course, UHAB made clear that homesteading alone could never be a pan- acea for all the problems of the urban poor, but the group attempted to craft politically persuasive arguments amidst the twin crises of abandonment and municipal cutbacks to assist homesteaders in gaining safe, stable, and afford- able shelter.

The notion that the poor needed to help themselves resonated among both conservatives and liberals. Indeed, the idea had animated the recent War on Poverty. Self-help was "a byword of the War on Poverty," as histo- rian Michael Woodsworth has written, reflecting the idea that "poor people would be offered not cash but opportunity."[47] Yet War on Poverty architects and proponents understood that it took major government resources to create opportunity (even if they did not substantively challenge the under- lying structural and racial barriers of wealth inequality). The War on Poverty therefore created an array of programs—food stamps, Head Start, Medicare and Medicare, and child care—as well as job training and direct employ- ment opportunities in order to provide "A Hand Up, Not a Handout."[48] Homesteaders, however, faced a vastly different environment in the 1970s by which time not only had resources officials were willing to spend on the poor diminished, but so too had faith in the ability of anti-poverty initiatives to succeed. Homesteaders asked for far less than the government resources afforded by the War on Poverty, but they did require support, whether via loans, tax exemptions, or legal channels through which to transfer ownership of tax-foreclosed properties.

Though homesteaders struggled to gain resources, they received con- tinuous praise in the media as well as from important political figures. The *New York Times*, along with the *New York Post* and New York's CBS tel- evision affiliate, endorsed the concept on several occasions, calling home- steading "one of the few hopes for reversing the disastrous trend toward disrepair and abandonment of sound apartment buildings."[49] Civic groups like the liberal New York Urban Coalition likened sweat equity to the brownstoning movement in Brooklyn, noting that such housing rehabilitation projects "restore capitalism and profit to the housing market" and work "because the people who are making it work have a stake in the product."[50] Homesteading also gained currency with national figures. Robert Kennedy's widow Ethel, for example, championed the Renigades at a UHAB organized luncheon of prominent business officials during which she proclaimed that her late husband and brother-in-law would have supported them.[51] The national CBS Evening News with Walter Cronkite also praised New York sweat equity homesteaders as a potential solution to the abandonment crisis plaguing cities nationwide.[52] Seemingly the ideal blend of sixties era demands for greater community control along with a simultaneous growing political climate that favored less reliance on government and more entrepreneurial initiatives for those needing services, the idea appealed to many as a propitious solution to urban ills.

Homesteading's momentum, however, ran headlong into the fiscal crisis at mid-decade that brought New York to the brink of bankruptcy. Under pressure from financial institutions strangling the city's access to capital, officials instituted a sweeping austerity platform. As the fiscal crisis seemed to foreclose on the potential for greater municipal resources, homesteaders and activists looked to novel tactics and new areas of fiscal support. These strategies enabled homesteading to continue to gain favor in the media and from figures across the political spectrum during the mid- and late-1970s. Such support would ultimately help homesteaders gain the attention of the president and the nation.

Homesteading on the National Stage

Abraham Beame came into the mayor's office in 1974 with the belief that homesteading had promise. During his mayoral campaign, Beame expressed support for the city rehabilitating in rem buildings and selling them "to tenants at prices they can afford to pay as new cooperative owners."[53] He continued the programmatic initiatives of the Lindsay administration, with Beame's Housing Commissioner Roger Starr noting in the *Times*: "We've got to move on [homesteading] because it's the only wheel in town."[54] But the fiscal crisis in 1975 curtailed municipal support. Most critically, officials suspended the loan program that had provided financing for homesteading projects.[55] Though officials did allocate federal dollars to a new loan program, funding was far lower what had previously been available.[56]

Aware that the city's financial position was deteriorating, the community housing movement redoubled existing strategies and turned to new ones. Several dozen groups, for example, formed the Association of Neighborhood Housing Developers (ANHD) to share knowledge, pressure officials, and raise funds from foundations, which became an increasingly important source of financial support in the face of municipal cutbacks.[57] Some homesteading groups also used direct action. Homesteaders at 519 East 11th Street, for example, had grown frustrated after they entered loan negotiations with the city for over a year and a half, only to be denied as a result of the fiscal crisis. These bureaucratic delays occurred during a period of rising inflation, jeopardizing the project as material costs increased 20 percent. But these homesteaders marched into municipal offices and said: "We, as Puerto Ricans, have been moved from one neighborhood to the next, and we're not going to be moved out of this one. We're going to stay and fight." With additional threats of protest and pressure from the media and community organizations, the city soon approved the loan.[58]

The fiscal crisis helped to expand homesteaders' target for resources to other levels of government. Homesteading required only "modest amounts of government support or funds," as UHAB's Charles Laven told state assembly members, but "reinvestment" in low-income neighborhoods required some "public sources," such as creating a "state bank for non-profit cooperative enterprises."[59] Supporters also began to seek out federal monies. "In spite of the apparent lack of funds in New York's neighborhoods," Rev. Norman Eddy, a cofounder of Adopt-a-Building described in 1975, "there is always money flowing from the federal government on down."[60] President Richard Nixon had imposed a freeze on federal funding for all housing subsidy programs in January 1973, but the spigot blocking federal funding was removed through the passage of the Housing and Community Development Act of 1974. The Act created the Community Development Block Grant (CDBG) program, which allocated broad funding directly to local authorities and replaced targeted grants under older programs such as Urban Renewal and Model Cities. Funds were to be used principally for projects under the rubric of low- and moderate-income community development.

CDBG funds, however, were filtered through municipal governments that could choose to loosely interpret federal guidelines. While New York administrators had designated some CDBG monies to a new loan program, officials struggling for capital in the wake of the fiscal crisis also used funds for matters as installing an elevator in City Hall, making curb improvements, and even paying Housing department salaries.[61] Such appropriations deepened frustrations with city officials and reinforced existing concerns about government dependability. Understandably, community housing advocates lambasted the city for not allocating more funding to low-income housing initiatives. UHAB's Philip St. Georges told the Board of Estimate, which oversaw funding designations, that they "should be ashamed" of themselves. "You talk about citizen participation and self-help efforts as the key to the survival of New York," St. Georges admonished. But "if you meant what you said, [CDBG] money could be used to encourage and support community self-help efforts." He demanded that funding go to low-income homesteading projects which projected to the community: "You can improve your home and your lives, you can get job training and skills, you can kick dope and get out of jail, and make our disaster area our home again."[62] Indeed, UHAB argued that "self-help" projects were especially critical in the wake of the fiscal crisis: "Now, more than ever, individual and community self-help efforts must fill the void left by the dozens of defunct official programs."[63]

As such decisions by officials were coupled with ongoing budget cuts, some housing advocates were not particularly surprised when in 1976 Housing Commissioner Roger Starr proposed de-emphasizing rehabilitation of some poor neighborhoods. Calling it "planned shrinkage," Starr suggested cutbacks in schools, housing, and hospitals to accelerate the population declines already underway, with the ultimate aim of consolidating poor residents. Though Starr, like Beame and other city officials, had expressed support for homesteading, "planned shrinkage" was a starkly different strategy for dealing with poor neighborhoods. The Beame administration distanced itself from Starr's comments, but to the low-income residents suffering under the city's fiscal retrenchment, planned shrinkage likely seemed to already be underway.[64]

Homesteaders looked to bypass the Beame administration by gaining funding directly from the federal government. For example, UHAB and ANHD, along with several community housing groups, successfully secured funding from Republican Gerald Ford's administration through the Comprehensive Employment Training Program (CETA) and the Criminal Justice Coordinating Council (CJCC), which allowed for homesteaders to be paid stipends while renovating projects and learning construction skills.[65] The fact that homesteaders received resources from a Republican-led federal administration—generally conceived of as being less receptive to the demands of urban grassroots activists—was not missed by advocates. It was the result of homesteading's emphasis on self-help, private ownership, and minimizing the need for ongoing government assistance. "We had loads of conservative right-wing support," the former executive director of UHAB from this era remembered. "Thought it was terrific, because we were encouraging self-help, boot strap, in retrospect what you call wealth building."[66]

Homesteading continued to grow in low-income neighborhoods. Projects were aided by neighborhood groups including the Renigades, Adopt a Building, the People's Development Corporation, Ocean Hill-Brownsville Tenants Association, Manhattan Valley Development Corporation, and United Harlem Growth. Additionally, ten recently formed housing groups gained Community Management contracts with the Housing and Development Administration, which worked toward cooperative owner-ship as its end goal.[67] Homesteading efforts were also buttressed by financing from foundations, including the Consumer-Farmer Foundation, which contributed the entirety of its resources toward assisting homesteading.[68]

Grassroots initiatives coupled with various forms of institutional, founda-tion, and state support helped facilitate an impressive array of fledgling low-income cooperatives. By 1976, UHAB was assisting forty-nine buildings. The Mosque of Islamic Brotherhood, for example, was renovating a building in Harlem that would include apartments, a day care/community center, and a mosque. One Bronx project was being rehabilitated as part of a work-release for those incarcerated in Greenhaven State Prison. A project in the Lower East Side was installing solar heating power and a windmill on the roof to provide energy for the building.[69] Compared to the staggering abandonment numbers in New York—about 150,000 units in 10,000 buildings by the mid-1970s—homesteading numbers were meager, but as the *Times* pointed out, each project had the power to provoke a "ripple effect" within its neighbor-hood. The windmill building, for example, initiated on an otherwise dan-gerous block strewn mostly with stripped cars and abandoned buildings, became "the flagship for the street . . . [with] three other buildings . . . now under construction . . . [and] a vest pocket park" built on an empty lot next door.[70]

These projects stood in stark contrast to the direction of municipal policy during the fiscal crisis, which only worsened conditions for low-income residents, especially those of color. Homesteaders not only alleviated dire housing conditions and increasingly provided job training and wages, but also rebuilt towering structures in their communities that served as phys-ical rejections of the notion that poor areas—and indeed, poor people—should be written off as the necessary price of navigating the fiscal crisis. Homesteading illustrated, in the words of one supporter, how poor people "will neither sympathize with nor tolerate 'planned shrinkage' or any other governmental effort to strangle their communities by curtailing essential services and accelerating the already disgraceful level of decay in the inner city."[71]

Participants also reiterated how homesteading projects enabled the poor to lead the projects designed to improve their neighborhoods. While "the voice of the poor is seldom heard by the City's planners," as one group put it, homesteading enabled "neighborhood residents to take control of their own destinies and chart the course of their future themselves."[72] As Rabbit Nazario of Adopt a Building explained of the group's approach: governments are "supposed to be saving neighborhoods, and we're doing it for them. And I hope we're doing it in a way which illustrates that the established process has failed."[73]

Perhaps no other area of the city needed rehabilitation initiatives more than the South Bronx. In addition to widespread abandonment, "fire and arson became a way of life" starting in the early 1970s, as landlords infamously set their buildings alight in order to collect insurance payments. The area was plagued by redlining, municipal neglect, and "the recurring cycle of drugs, crime, fires, abandonment, and more fires."[74]

One Bronx resident, Ramon Rueda, became inspired by the work of the Renigades and felt that homesteading had the potential to help turn around conditions in the area. In late 1974, he and a group of Bronx residents selected a six-story walk up building at 1186 Washington Avenue, which had been abandoned by its owner and fallen into city possession several years earlier. The building had no heat and was littered with garbage, syringes, dead animals, feces, and urine.[75] The People's Development Corporation (PDC), as the community renovators called themselves, labored for over six months on nights and weekends renovating the building before approaching the city for a municipal loan.

PDC members, however, were told by Housing officials that the twenty-eight-unit building was too big and that the neighborhood was "too far gone."[76] But members of PDC and UHAB gained access to another meeting with officials at which they arrived after a day of renovating the building, their "hair and clothes covered with plaster dust, wearing hardhats, and carrying crowbars and hammers." The group charged HDA—and Roger Starr especially—with racism and writing off the South Bronx and protested with a sit-in that resulted in thirty-one arrests.[77] Soon after, the group secured a city loan for $311,663. Working with ANHD, they also received a federal grant that allowed laborers to be paid for forty hours of work a week, with each participant required to "donate" an extra ten. The group had no trouble convincing federal officials that Bronx workers were formerly incarcerated individuals, a condition of the grant.[78] PDC started homesteading projects at five other buildings, along with helping to organize tenant groups in surrounding buildings threatened with abandonment. "The people of Morrisania—long used to the unfulfilled promises of successive governments and agency administrators," Rueda said, have "decided to generate their own programs, designed to meet the pressing needs of their community as no bureaucratic master plan could."[79]

Around the same time, UHAB, along with PDC and Adopt a Building, successfully convinced HUD to launch its first multifamily, sweat equity homesteading project.[80] While a limited demonstration, this marked a significant reorientation of recent urban policy: financing would be devoted to the poorest areas of the city. "It is important to attempt to save our neighborhoods," observed HUD's Cybil Phillips, "rather than write them off."[81]

The funding helped the People's Development Corporation to capture the media's attention. A group of low-income people of color in one of the most decimated areas of the nation had won financing and funding from the city and the federal government and were leading an effort to provide jobs and improved housing for themselves and community members in an area many felt was unsalvageable. Though PDC was working on less than a dozen buildings, their "self-help programs have extraordinary symbolic significance," as one article put it.[82]

Like other homesteaders, PDC crafted a nuanced political message. The group argued that "private abandonment and government cutbacks have forced neighborhood residents to take control of their own destinies."[83] These failures made clear that "revitalization for a community must be initiated from within, as a self-help program." Homesteading created "safe and decent housing affordable by community residents," the group emphasized, "without subsidy or hand-outs."[84] PDC made clear that these efforts required at least "initial public and private assistance," but stressed that the process would become one of "self-sustaining improvement," with the ultimate goal of "local self-reliance."[85]

The growing national attention on the South Bronx and PDC soon brought President Carter on an unannounced visit to the area in the fall of 1977. Accompanied by HUD officials, he made two major stops. One was to an abandoned and rubble-filled two-block area that the *Times* described as looking "like the result of wartime bombing." The other was to the area recently declared part of the multifamily homesteading demonstration. There he met with PDC, telling members "I'm proud of what you doing" and that he hoped "other people will want to do the same thing."[86] Rueda seized the opportunity to leapfrog municipal officials, telling the president: "What we need is more money from the federal government."[87]

The national press and nightly news covered the president's visit and the work of PDC in the days and months ahead.[88] Unlike the national publicity that accompanied homesteading earlier in the decade, this time the

FIGURE 1.4 The People's Development Corporation's homesteading projects in the South Bronx brought national attention to—and greater government support for—sweat equity initiatives, especially after President Jimmy Carter visited the group in October of 1977.

Courtesy of Neil Selkirk.

homesteaders featured in news reports were the urban poor. In the months following Carter's visit, PDC secured financing and funding from HUD, the city, and a consortium of four New York banks for renovating up to twelve multiple-unit, city-owned buildings into cooperatives, reflecting Carter's favoring of volunteerism and public–private partnerships to address urban problems.

Though PDC's nuanced proposals highlighted a range of issues—including public and private disinvestment and the need for community empowerment in poor areas—political supporters often focused on particular themes. Even the Democratic officials who supported providing some government resources for the poor held up homesteading as a means to diminish welfare, promote individual responsibility, and demonstrate the benefits of private-led revitalization. In a speech at the close of 1977, for example, Vice President Walter Mondale declared that "this administration is committed to the principle of homesteading" because "few programs better address at one time the problems of unemployment, urban squalor, and welfare dependence."[89] Mondale championed the work of UHAB, the Renigades, Adopt a Building, and PDC, citing their example of the power of people to "improve the quality of their own lives." Mayor Beame similarly declared that the project showed "what can be done by local residents to rehabilitate decent housing for themselves and their families, while at the same time restoring and preserving their neighborhoods." "It will," he made clear, "be up to the tenants to roll up their sleeves, [and] get to work."[90] "The self-help spirit is infectious," Juan Villanueva, a vice president at Chemical Bank, the lead bank on the PDC project, believed. "It is with the people, not government, that the responsibility lies for maintaining New York City's housing stock."[91]

Even PDC members themselves could depict the group's strength as breaking the supposed shiftlessness and dependence of poor people. Edward "Moose" Holmes, for example, described in one news article how he had previously been "hanging out, drinking, on welfare, doing nothing," before being transformed through his work with PDC.[92] In a *Saturday Review* cover story on the group, member Danny Soto contrasted PDC with area residents: "All around this area you see people sleeping in doorways, drinking all day . . . their fathers taught 'em nothing, and they don't know nothing. We want to change all that."[93]

PDC's homesteading projects were especially politically palatable because they were seen not as a handout, but as a bootstrap initiative that arose from among the urban poor. Homesteaders were among the worthy because they had demonstrated an ability to improve their own conditions. Their work spoke to the belief among both municipal and federal officials in the 1970s that government practices had changed from War on Poverty initiatives; even if some government assistance was provided, the overwhelming emphasis needed to be on private citizens and groups leading revitalization projects. To be sure, homesteading groups challenged government cutbacks. But the simultaneous emphasis on self-help and community control, the occasional distancing from welfare recipients, and even the emphasis on breaking from government support over the long term could be reinforced by political officials and in media portrayals of homesteading.

Indeed, government support for PDC's work was hardly generous. Much of the funding came from low interest loans that needed to be repaid. While the project enabled participants to become apartment owners, it required them to labor full time mostly at minimum wage, while also contributing ten uncompensated hours each week.[94] No doubt this was done to keep costs of apartments down in an era plagued by high construction expenses and inflation. But it also reflected both Democratic and Republican officials increasing equating of deservedness with entrepreneurial, nongovernmental, self-help initiatives in a time of diminishing government support of social provisions.

Homesteaders directly appealed to and in certain ways some-times encouraged this mentality, even as they simultaneously protested diminishing government support. PDC's message, no doubt shaped by the political and economic conditions of the era, was one that could be reduced to: government-led policies are ineffective; private-led initiatives are prefer-able; and only self-help models are worthy of government support, which should be short-term. As PDC member Paul Reyes put it: "What we have learned is that though the government does owe us a living, we have to work to collect it."[95]

Just as sweat equity gathered national media attention, the city began to grapple with a problem many officials and housing advocates came to see as more pressing than the ongoing crisis of vacant buildings: city-possession of *occupied*, tax-foreclosed buildings. In the late 1970s, more and more oc-cupied buildings began to come under city ownership through tax receiver-ship and overwhelmed, cash-strapped municipal officials did little to improve conditions. Tenants of these long-neglected buildings, housing advocates recognized, by and large faced the worst housing conditions. With this rap-idly accelerating stock of occupied in rem housing, the city of New York, housing advocates charged, had become Gotham's biggest slumlord.

"A Monster that We Are Seeking to Toilet Train"

As housing advocates witnessed this growing phenomenon, they began shifting their focus from the takeover of vacant buildings toward assisting tenants of in rem properties. Even UHAB—sweat equity homesteading's most ardent supporters—began at mid-decade to advocate for policies that would allow tenants "to cooperatively own and manage intact buildings that the City owns or that a landlord wishes to rid himself of."[96] City policy toward these buildings had not just been disastrously ineffective but put tenants in perpetual danger as no one properly oversaw their buildings or provided for their upkeep. The Beame administration relied primarily on auctioning buildings it took possession of through tax foreclosure, which oftentimes resulted in their abandonment by new landlords, continuing the cycle of neighborhood deterioration. "The city finds it easier to sell buildings for short term financial gains," Philip St. Georges of UHAB observed, than "to deal effectively with the long term problems of community revitalization."[97] As the housing movement shifted focus from private landlords to the city itself, the ongoing municipal economic crisis alongside the slow but sure retreat of federal urban policy would ultimately constrain the options available to those who acted on behalf of the city's most vulnerable residents. In the short term, however, the shift seemed to open new possibilities.

The continued problem of landlord desertion was exacerbated by the decision of municipal officials in 1977 to shorten the period in which nonpayment of taxes would result in city foreclosure from three to one years. Desperate for cash, officials thought that the decision would bring in $200 million by encouraging owners behind on taxes to pay. They also believed that for those who did not, properties would come into the city's hands before they deteriorated to the point of being unsalvageable.[98] The decision vastly increased the city's property holdings. The number of seized buildings rose from about 2,500 in 1976 to nearly 10,000 by the end of 1978—encompassing at least 35,000 occupied and 60,000 vacant units—nearly all of which were in economically depressed neighborhoods, especially those with high concentrations of African American and Latinx populations.[99] Officials increasingly came to see this extraordinary stock of publicly owned housing as "the worst problem facing the city right now."[100]

But in this crisis housing activists saw opportunity. The city, it seemed, had few viable options for these buildings. The private market had no productive interest in them. And both neighborhood housing groups and officials had no desire for city government to become the long-term landlord for these tens of thousands of apartment dwellers. Thus, even before the law passed, activists repeatedly pointed out that the city had several existing—albeit poorly utilized—programs in place for converting city-owned properties into tenant ownership or, for those less suited to cooperatives, nonprofit ownership and management.[101] In addition to the Community Management program, community and activist pressure engendered the creation of a municipal Direct Sales program that enabled tenants in properties that had come into city possession or that a landlord otherwise wanted to discard to form a cooperative and become the owners. The program, however, had suffered from tremendous bureaucratic delays and a paucity of municipal support; in 1977, only one building was sold through the program.[102]

With the election of Ed Koch at the end of 1977, activists hoped for more effective housing policies. Koch was aware of the complications of in rem housing. "We have inherited a monster," Koch wrote to his housing commissioner, "that we are seeking to toilet train."[103] Housing activists and many tenants of city-owned buildings began advocating for programs based on the idea that since this was housing that the market had failed, it should remain in the hands of residents and community organizations, not speculators.

Several activists and politicians formed The Task Force on City-Owned Property, which produced a report to serve as a blueprint for completely overhauling policy on in rem property. The report recommended a variety of programs that would facilitate the transfer of "as many buildings as feasibly possible to tenants groups, many of whom are already acting as de facto managers," including a vast overhaul and expansion of the Direct Sales and Community Management programs. "In an economic climate where residential real estate in low income neighborhoods has little or no market value," the report argued, "there is no choice but to build a new sector for low income residential management and ownership. . . . One that is based on various forms of non-profit and cooperative ownership, and has locally and democrativally [*sic*] controlled planning, management and development as its cornerstone."[104]

The Koch administration knew that continuing Beame's policies would be disastrous. Auctions were doing little to stem abandonment. For one, there existed little market for most of these properties. At an auction of Brooklyn properties in 1978, for example, half of the parcels had no bidders, although most were offered at under $200.[105] Even worse, auctions did little to stop abandonment. More than half of new owners made no tax payments on buildings bought at auctions.[106] A 1977 city report found "that four years after an auction sale . . . 94 per cent of the properties sold are in tax arrears,

54 per cent are again eligible for In Rem Processing, [and] 44 per cent no longer provide suitable housing for city residents."[107] It was not simply that none of these properties were economically viable. It was also that many landlords found it more profitable to purchase a building (nearly for free), collect rent, not pay taxes or for any building services, and then walk away from the building once the city took possession again. As one senior official of the newly named Department of Housing Preservation and Development (HPD) described, "if I were a cartoonist I would draw this [the in rem program] as a big bus, with windows broken and tires missing . . . And we'd be pushing from behind."[108]

Strident advocacy by the community housing movement, combined with pressure from HUD officials to formulate a plan and a clear need to shift course, pushed the Koch Administration to establish a Department of Alternative Management Program (DAMP) in 1978.[109] DAMP created or vastly expanded several programs activists had identified. Community Management, for example, grew substantially. Activists argued that nonprofit organizations were ideal managers of low-income housing, as they did not necessarily need to generate a profit on buildings that had failed in the private market.[110] Additionally, Direct Sales was transformed into the Tenant Interim Lease (TIL) program and became the first significant avenue for enabling tenants in city-owned buildings to form cooperatives. The program allowed tenants to purchase their apartments for $250 per unit after a tenant group successfully managed the building for eleven months. This price was no bargain; it was slightly higher than the average price of apartments for buildings in low-income areas sold at auctions in prior years.[111]

The city also agreed to formal contracts with many community organizations to help run these programs, including UHAB, which provided essential technical assistance and training to fledgling TIL cooperatives. From one angle, there was perhaps some irony in neighborhood housing groups taking such a prominent role in orchestrating DAMP for the municipal government that had they spent years accusing of failing low-income communities. But DAMP was, in fact, the culmination of years of initiatives pushed by community housing groups to elevate themselves as the private partners in government initiatives focused on low-income housing. These groups had spent years publicly criticizing the failures of government policy while working behind the scenes to propose new programs that would expand their role in city policy.

DAMP, of course, could not immediately reverse the problem of abandonment. However, it showed early promise as a solution once properties came into city possession. By late 1979, rent collections—perhaps the most significant measure of tenant satisfaction—were 85 to 90 percent in TIL buildings, 80 to 85 percent in Community Management properties, and 35 percent in city-managed buildings (where most properties remained).[112] "This much is clear," noted HPD Commissioner Leventhal, "these new tenant cooperative and community owners value their home ownership opportunity and see ownership as the single most important tool in their effort to stabilize and preserve blocks and neighborhoods in our low income communities."[113]

The Koch administration's creation of DAMP was a remarkable victory for housing advocates and low-income residents. DAMP shifted the direction from prior policies oriented around immediate cash influx from private auctions and increased municipal support for low-income housing programs. The powerful sentiment homesteaders and housing activists had expressed for years—that lower-income New Yorkers deserved decent, affordable housing they could control—proved critical to reshaping policy.

As the 1970s came to a close, however, the housing movement faced challenges that had previously been unimaginable: a rapid heating up of the housing market and unexpected constraints that emerged as the housing movement saw its programs and many of its groups adopted into government bureaucracy.

Housing Organizing in the 1980s

When Koch assumed office as mayor in January 1978 the city was still, as historian Jonathan Soffer has described, "a physical, financial, and administrative wreck."[114] Years of budget cuts from the fiscal crisis had left many agencies barely functional and yet the city still faced a severe budget shortfall. What's more, the Carter administration had continued a pattern of federal retrenchment from cities that had begun under Richard Nixon and Gerald Ford. New York, Koch administrative officials maintained, would need to rely on its own policy initiatives to ensure its economic viability.

As Koch began work on revitalization strategies, he looked for ways to rekindle what had long been a principal economic engine for the city: its real estate. He vastly expanded policies designed to attract middle- and upper-income residents, such as generous tax abatements and exemptions to subsidize new and renovated housing.[115] But Koch recognized that there remained large swaths of the city in which neither private developers nor gentrifying populations had interest. He supported alternative management programs less because of a concern for the economic and political empowerment of the lower classes than because there seemed to be no market-oriented solution for this housing stock. If nonprofit housing groups or tenants could prevent the further decay of buildings in low-income areas, then they represented the best hope for economic stabilization. Even if TIL and Community Management required some material resources in the short term, these programs, Koch administration officials rightfully believed, ultimately returned properties to private housing and restored them to "full tax paying status."[116] The emphasis on private ownership would not only absolve the city of further responsibility but also give "the people who live in the housing," as Deputy Mayor Herman Badillo noted, "a stake in keeping it up."[117] Additionally, projects like those of PDC broadcast the potential for private revitalization initiatives to take off in low-income areas. After all, as Koch told the audience at a press conference announcing federal funding for the South Bronx in 1978, it was the private sector that "does things quicker and better than government."[118]

But some of the areas with significant tracts of in rem housing—such as Chelsea, Clinton, and the Lower East Side—were by Koch's first year in office showing clear signs of private reinvestment and even gentrification, due to factors such as these areas' prime Manhattan locations and proximity to vibrant cultural scenes, as well as to lavish municipal tax incentive programs. This created the potential for in rem housing to be not simply a stopgap against economic decay, but a resource for fanning a growing real estate market. The Koch administration quickly halted any efforts to involve community groups in creating low-income cooperatives out of in rem buildings in gentrifying areas. "Where there is a market," assistant Housing Commissioner Jeffrey Heintz observed, "we're reluctant to become involved in deep subsidy programs."[119] For an area like the Lower East Side, where the city owned at least 50 percent of the housing stock—at least half of which was unoccupied—policymakers could use in rem housing to fuel the coming bonanza of private real estate development rather than use this public resource to create badly needed decent affordable housing.[120]

Additionally, beginning in early 1979 Koch began to push HPD to hire private real estate managers for its in rem properties across the city.[121] Koch used federal Community Development funds to operate and maintain the city's more desirable property, hired private managers to operate them, and gave managers the option to purchase these buildings on favorable terms after twelve months. The Task Force on City-Owned Property questioned "the fiscal sanity of taking scarce funds and applying them towards a management fee to the same private firms that originally wrote off these buildings."[122] Critics also correctly charged that the Koch administration was devoting more resources to the better city-owned buildings and handing them back to the private sphere, while giving fewer resources to the buildings in TIL and Community Management.[123]

Residents in Alternative Management programs in gentrifying areas soon faced difficulties in getting the city to sell them apartments as agreed, despite the fact that the average earnings in a city-owned apartment were firmly low-income ($6,865, or under $20,000 today) and that most housed families or the elderly.[124] In many cases, residents had also put considerable time and resources into repairing their buildings. One building in Clinton, for example, had endured years with an absent landlord, a drug trafficking superintendent, two suspicious fires, and a long rent strike after a lengthy period with no heat in the winter before taking over and managing the building beginning in 1977. Though most of the residents were elderly, they repaired the roof and major water damage caused by one fire. Even though tenants in the building entered into an interim lease with the city after it took control in mid-1978, the city soon refused to sell the building to them. Residents of city-owned buildings received letters explaining that it was now Housing Preservation and Development "policy to sell city-owned properties located in viable private market areas at market value." [125] As one anonymous housing official commented, "The problem is 'gentrification.' And [the housing department] is being asked to go along with it.... This is a hot area."[126] "We are low-income, Latino, Black and white tenants, mostly with families or senior citizens," one Chelsea resident facing similar city policies noted, asking, "don't we fit into the new look of the Chelsea real estate drive?"[127]

Nowhere, residents of these buildings and housing activists believed, was "the meanness of spirit of the Koch administration more sharply revealed" than in its reneging on the $250 sale agreement.[128] Though tenants and activist resistance initially forestalled a change in price, in 1981 Commissioner Leventhal declared that the city would no longer approve Clinton sales for $250 per unit.[129] The next year, the city made "offers" of over $10,000 per apartment in Clinton and Chelsea. HPD memos turned over to housing activists indicated that the increased sale prices were expected to spread beyond these areas.[130]

This struggle over pricing was compounded by debates over potential restrictions on the resale of these apartments. Coops under Community Management and TIL were governed by state law that required them to be sold to low- and moderate-income people. But officials began to exploit the law's imprecise language to facilitate properties quickly being taken out of the realm of low income.

The issue of resale prices divided the community housing movement. For much of the 1970s concerns over affordability of resold converted cooperative units were nonexistent; no one conceived that formerly landlord-abandoned properties in areas of Harlem or the Lower East Side might soon be out of reach even for very low-income residents. But conditions in many neighborhoods began to change late in the decade, sparking debates within the movement and individual cooperatives. Some advocates favored stern restrictions to ensure that the housing would remain permanently low-income. Others agreed that the housing should remain available only to low-income residents, but stressed that the decision needed to be made by each co-op. A third group felt that any restrictions would penalize the low-income residents who had fought so long for decent housing. "People who have struggled to save a building and are willing to assume their responsibilities as full taxpaying homeowners," the thinking went, "should not be told they must forgo the benefits available to everyone else."[131] The city attempted to exacerbate these tensions as HPD officials proclaimed that any restrictions on resale prices would limit residents' freedom.

The conflict came to a head when Deputy Mayor Nathan Leventhal announced that—after years of pressure by tenants and the housing movement—the city would agree to adopt the $250 sale price as policy, but demanded that the city recoup 40 percent of the subsequent resale.[132] This would allow tenants to make a profit, but take away their ability "to reap a huge windfall at the City's expense."[133] He warned that if the proposal was not approved, the city would cease selling buildings to tenants. An alternative proposal brought by tenants, activists, and several politicians would restrict the sale price, limit the amount received by the purchaser to the $250 price plus capital improvements, and allocate the small profit to the cooperative, which were generally capital-poor. Only if tenants sold at market rate would they be required to give the city 40 percent of the profit.[134]

The city refused the compromise. Advocates were outraged by the city's inflexibility. Koch's proposal, as Council President Carol Bellamy noted, "fails to ensure that the City's policy to preserve low income housing will continue in years ahead."[135] "At a time when Washington has turned its back on supporting low-income housing," Bellamy wrote, "it defies logic that the city would pass up this opportunity to preserve at least a few more units affordable to citizens of modest means."[136] This 40 percent "tax"—as critics called it—on each resale was likely to cause prices to rise higher than low-income populations could afford, as sellers and cooperatives sought to recoup

FIGURE 1.5 This January 1980 cover of New York housing movement magazine *City Limits* commented on the growing controversy over how any profits from resold units of formerly landlord-abandoned, city-owned buildings should be distributed.
Courtesy of City Limits News, Inc.

the capital they had invested, while accounting for the large portion the city would take from the sale.[137]

Koch saw no contradiction in encouraging vast increases in resale prices of apartments initially designated as low-income housing. This could only be the sign of neighborhood revitalization. Though critics like Bellamy pointed to the decline of federal aid as the reason why the city needed to devote its own resources to preserving affordable housing, to Koch, dissipating federal support for cities was precisely why New York needed to rely on the private sphere. "In the face of this virtual elimination of Federal aid," Housing Commission Anthony Gliedman noted, "the City must do all it can to spur private reinvestment if we are to save our housing stock."[138] Any measure to limit what housing might garner on the private market risked endangering needed private monies to maintain such housing, even for property legally designated as low-income housing. This was capital the city could not afford—and that the federal government was no longer willing—to provide. What's more, restrictions that aimed to help keep low-income residents in their neighborhoods potentially risked slowing or even reversing the economic rejuvenation of these areas. If failing to implement protective measures meant that low-income residents would be displaced from gentrifying neighborhoods, such problems, Gliedman noted, "are preferable to those created by decline and disinvestment."

The initial $250 sale price agreement was nonetheless viewed as a gain for tenants and activists, particularly as an anti-displacement measure for the initial purchasers. In gentrifying areas this meant that thousands of "low income, mostly minority residents won't be facing the threat of losing their homes."[139] Additionally, many buildings enacted restrictions on resales in their bylaws to ensure that the property would continue to serve low-income shareholders. As a tenant in one Clinton building said, "we refuse to make a profit on our resales. Where could poor working people go?"[140] But at other buildings resale prices quickly escalated, removing units from a dwindling supply of low-income housing. At one coop on West 121st Street, just months after tenants paid $250 for their apartments, the board of directors voted for minimum resale price of one hundred times that amount—a violation of the "moral basis" of TIL, as one observer put it, but not the law itself.[141]

The inability to ensure continued affordability of cooperative units and to prevent the city from directing in rem properties back into the private market were just two major unexpected developments for the housing movement. A third resulted from the severe limitations placed on many community housing groups as they became part of government programs. In the early years of the Koch administration many major neighborhood housing groups entered into contracts with the city through DAMP or the Community Consultant Contracts program or with state or federal programs to provide housing management, training, services, and rehabilitation in the low-income areas in which they were organizing. This reflected a significant counterpoint to the austerity policies of the 1970s, as numerous groups saw their budgets grow from five figures to several million dollars.[142]

But institutionalization also shifted the nature of some of the programs community housing groups had fought for years to see become policy. For example, programs like Community Management faced new criticism. Many groups helped to turn around conditions in rapidly deteriorating or drug-infested buildings and, in many cases, spurred strong tenant associations who came to manage their own buildings. However, city contracts de-emphasized tenant management and increased bureaucratic municipal-approval processes, often resulting in service delays that could put managing groups at conflict with tenant associations.[143] "The basic philosophy of HCC [Housing Conservation Coordinators] has been to educate tenants with the aim of tenant self-help, i.e. tenant-managed and tenant-owned buildings. . . . Community Management has instead made HCC into a typical landlord's agent," one group charged, in explaining its refusal to renew its city contract.[144] The program "does not allow the tenants to be in control of their own buildings."[145] Many housing activists claimed that Community Management "more than any other city effort, has changed neighborhood groups from local rabble-rousers into construction supervisors, developers, property managers and even landlords."[146] Creating a financially dependent relationship among community housing groups may have been part of its intention—or at least it was a welcomed outcome. An internal Housing department memo in 1980 positively described how the program "buys peace and cooperation from many low income communities."[147]

Such concerns went well beyond the Community Management program. A growing number of community housing advocates charged that nearly all city or state contracts with housing groups caused organizations to become increasingly disconnected from major principles that had driven the movement since its emergence a decade before: following community-initiated efforts to improve neighborhood housing conditions, connecting the control over housing to the need for greater community power over other local resources and institutions, and linking community organizing around housing to mobilizing for larger economic and political change. These goals became increasingly out of reach either because contracts explicitly forbade such activity or because there was simply no way to fund this work while juggling the demands of these contracts. As early as 1979, the housing movement publication, *City Limits*, observed how "organizations whose first priority was once advocacy—organizing tenants around different housing and neighborhood issues—are now putting the bulk of their energy into running government programs."[148] This, critics charged, prevented groups from being directed by poor residents themselves and caused groups to shed their "role of community agent, advocate and resource center." Grassroots groups had transformed from being "responsible locally" to being "responsible to institutional needs and where [their] money comes from," in the words of one long-term activist.[149] Groups "became service providers, agencies, landlords," with "funding and administrative demands" dictated by government and foundations driving organizations.[150] This also allowed the city to more easily direct the end goal of groups toward the economic stabilization—if not rapid market escalation—of low-income areas.

By these important measures, the incorporation into government bureaucracy significantly changed the nature of the community housing movement in the 1980s. By decade's end, even the *New York Times* recognized the widespread change that had occurred. Many housing groups had "transformed from tenant-rights advocates, community organizers and thorns in the sides of city officials into builders, property managers and landlords in New York City's poor neighborhoods."[151] The group Banana Kelly was indicative of such change. Started in the Bronx in the late 1970s as a homesteading initiative inspired by the Renigades, by the end of the 1980s it had become a seven-million-dollar, hundred-employee organization that managed twenty-six buildings.[152] Tenants in buildings renovated and managed by the group often found conditions improved, but some still suffered from slow repairs and catastrophes like ceiling collapses. "They've got too many buildings, now" one resident said. "Now they're like a corporation."[153] In order to secure and maintain city and foundation funding, its executive director stated plainly, "we gave up our right to advocate and organize in this community."

The growing place of the community housing movement in government nonetheless did lead to a number of achievements. This was particularly notable in the case of TIL and low-income cooperatives. In the 1980s, the cooperative conversion of multifamily, landlord-abandoned buildings in poorer neighborhoods grew significantly, especially through TIL. Even though TIL's budget represented just 3 percent of what the city spent on tax-foreclosed housing programs in the early 1980s, by 1982, the program had become the largest tenant self-management program in the country, with over one hundred low-income multifamily cooperatives formed.[154] By the end of the 1980s, approximately 350 buildings with 8,500 apartments had been sold to tenants through TIL or Community Management. These cooperatives not only helped to provide decent and affordable housing to low- and moderate-income residents, but often served as the lynchpins in stabilizing many lower income neighborhoods. As one co-op resident on Hoe Avenue in the South

Bronx explained, she and her neighbors had worked for years to renovate their landlord-abandoned building, turn the basement into a community space, and combat local drug dealing "so that we could join people one to another, so that we could be a neighborhood."[155]

Cooperative ownership has also helped serve as stopgaps to shareholders' displacement as neighborhoods began to gentrify in the 1980s. "I feel proud of the fact that we are truly in control of our living space," noted one Harlem co-op resident on 114th Street. "*We* can control how much we pay, and *we* can insure the fact that we will be able to afford to live on the island of Manhattan" in the future.[156] Studies also showed that TIL residents were happier with their housing than those in any other management program, citing "resident satisfaction, social support among residents, a sense of belonging, and ability to control housing conditions and cost" and, for many residents, "the process of organizing collectively to take control of and manage their buildings."[157]

LOW-INCOME NEW YORKERS AND activists in the 1970s demonstrated how, even in the midst of crisis, people were determined not to give up on where they lived. Though homesteading and other initiatives to facilitate poor and low-income people gaining greater control over their homes and communities did not always fulfill proponents' expectations, they captured peoples' imagination and in doing so refocused attention on the poorest areas of the city.

Homesteaders and advocates navigated the crises of abandonment and affordable housing with ingenuity. Recognizing the tumultuous history both of government and private investor involvement in low-income areas, they forged an alternative path forward—one that relied on and empowered low-income residents themselves. They saw homesteading as a self-help initiative that arose from—and that would be directed by—those outside both municipal and federal government. Attuned to the political currents of the 1970s, they also crafted a nuanced political message that won homesteading important allies among elected officials from across the political spectrum. And by strategically looking to the federal government during the city's fiscal crisis and to city officials as federal withdrawal from urban areas accelerated in later years, homesteaders and advocates improved housing and empowered low-income New Yorkers.

However, the message homesteaders and advocates promoted ultimately enabled officials from across the right and the left to champion homesteading as a private-based, self-help rejuvenation effort that could persevere where government had failed. This gave greater credence to a broader governing ideology gaining ground over the decade that favored private-led rejuvenation efforts. After all, to a casual observer, it seemed that even low-income people themselves preferred less government and for development to be led by actors outside of the state. Officials were able to seize upon homesteading and selectively promote its politically alluring characteristics—a message furthered by media coverage. Homesteading, Democratic officials like Mayor Beame and Vice President Mondale proclaimed, demonstrated the success of relying on the reduced role of government and the promotion of private and market-based solutions for rejuvenating neighborhoods. In attempting to navigate the shifting economic and political conditions in the 1970s, everyday residents helped facilitate New York's turn to the market and private sector in ways they did not intend.

Mayor Koch accelerated the vision of turning toward the private sector and market upon taking office. Though low-income activists and housing advocates won remarkable victories that limited or entirely prevented in rem housing's exposure to the market, Koch was able to implement policies that overwhelmingly favored private development, boosted in part by the recent championing of private-led rejuvenation initiatives like homesteading.

Koch's vision was also abetted by growing use of city and state contracts that helped transform many housing advocacy groups into municipal program administrators, forestalling their agitation for broader economic and political transformations of low-income neighborhoods. With a major element of the housing crisis by the late 1970s centered on a municipal-owned resource, the city could more easily dictate the conditions of this stock's (ultimately, market-oriented) future. Unsurprisingly, when city resources for initiatives promoted by the neighborhood housing movement increased substantially in the late 1970s, many groups clamored for such support. A movement engendered in part by government inaction was perhaps bound to recognize an influx of resources as the fulfillment of long-standing goals. But in ways largely unexpected, the terms of this incorporation helped transform many housing groups into program administrators, forestall their agitation for broader economic and political transformations of low-income neighborhoods, and still allow the city to rely as much as possible on market-based solutions for the crisis of city-owned housing. These contracts were designed to shift responsibility for in rem housing to those outside government, but they also had the effect of altering the focus of the movement away from prior key tenets, such as increasing poor peoples' control over their housing and neighborhoods and connecting conditions in poorer minority areas to larger economic and political systems. As a result of these factors, early in his first term Koch was able to institutionalize as city policy private-led rejuvenation initiatives and narrow the seeming viability of limiting market-exposure to the stock of affordable housing.

2

From Renters to Owners

SHORTLY BEFORE CHRISTMAS in 1969, an anonymous tenant of 360 East 72nd Street wrote to Mayor John Lindsay in a fury.[1] For the building's middle-class, rent-protected tenants, the security and stability of home had been upended by a surprising proposal they had recently received from their landlord: he wanted to convert the building to a cooperative by selling each tenant their apartment. Unlike the homesteaders who at the same time were taking over buildings in low-income neighborhoods, these middle-class New Yorkers wanted no part in owning their home. The conversion plan, the letter writer claimed, was merely a way for the landlord to "nullify" government-enforced rent protections, while making an "extravagant and unconscionable" profit. Especially alarming was that tenants who did not buy risked eviction. The author believed that these kinds of landlord-initiated cooperative conversions would result in the end of New York's middle class. Not wanting to be burdened by ownership, losing the security of rent protections, and facing eviction in a tight housing market, these residents would be forced to flee the city. "IT IS IMMORAL," the author wrote, "for landlords of the city to drive the middle class out of New York and leave it a haven for the very rich and a jungle for the very poor." With landlord-initiated conversions beginning to grow across the city, the writer pleaded with Mayor Lindsay to launch an investigation into "how many families will be driven out of their apartments and from the city because of these actions."

New York's landlords and real estate boosters saw the matter of converting middle-income rental buildings into cooperatives quite differently. To Rexford E. Tompkins, for instance, president of the Real Estate Board of New York (REBNY), the industry's most important trade organization, and head of a leading real estate firm, Brown Harris Stevens, cooperative conversions would address several of the most important problems facing the city. One was the condition of the housing stock, 60 percent of which was over forty years old. Tompkins worried openly about the ongoing "housing decay and disaster in our city."[2] Building abandonment in low-income areas was one sign, but prominent real estate figures like Tompkins expressed great concern with the declining condition of the housing stock in middle-income neighborhoods, which municipal officials seemed to be ineffective in stemming. Real estate men principally blamed the robust rent protection laws that limited landlord capital for continued upkeep.[3] It was true that conversions would allow landlords to escape the rent regulation system, but in seeking to convert their buildings they would underwrite improvements to induce tenants into assuming ownership, as the potential sale created a financial incentive to do so.

Tompkins also believed cooperative conversions would in fact help retain the middle class. Nearly 900,000 white residents left the city during the 1960s, mostly for its surrounding suburbs.[4] While the suburbs were burgeoning with fledgling homeowners, New York remained a city of renters, bucking the powerful postwar trend toward homeownership.[5] Dominated by multifamily rental buildings and with new construction at a standstill, the city offered few opportunities for middle-class populations to own their home, distressing leaders of the real estate sector.[6] Conversions would address this lapse. "The fundamental drive toward home ownership," Tompkins believed, "can only be satisfied in an urban economy through co-op ownership."[7] Without homeownership opportunities, men like Tompkins believed, the middle class would continue to abandon New York. Throughout postwar America suburbanization drew middle-class residents—and their incomes and property taxes—out of major cities, but New York's particular version of postwar decline was striking, because real estate had long been one of its dominant industries.

Alongside other prominent real estate figures, Tompkins championed converting rental buildings to cooperatives as a creative solution that—despite the concerns on 72nd Street—would solve the two perilous conditions pulling the city deeper into an economic and housing crisis as the middle-class tax base and housing stock eroded. Conversions, Tompkins declared, were "the only genuine hope for any salvation for the city's housing supply."[8] Real estate boosters like Tompkins helped launch a campaign in the late 1960s to convince city-dwellers that converting rental buildings into cooperatives would benefit them, their neighbors, and the city as a whole.

A number of prominent political officials, housing experts, and civic leaders also became convinced that conversions would improve the housing stock and advantage all involved. Landlords would not only profit hand-somely, but residents would be able to own their homes and the city would retain its middle-class base, keep property taxes stable, and gain from income taxes. "Cooperative ownership represents a valid and valuable approach to the preservation of good housing and a way of encouraging middle-class families to remain in the city," Herman Glaser, Chairman of the recently-formed con-sumer advocacy group New York Council for Civic Affairs, proclaimed.[9] Greater homeownership opportunities might even induce some of the over 600,000 commuters into New York City from its suburbs to take up resi-dence within the city.[10]

Unfortunately for supporters like Tompkins, the tenants of 360 East 72nd Street were not alone in their opposition to conversions. Indeed, enthusiasm for conversions hardly extended to the population whose endorsement was necessary for them to proliferate: tenants. "Doesn't every New Yorker really want to own a co-op?" Louis Smadbeck, president of the realty concern Wm. A. White & Sons, asked a crowd of tenants at a 1972 hearing on conversions. His question provoked only "a chorus of noes."[11]

There were many reasons middle-class tenants might reject the opportu-nity to own their apartments. Because laws protected many residents from significant rent increases, fixed-rate mortgage payments were a less obvious advantage, especially when coupled with a sizeable down payment. Others felt little assurance that their investments would grow, a not illogical senti-ment given that cooperative unit prices fell steeply in the late 1960s and that the city's future increasingly looked precarious to many residents. Tenants also often maintained that they or their neighbors could not afford to pur-chase their apartments and rejected any proposal that forced the choice to buy or vacate. For this complicated but understandable set of reasons tenants commonly banded together to block proposed conversions. Their cause was aided by a state law that required that a specific percentage of existing tenants in a building (35 percent in 1968) had to agree to purchase their apartment in order for a conversion to receive state approval.

For over a decade beginning in the late 1960s, conversions became fraught terrain with the stakes involving nothing less than people's home. The con-test over conversions involved two competing ideas of how best to secure the city's future. On one side were landlords and real estate leaders who saw conversions as an opportunity to dismantle the rent regulation system. Joining them were politicians, heads of civic associations, and business leaders who viewed increased homeownership as the means to improve the housing stock and expand the middle class. On the other stood tenants who organized within and across buildings to assert the opposite: conversions would lead to the eradication of the middle class, in no small measure by decimating the rent regulations that kept housing costs within its reach.

Over the 1970s, however, tenants' receptiveness to conversions slowly shifted. While initially few middle-class residents jumped at the chance to own their apartments, as strident tenant organizing increasingly stymied conversions, tenants began to win greater concessions designed to induce them into ownership. Though oftentimes the goal of tenant organizing was to stop conversions—not simply to obtain better deals—over time, fierce renter opposition led to legislative changes and shifts in landlord practices that brought economic advantages to tenants-turned-owners in a conversion. This change was compounded by the emergence of a new voice in the conversion debates in the late 1970s: fledgling cooperative owners. These owners formed organizations and launched publications that advocated for—and educated residents about—cooperative ownership, helping to normalize middle-class apartment ownership in New York, and further quell tenant opposition.

By the early 1980s, the shifting sentiment toward conversions became more widespread. This changing attitude was the linchpin for the dramatic expansion of conversions and the larger acceptance of apartment owner-ship, which underwrote a momentous turnaround in the real estate market. Conversions also enabled the real estate industry to attain a goal that for years it had struggled to achieve: diminishing the grip of rent regulations over the housing stock. This marketization of rent-regulated apartments was not simply imposed from above by the real estate industry and municipal officials. While the real estate industry initially pushed conversions, they proliferated only once they were embraced by the very regulated tenants who came to benefit in the process. What had begun in the late 1960s as a tenant move-ment opposing conversions had increasingly become by the early 1980s one in which tenants aimed to secure the most lucrative conversion deals possible. This shift enabled conversions to spread and for market-rate, owner-occupied apartments to begin to flourish in the city.

Promoting Homeownership in the City of Renters

Leading real estate figures like Tompkins were not foolish for thinking that tenants might find conversions attractive, given the potential benefits. In ad-dition to the opportunity to own and have control over one's home, federal, state, and city laws offered cooperative owners tax deductions similar to those available for homes in the suburbs.[12] Though much of the rental stock was

protected from substantial rent increases by government regulations, ownership would enable residents to improve their building in ways the landlord
had been unable or unwilling to do. For unregulated apartments, conversions
would protect against unpredictable rent increases.

Conversions, however, promised even greater gains for the real estate industry. Prominent industry figures and major real estate organizations who
championed conversions believed increasing homeownership opportunities
would benefit all residents by improving the city's long-term health. But they
were principally compelled to act because of the concern that their industry
faced the gravest threat as a continued middle-class exodus weakened the economic stability of the city and its real estate. Additionally, landlords—from
owners of single buildings to real estate barons—overwhelmingly supported
conversions because they promised enormous profits. Selling off a building
through sales of individual units to tenants produced far greater sums—
generally three to four times more in the early 1970s—than selling one's
building to another landlord. As in retail, property owners could make far
more by selling directly to consumers than by operating as wholesalers.

Conversions were particularly appealing to owners of rent-controlled
properties, which made up 77 percent of the rental stock in 1960.[13] No issue
provoked the ire of landlords quite like rent control, which owners viewed
as artificially constraining profits by significantly restricting rent increases.
Federal officials had introduced rent regulations as part of price and inflation control measures during World War II, but they continued into the
postwar decades in New York because of the city's strong tenant movement.
Landlords had by the 1960s formed various organizations whose principal
aim was to eliminate rent control. On January 20, 1967, for example, more
than five thousand property owners came to the Manhattan Center to hear
representatives from a newly formed New York Realty Owners Association
(NYROA). The group brought together more than forty smaller landlord
organizations under the "common goal of aiding property owners who
have suffered losses under the 'oppressive' rent control laws." One speaker,
Reverend Walker, felt the injustice of rent control to be so great that he called
upon God to bring about its end. Another deemed Mayor John Lindsay and
Governor Nelson Rockefeller thieves, warning them: "Either you give us justice or you give us jail."[14] But even coalitions like NYROA could not provide a sufficient counterweight to the collective political strength of millions
of rent protected tenants. Cooperative conversions thus seemed at first to
offer landlords a politically tenable and highly profitable escape from rent-
regulated housing.

The real estate industry actively encouraged the spread of conversions through its major trade organization. The Real Estate Board of New York (REBNY) offered landlords educational seminars on "how to co-op your rent controlled apartment house" and prophesized to political officials about the fortunes conversions would bring.[15] Conversions allowed landlords to sell their buildings "at a fair price to the tenants," Rexford Tompkins declared.[16] They were, he told members of the City Council in 1969, the "only possible escape" from urban ruin.[17]

Though conversion boosters like REBNY struggled to make immediate gains among tenants, they helped convince Mayor Lindsay of its potential benefits. By the late 1960s, Lindsay took a keen interest in promoting conversions for several reasons. For one, he shared the concern about retaining the middle class. Anxiety over an evaporating middle-class white population had fueled many of the urban renewal and Title I projects in the years after World War II, when many white families left for the suburbs.[18] At the dawn of the 1970s, with no federal resources that paralleled an initiative like Title I, Lindsay needed new solutions. Administration officials hoped that by increasing homeownership, conversions might stabilize the exodus and "contribute toward keeping the middle class in the city"—a population, as during the era of urban renewal, that was understood to be white.[19]

Lindsay was also concerned about the effects of rent control. His head of the Housing and Development Administration (HDA), Jason Nathan, had commissioned several studies to assess the effects of rent control. One by the Rand Corporation blamed rent control for the staggering number of apartments being abandoned by owners in low-income neighborhoods.[20] Another study by Rutgers University's George Sternlieb suggested that rent control had deleterious effects even outside lower income areas.[21] Defenders of rent regulations pointed out that the problem of abandonment extended to cities throughout the country with no such laws. Nonetheless, these studies, along with growing pressure from landlords who were becoming "more organized" and "more adamant," convinced Lindsay and key members of his administration that rent controls were the leading cause of building abandonment and would soon cause the decline of middle-class neighborhoods as well.[22]

But with millions of residents protected by rent control, Lindsay recognized that it was politically impossible to remove them in a single stroke. He instead looked for ways to reduce their supposedly harmful effects. Commissioner Nathan and other housing officials believed that converting rent-controlled buildings to cooperatives was a viable means to do so. Conversions, one HDA report optimistically declared, would satisfy all parties: rent-controlled tenants who were "dissatisfied with building maintenance and deterioration," landlords who "would like to be absolved of the problems of managing property under the provisions of rent control," and city officials who sought low-cost means to improve housing and retain the middle class.[23]

Lindsay administration officials, however, struggled to find ways to proactively facilitate conversions in middle-income areas beyond providing "public information/education."[24] This changed with the passage of rent stabilization in 1969. Rent stabilization resulted from years of bitter debate between real estate and tenant advocates over the growing number of apartments that were unprotected from rent regulations (principally those build after 1947), which largely housed middle-class tenants. Many tenant advocates applauded the law because it instituted rent regulations for these 400,000 units, even if stabilized apartments faced much more significant yearly increases than rent-controlled units. Landlords, however, were alarmed that the law would restrict profits on these newly regulated buildings, leading conversion proposals to spike.[25] Additionally, the mayor's office and City Council had included an initially little-noticed provision that lowered the number of existing tenants needed to agree to purchase their apartment from 35 percent to 15 percent for a conversion to be allowed to proceed in a rent-stabilized building, greatly increasing the likelihood of success.

The rent-stabilization law kick-started a battle over conversions that would last for well over a decade. Though there had been some opposition to conversions earlier in the decade, resistance swelled into a full-fledged movement only at the end of the 1960s. Previously, conversions were infrequent and limited to only one area of Manhattan: the Upper East Side, home to much of the borough's affluent housing.[26] But the number of proposed conversions growing and spreading from affluent to middle-class buildings following rent stabilization buoyed opposition.

Although Mayor Lindsay and the real estate industry had hoped that residents would welcome the opportunity to own their apartments, tenants commonly responded to the increasing number of conversion proposals with outrage and fear. Rita Savoy, for example, an elderly tenant of 250 West 94th Street, wrote to political officials in a "desperate situation" in 1969. A number of "wealthy tenants" of her rent-regulated building supported a conversion.[27] The building, Savoy acknowledged, was in "poor shape" and the conversion would result in needed improvements to the pipe system, roof, and building interior. These seemed to be the exact circumstances conversion boosters pointed to in making their case. But the monthly maintenance costs for a cooperative would be "out of the question" for her and many of her neighbors. These residents, Savoy wrote, included "Social Security recipients, city pensioners, widows, invalids in chairs, sufferers from heart ailments. . . . Refugees from Nazzi [*sic*] concentration camps, and some, like myself, although *past seventy* continue working to meet ends." She feared that she and her neighbors would have to leave their homes. "Why should rich tenants," Savoy wrote, "have the right to throw out those who have no money?" The new law made it possible for 15 percent of residents to force a conversion on the entire building, leaving those who did not purchase their apartment open to eviction proceedings. Savoy's fear was understandable.

With the provision supported by the City Council and mayor, tenants hoped another powerful figure would come to their aid: the state Attorney General. New York was unique in that its Attorney General was charged with overseeing offerings of cooperatives and condominiums.[28] Attorney General Louis Lefkowitz was widely admired, winning each of his elections handily since 1958, and much of his popularity rested on his strong reputation as a consumer advocate. Lefkowitz and his Assistant Attorney General, David Clurman, recognized cooperatives as potentially beneficial both to tenants and the city but saw themselves as public advocates responsible for protecting tenants in the process. Neither Lefkowitz nor Clurman believed that requiring only 15 percent of residents to approve a conversion afforded ample protection for tenants.

Taking matters into their own hands, they refused to approve any conversions proposed for a rent-stabilized building unless the owner received the endorsement of 35 percent of tenants. Lefkowitz wrote to Mayor Lindsay and the City Council president that the reduction to 15 percent "represents a clear danger to the public interest."[29] His actions sparked several supportive *Times* articles, no doubt embarrassing the mayor who personally intervened to implore Lefkowitz to see that the city's future required greater homeownership.[30] But Lefkowitz would not budge. With the Attorney General's office refusing to approve conversions, the council and mayor backed down, agreeing to establish a 35 percent threshold in rent-stabilized buildings.[31]

The struggle over the rent-stabilization provision was representative both of the broader awakening of tenant opposition to conversions well as a greater fission within New York's socially democratic tenets. Tenant opposition, steeped in this tradition, proclaimed that government's responsibility was to protect its residents, even if doing so impeded the market. This view, however, was increasingly coming into conflict not just with long-standing market

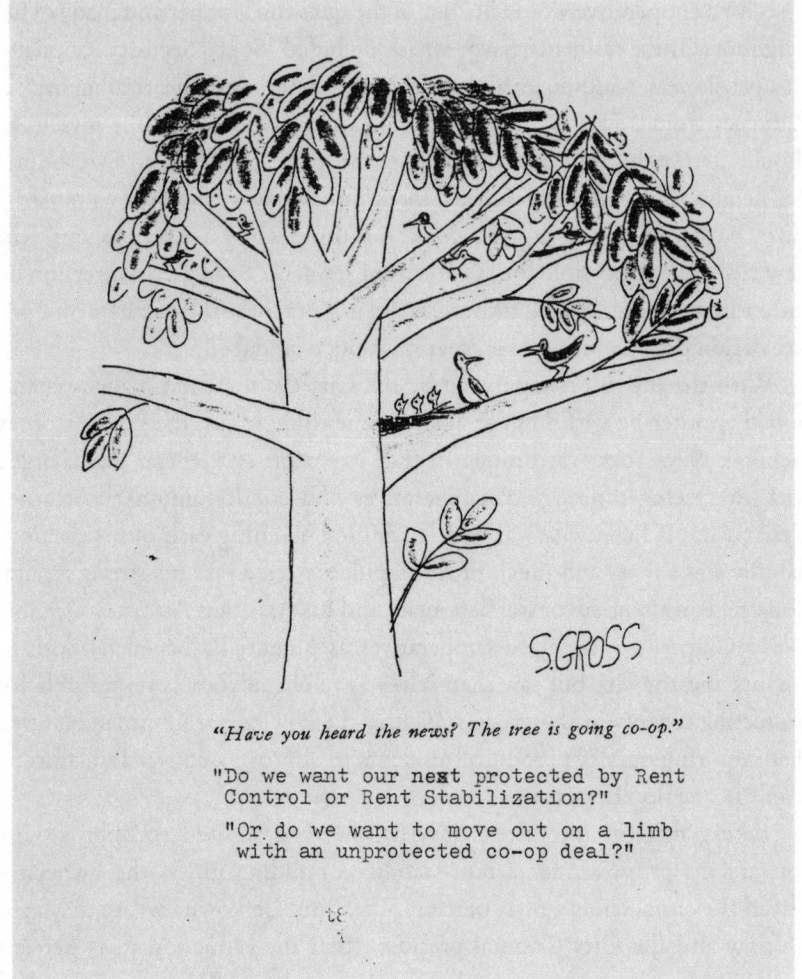

"*Have you heard the news? The tree is going co-op.*"

"Do we want our nest protected by Rent Control or Rent Stabilization?"

"Or do we want to move out on a limb with an unprotected co-op deal?"

FIGURE 2.1 For many moderate and middle-income tenants, news that their landlord would be attempting to convert their building into a cooperative was hardly welcomed. Many believed that renting offered more security, especially if their building was rent-regulated.

Jack Newfield Papers, di_11925. Courtesy of the Dolph Briscoe Center for American History, The University of Texas at Austin.

advocates from the real estate industry but even in the position liberal officials like Lindsay took toward promoting ownership and undoing rent control, long viewed as a hallmark of the city's left exceptionalism. This conflict over the government's role as protector from—or facilitator of—the market would deepen in the decade ahead.

In the interim, tenants banded together. As landlords proposed conversion plans for an increasing number of middle-class buildings, tenants began to organize, first in their buildings and then citywide. Rejecting the notion that conversions would enable the city to retain a healthy middle-class population, these residents offered themselves as examples of how conversions would in fact have the opposite effect.

Middle-Class Opposition to Conversions

Though tenants saw Clurman and Lefkowitz as allies, residents opposing conversions did not rely on political officials alone. And while the Attorney General's office sought to make the conversion processes fairer for tenants, there was a growing sentiment among some tenants that conversions should instead be stopped entirely.

The group Tenants Against Cooperative Conversion (TACC), formed in 1969, led this effort. "There exists a powerful Real Estate lobby," the notes from one early TACC meeting observed. "Tenants must all join together to create a stronger lobby."[32] The group called for a moratorium on all conversions until the vacancy rate increased, demanded that no conversion proceed without the approval of two-thirds of active tenants, and stipulated that if the plan were not approved by tenants within ninety days of its offering the landlord be prevented from issuing another plan for three years. As the group no doubt knew, these provisions would likely bring an end to nearly all conversions.

Within just a few weeks, forty-four buildings facing or expecting conversion plans unanimously accepted TACC's platform and an additional sixty-seven buildings were in the process of doing so.[33] These were middle-income buildings primarily on the Upper East and West Sides of Manhattan, where conversion proposals first proliferated before spreading in the early 1970s to other parts of Manhattan and gradually to Brooklyn and Queens. The group organized protests at politicians' offices and spoke out at hearings for legislation that affected conversions. "Stop Cooperative Coercion Now!," one early flier proclaimed bluntly. It continued: "We will take our fight to the local, state, and federal governments. We will fight through the courts and legislatures. . . . WE MUST SHOW THE POLITICIANS THAT WE MEAN BUSINESS."[34]

Though TACC had begun to successfully mobilize residents through protest activities, residents most often organized through tenant associations within individual buildings after their landlord proposed a conversion. For example, residents at Park Terrace Gardens in Inwood, the northernmost

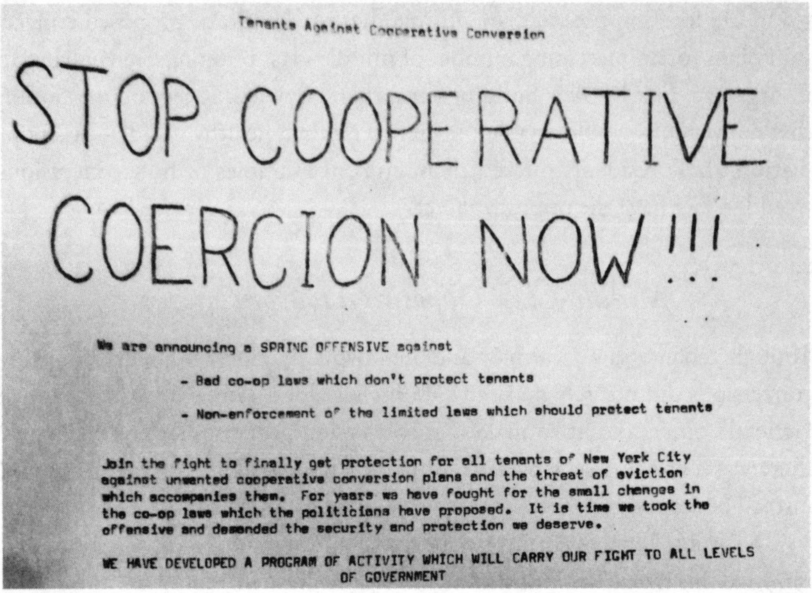
Tenants Against Cooperative Conversion

STOP COOPERATIVE COERCION NOW!!!...

We are announcing a SPRING OFFENSIVE against

- Bad co-op laws which don't protect tenants
- Non-enforcement of the limited laws which should protect tenants

Join the fight to finally get protection for all tenants of New York City against unwanted cooperative conversion plans and the threat of eviction which accompanies them. For years we have fought for the small changes in the co-op laws which the politicians have proposed. It is time we took the offensive and demanded the security and protection we deserve.

WE HAVE DEVELOPED A PROGRAM OF ACTIVITY WHICH WILL CARRY OUR FIGHT TO ALL LEVELS OF GOVERNMENT

FIGURE 2.2 For some tenant groups, making cooperative conversions fairer was insufficient; *all* landlord-initiated conversions needed to end.

Metropolitan Council on Housing Records. Courtesy of the Tamiment Library, New York University.

neighborhood in Manhattan, formed a tenants' association to block the plan their landlord had initiated. When the landlord put up a large sign advertising cooperative apartments for sale, tenants responded with smaller signs in windows throughout the complex that asserted: "I AM NOT CO-OP."[35]

Tenants like those in TACC and in tenant associations like at Park Terrace Gardens opposed conversions for a multitude of reasons. In the early 1970s, it was by no means assured that cooperatives would increase in value. Following a remarkable growth in prices between 1967 and 1968, cooperative values declined precipitously the following year, as a national recession and a steep fall in the stock market dragged housing values downward. At Park Terrace, the tenants' association likened purchasing an apartment to a car and believed that their building—which was over thirty years old—"will become less and less valuable in the immediate future."[36] Tenants also rejected the claim by conversion boosters that co-oping would help to stabilize middle-class neighborhoods. As Park Terrace tenants observed, "our houses are not isolated from the socio-economic problems of our local community or the overall urban community."[37] Neighborhood parks "are no longer maintained, policed, or cleaned as they were ten years ago" and "parents no longer look forward eagerly to having their children attend the local schools." Amidst widespread deterioration of municipal services and ongoing economic troubles, they wondered if homeownership represented the boon to residents claimed by real estate boosters. Renting offered flexibility, a virtue potentially greater than putting substantial capital into what looked to be an increasingly uncertain investment in New York City.

Conversions also asked tenants to make the biggest financial decision of their lives with the person they often trusted least: their landlord. Park Terrace tenants believed that their landlord had underestimated the expense of maintaining the buildings, understated their declining physical condition, and inflated the tax benefits of purchasing. Many were aghast at the likely profits the owner—required by law to be in the offering plan—would realize. These robust profits signaled to tenants that the prices the landlord had offered them for their apartments were excessive, whether measured by market values or by moral ones. Park Terrace residents were horrified that the conversion would allow their landlord to make "a huge profit . . . in excess of $5,000,000—FIVE MILLION DOLLARS."[38] The landlord, tenants believed, was already made a good living; that he sought to reap a monetary windfall while upending the security of home was an affront of the highest order.

Tenants also rejected co-oping out of concern for their neighbors who might be forced to move if they could not afford to purchase their apartments. The transition was not simply unsound "from a financial standpoint, but also from an ethical and moral point of view," Park Terrace residents noted, echoing many tenants facing conversions. What would happen to those who could not afford to buy, particularly the elderly, widows, and younger tenants? "We would never speculate on the misery of others," as one tenant put it.[39] The city's vacancy rate in 1970 was 1.5 percent, daunting to those seeking new apartments.[40]

Affordability was not just a concern for those with limited incomes. Rather than solving "the urban crisis by keeping middle-income families in the city," one tenant wrote in the *Times*, "conversions have exactly the opposite effect now."[41] With the city's "bad housing shortage," another tenant wrote, conversion proposals had forced "a number of friends of mine" to leave "the city for other places and the city is the loser of good, middle-class citizens."[42] These assertions severely undercut claims by the real estate industry that conversions were key to retaining the middle class.

Opposition was not confined only to rent-regulated buildings. At the Vermeer, a market-rate rental building on the outer edge of Greenwich

Village, tenants formed the Vermeer Tenants Organization (VeTO) to oppose a cooperative plan in early 1972. The group was "firmly and completely opposed to the conversion of this building *on any terms*."[43] Tenants believed that the possibility of increased maintenance costs, a declining real estate market, and "the physical condition of this building makes the purchase of an apartment herein financially unattractive."[44] After all, they had a good deal. Rents in Manhattan were "considerably higher than we are paying here," VeTO reminded tenants.[45] The group passed out fliers at the sales office, invited speakers from TACC, hired attorneys, gathered tenant signatures for a "no buy" pledge, and ensured all members wore their VeTO Buttons. "We will not move. We will not buy our apartments," the group proclaimed. "We will stay and fight this plan, and we will win."[46]

Conversion proposals nonetheless tended to provoke the fiercest opposition in rent-regulated buildings like Park Terrace. Why, one tenant asked, should residents pay a premium for their apartment when "they have the alternative of continuing under a landlord with rents subject to control or stabilization?"[47] A tenant at 205 West 89th Street denounced conversions as nothing more than "a beautiful way for landlords to get out from under rent control," calling the plan to convert her rent-controlled building "absolutely ridiculous."[48]

Solidarity among tenants, however, was not easy to build or sustain. New York's large apartment buildings frequently contained residents in different social and economic circumstances.[49] Tenants at the Excelsior on East 57th, for example, asserted that they were united against the offering plan they received early in 1970. Tenant leader Joseph Eckhaus denounced the plan as "avaricious." Just a few months later, however, Eckhaus agreed to purchase his apartment, lured by a substantial price drop. "There were very few comparable apartments around" for the price, he noted in his defense.[50]

Indeed, despite mounting opposition, not all tenants were opposed to purchasing their apartments. The twenty-story building at 165 East 72nd St, for example, was converted with "barely a hint of controversy" after the owner agreed to provide $500,000 in upgrades and $50,000 in start-up capital for the fledgling co-op.[51] These kinds of concessions typically came only after tenants banded together to oppose a conversion. Sweetened offers that followed tenant opposition campaigns had the potential to radically alter residents' responses. At the Excelsior, the vast majority of tenants had joined Eckhaus in opposing the conversion, but after the owners reduced apartment prices by 25 percent and nearly doubled the building's capital and repair funds to $675,000, over half agreed to purchase their apartments.[52] These examples marked the beginnings of a trend that would become increasingly common over the decade: organizing to block conversions led to improved offerings that ultimately compelled a greater number of tenants into supporting conversions.

But in the early 1970s, such incentives were often insufficient in overcoming tenant opposition. These fledgling cooperatives nonetheless signaled to landlords and others in the real estate industry that, despite growing opposition, hope for conversions was hardly lost. The real industry thus began to look to other strategies that would promote conversions, expand homeownership opportunities in the city, and increase their profits.

"Even if They Drop a Bomb on it . . . the Property will Still Go Up in Value"

Widespread tenant outrage signaled to many conversion advocates that they needed to do more to make their case about the importance of conversions and homeownership. Real estate executives and industry organizations turned to the media to convince city-dwellers of the benefits of apartment ownership.

To some industry figures, this meant better advertisements to induce buyers. Leona Roberts—who was then vice president of Brown Harris Stevens and would later marry real estate mogul Harry Helmsey—reported with envy to her colleagues of an advertisement for an owner-occupied building in the *Los Angeles Times*. The ad included a photo of an atomic bomb with text noting "even if they drop a bomb on it (your land or building) you still own the hole. And when the dust settles, the property will still go up in value."[53] Roberts, unlike some tenants, had an enduring belief in the economic sense of investing in real estate.

Other real estate boosters wrote or were quoted in articles evangelizing homeownership's benefits. Henry Hart Rice of the real estate consultant firm James Felt & Co. asserted in the *Times* that with a conversion "the tenant knows exactly where his money goes and what it will cost to increase services."[54] Other advocates proclaimed that purchasing one's home was not only a good investment, but that the building would also be better maintained, monthly expenses would go down since former renters would no longer be paying for their landlord's profit, and ownership would foster relationships within buildings and communities.

Conversion boosters also prophesized about how homeownership would benefit the city as a whole. "An apartment owner, like a home owner," Arnold Witte of the Commerce and Industry Association described, "cares for his property, develops an interest in his building, his community, his city, the future of that city and the stability and values of that city."[55] Apartment owners, Roberts believed, "have a common interest. . . . They want the best schools, the safest district, well-maintained houses of worship, adequate policing of the areas, cleaner surroundings, etc."[56] To conversion advocates, the links between homeownership, a vibrant middle class, and a healthy city could not have been clearer. "The only way New York will retain its middle class," another proponent proclaimed in the *Times*, "is to permit them to own a piece of it. People have given up on the city, but you don't give up when you have money in it."[57]

Conversion boosters looked for other ways to facilitate homeownership, including legislative changes that would be less controversial than the 15 percent reduction. Even tenants who wished to purchase a cooperative apartment had long been stymied by limited financing. Suburbanites benefited from federally backed bank loans that put their homes within reach of moderate- and middle-income white male suburbanites. By contrast, cooperative shares were generally not seen as adequate collateral by banks.[58] After all, if an owner faced foreclosure and the bank took over the apartment, there was nothing to stop the cooperative board from rejecting potential new owners, all while keeping the banks on the line for maintenance fees. As a result, "it's always been easier for an $8,000-a-year deli man to finance a home in Levittown [Long Island]," one broker explained, "than it's been for an executive to buy a home—a coop, that is—on Park Avenue."[59] Simply put, none of the fiscal and social advantages promised by ownership would lure a tenant into purchasing if he lacked the financing necessary to do so.

To address this, in 1971 Governor Nelson Rockefeller signed legislation that made financing for cooperative apartments more readily available. While widely supported by the real estate community, the law was shepherded by a prominent figure whom some in the industry considered a foe: Assistant Attorney General David Clurman. New Yorkers who wanted to buy a cooperative, Clurman believed, deserved access to the same type of financing available to purchasers of single-family homes.[60] With his urging, the state legislature passed a law that allowed financial institutions to make loans at 1.5 percent above the rate allowed for conventional mortgages.[61] The availability of financing began to put purchasing an apartment within greater reach of the middle class. Observers recognized the magnitude of the change. "Many in the [real estate] industry," one reporter described, "see the law as nothing less than the savior of the city as a place where middle-class families can live."[62] As a Central Savings Bank advertisement in the *Times* soon declared: "Our New Co-op Loans . . . could change your mind about moving to the suburbs."[63]

This landmark change would mean little, however, if opposition to conversions remained widespread. Indeed, just as Clurman and the real estate industry had successfully induced a major legislative change that would help ease conversions, tenants began to demand that the percentage of tenants needed to purchase their apartments for a conversion to be successful be raised from 35 to 51 percent. Doing so, a tenant of 505 E. 79th Street wrote to the City Council, would "remove the tyranny of a minority over the majority."[64] Tenants' majority-rule logic baffled owners who believed that it was their right to do what they wished with their property. Nonetheless, support for the increase in the heavily tenanted city spread, gaining the endorsement of the Attorney General's office and the *New York Times*. Though conversions were "a good thing for the city," the *Times* editorial board believed that "the situation in which a majority of tenants in a building faces eviction unless it falls in line with a minority must end."[65]

Political support for the measure also grew because landlords were increasingly found guilty of techniques that went far beyond offering deals to force conversions. A later federal report found that in the early 1970s "harassment of tenants was relatively common in New York conversions," including evictions, bribes, cutbacks on maintenance, and even personal harm.[66] Another "common practice" was for the owner to "buy" a tenant to convince other residents to purchase their apartments or to move.[67] At 150 East 61st Street, the Attorney General found that the landlords had reached the 35 percent requirement through "phony leases and purchase agreements signed by friends, relatives, business associations, and employes [*sic*]" of the landlords.[68] Though many tenant groups wanted to dissuade landlords from attempting a conversion at all, the Attorney General's office believed that the change to 51 percent would "eliminate the tremendous fear and pressure and antagonism and tension that is occasioned in a rental apartment house upon the first delivery of a cooperative plan," as Clurman told City Council members.[69]

These proposals reached a standstill in the early 1970s as legislators were unable to agree upon the best course of action for a tenant-dominated city with a powerful, and, many officials acknowledged, troubled real estate sector. When real estate representatives made their case against a 51 percent requirement, they reminded officials that ownership would retain middle-income families and stabilize neighborhoods, in addition to the dangers of legislation that would further stymie the industry. New Yorkers were not only suffering under an economy that had declined significantly since in the late 1960s (the city lost 257,000 jobs between 1969 and 1973), but also a housing crisis.[70] New construction had fallen to less than 2,000 units per year. The costs associated with housing were rising rapidly due to inflation, fuel, labor, and debt service costs of building mortgages. With building abandonment in low-income areas ongoing, New York was suffering a yearly net loss of housing.[71]

With this clear retreat of investment capital from housing, real estate owners asked, how could legislators risk deepening this crisis by preventing the benefits brought by conversions? Successful conversions very often led to building improvements as tenants pressured landlords to fund repairs as a condition of approving the conversion. These improvements made to fledgling cooperatives put them in stark contrast to much of the housing stock. Additionally, despite the ongoing abandonment of tens of thousands of units of rental housing, there was not, advocates pointed out, a single failed cooperative in the city.[72] "At a time when all the resources of the private sector are needed to stem the decline in our housing inventory," one group of real estate owners wrote to officials, "legislation of this kind . . . is clearly not in the public interest."[73] The president of the Great American Realty Corporation wrote the council to express his opposition to the 51 percent legislation and to inform them that his company had recently liquidated 90 percent of its holdings in the city and was now building $10,000,000 worth of housing in surrounding states. "Perhaps you could encorage [sic] builders to return to New York City," he noted, "if you would let up on additional landlord repression."[74] These words no doubt weighed heavily on officials who were struggling to find ways out of the housing crisis.

Though Lefkowitz recommended the 51 percent proposal in every legislative session between 1971 and 1973, each time it failed. "There has been," one politician acknowledged in 1973, "some very heavy pressure against the proposal from the real-estate industry."[75] The industry had convinced many officials that the law would "sound the death knell of conversions," as REBNY's John O'Donoghue put it in a letter to legislators.[76] Disagreements over altering the laws governing conversions continued, but the 35 percent threshold stood. It would take a conversion battle unprecedented in size and stature involving one of the most powerful real estate men in the country and a fiercely organized group of tenants in the Bronx to shift the direction of conversions for the entire city.

The Battle at Parkchester

Parkchester was the largest rental apartment complex in the nation, with 12,270 rent-controlled units on over 125 acres in the Bronx. The complex had been developed by the mammoth Metropolitan Life Insurance Company

(MetLife), which opened Parkchester in 1942 for "the middle class who longed for the affordability and community life of a small town, but couldn't bring themselves to abandon the convenience of urban life," as historian Samuel Zipp described.[77] MetLife aimed not just to make a sufficient return on its investment, but also to improve the public welfare by creating a healthy and happy community for the thousands of existing and potential life-insurance policyholders at the complex.

In 1968, however, MetLife sold Parkchester to Harry Helmsley, who saw in the complex the potential for profit but also a very different vision of how it could promote public good. Achieving both, Helmsley believed, would come only through converting Parkchester into owner-occupied units. Helmsley, best known as the owner of iconic Manhattan properties like the Empire State Building, typified the pro-conversion boosterism of leading real estate figures. Believing both in the importance of homeownership and that the economic incentives for landlords to maintain their buildings had diminished, Helmsley proclaimed that "the exodus from the city will be stanched" only through conversions. "I would hope," Helmsley continued, "that in 20 years landlords would be a rarity in New York, that everyone would own his own home."[78]

Helmsley proposed a conversion of the first of Parkchester's four quadrants in 1972, three years after acquiring the property. If he could successfully convert this vast rent-controlled complex, many observers believed, there was little doubt that a tide of conversions would soon sweep over the city, ushering in "a revolution in New York real estate," as Helmsley himself predicted.[79] As a rent-controlled complex, the law required 35 percent of existing tenants to agree to purchase before a conversion would be approved. However, Helmsley used an innovative strategy in which his conversion plan was allowed to proceed based on his agreement to sell apartments as they became vacant and not to evict any tenant who wished to remain a renter.

Helmsley's tenants by and large wanted no part in owning their apartments and fought the conversion with an unprecedented fervor. Residents formed the Parkchester Defense Fund, which strategized with other tenant coalitions, protested outside of Helmsley's home, conducted their own surveys of apartments and buildings, and hired lawyers to file suit against Helmsley, all "at tremendous financial sacrifice to our beleaguered neighbors."[80] They believed that Helmsley was selling them an "inferior product": a thirty-two-year-old building with faulty elevators, lax security, and no wiring for air conditioning. Lifetime Parkchester resident and tenant leader John Dearie asserted it would give tenants "all the headaches of homeownership without any of the advantages."[81] That Helmsley pledged not to evict any tenants was of little comfort. "If Helmsley succeeds with this and I have to call him to fix a broken pipe," one tenant believed, "I'll be at the mercy of a man who knows the sooner he can get me the hell out, the sooner he can sell my apartment."[82] Dearie called the noneviction plan an outrage as it allowed Helmsley to proceed with his conversion even though nearly all existing tenants initially turned down Helmsley's offer. The plan, Dearie exclaimed, required "no minimum tenant approval—not five percent . . . not ten percent . . . not zero percent!"[83] Helmsley's proposed profit also infuriated residents. Though Helmsley had bought the entire complex in 1968 for $90 million, converting just 32 percent would net him over $120 million.[84] The profit he was poised to make from converting the entire complex signaled to tenants that they were being swindled.[85]

Helmsley likely underestimated how great a foe he had in John Dearie. "Tall, articulate, and movie-star handsome," Dearie capitalized on his overwhelming support in Parkchester by running for a seat in the State Assembly in 1973, making conversions and tenant protections central issues in his campaign.[86] Once elected, he worked quickly to forge contacts and support and used his position to broadcast tenants' opposition in the press. "So you thought the domino theory of successively collapsing communities applied only to Southeast Asia? Forget it," Dearie began one article. "Harry B. Helmsley—and his companions—are diligently at work calculating to knock over one established neighborhood after another while reaping incredible financial profit." He pointed to the list of developments confronting or reported to be soon facing a conversion, which included the major middle-class, rent-regulated complexes in the city: the 1,830 apartment Windsor Park in Queens; Peter Cooper Village and Stuyvesant Town in Manhattan, which together totaled nearly 20,000 apartments; and the recent Helmsley purchases of Parkchester, Tudor City (2,800 apartments on Manhattan's East Side) and Fresh Meadows (3,285 apartments in Queens). After outlining why conversions were "the single most critical housing issue requiring attentive legislative action," Dearie ended his article with a warning from tenants: "Look out, Harry Helmsley and Company, we're coming on strong!"[87]

Dearie worked to elevate tenants' collective political strength by formulating legislation to give them more leverage in a proposed conversion. The legislation's "origin, concepts, and drafting emanated at the grass-roots levels," Dearie explained, "from a new breed of tenant leaders who have rallied their respective tenant associations around legislative reforms in the conversion field."[88] Indeed, while TACC sought to bring together tenants from individual buildings of varying sizes that were primarily in Manhattan and, prior to the proposed conversion, often had no collective associations, Dearie augmented this strategy by organizing alongside tenant leaders from the major rental complexes threatened by conversions. These complexes spread across several boroughs, often had well-organized tenant associations, and collectively offered the potential of mobilizing well over a hundred thousand residents.

With such extensive tenant support behind him, Dearie found a cosponsor in powerful state senator Roy Goodman, who helped push the law through the state Assembly and Senate. Among several other provisions that benefited tenants, the bill required landlords to gain at least 35 percent of existing tenants' approval within one year for all plans. Previously, landlords could proceed with conversion plans if they agreed not to evict any tenants in residence. The Dearie-Goodman law would create major impediments to successful conversions.[89]

The real estate industry vehemently opposed the bill. Many argued that it interfered with property rights and due process requirements, making it unconstitutional. "I believe the right to own property and invest in it," one owner wrote to Governor Malcolm Wilson, "presupposes the right to dispose of it."[90] The bill essentially transferred "the powers of basic property ownership rights" to the tenant. "Why should the economic future of an owner's investment be controlled by people who do not have an equity position in the project?" another flummoxed landlord asked.[91] Owners claimed that by giving tenants too great of a hand in the negotiating process, the bill removed any economic inventive for landlords to convert their buildings.

Impassioned tenants countered. Several of the tenant associations of major rental complexes joined a recently formed lobbying group, the New York Tenants Legislative Coalition, which organized trainings for residents.[92] Leaders at the Helmsley-owned complexes mobilized busloads of tenants to attend rallies, legislative hearings, and lobbying sessions at City Hall and in Albany. Tenants also flooded legislators with fervent letters supporting the legislation. John Whalen, the president of the Parkchester Defense Fund, wrote to Governor Wilson that without his approval of the bill, "you will give carte blanche to all the Helmsley's lurking in the shadows. . . . [to] make scandalous profits at the expense of those least able to pay." He continued,

> To Helmsley, Parkchester is 12,500 [*sic*] apartments but to us it is a community of 12,500 families. To Helmsley, each room in each apartment represents a portion of the unconscionable profit he seeks to reap, while

to us, it is home—for some the only one we have known—for many, the only one we can afford on our pitifully small fixed pensions— for many too, recently enticed to Parkchester without knowledge of Helmsley's secretly prepared prospectus, now faced with the trauma of eviction, it is the destruction of a dream of a decent home in a viable community.... 45,000 tenants of Parkchester await your answer.[93]

The bill passed, enacting Dearie's law for a two-year period. Attorney General Lefkowitz blocked the conversion plans for Parkchester, determining that Helmsley's plan to offer vacated apartments for sale violated the new law, as he had not yet secured the approval of 35 percent of existing tenants. The law also caused Helmsley to delay his conversion plans for his other recently purchased complexes.[94] "Tenant power!" Helsmley jeered. "If they want tenant power, let them own the building."[95]

Homeownership and the Fiscal Crisis

New York tenants were not alone in resisting what they believed were un-just conversions in their city. In the early 1970s, conversions were rapidly increasing in cities like Boston and Washington, DC, and by mid-decade, they began growing in dozens of cities throughout the country. As in New York, many tenants complained that conversions were causing undue hardship and displacement. One 1975 federal report found that nationally 80 percent of tenants were displaced during a conversion, totaling over 100,000 households over just a few years.[96] Conversions also compounded housing losses resulting from abandonment, leading some to raise concerns about dissipating rental housing. D.C., for example, lost 11,000 rental units between 1970 and 1975, half to conversions, resulting in a vacancy rate under 2 percent.[97]

Dozens of cities—such as Baltimore, Chicago, and Miami Beach—enacted protections for tenants during proposed conversion.[98] But to Benjamin Rosenthal, a liberal congressman from New York City, conversions posed so great a threat that federal intervention was needed. Rosenthal introduced a bill in Congress to provide tenant protections nationwide. Calling the re-cently passed New York law "the best in the country," Rosenthal hailed it as a model "for the kind of national legislation that I think is absolutely urgent."[99] Testifying at a federal hearing on conversions, Rosenthal claimed that they not only had led to many tenants being "dispossessed and unable to find de-cent substitute housing," but also to thousands of purchasers being "misled or defrauded."[100] Rosenthal's proposal, however, gained little steam. Similarly, although the Department of Housing and Urban Development held hearings and produced several detailed reports on conversions, these also failed to result in federal legislation, leaving regulation to municipal and state governments.

While New York never passed a formal moratorium on conversions, the Dearie-Goodman law proved nearly as efficient. Even before the law passed in 1974, the percentage of conversion plans defeated by tenants had risen from around 10 percent in 1968 to nearly 50 percent by 1973.[101] Conversions plummeted after the law's passage. Few landlords were willing to take the financial risk, as offering plans cost thousands of dollars to prepare. There were only thirty-six plans submitted to the Attorney General in 1974 and seventeen in 1975; most were tenant-initiated conversions in small buildings that tenants feared owners might abandon.[102]

The law's passage also coincided with the beginning of the fiscal crisis, which lessened the appeal of co-op apartments as investments. Worsening economic conditions reached their lowest point in the mid-1970s when the city teetered on the brink of bankruptcy and political collapse. Though the austerity measures financial and political leaders implemented during the crisis—municipal layoffs and reduced services, funding cuts to parks and schools, increased subway and bus fares—were most punishing to the poor and lower classes, decimated public services did little to encourage the middle class that the city was worthy of a personal and financial investment as substantial as purchasing a home. While some in the real estate industry pointed out that a shrewd purchaser could find bargains amidst the crisis, others more candidly noted that such purchases would only be deals if conditions in New York improved. There were few reasons for such optimism at the time. Prospective buyers were more likely to ask, as a partner in Orsid Realty acknowledged in late 1975, "why should we buy, if we don't know what's going to happen to the city?"[103] Such concerns were deepened by rising monthly maintenance fees, which had greatly increased in recent years due to inflation, fuel, labor, and debt service costs.[104]

The combination of Dearie-Goodman, the fiscal crisis, little new construction, stagnant real estate values, and increasing maintenance fees no doubt caused many to believe that apartment ownership in the city was a lost cause. Yet all was not bleak for the real estate industry during the fiscal crisis. Two major developments in particular signaled not just the possibilities for successful real estate development but also how homeownership could drive revitalization.

The first was the emergence of luxury condominiums. Unlike a cooperative, a buyer of a condominium owned the apartment outright and could sell it without the approval of a building's board. Though a "condominium craze" was sweeping the nation in the mid-1970s—condominiums accounted for 25 percent of all new housing nationwide in 1973 and 1974—the cooperative's long-standing history in New York helped ensure that they continued to be overwhelmingly favored in the city.[105] Though nationally the number of condominiums grew from under 450,000 to over 1,500,000 between 1970 and 1975, there were only a half-dozen condominium projects in New York by 1975.[106]

But some shrewd developers sensed a potential market for luxury condominiums, particularly among wealthy foreign purchasers who had long looked to maintain a nonprimary home in New York and who were often more accustomed to condominiums in their home countries. Few observers would have likely anticipated that buildings with unprecedented luxury amenities and apartments priced at over a million dollars during the height of the fiscal crisis would prosper. Their success became powerful illustrations of how even in the midst of crisis New York retained elements of its long-standing desirability, at least for the ultra wealthy. At the Galleria on East 57th Street, for example, apartments cost up to $1.2 million and the building included a 34,000 square foot club with a year-round swimming pool, cocktail lounge, athletic facilities, and a "sky terrace" with indoor and outdoor butler-attended areas.[107] Over 50,000 prospective purchasers viewed model apartments when the Galleria opened in 1975. That most purchasers were corporations or superrich foreigners buying their second or third homes did little to dampen the enthusiasm of developers.[108]

With such success, others looked to condominiums for salvation. The Museum of Modern Art (MoMA), for example, was operating in the mid-1970s with a million dollar a year deficit and no means to fund a desired expansion. To ensure stability, MoMA's board proposed leasing the air rights over the museum for the construction of a forty-eight-story luxury condominium in a complex arrangement whereby the real estate taxes would go directly to a museum trust that would then fund the museum's expansion and balance its operating budget. Detractors called the proposal a "giveaway to the rich" and labelled the diversion of taxes "robbery."[109] State Assemblyman Oliver Koppell proclaimed: "We can't build palaces of gold when we can't feed our children, finish building new schools and keep hospitals open." The condominium project nonetheless was approved in order to make MoMA solvent, thanks to "massive lobbying" by Mayor Abraham Beame and other political supporters.[110]

Condominiums were not the only bright spot for real estate during the fiscal crisis. Though artists had been living in a small Manhattan neighborhood south of Houston Street for decades, it was not until 1960s that the area—by then called SoHo—began to emerge as a hub of artistic activity.[111] Artists moved into large lofts that were slowly opening as the area's traditional light industry declined. Though these actions were illegal—as the area was not yet zoned for residential use—they were largely cheered in local newspapers, which depicted artists as a perfect replacement for declining manufacturing.[112] By the mid-1970s, SoHo had become home to an increasing number of middle-class residents who were less likely to make their living through art.[113] A 1977 study of converted Manhattan loft buildings found that 33 percent of residents had moved to their apartments from outside the city and that they had household incomes twice the city's median, even though the median age of residents was twelve years younger (31.8) than the city-wide median (44.4).[114]

While most lofts remained rentals, many were converted to cooperatives. These spaces, many real estate experts and officials believed, were the "most important."[115] So vital were these cooperatives to the area's revival that in 1975 the Attorney General took the unprecedented action of "legalizing" the thousands of cooperative apartments that had been formed, even though few had been sold in accordance with state law.[116] As one housing expert proclaimed, "the occupants of coop lofts emerge as the most committed to living and working in New York City. They are drawn to loft living by the ample space, the chance to customize it, and the opportunity for home ownership."[117] This "neighborhood revitalization" of SoHo demonstrated to many officials and real estate executives "that older inner cities could be attractive to middle-class households."[118]

Real estate officials were quick to point to the significance of these successful homeownership initiatives. Brewster Ives, the long-standing chairman of the leading real estate firm Douglas Elliman, wrote in his company's newsletter that the "substantial number" of condominium and cooperative purchasers coming from Western European and South America as well as "many parts of the country, including the outlying suburbs" signified New York's reemergence as the world's "financial center[,] . . . cultural center, . . . [and] most exciting city." These initiatives signaled the ability "for more cooperative and condominium conversions to replenish the dwindling supply of desirable apartments and to reverse the deterioration" of the housing stock. There was, Ives wrote, "hope for the future of the City of New York."[119]

The success of luxury condominiums and loft cooperatives fueled support for allowing the Dearie-Goodman law to expire. The real estate industry, unrelenting in its opposition to the law, compounded the political pressure to do so. "Cooperatives and condominiums are the way of the future and the salvation of this city because it means that these properties will be preserved and well maintained," Ives told state officials in a statement against the law's extension. "The movement toward cooperative and condominium ownership, which has become such a large source of strength in our better residential areas, should be allowed to grow unhampered by legislative restraints—all for the greater good of our City and our State."[120]

Legislators granted only a one year extension in 1976 before allowing the law to expire in 1977.[121] Pressure from the real estate industry was a factor, but many politicians also came to believe that the law effectively ending conversions was too extreme a step, particularly as conversions offered "hope that decent but deteriorating rental apartment houses might be saved by converting them into cooperatives," as the New York Times noted in one of its several editorials against the law's extension.[122] Although the law retained tenant support, many officials also came to trust that rent stabilization and control laws protected tenants sufficiently, a position reinforced by media commentators and experts like David Clurman.[123]

In the wake of Dearie-Goodman's expiration, many tenants continued to view their landlord proposing a conversion as a "traumatic experience," as the Times reported.[124] But some found that years of intense tenant organizing—which had effectively caused conversions to grind to a halt—caused landlords to take a more conciliatory approach. For example, an initial conversion attempt at Carnegie House on West 57th Street in 1974 had failed. After Dearie-Goodman lapsed, the owner switched to a noneviction plan—something the law had prevented—which enabled nonpurchasing tenants to remain in place but lowered the requisite tenant purchasers to 15 percent and gave the plan more time to succeed. The owner also offered tenants a deeper discount: 25 percent below the price at which they were sold to outsiders.[125] Though opposition remained, the building began gradually converting to a cooperative, with a third of the 321 apartments being sold over the next ten months. After tenant opposition thwarted conversions citywide, some landlords anxious to see their expensive conversion plans succeed become more willing to assure still-hesitant tenants that they too would profit from a conversion and from becoming homeowners.

Alongside this development, new voices began to emerge in the longstanding battle over conversions: happy postconversion, middle-class cooperative owners. An increasing number of owners began to join what had for years been a debate largely limited to pro-conversion landlords and resistant tenants. Unaffiliated with conversion's long-term—and long suspect—boosters in the real estate industry, these middle-class residents challenged the idea that it was only landlords who benefited from conversions. They educated tenants about the conversion process and the cooperative market, aiming to empower residents to profitably navigate through conversions and into cooperative ownership. They also extolled the virtues of apartment ownership, advocated publicly for conversions, and championed their own contribution to the city as middle-class property owners. Their work helped conversions to spread in the late 1970s, especially as their advocacy gained the backing of pro-conversion Mayor Ed Koch.

The Growth of Middle-Class Cooperative Owners

The voice of middle-class owners was most powerfully evident in the formation of organizations and publications by and for fledgling cooperative owners. The most prominent of these groups formed simply when a small number of new cooperative owners gathered in a basement on West End Avenue in 1974, each seemingly confounded by how to run their buildings. "We realized we had all the same problems—and no answers," Marc Luxemburg, the group's first president, recalled.[126] Calling itself the Council of West Side Cooperatives (CWSC), the group exchanged information on matters mundane (who should service the laundry room?) to the complex (what potential legal changes might affect the building?).[127]

Though principally devoted to educating owners about running buildings, CWSC soon began to take a more public role as the face of postconversion, middle-class cooperatives. For example, it corrected negative sentiments about apartment ownership in the press. When an article in *Our Town*, a popular Manhattan weekly paper, left readers with the "discouraging" impression that cooperative residents suffered under high monthly maintenance changes, Luxemburg replied with the findings from its member survey, which proved them to be much lower. He also disputed the claim that families escaping the suburbs for the city would not want to live in a co-op. "The principal burdens of house ownership usually involved physical maintenance of the structure and the surrounding acreage," Luxemburg replied, "and such unpleasant tasks as mowing the lawn, raking the leaves and shoveling the snow. A co-op owner does not have those problems, and yet enjoys the ability to have a voice in the management of the building, and the tax advantages of home ownership."

In contrast to such articles, Luxemburg wrote, *Our Town* should instead be advocating for "active assistance at all levels of government to encourage and increase the growth of the co-op movement in Manhattan and to greatly increase the number of co-ops."[128]

That is just what the CWSC had begun to do. The group, for example, spoke alongside landlord and builder representatives in hearings and in the media against the extension of the Dearie-Goodman law in 1977. Speaking with confidence from their own experience as new cooperative owners and with the belief that more homeownership would benefit New York, the group proclaimed that "in this time of fiscal crisis no policy can be more destructive than one which discourages private investment in the city."[129] The law, in short, "has no good provisions," Luxemburg declared.[130] After the law expired, the CWSC began to host free public meetings giving "advice to tenants on how to convert from rental building to cooperative."[131]

The CWSC joined similar kinds of groups that were emerging to represent the interests of middle-class residents. Although small numbers of white middle-class professionals had been purchasing and restoring Brooklyn brownstones for decades, this trend accelerated in the 1970s and produced several neighborhood and citywide organizations to promote their efforts. These groups worked to shift municipal, banking, and insurance policies to facilitate brownstone ownership, as Sulieman Osman has chronicled, and organized public events such as the first Brownstone Fair in 1973, which promised to tell attendees "Everything You Always Wanted to Know About Brooklyn Brownstones."[132] Similarly, in 1970, SoHo owners and tenants formed the SoHo Artists Association to create a voice for loft residents "in any dealings with any private or government agencies" and to organize public events like street festivals that brought attention to artists' work and to aid "advocacy efforts for zoning laws that would allow them to live and work in SoHo lofts," as Aaron Shkuda has described.[133]

Cooperative owners soon engaged in similar kinds of public advocacy. By 1980, the CWSC's widening focus led the group to change its name to the Council of New York Cooperatives (CNYC). It represented over nine hundred co-ops with over a quarter-million residents and aimed "to act as a clearing house for co-op information, to provide for the common needs and interests of co-op apartments.... to establish cooperatives as a united community with interests that are separate and distinct from rental apartments; and to participate in political action favorable to this co-op community."[134] The CNYC's newsletter included information for fledgling owners on matters like energy conservation, insurance, as well as legislative developments the group encouraged residents to contact representatives about to ensure that officials knew there was "a growing and active constituency of New York cooperators."[135] Additionally, the CNYC hosted yearly conferences, the first of which attracted close to four hundred representatives from cooperatives and included over twenty-five workshops on topics including organizing a cooperative, building management, and taxes and abatements. CNYC's president Ray Hoey cheered the participants in the "cooperative movement," telling them that their "presence here today attests to the growing interest in cooperatives in our city," which "have been a major factor in bringing stability to New York neighborhoods that were faced with decay, abandonment, redlining and lack of community interest."[136]

Such efforts to inform and organize the fledgling cooperative community were extended through new publications. *The Manhattan Cooperator* launched as the first citywide co-op newspaper in April 1981. Its publishers, Vicki Chesler and Matt Kovner, noted in the inaugural issue that that the publication sought to "create an integrated and well-informed co-op community" where none existed.[137] "By moving into a co-op, or helping to convert your building to one," the editorial praised, "you have shown that you believe in the future of New York City; that you feel it to be a vital, thriving place in which to live and work—a place worthy of investment, and worthy to be called home." The next year, Carol Ott launched *New York Habitat*, "a magazine for co-op, condominium, and loft living." Ott had previously published a how-to book on buying and living in a loft as well as a newsletter, *The Loft Letter*, for "people like me who were middle-class people who were buying lofts and weren't artists."[138]

Cooperator and *Habitat* each had a slightly different approach—*Habitat* was more journalistic and *Cooperator* had a lighter, more lifestyle oriented focus—but they shared important characteristics. Both included critical but difficult to access information for new and potential apartment owners. They published articles on taxation, insurance, building staffing, real estate law, and potential legislative changes. They also kept pace of market developments. While *Cooperator* published articles on "Co-op Availability: The Market Today" and "Condominiums: Wave of the Future," each issue of *Habitat* listed all available mortgage rates, along with recent sales, the latest approved conversions, and all new and rehabilitated condo and co-ops on the market in Manhattan.[139] Such information ensured buyers had a more sophisticated awareness of the market at a time when such information was generally held only by real estate firms. Both also tracked ongoing market upticks. *Cooperator* published features like "The Renaissance of the West Side," while an early *Habitat* article told readers how to recognize signs of "neighborhood transformation," which "can happen quickly—and to your advantage, if you recognize the signs."[140] These publications encouraged New Yorkers to see their home as an economic investment, a view that could bring benefits far greater than the security afforded by rent-regulated housing.

These publications aimed not only to educate new apartment owners, but also tenants who were considering a conversion offering or otherwise looking to buy a cooperative. In their first few years, *Habitat* and *Cooperator* published articles informing tenants how to understand a conversion prospectus, organize with fellow tenants, negotiate discounted prices, find legal representation, and even initiate their own conversion—all with the intention of making the process both comprehensible and as profitable as possible.[141] "There are a number of things you should know first," one *Cooperator* article for tenants those landlord had recently initiated a conversion advised, "but in the long run, you stand to make a great deal of money, even if you don't have a dime to spare."[142] A conversion prospectus, these publications made clear, should be greeted not with fear or antipathy, but with the confidence that one's home could become a lucrative financial asset.

These new groups and publications offered an increasingly prominent counterpoint that came from regular New Yorkers, rather than politicians or the real estate industry. They empowered residents to navigate a cooperative conversion process with fiscal prowess and emerge on the other side with the knowledge to successfully own and run their homes at significant financial gain. They proselytized about the benefits of ownership and tracked an accelerating real estate market. They also helped to inform, assure, and normalize cooperative living in the city, ushering in a changing attitude toward—and the successful navigating of—cooperative and condominium ownership in a city historically dominated by renters. The growing conversion of buildings created swaths of new owners charged with running their buildings with no experience and little sense of what was required in owning a share of an entire building. Many of these buildings could have failed as cooperatives. But none did, in part because a movement to education and advocate around these fledgling cooperatives formed to help ensure their success.

Mayor Ed Koch, who took office in 1978, was an enthusiastic supporter of these efforts. Koch's Housing Commissioner Anthony Gliedman gave the opening remarks at CNYC's first conference, telling attendees, "I have never seen an association more appropriate in time or place than this," and adding: "Both the Mayor and I want to see this effort continue and expand."[143]

FIGURE 2.3 New publications such as *Habitat* and *The Manhattan Cooperator*, along with groups as the Council of New York Cooperatives, worked to inform, organize, and advocate on behalf of fledgling apartment owners. Their proselytizing about the benefits of conversions and apartment ownership was especially powerful because they represented middle-class residents, rather than landlords or politicians.

Courtesy of *Habitat Magazine*.

Koch even sent a letter praising an early *Habitat* issue, noting that he had "shared the magazine with members of my staff in charge of development."[144]

Despite offering only tempered support for low-income cooperatives, Koch saw conversions of middle-income rentals as a means to infuse capital into these buildings and expand homeownership opportunities that would attract additional white monied residents. Like many other big-city mayors in the late 1970s, he believed that the only way cities could revitalize was to lessen their appeal to lower classes and increase their ability to draw in those with capital. Koch even used his inauguration address not just to promise "better services for the middle-class," but to appeal to "urban pioneers"—as the *Times* described them—to "come east and join us" in revitalizing New York.[145] His certainty was reflected both in the rhetoric of his appeals to these residents as well as in his support for housing policies that he believed would attract them.

In the suburban locations as well as many of the urban areas from which Koch hoped to attract these residents, homeownership was the norm. Koch was a strong advocate for measures that might increase homeownership opportunities and facilitate the shift in the economic composition of residents. He championed conversions, believing that "a tenant's ownership of his or her apartment fosters commitment and stability to our neighborhoods."[146] Conversions "were a 'positive' trend that had helped to stabilize neighborhoods and the city's tax base."[147] Several studies at the time demonstrated that those purchasing apartments in converted buildings in the wake of the expiration of Dearie-Goodman were exactly the types of residents the Koch administration hoped would commit to making the city their long-term home. In the late 1970s, a major HUD study found, cooperative residents in Manhattan were most likely to be dual-earner professionals between thirty and forty years old.[148] A 1981 survey of *Cooperator* readers found that 63 percent earned incomes between $40,000 and 75,000, well above the city's median.[149] Additionally, nearly 80 percent of the owners of units converted between 1978 and 1984 were white, even though whites made up just over 50 percent of the city's population.[150] Koch recognized that as rental buildings turned into cooperatives, they would create greater homeownership opportunities for existing and new middle-class residents. Though several legislative proposals to raise the number of tenants in eviction plans to 51 percent were made in city and state government, Koch's opposition helped ensure that none were successful during his first few years in office.[151]

These policies encouraged an increasing number of middle and upper-class people at the end of the 1970s to do what would have been largely unthinkable just a few years earlier: move to New York. While many new urban transplants were content to rent, many others desired the owner-ship opportunities feasible in the suburbs and other cities. With New York emerging from its fiscal crisis, as the *Times* reported in early 1979, it had quickly become "a much more desirable place in which to work and live—at least for people with money."[152] Anecdotal evidence, which the *Times* seized on, suggested that many of these new residents had grown up in the suburbs and were willing to endure New York's crime, grit, and smaller abodes to live in areas that offered more expansive options for restaurants, culture, and en-tertainment. Suburban home costs remained high, while co-ops and condos, along with lofts, seemed to many to be comparatively affordable. By the late 1970s, city property taxes were generally lower than those in the neighboring suburbs.[153] Thus conversions as a perfect lure for a new class of residents.

Drawing in new residents, however, was not enough to make home-ownership succeed. With new construction still slow, homeownership opportunities would lag unless more rental buildings could be converted to cooperatives. Landlords still needed to convince 35 percent of rent-regulated tenants to purchase their apartments if they proceeded with an eviction plan.

Though opposition to conversions continued into the 1980s, the growing prominence of cooperative owners helped begin to shift the tide of co-operative conversions. This development, combined with new laws and conciliations from landlords, along with the support of Mayor Koch, helped to forge a place for homeownership in the city of renters and encourage its proliferation in the years ahead.

Owning a Piece of New York

Continued tenant organizing and greater tenant knowledge about navigating conversions led an increasing number of landlords to augment their ap-proach to conversions to ensure that they were less contentious—and more successful—than in the past. The most important tactic was insider pricing. Offering below-market discounts to tenants was not new, but a decade of tenant opposition, as well as a rapidly heating up real estate market that raised the potential profits of conversions, encouraged owners to offer much greater discounts than in the past. In addition to continuing to underwrite building repairs and improvements, especially in larger buildings, landlords could sell apartments to existing tenants at one-third their market rate and still profit significantly. Rent-controlled tenants could receive even larger discounts. Though the required 25 percent down payment ensured purchasing remained limited to those with capital, insider pricing made apartments affordable to a far greater range of tenants than in the past.[154] It also created the potential for windfall profits. It was not uncommon for a tenant to purchase an apartment at an insider price and initiate a sale quickly after at double that price. Tales in the media, at the office, and at cocktail and dinner parties of the windfall profits neighbors, coworkers, and friends could make through a conversion became a huge asset for landlords in reaching the requisite number of tenant sales to turn a building into a cooperative. The prominent new role of enthusiastic middle-class cooperative owners along with this potential for profit made it easier for the real estate industry to point to what they had long claimed: co-oping was good for the middle class and the city.

Legislative battles continued in the early 1980s between representatives who wanted conversions to proliferate and those who sought greater protections for tenants. In 1982, the two parties finally came to an agreement. Under pressure from tenants, senate Republicans from New York City finally agreed to raise the number of bona fide tenants needed to agree to purchase their apartments in order for an eviction plan to be approved to 51 percent. This hurdle was a major deterrent to landlords, leading the *Cooperator* to title their article about the law "An End to Eviction Conversions."[155] But Republicans also forced pro-tenant politicians to change a requirement in noneviction plans to make them easier to achieve. The new provision allowed for apartments sold to people who did yet not live in the building to count toward achieving the 15 percent of sales needed for a noneviction plan to be approved. Owners could hold vacated apartments before a planned conversion and then sell these to nonresidents, making surmountable the already low threshold of selling 15 percent of apartments for a conversion to be approved.[156] Tenant leaders therefore won a long-standing goal of making eviction plans exceedingly difficult to accomplish—thereby greatly discouraging their use—but in so doing allowed "the Republicans to get away with leaving the non-eviction loophole," in the words of one critical tenant advocate.[157] The change all but assured most plans going ahead would be noneviction ones and that these plans would be easier to win.

These developments were reinforced by shifts occurring in the city's rent regulations. Various changes in rent protection laws at the end of the 1960s and early 1970s diminished the number of rent-controlled apartments from over one million in 1970 to less than 285,733 by 1981.[158] Though many of these units remained protected by the far less powerful rent stabilization, the change meant much greater rent increases for hundreds of thousands of tenants. Thus, the benefits associated with ownership appeared only to grow, leading even tenants in buildings with rent protections to look at ownership more favorably.

Conversions also compounded other policies that directly diminished rent regulations. Even if a rent-controlled or -stabilized tenant refused to purchase her apartment and was not evicted during her building's conversion, once she vacated the apartment, it was de-regulated and could be sold or rerented at market rates. That is, a conversion assured the eventual deregulation of all units within that building, even if that process might take time. Indeed, nearly 90 percent of the units converted between 1978 and 1984 had been rent-regulated.[159] With noneviction conversion plans relatively easy to achieve after 1982, landlords were further encouraged to initiate conversions as a deregulation mechanism. In a number of buildings, few tenants beyond the initial 15 percent of purchasers actually came to own their apartments after a conversion of a rent-regulated building, as vacated apartments of non–purchasers were simply rerented at market rates.[160]

The combination of these factors helped shift the tide of conversions and of apartment ownership more generally. Tenant opposition facilitated legal changes and softer landlord tactics like noneviction plans and insider pricing that ameliorated some of the most objectionable aspects of conversions. Ambitious early converters rose to proclaim that conversions had benefited them, to ensure greater sophistication about conversions, to encourage the growth of apartment ownership, and to normalize the place of middle-class owners in the city. And a rising real estate market—fueled in part by conversions—increasingly made purchasing one's home look like an economic opportunity worth pursuing even within a city that only recently been in financial crisis.

THOUGH SOME OPPOSITION to conversions remained, by the early 1980s, the sentiment toward homeownership and its place in New York City had changed. There was perhaps no greater indication of this than at Parkchester. At the complex where tenant opposition eleven years had led to conversions being shut down across the city and state, Harry Helmsley filed a noneviction conversion plan for the remaining three quadrants in 1983 and their tens of thousands of residents. The tenants' committee took a new position: neutrality. John Dearie, who remained president of the tenants' association, said, "Now we are neither for nor against. Our responsibility is to convey the facts on the tenants' rights."[161] Though apartments were still overwhelmingly protected by rent control or stabilization, tenants no doubt observed that outsider prices were 110 percent higher than they had been when sales began.

As such, the tenants' association saw its responsibility as helping tenants who want to buy to "strike a better deal."[162]

Conversions proliferated throughout the city in the late 1970s and early 1980s. The number of building plans submitted to the Attorney General rose from 117 in 1976 to 403 in 1980 and then jumped to 1,029 in 1982.[163] Cooperative housing units in New York went from 138,000 to 233,377 between 1975 and 1982, with over 11,000 new condominium units.[164] Conversions also continued to spread to the outer boroughs, particularly Queens and Brooklyn where, the *Times* wrote, cooperatives were "leading [the] latest renaissance."[165] By the early 1980s, the overwhelming success of co-ops and condominiums led to predictions among some real estate experts that "no one will ever build rental housing again."[166] By the end of the decade, the percentage of homeowners had grown to 28.4 percent, the highest in the city's history.[167]

The conversion of rental housing helped usher in a remarkable real estate turnaround. "The push to co-op," in the words of one observer in 1980, "has outstripped the garment industry as the city's number one industry."[168] This was especially true in Manhattan. The average per room selling price in luxury Manhattan buildings increased two and a half times between 1974 and 1978, and increased another 50 percent between 1978 and 1979.[169] By 1981, prices in the more desirable cooperatives had quintupled from 1973.[170] "Do you ever wonder if there's any limit to the sky-rocketing prices in Manhattan?" remarked the editor-in-chief of the *Cooperator*.[171] Rents also substantially increased; median rents doubled in Manhattan between 1975 and 1984, an only slightly greater percentage increase than across the rest of the city.[172] The growth of cooperatives through conversions and continued development of new condominiums were drivers of escalating real estate prices in the early 1980s: swelling demand for housing from moneyed newcomers and current residents (who now had greater ability to own their apartments), meager construction of new housing other than condominiums, and a diminishing stock of rent-regulated housing.[173]

Not everyone applauded the effects of these changes. Representative Benjamin Rosenthal, who continued to oppose conversions, said in 1981, "I am concerned that the middle class is being pushed out of the city and that Manhattan may become an enclave for the wealthy."[174] But it was not only long-standing critics like Rosenthal who saw New York changing for the worse. Conversions had no greater advocate than Brewster Ives of Douglas Elliman, who was widely recognized as the "elder statesman" of the cooperative and condominium movement and "the uncrowned co-op king." But he too had become alarmed at the effects of the explosive growth of cooperatives and condominiums. "I hate to say it and I hate to think it," he noted in 1981, "but I don't see how we are going to hold the middle class in Manhattan. The New York of the future will in large part be for the wealthy—be they Americans or foreigners—and for the subsidized poor."[175] While conversions had so recently been hailed as the solution for retaining the middle class, now even real estate elites worried that accelerating homeownership and real estate values would drive them away.

It is tempting to attribute these developments solely to the real estate industry or to the unabashedly pro-gentrification policies of municipal leaders like Koch. While these were powerful forces indeed, the growing acceptance of conversions and ownership by tenants was critical. Similarly, the mounting disparities associated with the economic revitalization of New York in the 1980s did not occur solely as a result of top-down policies by political leaders who embraced urban neoliberalism, but also through grassroots support from those who benefited economically. In the case of cooperative conversions, this included the very people who had earlier led campaigns to preserve economic diversity and rent-regulated housing especially as they came to see how they could personally benefit.

New middle-class cooperative owners encouraged a shift in the relationship to one's home as a New Yorker. As the momentum against conversions dissipated in the 1980s and was replaced by a movement of cooperative converters, tenants still organized in great numbers in response to the proposed conversions of their buildings. Increasingly, they did so not to block the conversion but to win as lucrative a deal for themselves as possible. As renters became owners and neighbors became investors, refrains common among those who ferociously battled conversions in the 1970s, such as the importance of preserving rent regulations for retaining moderate and middle-income residents, diminished.

Instead, owners used their growing presence to influence political and economic life along their preferred terms. Owners, for example, joined their suburban homeowning counterparts in fighting to maintain already low property taxes. Despite the fact that city tax assessments were "hideously inequitable," and greatly favored owners over renters and wealthier white areas over poorer areas of color, new middle-class owners used their organizations to vigorously oppose new assessment mechanisms that may have increased the tax burden on cooperatives.[176] Middle-class apartment owners, as the administrator of the Council of New York City Cooperatives perceptively noted in 1982, represent a "tremendous block of voters and influence in the city," which are "just beginning to raise consciousness" to get their voices heard.[177] Indeed, their success contrasted sharply with the struggle of low-income residents of color occupying in rem housing to win political gains such as the $250 sales price.

Though New York would remain largely a city of renters, the growth of homeownership contributed to a restructuring of the built environment and economic composition of the city. It also helped facilitate what had for decades been a politically untenable goal of the real estate industry: diminishing the rent-regulated status of much of rental housing. In so doing, homeownership compounded the shift away from an era of state intervention and regulation toward one of "free" markets and privatization. The result was a process not unlike other neoliberal initiatives—say, the imposition of tuition throughout the city university system in 1975—in which the state effectively transferred the "costs" of regulating the market or diminishing its harmful effects directly to residents and the private sector. But conversions allowed everyday residents to directly take part in and benefit from this process, even though the ramifications of doing so spread far beyond the individuals initially involved.

Indeed, the changing attitude toward apartment ownership, a mayor willing to privilege real estate development, and the reinvestment of capital by the real estate industry would finally lead to the "revolution in real estate" observers sensed when Helmsley made his initial Parkchester offering in the early 1970s. It was a transformation in which real estate emerged from crisis and regained its place as the leading edge of the economy, with a growing presence of affluent apartment owners able to shape city life.

Remaking Public Parks

WILLIAM STUHLBARG WAS fed up. A prominent figure in New York real estate, he also served in the mid-1970s as Chairman of the Community Planning Board for Manhattan's midtown business district. Stuhlbarg was especially anguished by the conditions of midtown's major public space, Bryant Park. Drug dealing, public intoxication, and drug use had grown so prominent that a few years earlier the city's Parks Commissioner, Richard Clurman, had declared Bryant Park lost to "gamblers, junkies, brown-baggers sucking at wine and liquor bottles, derelicts, panhandlers and menacing rip-off specialists."[1] Many businesses in the area advised employees to stay out of the park other than at lunchtime, when office workers had protection in their numbers.[2] "The whole area is affected by the fear generated in the park," Jerome Gartner, another member of the Community Board, described. "We're not just dealing with another park," he continued, "we're dealing with how unsafe the central business district is." After a Union Carbide executive was robbed in Bryant Park in 1976 while walking to the company's nearby headquarters, the company's leadership informed Mayor Abraham Beame that they were relocating their company, with its more than three thousand employees, to Connecticut.[3] That same summer, a thirty-four-year-old man was stabbed to death. The murder, to Stuhlbarg, was the final straw. "If we can't clean up the park, and apparently we can't," he announced following the stabbing, "then let's close it."[4]

Though New Yorkers had long expressed dissatisfaction with the city's parks, the park system by the 1960s had become widely disparaged. When John Lindsay ran for mayor in 1965, he described it as "among the most poorly maintained in the entire United States," with "an appalling number of the city's parks . . . decayed and filthy."[5] Surveys of park users showed that New Yorkers agreed.[6] Though Lindsay promised to clean up the system as mayor, the city's financial troubles at the end of the decade brought only cutbacks. The ensuing fiscal crisis further reduced already thinned municipal resources. The budget for the Parks Department was decimated between the late 1960s and late 1970s, with the number of permanent workers plummeting from 6,000 in 1968 to 3,000 in 1978. Essential equipment was not replaced. "Park maintenance is almost abandoned and corrective work impossible," the *New York Times* reported in 1976. "The fiscal crisis has meant cutbacks on cutbacks."[7] The Parks Department cycled through five commissioners in five years at mid-decade.

The future of the park system looked increasingly uncertain during this tumultuous period. Indeed, to Stuhlbarg and to others like Lindsay's final Park Commissioner, Richard Clurman, who also supported park closures, these circumstances should have foreclosed the possibility for some parks even to have a future.[8]

At the same time as calls for park closures proliferated, neighborhood residents proposed an alternative solution, one that would radically reshape the park system in the years ahead. New Yorkers who were deeply troubled by inadequate government action began to pledge their time and labor and initiate creative proposals to improve parks. Dwellers feared that parks—the city's quintessential public spaces—were being lost, perhaps irreversibly. This perception became powerful enough to dramatically increase the involvement of citizens and, eventually, the private sector—particularly businesses and foundations—in the care of parks. By the beginning of the 1980s, their momentum grew so significant that it engendered extraordinary policy changes that officially opened the care and management of parks to those outside of government.

The drive for greater involvement in parks first began in earnest in the 1960s with the widespread formation of volunteer groups that performed maintenance, planted grass and shrubbery, and raised funds for neighborhood parks that they saw as rapidly declining. These grassroots groups labored intensely to forestall and, in some cases, even reverse the decay local parks suffered under government cutbacks. These initiatives promoted the idea that the city could not care for its parks, a sentiment that park advocates and even city officials reinforced. These community-based volunteers were hardly seeking to permanently diminish the role of government but simply wanted to step in when they saw government failing to improve a critical neighborhood resource. Their efforts nonetheless helped to lay important groundwork for subsequent policy changes that opened financing and management to those outside government.

The environment of austerity during the 1970s was critical to this transformation. The Parks Department grappled with very real cuts that darkened the outlook for the park system years before the fiscal crisis. Facing tightened budgets, park advocates and municipal officials began to proclaim that the city could "no longer afford" to adequately care for its parks. Park advocates anticipated the claim that federal officials and the financial community would express during the fiscal crisis about what the city could no longer afford. Instead of demanding greater municipal resources, park advocates sought solutions that relied less on government. Indeed, it was park advocates themselves—not the political officials and bankers who imposed austerity on the city during the crisis—who championed turning to the private sector as the potential salvation for parks.[9]

The initiatives to increase private sector involvement in parks that took off in the mid-1970s commenced only after residents had already come to believe that city government was failing parks and began organizing community efforts to improve them. That citizen groups came to such conclusions first was critical to the eventual involvement of the private sphere—including businesses along with their supporters in foundations and major cultural institutions—in improving and even controlling parks by the early 1980s. These community efforts helped legitimate the notion that government alone could no longer care for parks and created openings for greater private involvement once the fiscal crisis hit.

The growth of private sector involvement in parks did not come easily, however. It was one thing for neighbors to volunteer their time to improve local parks, but quite another for corporations to begin to devote their resources to park maintenance and even management. Why would businesses volunteer to take on fiscal responsibility for a realm for which government had long been responsible? The notion struck many as absurd, akin to a voluntary tax increase. The business, corporate, and real estate spheres were initially highly resistant to efforts to bolster private sector involvement. Indeed, several early efforts to increase their role in improving parks faltered.

This sentiment slowly changed in the late 1970s and 1980s principally through the actions of a small number of actors, most from outside of business. As it became ever clearer that parks were continuing to decline and that grassroots citizen revitalization efforts could not muster adequate resources to sufficiently improve parks, a variety of supporters—park advocates, former Parks Department employees, philanthropic organizations, and cultural institutions like the New York Public Library—labored in the 1970s to convince business that it was in their interest to provide resources to improve greenspaces. Revitalized parks could increase real estate values, attract commercial tenants, appeal to prospective employees, and garner positive press. As business interests came to see how their involvement reaped financial benefits, many also came to believe that their contributions would go even further if they took on actual responsibility for day to day operations and long-term planning of parks. Mayor Koch encouraged these efforts just as he embraced policies that would marketize in rem housing and promote cooperative conversions.

The late 1960s and 1970s thus marked the beginnings of a radical reconceptualization of the role both of private citizens and the private sector in supporting parks. In the mid-1960s, there were only a handful of groups working to improve conditions in parks. By the early 1990s, community groups helped care for nearly a quarter of parks, principally through volunteerism and small-scale fundraising. By that time there were nearly a half-dozen professional organizations involved not simply in providing supplemental care but also managing parks, a number that would increase to at least fifty by the early 2000s, as the park system transformed into one dependent on private funding and management.[10]

The Parks Department "Cannot Do the Job"

When urban parks emerged during the mid- and late nineteenth century, they were inspired by a vision that was both democratic and elitist. Recognizing the need for spaces for quiet reflection and simple recreation, designers aimed to create bucolic landscapes in which residents across classes and ethnicities would come together in refuges from an increasingly chaotic urban landscape. This, planners hoped, would also enable immigrants and the lower classes to "emulate the behavioral patterns, the refinement and culture, of an educated class."[11]

By the turn of the century, the vision of parks as pastoral landscapes began to give way to equipping parks with greater recreational activities, such as tennis courts and picnic areas.[12] In New York, the New Deal accelerated such provisions, as the Parks Department—infused by extraordinary federal monies and the overpowering leadership of Robert Moses—built hundreds of playgrounds, enormous swimming pools, and a vast array of sports facilities, while expanding park acreage.[13]

The continued enlargement of the park system, however, should not mask its lackadaisical administration and inconsistent funding. Before the New Deal—when federal funding for parks reached more than eight times the budget provided by the city, allowing for a thorough restoration of the entire system—New Yorkers had reason to grumble about park maintenance.[14] During Tammany Hall's political dominance in the late nineteenth and early twentieth centuries, for example, parks harbored the most egregious appointments of the machine's patronage system. Waste and favoritism left parks as "scabs on the face of the city," as writer Robert Caro put it, administered by "fiefs" who employed "the dregs of its barrel of ward heelers."[15] Yet there were few serious suggestions that financial support for or management of parks should be the responsibility of any sector other than city government.[16] Nor were there sustained, widespread resident-led movements to supplement city care. This continued to be the case even as federal support all but evaporated in the postwar period. During Moses's twenty-six year autocratic reign as Parks Commissioner (1934–1960), he continued to vastly increase parkland, but favored boosting recreational facilities over parks' continued upkeep. Park acreage increased almost 250 percent, from 14,000 to nearly 35,000 acres, but in the 1940s and 1950s, department funding declined as a percentage of the municipal budget, as did park conditions.[17]

Like so many municipal services, parks had long been maintained at lower levels within poorer communities and neighborhoods of color, but by the early 1960s, "dissatisfaction with maintenance and supervision of parks" had become near universal.[18] Complaints dominated user surveys from low-income neighborhoods, where "the worst conditions of park maintenance were reported," all the way to the city's "show-piece parks"—sentiments confirmed by park advocates' site visits.[19] Asked to give suggestions to officials, one park user noted simply: "Try cleaning them up."[20] New Yorkers at this time were more likely to avoid parks than actively participate in their upkeep.

When Mayor John Lindsay took office in 1966, he promised not just to "bring existing parks up from decay to high standards of maintenance," but to reverse severely declining park usage.[21] His Commissioners, Thomas Hoving (1966–1967) and August Heckscher (1967–1972), encouraged non-traditional use that they believed would broaden parks' appeal, such as hippie "be ins," art games, puppet shows, and large musical performances. These new programs worked. People "are coming back to [parks] in droves just because of our innovations," Heckscher put it in 1967; they have newly "fallen in love with the city's parks."[22] Though many observers argued that such uses compromised maintenance, Heckscher firmly believed that "what counted was that . . . the green places of the city had become the democratic place of a vast seething metropolis."[23]

Heckscher's efforts to balance increased usage with improved conditions began to falter late in Lindsay's first term when budget cuts led to significant contractions in resources and employees. As usage remained strong, many parks that had only just begun to improve started to atrophy. Decreased maintenance was heightened in the late 1960s by frequent instances of vandalism—what Heckscher called an "absolutely senseless sort of destructiveness and of violence"—bewildering the Commissioner who was convinced his policies had revived people's affinity for greenspace.[24]

Budget woes only worsened in the 1970s. A city-implemented hiring freeze throughout nearly all of Lindsay's second term resulted in the Parks Department losing an average of one employee a day by attrition. The number of full-time employees declined nearly 40 percent between 1968 and 1975. By that time, the backlog of work orders for Manhattan and Staten Island parks was over two years long.[25]

These conditions alarmed park advocates. The park system "as it exists today cannot last until the end of this century," Herschel Post Jr., the executive director of the city's largest park advocacy group, the Parks Council, remarked in the early 1970s.[26] With few signs of the problems of "little money, inadequate maintenance, vandalism, overuse, and litter" abating, Post suggested that some parks might need to become commercially operated with entrance fees.[27]

Residents of many neighborhoods, however, were already at work on a different solution: organizing to improve local parks. Beginning in the late 1960s, community efforts devoted to improving parks began to grow in number and breadth. These groups organized regular maintenance and fundraising initiatives to supplement declining city resources. "In the last few years, even while the park facilities have reached new depths of physical deterioration . . . we have seen a new attitude on the part of New Yorkers," two prominent park advocacy groups described at the time. "New Yorkers have come to realize today that if they wish to restore and revitalize their neighborhoods and their parks, they themselves are going to have to take initiatives and contribute their own time and effort to the task. . . . The [Parks Department] alone . . . cannot do the job."[28]

Residents in Manhattan's Yorkville, for example, had grown exasperated by the continued decline of their local greenspace, Carl Schurz Park. Despite the park's location next to Gracie Mansion, the mayor's official residence, it suffered from the same neglect and vandalism that was alarming park users all over the city. In response, local residents formed the Carl Schurz Park Association in the late 1960s "on the premise," as one article put it,

FIGURE 3.1 By the late 1960s, the entire New York City park system suffered from litter, vandalism, and insufficient maintenance.
Courtesy of the NYC Municipal Archives.

"that community involvement is the key to securing a safe, clean, and well-maintained park."[29] Members volunteered their time to clean up litter, plant, landscape, and pass out plastic bags as part of a dog control committee. Membership grew into the thousands, with each member contributing $5 annually to pay for fencing, cleaning supplies, and landscaping and horticulture experts. The group raised an additional $25,000 through bake sales and fundraisers for a restoration project.

The Carl Schurz Park Association was not the only grassroots park advocacy initiative in Yorkville. Other residents formed the Neighborhood Committee on the Asphalt Project, which advocated for a shuttered municipal asphalt plant to be turned into a new green and recreational space. The group collected 29,000 signatures and $700,000 from community members, with an average contribution of $14, throughout Harlem and the Upper East Side.[30] Volunteers also hauled away more than twelve tons of wreckage and garbage from a one-and-a-half-acre park on the northern border of the site. The group asked for no financial government resources from the city, instead supplementing community fundraising with support from foundations. The emphasis, the group's leader George Murphy noted, was that the facilities "would be created and thereafter maintained as a *public* recreation park with *private* funds to be raised by the Neighborhood Committee."[31] With municipal resources constrained, Murphy believed, "community improvement by the community itself is of greater importance to the City's viability than ever before."[32] After several years of demonstrating their commitment through their own labor and fundraising, the group convinced the city to turn the land into a park and sports center called Asphalt Green. What make the effort "all the more magnificent," Mayor Beame proclaimed in 1975, is that residents "have done it without City help, except for the land."[33]

These two community efforts in Yorkville were representative of a larger movement that extended across region, race, and class in which neighbors increasingly came together in the early and mid-1970s to revitalize greenspaces. New Yorkers organized clean ups, planted flowers and trees, weeded, painted, and formed safety patrols. "New York parks are getting cleaner these days," one paper described, "and volunteers are doing it."[34] Members of senior communities in the Bronx painted benches and planted flowers at Mount Eden Park.[35] A group of almost two dozen mothers in Queens organized the Community Volunteers for Yellowstone Park and raised $1,000 to pay the architectural expenses for a community center after the city said it had no budget for such fees.[36] At Castle Hill in the Bronx, volunteers painted handball courts and planted 1,200 marigolds. African American residents in southeastern Queens succeeded in an even more extraordinary endeavor. After the city refused to accept the federally bequeathed grounds of a closed naval hospital in 1974—knowing it had no money to pay for its existing parks—the community formed the Southern Queens Park Association (SQPA), which raised funds to take over the land. By 1976 they entered into an agreement with the Beame administration whereby the city acquired the land, but entrusted the SQPA to take responsibility for it and raise all monies for the creation of the park.[37] "There wasn't a community that wasn't trying to do something," one Parks Commissioner at the time remembered, "knowing the Parks [Department] couldn't do it."[38]

These groups rarely asked for more resources from the city, believing such support to be improbable in the midst of budget cuts. Instead, groups

FIGURE 3.2 In response to inadequate upkeep, residents throughout the city began to volunteer to improve local parks themselves. Some residents even created new parks on vacant lots or unused government land, as these teenagers in Williamsburg did in 1977. *New York Daily News*, August 18, 1977. Courtesy of Ed Molinari / *New York Daily News*.

primarily fundraised within their own community, with some more ambitious efforts also turning to nonprofit foundations and civic associations. "We have to take matters into our own hands," Pauline Walsh, who helped coordinate a project in Mount Eden Park, put it. "The idea is to clean up an area we have to sit and look at. And we're doing it ourselves."[39]

City officials were initially wary of unleashing untrained volunteers into parks, and the municipal employees union voiced objection to the prospect of unpaid volunteers being used to replace full-time unionized workers.[40] But as both the city's economy and park conditions worsened, officials increasingly supported public involvement.[41] Richard Clurman, Lindsay's final Parks Commissioner, used his swearing-in ceremony in 1973 to announce that the Department would "withdraw" all maintenance and services for parks that were repeatedly vandalized and for which there were no signs of community involvement. He established the Office of Parks Partnership to bring "a pre-organized, vocal and sophisticated constituency in the form of park groups. . . . directly into the process of running, planning and programming neighborhood parks."[42] Clurman's initiative, however, offered little in the way of direct resources for volunteers. Indeed, officials in both the Lindsay and Beame administrations encouraged resident involvement but provided few means to assist their efforts.

Officials' rhetorical support for volunteerism likely remained high because no major department had a greater percentage of personnel reductions than Parks during the peak of the fiscal crisis.[43] Indeed, volunteerism was increasingly framed as necessary to the very survival of the parks system. Parks "will survive," Commissioner Martin Lang (1976–1977) noted, if the system continued "to tap the last great resource of the city—people."[44] "We encourage" local groups working in parks, his deputy commissioner, Mohan Jethwani, proclaimed. "Their commitment means the parks have a better chance to survive."[45]

Though municipal resources for volunteers remained immaterial, community efforts began to receive support from private organizations. The most important was the Citizens Committee for New York City, which formed in 1975 to fill "gaps in the city's bureaucracy with volunteers and working with existing community organizations to provide services lost in the budget cuts."[46] Citizens offered community groups willing to carry out park maintenance $100 grants to purchase materials like rakes, paint, and plants. Soon, nearly two hundred groups throughout the city, such as the Committee to SAVE Smokey Park in Queens and the Friends of Inwood Hill Park, received such grants.[47]

Established groups like the Parks Council also aided these community initiatives. The Council started a Community-Volunteers-in-Parks program in 1976 "when budget cuts made it apparent that the users of city parks would have to assume greater responsibility for the care of city parks."[48] In its first three years the group helped over 1,800 volunteers across all five boroughs take to one hundred sixty five local parks—a substantial figure, given that the Parks Department only had 3,400 employees at the time. The Council provided training and supplies, helped groups raise money, and coordinated efforts with the Parks Department. These projects "ranged from simple clean-ups and garden plantings to ... converting a dumping area into a picnic ground in Springfield Park, Queens," the Council noted.[49] "Some groups work once a week, others almost daily," explained the Council's Norman Cohen. "None of the cost of the materials or tools is borne by the city." Funding came instead from the state and some private donors as well as through the volunteers themselves who "in many cases ... raise money or get tools donated by local merchants for the work."[50]

These efforts helped to stem, and in some cases reverse, the deterioration of many parks. They hardly sought to replace government, but rather aimed to supplement municipal services because the continued viability of a local park seemed threatened. The belief sweeping across 1970s New York that the city could no longer care for its parks was evident not only the formation of these groups, but increasingly in the statements and actions of major citywide park advocates, in nonprofits that helped to support these efforts, and even in public pronouncements and policies of Parks Commissioners.

Most of these efforts involved small neighborhood parks. What would happen to the city's most important parks—ones that transcended allegiance from any one neighborhood—and whose revival would require greater involvement than weekend clean-ups and small-scale renovations? These questions were at the forefront of revitalization efforts around the crown jewel of the park system: Central Park. Two major groups formed during this time with the similar goal of revitalizing the park, but each initially took a slightly different approach. The Central Park Task Force aimed principally to promote volunteerism and public awareness, while the Central Park Community Fund focused on improving park management and obtaining donations from the private sector. Both saw securing the involvement of those outside of government as necessary for Central Park's future. Over time, these two groups not only increased the involvement of residents and the private sector in aiding Central Park, but ultimately opened up the financing for and authority over the park to those outside of government.

"Saving" Central Park

Central Park, an 863-acre expanse that spans midtown to upper Manhattan, had since its opening in 1873 been among New York's most renowned and frequently visited parks. The deleterious effects of increased use and deferred maintenance in the late 1960s became especially notable there, as no other park faced such a significant increase in visitors. "It is doubtful whether as many people have ever derived as much quiet enjoyment from the place," the *Times* opined in 1968."[51] Just a few years later, with staff reductions ongoing, a *Times* editorial proclaimed that the park was "becoming a victim of abuse, of the losing battle between maintenance and decay."[52]

Faced with a constricted budget, the Department struggled to maintain resources even for its most valued park. Central Park gardeners, for example, had numbered forty-six for most of the period after World War II, but were reduced to three in 1973. That year, a department survey reported "heavy erosion," horticulture in a "deplorable state," and many roadway bridges, perimeter walls, and other structures "crumbling with age" or "badly vandalized." The park, as one observer described, was "overused, trampled upon, neglected, disrespected and abused."[53]

Alarmed residents began coming to the park's aid, just as they did for local parks.[54] Groups of parents living around the park, for example, began to raise funds for the creation and continued care of playgrounds. Parents often worked for years to raise the requisite funds and then volunteered to provide maintenance and cleanings after their creation.[55] Additionally, residents concerned with growing instances of crime and vandalism formed the Central Park Precinct Community Council in 1973. The initiative involved volunteers from throughout the city "who feel that Central Park is the jewel of the city's park system and that its preservation is of paramount importance."[56] The extraordinary effort involved hundreds of volunteers on foot, horseback, and bike, along with a medical rescue unit.

As important as these and similar efforts were to improving conditions in the park, the Task Force and Community Fund would ultimately do much more to promote turning to private citizens and the private sector. The groups believed that the park's very existence was threatened by diminished municipal resources. They argued that enhancing the role of those outside of government was not just needed to revitalize Central Park but to save it.

The first of these groups, the Central Park Task Force, was formed in 1974. The Task Force expanded on the same strategy as grassroots park initiatives: volunteerism and fundraising. While only some New Yorkers saw Central Park as their local park, the Task Force capitalized on the connection many residents felt to the park, whether they lived near it or traveled to it from across the boroughs. Though technically established within the Parks Department, the Task Force was funded by philanthropist Brooke Astor's foundation and therefore operated largely independently. It identified park needs and organized volunteers and raised private funds to meet these needs, thereby serving "as a bridge between the Parks Administration and the private sector."[57]

The Task Force hired Elizabeth Barlow as its executive director. Barlow had arrived in New York in the mid-1960s after receiving a graduate degree in City Planning from Yale and worked at the Parks Council, where she advocated for greater public funding for parks, and also authored several books, including one on Central Park designer Frederick Law Olmsted.[58] Barlow had grown alarmed by Central Park's declining conditions, which she witnessed on regular visits with her young children, and believed that the city's ongoing budgetary turmoil necessitated garnering greater support from outside government. At the Task Force, she spearheaded a strategy of cultivating volunteers and donations by fostering a deeper sense of public investment in the Park's future and by proclaiming that the city could not safeguard Central Park with its existing staff or budget. "Abandon Central Park?" asked the cover of one CPTF fundraising pamphlet that also included a picture of an eroded and tarnished park landscape. "Never!" the next page answered. "Can anyone imagine New York without Central Park?" the pamphlet continued, "Central Park is in trouble. It needs help. Your help."[59] The group invited New Yorkers to become involved in its volunteer initiatives, such as weeding and planting patrols whom the Task Force provided with tools and teamed with landscaping and horticultural experts. Litter brigades used refuse bags with tags that read: "This litter was bagged by a volunteer." "Now is the time," the Task Force proclaimed, to put "energy and spirit of cooperation into helping our short-handed Parks Department maintain the appearance and beauty of the city's public open spaces."[60] These efforts, of course, would only succeed if New Yorkers responded; hundreds—and ultimately thousands—soon did. "Every day the phone rings with people who want to be city gardeners. That resource needs to be utilized," Barlow told the *Times* in 1975.[61]

The group combined these volunteer initiatives with education about misuse that it contended had tarnished the park. The Task Force informed park users that "whether the park remains a great theater for outdoor life, or . . . a shabby relic of former good times, is up to us, the people of this city."[62] It developed a School Program that allowed children to improve the park while also educating them about proper usage.[63] "If kids understand the park as a work of art," the program director noted, "they don't have to read the rules."[64] By 1976, twenty surrounding schools had "adopted" an area to care for, with the Task Force providing professional training and supervision.[65]

FIGURE 3.3 AND FIGURE 3.4 The Central Park Task Force garnered volunteers and individual donations for Central Park by proclaiming that city government could no longer safeguard the park on its own.
Central Park Task Force Pamphlet and Tag for Trash Bags. Courtesy of the Central Park Conservancy.

While the Task Force sought to encourage everyday users to volunteer their time or dollars to improving the park, the second group, the Central Park Community Fund, prioritized enhancing management and capturing large-scale donations. The seeds of the Community Fund were planted during daily walks to work Richard Gilder took across the park after he moved his stockbrokerage firm to midtown from Wall Street in 1969. Those walks left him "totally horrified" by the park's conditions.[66] Gilder soon partnered with another Wall Street titan who had expressed similar alarm from his office that overlooked the park: George Soros. Gilder and Soros had each recently formed their own investment firms and their rising stature in the world of finance no doubt opened the door to initial meetings with Lindsay's Commissioner Richard Clurman. While in subsequent decades, each man's philanthropic endeavors would reflect his distinct politics— Soros would become the most renown philanthropist of progressive causes, while Gilder supported conservative endeavors like the Manhattan Institute and the Club for Growth—their involvement in Central Park gave little sign of being motivated by a politics of either the right or the left. Gilder and Soros agreed with Clurman "that the main responsibility for capital and maintenance support for Central Park belongs to the city" and worked with officials to "mobilize both public and private financial aid . . . to insure a continuing flow of funds. . . . which will be necessary to keep the park beautiful, enjoyable and safe."[67]

As a first step, Gilder and Soros proposed they principally fund a study undertaken with the city to document the physical condition, usage, maintenance, and management of Central Park.[68] The resulting report, led by Columbia University business professor E. S. Savas, painted a picture of the park being lost to decay and mismanagement. The chronicling of the park's aging, decrepit greenery and built environment would not have surprised anyone who had visited the park. More novel and influential was the study's discussion of management. No one in the Department, the report found, could say how much the city spent on the park. There was no organizational chart delineating responsibility for what Savas estimated involved 346 workers and $10,000,000 spent annually.[69] No one was charged with long-term planning. "Responsibility is so fragmented and diffuse," the report concluded, "that no one below the Commissioner himself (or his deputy) has an identifiable responsibility for planning and managing" or even the park's day-to-day operations. In some cases, "supervisors simply admitted that they were somewhat confused about how their individual positions and responsibilities fitted into the larger picture."[70]

To fix these problems the report pointed principally not to more funding, but "better management."[71] Central Park should be managed as a single organization under a new position of Park Executive who would have authority over administration, personnel, maintenance, and long-term planning. Additionally, a Board of Guardians should aid the Administrator to "assure responsible attention to [Central Park's] needs and its future condition." The Board would increase "citizens' role in park planning, policy formulation, and performance monitoring," oversee a major rehabilitation effort, and ensure greater long-term planning.[72]

Alongside the study's release in 1974, Gilder and Soros announced the founding of the Central Park Community Fund. The group's agenda reflected how much Gilder's and Soros's approach had changed since they first began discussing how to improve Central Park a few years before. While their initial discussions included how to increase municipal funds, such goals diminished once Beame took office and the depths of the economic troubles grew more apparent. While the two had earlier also promoted volunteerism, the Community Fund soon concluded that rescuing the park would occur not through masses of volunteers, but through gaining institutional support from businesses, foundations, and civic organizations.[73] Additionally, while their earlier efforts had emphasized the need to improve the park, the CPCF began to promote a new logic: private-citizen and private sector involvement was necessary to save the park. The Community Fund put this in the starkest terms: "The City can no longer maintain Central Park alone," the group wrote in a fundraising letter. "This has left the park dying,—choked by trash, swamped by clogged drains, marred by vandalism and neglect."[74]

While Soros and Gilder were convinced of the type of support needed to ensure that the park did not suffer irreversible decay, others were less certain. No one had previously suggested that private guardians and donations were necessary to save the park; the care of Central Park had long been understood to be the city's responsibility. Indeed, when Gilder and Soros announced their goal of raising a million dollars for the park over the next five years, as Gilder remembered, one reporter responded: "Are you kidding? You really think you can raise a million dollars for Central Park? You've got to be nuts."[75] Even Beame administration officials were initially much less receptive to assistance than Clurman had been. Though Beame's Park Commissioner Edwin Weisl (1974–1975) accepted many conclusions of the Savas report, he rejected the idea of a Board of Guardians or that the park be organized under a "single organizational unit" headed by a Park Executive. "I am certain," Weisl noted, "that we can work out the park's problems within the existing system."[76] Such resistance even extended to the group's donations. The Task Force raised an initial $25,000 "and the city didn't want it," Gilder remembered.[77] Desperate as Beame's administration was for financial relief, parks officials were likely hesitant because of concern that the recommendations and donations might diminish department autonomy.

As Gilder and Soros raised additional funds and as the city's fiscal position declined, officials became more receptive to private contributions. The

Community Fund's solicitations, often from business associates of Gilder and Soros, soon financed tree plantings, soil and tree care, and facility improvements.[78] The group also raised money for the fleet of trimmers, mowers, and sweepers, many of which were broken and idle. "With each unit that CPCF can help to put back into the park," the group told potential donors, "manpower can be freed for other uses and the efficiency of the machine operators increased considerably."[79]

These initiatives began to dovetail with Barlow's work at the Task Force. While Barlow had successfully garnered greater volunteers and small donations, her most significant step in rallying the public came in 1976 when she authored a *New York* magazine cover article titled "32 Ways Your Time or Money Can Recue Central Park." "New York can no longer afford its parks," the article began bluntly. "Not even Central Park."[80] The article was not a call to arms for increased government support of parks in the face of the fiscal crisis. Instead, it echoed the message being promoted by the political and banking officials about what the city could no longer support. Indeed, Barlow deliberately looked elsewhere. Yet she simultaneously raised—and rejected—the idea that the management of Central Park be "contracted out to private agencies." Instead, she proposed that the best solution was "the volunteer sector. The survival or ultimate death of the city's parks depends entirely on how much people care about them." The article included several suggestions for how readers could donate their time, such as volunteering for a litter patrol. Institutionalizing greater volunteerism for the care of public space "is a tall order," Barlow conceded, "but if it works, Central Park might yet be saved in spite of (or perhaps because of) this age of austerity."[81] The implication of her language was clear: Central Park was dying in the city's hands.

Barlow's article was not just about increasing public support for volunteering and small donations. The piece was also the Task Force's first major attempt at changing sentiments among the affluent and philanthropic classes. Barlow hoped the article would allow potential donors to see that the park was a "New York institution" on par with "the Metropolitan Museum or Broadway" and that it could not be saved without their participation.[82] Though much of Barlow's article was devoted to calling for volunteer efforts, nearly all of her thirty-two suggestions directed readers to make fiscal donations for park improvements. While a few were small—($10 to plant a shrub)—many more were sizeable, including providing new granite vases for the mall ($7,500), restoring Bethesda Foundation ($575,000), and dredging and relandscaping the 59th Street Pond ($2.5 million).

The response to Barlow's call was immediate, though donations primarily came in small amounts rather than in larger sums. Readers accepted her
premise that responsibility for saving the park now fell to those outside government. Tens of thousands of dollars poured in from readers throughout
the city as well as from ex-New Yorkers across the nation.[83] "The people of
New York and the country," Barlow proudly exclaimed, "will not allow our
chief municipal amenity to be written off like a bad debt because of fiscal
austerity."[84]

While the Task Force continued to secure volunteers and modest
donations, the Community Fund had growing success in obtaining large-
scale contributions. The group announced a Second Century Fund campaign that sought to raise $2 million, especially targeting corporations and
businesses from which the group had previously struggled to raise funds.
"While corporations have given handsomely to the arts over the past several
years, Central Park is also a living, magnificent, and grand work of art that
also needs to be helped," the Fund's executive director argued.[85]

These campaigns reflected how the strategies of the Task Force and
Community Fund increasingly complemented one another. While the Task
Force's greatest strengths were in promoting volunteerism and small-scale
donations, the Community Fund was having greater success with outreach
to businesses and corporations. Collectively, the Task Force and Community
Fund sent the message to residents of all income levels, to foundations, and to
businesses that the city could no longer support the park on its own and that
their time and resources were needed to save the park. The Task Force and
Community Fund built on the grassroots park revitalization initiatives that
had been proliferating since the late 1960s, and reproduced these strategies on
a much grander scale.

However, the Central Park groups also deviated from these local initiatives
in important ways. For one, both the Community Fund and the Task Force
increasingly believed that the park's greatest hope for salvation lay in securing
support from elites—whether businesses and corporations or its philanthropic
class—rather than just grassroots volunteerism and donations. The Central
Park groups also increasingly differed from community efforts in their end
goals. While neighborhood initiatives formed as a temporary measure to reverse park deterioration, the Community Fund pushed to permanently expand fiscal responsibility for and even authority over the park to those outside
of government, a notion the Task Force would soon embrace as well.

Despite their accomplishments, the combined efforts of the Community
Fund and the Task Force could not outpace the severe cutbacks that occurred

during the fiscal crisis. Park appropriations fell from $4.5 million to $1.7 between 1973 and 1977.[86] The number of seasonal workers in Central Park declined 80 percent, from an already reduced number, between 1975 and 1976. The Department had suffered the loss of half of its permanent personnel since the late 1960s and was on its seventh commissioner in six years by 1978.[87] There "simply are no longer enough job lines to cover all the work that needs to be done in Central Park," the Task Force reported in 1976.[88] Severe decreases in city funds for repairs, labor, and maintenance had transformed the park "into 840 acres of bare ground, trash, and dog dirt."[89]

Continued municipal cutbacks, however, ultimately gave the Task Force and Community Fund the leverage they needed to radically change policies governing Central Park's funding and management. The crisis helped to shift the notion that the private sector could better provide services closer to the mainstream of government thought in the late 1970s. Their proposals also took on new relevance as others concerned about the park began to advance solutions considered by many to be far more drastic: transferring responsibility to another branch of government. As federal and state officials began discussing the idea of taking control of Central Park, a growing number of city policymakers and park advocates warmed to the notion of turning to the private sector.

Establishing the Central Park Conservancy

As alarmed as city officials and park users were by conditions in Central Park, many New Yorkers became even more disturbed by calls for the park's federalization. The idea was advanced by New York Senator Patrick Moynihan during his campaign in 1976. "To leave the park in the hands of the City leaves the park to eke out a living in a bidding system that has become increasingly competitive as resources have become increasingly scarce," Moynihan said. "To follow this path . . . is to accept defeat."[90] Several prominent representatives endorsed Moynihan's proposal.[91]

This and other proposals to save Central Park were fervently debated in 1978 in a public forum on the "Future of Central Park." The event, organized by Manhattan Borough President Andrew Stein, featured prominent politicians including Moynihan, Congressman Charles Rangel, and numerous city officials, as well as leading park advocates. Participants debated a range of ideas that had surfaced to save the park: federalization, state control, and transferring the park to an independent board that would operate the park along the lines of the Public Library and the Botanic Gardens.

Despite the divergence of opinion, many attendees and park advocates agreed on two broad sentiments: the Parks Department was unable to care for the park on its own and control of the park should not be wholly transferred away from the city. To the Community Fund, the solution was clear. The group's new study, "Alternative Governance Proposals for Central Park," reiterated its proposal to appoint a professional administrator responsible for operating and planning as well as a Board of Guardians, which would solicit donations from the private sector.[92] Threatened with losing control over the park, city officials paid greater attention to the Task Force's proposal than they had previously.

The plan also gained popularity because its release followed the election of Mayor Ed Koch, who brought to the office a new enthusiasm for market and private sector based solutions. Both Koch and his Parks Commissioner, Gordon Davis, took immediate interest in the proposal. Paralleling the approach to housing, Koch and Davis believed that the city needed to look to the private sector to support and even run department operations to relieve municipal resources in a time of fiscal strain and federal retrenchment.

Davis made no attempt to defend his department's ability to adequately care for the resources with which it was entrusted. Early in his tenure, Davis ordered a systematic study of all department facilities—such as its thirteen golf courses, seven skating rinks, and over 500 tennis courts—to determine which could be run by private operators. Davis also worked to ensure that the city's three zoos were turned over to the New York Zoological Society.[93] "Almost without exception the Parks Department's fee charging special facilities were . . . being managed inefficiently and uneconomically and, equally important, day to day upkeep of these high maintenance operations had declined seriously," Davis stated. "To reverse this situation would have required resources, both time as well as money, that the Department simply did not have."[94]

Turning Central Park over to private operators would have likely been too drastic a measure for most New Yorkers to accept; it was just as politically unpopular as federalization. Davis instead embraced the more moderate recommendations of the Community Fund. Not long after his appointment, Soros and Gilder met with Davis and offered to pay for the administrator position.[95] Davis soon agreed to create the position of Central Park Administrator in February 1979. To fill the position Davis turned to Betsy Barlow, who had become the best known advocate for the park and for soliciting private resources. Barlow was charged with overseeing the "rehabilitation, management, and horticultural management of Central Park" and with encouraging more private, state, and federal support.[96] Two-thirds of Barlow's office, including her salary and supporting staff, was funded through the private sector.[97] The city had had never in the twentieth century turned to the private sector to fund the administrative head of a public park nor had there been a park administrator appointed to fundraise from the private sector.

Barlow implemented administrative changes, initiated long-term planning, and capitalized on the years of work of the Task Force and Community Fund by garnering private donations. Bolstered by what was seen as the first serious commitment of the city to the park in years as well as the tactics and relationships that the Task Force and the Community Fund had developed, Barlow helped facilitate the types of major donations that she, Gilder, and Soros had sought but not often succeeded in securing. Lila Wallace, co-founder of *Reader's Digest*, for example, committed $500,000 to repair the Egyptian obelisk.[98]

Though Barlow's success seemed to reinforce the fruitfulness of turning to the private sector, in the eyes of the Community Fund, it was not enough. "The long-term, non-political, appointment of a professional park director is only a first step," noted the Community Fund newsletter. The fiscal crisis, the group argued, had proven overwhelmingly that municipal management jeopardized the park's future. "Central Park demands a managerial continuum, permanent manpower and funds as insulated as possible from the ebbs and flows of fiscal crisis."[99] This no doubt spoke to Davis's desire to utilize to the private sector. Additionally, Barlow's successful fundraising had demonstrated an important change had recently occurred: wealthy individuals, foundations, and corporations were willing to provide substantial monetary support for something that had previously been understood as government's responsibility. Davis saw no reason not to accept as much support as they were willing to offer.

Davis, after all, was still charged with improving conditions across the park system and, despite the work of community groups, they proved unable in many parks to offset decimated municipal resources. As extensive as these community initiatives were, they never extended to all of the system's 572 parks. A month-long *New York Times* investigation reported that this system at the end of the 1970s was "a dirty, unkempt, vandalized shadow of its former self."[100] "Vast swatches" of parks "are near ruin."[101] "Many of these once glorious urban oases," a *Times* editorial about the series described, "are now unsightly and dangerous dumps. . . . routinely ravaged by vandals and staved of funds for both maintenance and security."[102] So alarmed by what it termed the "chronic crisis" of parks, the *Times* editorial board asked: "Are there not some parks, or parts of parks, that should be fenced off indefinitely to let nature preserve what this generation of custodians so obviously cannot?"

As in other areas of municipal government, federal cutbacks only seemed to foreclose other government-based solutions for improving the parks systems. The Parks Department had relied for a number of years on several federal programs to offset dwindling municipal resources. Since 1973, for example, the Department had compensated for cutbacks in permanent employees with the Comprehensive Employment and Training Act (CETA), a program in which the federal government paid for low-income workers in public employment or nonprofit agencies. By 1978, Davis's first year in office, Parks employed 2,600 CETA workers, but changes in CETA regulations implemented that year resulted in the loss of nearly 1,000 such employees; the program was eliminated soon after Ronald Reagan's election.[103] "It was almost as if," Davis remarked, "somebody in Washington said, 'let's see how we can destroy the New York City Parks Department.' "[104] These changes were further exacerbated by extensive reductions in federal funding. When Davis took office, roughly one-third of the Parks budget came from the federal government; by 1983, this had declined to less than 4 percent.[105]

These conditions only reinforced for Koch administration officials the idea that the private sector could be the park system's salvation. In 1980, Davis announced the formation of the Central Park Conservancy. The Conservancy effectively merged the Community Fund and Task Force, providing "a unified voice within the private sector on behalf of the park," stated William Beinecke, the Conservancy's first chairman.[106] Conservancy officials aimed to raise private funds by adopting the strategy that the two groups had pioneered over the previous decade. The Conservancy would include largely wealthy "public-spirited citizens," Koch described, who "believe that Central Park is a cultural resource that deserves the kind of support as our great museums, botanical gardens, and other institutions."[107] "There's a great untapped resource of donors out there who have never contributed to the park or the city before," Davis explained. "But while the museums and other cultural institutions don't hesitate to hold out their cups, there's been no institutionalized begging on behalf of the park."[108] Indeed, the Conservancy's earliest fundraising materials proclaimed that the park should be seen "as a civic institution in much the same way that Lincoln Center, the Bronx Zoo, and the Metropolitan Museum are seen as institutions whose well-being directly enhances the quality of life in the City. Indeed, the park may be the most important: it serves the widest constituency."[109]

The Conservancy marked an exceptional change in city policy by embracing private sector involvement in the park, but business elites remained skeptical. Many viewed the proposal as a request that the wealthy fill fiduciary and fiscal roles for which the state should be responsible. As Barlow remembered, "There was that mentality: Aren't we taxpayers?"[110] Several former CEOs turned down Davis's request that they serve as the Conservancy's chair. The idea of raising extensive funds for a public park from businesspersons, corporations, and wealthy individuals was seen by many as foolish. "They all thought we were crazy," Davis remembered."[111] Once Beinecke took the position, he too faced difficulty in recruiting "names that people in our city would recognize" for the Conservancy's board.[112] As Beinecke approached prominent financial and corporate leaders, he encountered resistance from those who told him "parks are public property, and should be supported by public money."

Beinecke eventually convinced powerful business and financial figures to join the board by impressing upon them that the park could be saved only through the assistance "of private citizens who would raise money to augment city funds."[113] Beinecke and Barlow also stressed that that "the Conservancy will not provide support that can and should legitimately be provided by the City," making clear that the Conservancy would supplement—and not supplant—city funding.[114]

As the Conservancy took form and began facilitating park improvements, contributions grew tremendously. Some came from everyday park users, who committed small donations in numbers unheard of in prior decades. Indeed, its first two public campaigns yielded 4,000 contributions averaging $41 per gift for $165,000. But these were vastly overshadowed by corporations, wealthy individuals, and foundations, whose contributions totaled nearly $3,000,000 during that same period.[115] Though some potential donors no doubt remained skeptical of contributing to an endeavor their tax dollars already supported, the Conservancy's nonprofit status made such donations tax deductible, providing a compelling financial incentive for giving.

In just a few years, campaigns for Central Park helped to shift views and policies about citizen and especially private sector involvement in a public park. The Conservancy successfully tapped into New York's tradition of cultural institutions—museums, performance centers, and even greenspaces like Botanic Gardens—that relied on funding from the wealthy, either as individuals or through private foundations. In reconfiguring Central Park to be accepted into this model, the park underwent a significant conceptual shift from being understood a space entrusted to government to one "guarded" by elites.

This revitalization effort facilitated the beginnings of a transition from resident groups leading park revitalization initiatives that began in earnest early in the decade to "guardians" comprised of the affluent, corporations, and major foundations. Extraordinary political currents helped to facilitate this change, as the private sector began to see the fruits—tax deductions, positive press, increasing real estate values—of greater involvement in parks. Nonetheless, the Community Fund, Task Force, and Conservancy all faced significant hurdles in changing sentiment among residents and the private sector regarding the city's premier park, which provided little assurance that efforts at other parks to harness the resources of the private sector would prove successful.

The Corporate Campaign for Madison Square Park

Some of the city's most neglected parks were unexpectedly located in centers of commerce. Severe cutbacks in maintenance did not spare parks in business districts; their conditions declined significantly. Additionally, these parks were principally used during lunch hours of the work week, creating the opportunity for them to at other times become inhabited by drug sellers (who found an ample market among white-collar workers) as well as those struggling with addictions to alcohol and narcotics. As residents rallied around their neighborhood parks and people throughout the city joined the effort to save Central Park, who would come to the aid of these parks?

Madison Square Park, for instance, sat between two of Manhattan's renowned avenues of commerce and wealth: Madison and Fifth. The headquarters of several major national corporations overlooked the park, including New York Life Insurance and Metropolitan Life Insurance (who were also major landlords in the area). But by the late 1970s, the park, whose deteriorating conditions the city had "long neglected," had also became "the site of daytime drug dealing and a place where derelicts drink and sleep on the benches," the *Times* noted.[116] Though race was never explicitly evoked in calls to clean up the park, most of the park users deemed "undesirables"—those drinking, sleeping, or selling drugs—were African American, whereas most of the office workers—and drug purchasers—were white.[117] The very presence of these "undesirable" park users was often sufficient to discourage white office workers from spending much, if any, time in the park.[118]

Madison Square Park's setting was exactly what Donald Simon, an ambitious former Parks Department official, believed would be the foundation for its revival. Simon thought that the park's salvation could come from its corporate neighbors. Such funds could provide the maintenance, management, and security to revitalize the park. These corporations, Simon believed, would recognize that devoting resources toward the "reversal of the park's decline" was a smart investment, as it would be "mirrored in a stronger demand for rental space."[119] Improvements would also lead to "a better employment situation, easing the task of attracting competent personnel."[120]

Simon found an ally in his former boss Richard Clurman, who was "instrumental" in providing early support for Simon's idea. "It's a concept we had in government, one we spoke about quite a bit," Clurman explained, "You pick a park, one in bad condition, and you treat it as a company would treat its corporate plaza, completely with private sector funds. And it can be duplicated throughout the city." The private sector could provide "the funds and the people to relieve the Park Department of a responsibility it can't meet because of budget strictures."[121] The Ford Foundation also endorsed Simon's plan and awarded him $25,000 in seed money to create Urban Park Plazas in January 1979. These provided Simon with startup funds as the project moved toward being supported by the corporations surrounding Madison Square Park; the model would then be reproduced with other parks throughout Manhattan.[122]

The vision of Urban Park Plaza was at once simple and profound. Simon believed parks could be vastly improved without the millions of dollars a major renovation would require, funds difficult to raise from corporate neighbors. Urban Park Plazas "does not agree that in the absence of large-scale rebuilding of the park, nothing can be accomplished."[123] Instead, the principal idea, as Simon described, is to drive out "the unwanted elements" by getting more people to use the park through providing programming such as free music.[124] "Large numbers of people," the group believed, "tend to drive away the drug dealers and derelicts who by their very presence give the site a dangerous appearance."[125] What's more, vast improvements could come to the six acre park simply by hiring a few private maintenance workers to supplement municipal pruning, painting, and trash removal. Finally, by providing centralized management where none then existed, Urban Park Plazas would coordinate these efforts and ensure that the park would not fall back into disrepair.

But Simon's idea was also profound. In an era in which corporate donations for parks were rare, no one had proposed that their efforts alone could—and should—revitalize a public park. What's more, as the UPP explained to potential corporate supporters, the goal was not simply renewal but "taking the management and maintenance of Madison Square Park out of the hands of the City which does not and cannot afford to maintain it and putting that management into private hands for private profit but for public use."[126] "In the future," Simon believed, "other companies will be paying to supplement city services, because the city just doesn't have the money anymore."[127]

With the Ford Foundation's support, the UPP approached Madison Square Park's four major corporate neighbors. "This plan," Clurman wrote to the president of Met Life, should be seen as "a commercial venture for the four companies involved, not as a piece of philanthropy," explaining that reviving the park could in short time "raise the value of real estate in the participating buildings as much as $2.00 a square foot." The improved park would "please your employees, improve the whole neighborhood, increase the value of your property and set an example which would likely be followed in as many as ten or twenty other locations around the City."[128] Simon and Clurman depicted themselves as public servants who recognized that parks in business districts could flourish with support from the corporate sphere, advantaging all involved. "You would be right in not expecting me, primarily, to be interested in increasing the value of your real estate," Clurman explained to one corporate executive. "But I *am* very interested in the proposition that in some cases the private sector, for its own benefit alone, can take on certain municipal functions that the City is too broke or too tangled to undertake effectively and in so doing actually enrich themselves at the same time they improve the City."[129]

The corporations, however, were hesitant to take on the role of fiscal benefactors of the Parks Department. Urban Parks Plaza proposed that each of the four corporations contribute $100,000; they offered far less. The UPP raised only $64,000 in its initial fundraising campaign.[130] "We are pleased and excited about this unique effort by the private sector to rehabilitate and enhance this historic portion of New York City," professed the president of Metropolitan. But his support was tempered by a reminder that private initiatives could not fully substitute for public services. City involvement was necessary to successfully "clean up the park," the vice president of Metropolitan proclaimed.[131]

The corporations neighboring Madison Square, however, warmed to the idea of participating in the park's renewal. While the UPP continued to fall short of its fundraising goals, seventeen landlords and companies surrounding the park contributed to its $100,000 budget in 1980.[132] "We're doing this because we can't wait for government to do the things that have to be done," the principal in one major real estate firm with headquarters on the park noted.[133] Parks officials were so encouraged by the UPP's efforts that they allowed the group to take over "tree care, fence repairs, horticultural improvements, bench repair, replacement and panting" in return for the Department adding personnel for basic maintenance, supplies, and litter pick-ups.[134] The UPP's success was, the *Times* wrote, a scarcely noticed "pleasant little revolution."[135]

It was, however, short-lived. Despite its initial momentum, the UPP found that corporate funds could not produce enough improvements to convince donors to provide ongoing support. The organization folded in the early 1980s.

But Simon's vision for greater corporate involvement in parks was prophetic. Simon was instrumental in helping to promote a nearly identical program exactly one mile north of Madison Square in Bryant Park. The plan—led by the Bryant Park Restoration Corporation (BPRC)—included securing the support of respected institutions, foundations, officials, and park advocates, which strengthened its reception from the business community. This broader constituency allowed the Restoration Corporation to accomplish what the UPP could not: a private group gaining control of a public park.

"A Grand Experiment in Urban Governance"

Although Central Park's deleterious state received the greatest public attention in the 1970s, many New Yorkers would have likely pointed to Bryant Park as the park in which conditions had declined most severely. What made Bryant Park's state particularly striking—and so frustrating to people like William Stuhlbarg—was its setting: it was in the center of Manhattan's midtown business district, just a few blocks from the major transportation hubs of Grand Central Terminal and Penn Station, and half of its nine acres were filled by the renowned main branch of the New York Public Library.

In addition to its dilapidating conditions, many observers blamed Bryant Park's design for enabling illicit activities to flourish there. The park sat about five feet above street level, surrounded by walls and thick shrubbery, with narrow, spaced out entrances and exits, which obscured it from street view. Drug and alcohol use and drug dealing had over the prior few decades grown increasingly common. As in Madison Park, the park users deemed responsible for these activities were largely African American men whose presence no doubt heightened racialized fears about conditions in the park.

Corporations and businesses in the area consistently expressed alarm about the park but took little action. The private sector finally took significant steps in 1977 when local businesses and the City University of New York formed the Bryant Park Steering Committee. The group aimed to organize programming and "fix ups," to improve safety, and ultimately to plan a major park renovation.[136] The committee also helped create a Bryant Park

Community Fund—no doubt influenced by efforts in Central Park—to so-licit donations from corporate donors.[137] "Essential in these days of fiscal crisis," Parks Commissioner Martin Lang wrote in applauding the initiative, "is the formation and continuing commitment of private groups devoted to the improvement, upgrading, and operation of specific park properties. It is our hope that such coalitions of local residents and business interests will be-come established institutions within the New York City Park system."[138]

But the group found raising significant support from surrounding businesses difficult. Just as Urban Park Plaza and the Central Parks groups had discovered, business interests were hesitant to step in to provide fiscal support or take on managerial responsibility for a realm considered to be the duty of the city. Although many local corporations initially expressed interest, the group only raised $5,000 in its first six months because, as one participant described, "there's a feeling that they shouldn't be forced to do the city's job."[139] The Steering Committee's other initiatives were equally in-effective. The group's summer concerts—designed to get more people in the park—first proved popular, but had to be put on hold after the sound system was stolen. Other events simply enlarged the market for drug dealers.[140]

These and other revitalization efforts during the decade were essen-tially ignored by the institution most intimately connected to the park: the New York Public Library (NYPL). But in the late 1970s, several of the library's funders grew so concerned about the park's conditions that they refused to make contributions to the library's $45 million restoration cam-paign. "'Why,' they asked," as Andrew Heiskell, the vice chairman and trustee of the NYPL and Chairman of *Time*, remembered, "were we raising money for improvements that nobody would ever notice? For who would fight his or her way through the corps of drug sellers and other hustlers who ringed the building?"[141] Several long-term funders informed the library's board that they would only continue to give if the library actively improved Bryant Park.

Under pressure, library officials turned their attention to the park. Heiskell approached the Rockefeller Brothers Fund, which had denied the library a $1 million donation, to provide $75,000 in seed money for a new or-ganization, the BPRC. He also hired Daniel Biederman, a young graduate of Harvard Business School, who was serving as Chair of the local Community Board, as the group's first executive director. Such boards were largely advi-sory, but their endorsements were generally required to receive support from key political bodies like the Department of City Planning.

The group's revitalization plan was similar to the one developed by Donald Simon, whom the group hired as an early advisor. "The problem in Bryant Park is under-use," Biederman explained, echoing Simon.[142] "The void of activity permits a variety of law-breakers to operate there with little fear of apprehension," the group's early promotional materials stated, leading "many to believe that Bryant Park has been abandoned by its caretakers and neighbors."[143] The group developed a four point plan, all of which required turning to the private sector: creating facilities and activities to attract visitors, developing a privately funded workforce to provide maintenance that was "beyond the capability of the dollar-starved Parks Department," increasing policing either through hiring a private security force or pressuring the Police Department, and, eventually, facilitating a major redesign of the park.

Many of the ideas the BPRC advocated had been attempted or proposed previously for the park. But most of these earlier efforts also depended on increased municipal resources, which the BPRC believed to be fruitless. The Restoration Corporation's initiatives, they made clear, would rely almost entirely on the private sector.[144]

Biederman and Heiskell found the corporations surrounding the park much more receptive to their outreach than their predecessors there or the UPP had. It is likely that executives had read press accounts of Barlow's work in Central Park, which gave an encouraging picture of how greater private sector involvement could improve a park. This warmer reception was also likely due to Bryant Park's conditions—which by the late 1970s were far worse than Madison Square—as well as a growing concern about its effects on corporate bottom lines. "Bryant Park is no longer a place where one can spend his lunch hour without being solicited to buy drugs," Walter Weiner, the Chairman of Republic National Bank, wrote to the president of New York Telephone, J. R. Mulhearn. The headquarters of each company bordered the park.[145] Republic executives similarly bemoaned how prospective commercial tenants for its new headquarters saw the park as a liability.[146] Corporate leaders also worried about how park conditions affected employee recruitment. The presidents of Republic National Bank, New York Telephone, and American Standard directly lobbied companies adjacent to Bryant Park to see it as their "front yard" and support its revitalization.[147]

The early success of the BPRC also resulted from its ability to garner political and financial support from a wide array of actors. Indeed, the initiative was driven by the NYPL, a trusted cultural institution with an affluent, politically connected board, which gave the effort credibility in the eyes of its corporate neighbors. The group had also been endorsed by a major foundation, the Rockefeller Brothers Fund, helmed by financial titans Laurance and David Rockefeller. Additionally, unlike the UPP, the Restoration Corporation worked quickly to forge additional alliances, including an early partnership with the Parks Council, which led the group's efforts to bring more individuals into the park, particularly outside of lunchtime hours. The Council helped open bookstalls, a small café, and a flower stand, organized entertainment, and underwrote a landscaping program. These helped the park to "become known a bit less for its muggers and drug sellers and more for its flowers, trees, and books."[148] The *Times* likened these efforts to "take back" the park to those of the recent feminist "take back the night" actions against sexual violence.[149]

The BPRC's broad support was also evident in the group's board of directors. The board included Commissioner Davis; Heiskell of the NYPL; real estate mogul Marshall Rose; the executive director of Parks Council; the president of the nearby CUNY Graduate School; and Biederman. This backing from a variety of sectors—the mayor's office, cultural and educational institutions, real estate, park advocates—reinforced that rallying the private sector around Bryant Park was prudent and necessity.

Such support was critical not just to receiving donations from neighboring corporations, but from major philanthropists and foundations as well. Indeed, as with Central Park and Madison Square Park, the philanthropic community provided necessary early capital; these efforts would not have gone far otherwise. Of the $711,750 the BPRC raised in its first three years, sizeable donations came from the corporate neighbors, especially those that owned real estate surrounding the park. However, these were significantly outpaced by grants from foundations, such as the Rockefeller Brothers Fund and Rockefeller Foundation ($260,000), the Henry Luce Foundation ($180,000), and the New York Community Trust ($50,000), who endorsed the group's efforts as credible and commendable.[150]

These resources enabled the BPRC to carry out the first sustained improvements to the park in recent memory. By 1982, the Restoration Corporation paid for the trees to be pruned for the first time in years, helped plant 3,000 square feet of begonias, restored Bryant Park's three fountains, and fertilized and replanted the main lawn.[151] The BPRC also eliminated much of the park's graffiti. It purchased a graffiti removal machine, which it donated to the Parks Department, but required the city's graffiti removal crew to "give Bryant Park top priority in the use of that equipment."[152]

Despite these successes, BPRC officials like Biederman and Heiskell remained frustrated by how much remained to be accomplished. The park attracted large crowds of "desirable" users predominantly during workday lunchtimes in nicer weather. They were also still troubled by the park's crime rates, though these were declining, and believed that the park remained in need of several maintenance projects and a thorough renovation.[153] Biederman and Heiskell had also grown concerned that BPRC's funding derived primarily from "ad hoc donations from the area's corporations, realty owners, foundations, and individuals . . . solicited with the implicit promise that a long-term source of funding would be found to secure the park's future."[154] This funding remained elusive.

The solution, Biederman and Heiskell believed, was to " 'privatize' the park, to take it away from Parks Department ownership and management," as Heiskell remembered.[155] This plan to take over day-to-day control was principally fueled by Public Library officials who felt it was the only way to ensure the park's—and the library's—future. "Our backyard has to be as secure and as clean and as decent, symbolically and actually, as our front, the library itself," Vartan Gregorian, the NYPL's president asserted. "Otherwise we can restore the library in front, the back will drag us down and I don't intend to allow that to happen."[156]

The BPRC developed three initiatives to ensure the group's ability to care for and to take control of the park. The first was to enter a management agreement with the city.[157] The second was to develop a "first class" restaurant to attract more desirable middle-class and affluent users throughout the day and evening.[158] With 1,000 seats, the restaurant would become the biggest in the city, and it would pay its rent directly to the BPRC.

The third component was to make the blocks immediately bordering the park into a Business Improvement District (BID), which allowed property owners within a designated district to enact a mandatory tax or special assessment on all owners. Most commonly, BIDs used such funds to support maintenance, marketing, and even security and capital improvements within the district. Nationally, BIDs were new—in New York they had only been allowed by the state legislature since 1980—but in the years ahead they would begin to spread rapidly to supplement government services.[159] The BPRC aimed to create a BID for the four frontage borders of the park and to use the resulting assessments for their improvement efforts. "The prime advantage of a business improvement district is that money can be collected for street and park improvements using the coercive mechanism of the City's real estate tax collection," Biederman wrote to Heiskell and Marshall Rose. "In other words, we would no longer have to go door to door soliciting funds for our park maintenance programs. Those funds would instead be collected quarterly by the City" and then transferred to the BID.[160]

The management agreement, restaurant, and BID, the BPRC stated, would secure the "long-term operation of Bryant Park that will make the park accessible and safe around the clock and in all seasons, and will link the Library and the park for the first time."[161] It would also establish ongoing funding streams for the BPRC's work. The organization estimated the BID, restaurant, and city funding would generate upward of $1.5 million each year, more than five times what the city alone provided in the early 1980s.

Municipal officials enthusiastically supported the plan. In early 1983 Mayor Koch and Gordon Davis signed an unprecedented management agreement with the BPRC, a stunning indication of just how willing Koch administration officials were to increase the private sector's role in parks. The City agreed to lease the park to the BPRC for thirty-five years, with renewal options at BPRC's discretion for up to an additional twenty years. The agreement also allowed the BPRC to sublease the terrace area of the park to the proposed restaurant operator. The city committed a million dollars toward Bryant Park's renovation and agreed to pay the Restoration Corporation what it would have designated for yearly upkeep. BPRC would assume responsibility for repairs, cleaning, landscaping, and graffiti removal, as well as "supplemental services" such as security. While the Parks Commissioner retained veto power over such matters as capital improvements, budgeting, and changes in hours, the BPRC was given limited authority to create and alter park rules and regulations and to host and permit others to put on special events. The agreement, Gregorian noted, had come together with the endorsements of "the City of New York, the New York Department of Parks and Recreation, the New York Public Library, the New York Botanical Garden, private foundations, and the neighboring business community. In short, it is a creative public/private partnership."[162] It was, Biederman rightly exclaimed to bankers, "a grand experiment in urban governance."[163]

Some New Yorkers who took a keen interest in parks, however, were troubled, above all the Parks Council, whose involvement in the BPRC had wound down the prior year. The transfer of responsibility from the city to a private entity over the management, rules, alterations, and events was undesirable and unnecessary, the group believed.[164] "Handing over to private entities city property and city responsibility for services," the group wrote, "is a stopgap expedient, the relic of the city's fiscal crisis, not a long-term solution for problems facing the Parks Department. It threatens to create a two-tier parks system, in which parks in prime neighborhoods are embellished by affluent private organizations, while those elsewhere are maintained at a far lower level and permitted to deteriorate."[165] What's more, "if you have a private entity running a public park," the Parks Council president asked, "who is to say that you and I may not be the undesirables next year?"[166] The Commissioner's veto power over was insufficient. Public officials "need to participate in the decision making, not to be just in the position of vetoing things," believed Jeanette Bamford, the group's director.[167]

Such criticisms simultaneously spoke to how significantly the thinking about park governance had changed over the previous decade. They did not question whether there was a need for greater private sector involvement; there was widespread acceptance of this in the case of Bryant Park. Indeed, the Parks Council had itself for years encouraged greater involvement from those outside government, not just by increasing volunteer efforts, but also private sector donations. The only substantive questioning about the agreement concerned the extent of private involvement and whether it should extend to the control over public parkland. "It's a very knotty problem," Bamford remarked. "We're trying to resolve how to bring private resources into a public facility" and maintain "the public nature of that facility. . . . It's important to bring private resources into the parks, but it is also important to safeguard our public parks."[168] The Council advocated for terms similar to the Central Park Conservancy, which allowed the Parks Department to retain greater authority. "We admire the aims of the Restoration Corporation," one Council board member noted, "We're saying 'how can you achieve those ends without removing the park from the public domain?'"[169]

But even this moderate criticism struggled to gain widespread traction. Indeed, early press coverage of the agreement voiced little concern about turning Bryant Park over to private operators. It was a stunning change from the reaction Gilder and Soros had received from the press to their proposal simply to raise funds for Central Park less than ten years earlier. No doubt the experience of the fiscal crisis convinced many of the fruitfulness of turning to the private sector. The amount of capital the Central Park Conservancy had successfully raised likely engendered confidence. Additionally, media commentators pointed to the small but significant improvements in appearance and safety and greater public use as evidence that the Restoration Corporation would be a better operator than the city. While acknowledging that many park advocates found the idea of private management "repugnant," one *Times* article wrote that Bryant Park should be viewed as "an exception because the park has stubbornly defied all attempts to make it a place where the public can feel safe."[170] "There will be naysayers who object to the idea of permitting a city park to be managed by a private group," *The Daily News* wrote in an editorial. "They're wrong. It will remain a *public* park, but for the first time in recent history it has a fighting chance to become a glorious place for New Yorkers to relax—instead of a happy hunting ground for drug users, pushers, and drunks."[171]

Most articles also commented approvingly that the city would contribute only a portion of funding for the $18 million project. With the city still grappling with a struggling economy alongside diminishing federal support, some wondered how it could turn down a private sector willing to impose a voluntary tax upon itself to support a long-tarnished public park—even if they wanted to control the park in return. Supporters from the business sector reinforced this sentiment. Criticism of private management "might be understandable in a world where there are unlimited public funds for park maintenance and improvement, but there is no such world, and I doubt that New York will ever again enjoy that world," Mobil Oil's Herbert Schmertz remarked in a televised editorial.[172]

The controversies over the plan delayed its implementation for two years and altered many of the details, though not the spirit, of the agreement. Most substantively, due in large part to the Council's objections, the BPRC received a permit to run the park instead of a lease. But the agreement paved the way for the privately run group to take authority over matters such as maintenance, repairs, events, concessions, security, and overall operations and management. "They're acting as our agents to manage the park," praised Henry Stern, who became Parks Commissioner in 1983, "and we think it's important because we want this to be a model for others, if it works."[173]

THE 1970S PROVED a transformative decade for New York's parks. Beginning in the 1980s, the number of organizations that formed to take a role in the care of parks grew exponentially. These included groups of community members that conducted clean-ups, horticultural care, painting, and small-scale fundraising, such as the Friends of Tompkins Square Park and the Friends of Fort Tryon Park, both founded in the early 1980s.[174] Such efforts helped supplement municipal support through volunteerism and small-scale fundraising in order to provide the desired level of upkeep of neighborhood parks.

For the first time, a significant number of professional organizations also emerged to raise large sums and exert greater control over the management of parks. These groups followed the examples of the BPRC and, especially, the Central Park Conservancy, which the Parks Department described as the "model for other public-private partnerships in the city's parks."[175] They were typically formed for larger parks by residents in middle-class and affluent neighborhoods, often ones that were experiencing a boon in cooperative conversions and condominium development.[176] Recently marketized homes encouraged owners to see new fiscal benefits of improving nearby public spaces, especially the effects on home values. The Riverside Park Fund, for example, formed when residents of the Upper West Side "spent the summer of 1986 going up and down Riverside Drive, the wealthy part," soliciting co-op board presidents for park funds by asking them: "If you don't fix up your front yard, who will?" Such donations and a major grant from the J. M. Kaplan fund raised $400,000.[177] By and large the groups proved to be remarkably successful at raising funds and in forging private management agreements with the city. In 1989 alone these types of groups helped to raise an astonishing $53 million in private funds for public parks.[178] The Conservancy especially was soon heralded as the model for the proliferation of private park conservancies across the country.[179] "There was a time when urban parks were firmly considered the pride, joy and responsibility of taxpayers . . . to be carried on the shoulders of city government. No longer," one report on this national transformation recently summarized.[180]

The Conservancy, BPRC, and similar organizations were championed by officials, the media, and the business sphere for "saving" parks, increasing tourism, attracting moneyed residents, raising property taxes, and reducing so-called undesirables. Their efforts were widely regarded as critical to the gains in the city's economy during the 1980s. This was particularly notable in enhancing real estate values. By the early 1980s, major real estate firms pointed to the efforts of the Central Park Conservancy and BPRC in their newsletters and in advertisements for their holdings in these areas.[181] "Property values south and west of the park are exploding in anticipation of the . . . Bryant Park plans" and redevelopment efforts in nearby Times Square, one Restoration Corporation board member remarked in 1985.[182]

City officials continued to encourage the growth of these resident and private sector–led efforts, which ranged from small-scale groups devoted to improving local parks to major private nonprofit organizations modeled on the Conservancy. These groups not only alleviated fiscal and fiduciary burdens on city government but also furthered the business, affluent, and tourist friendly climate that officials desired to create.

As these groups multiplied in subsequent decades, particularly in wealthier areas and business districts of Manhattan, city leaders chipped away at the Parks Department budget. During the early and mid-1980s, Parks finally began to make gains in hiring employees and increasing budgets, but these declined—and never recovered—when the city suffered another economic downturn at the end of the decade.[183] This downturn continued, in part, as a result of the major reconceptualization by municipal officials of public parks, which went from being understood a common property of the public to property that could instead be safeguarded by well-resourced populations outside of government. Indeed, with the enthusiastic support of officials, conservancy-type organizations often formed in capital rich areas to insulate particular parks against cuts in public funding.[184] But the many parks in parts of the city that were unable to garner significant amounts of private sector support suffered.

The experience of the two largest parks in the Bronx is instructive. After several years of declining Parks budgets, two groups formed at the end of the 1980s: the Friends of Van Cortland Park, located near the largely white and affluent neighborhood of Riverdale, and the Friends of Pelham Bay Park, located in a much more racially and economically diverse area in the northeastern part of the borough. The Van Cortland group raised $100,000 in its first three years, enough to hire eighteen full time employees for the summer. The Pelham Bay Park group, in contrast, struggled to raise significant sums and relied mostly on volunteer cleanups.[185] The latter group soon disbanded, leaving the 2,700 acre park cared for by a staff of only thirteen city employees. In contrast, Central Park, less than a third of its size but the beneficiary of the Central Park Conservancy, at the same time had over 350 workers.[186]

These kinds of disparities across the park system worsened in the years ahead. As one report on city parks from the 2000s found, the result of declining municipal funding has been that "it's the parks that need to rely solely on public funding and not private funding that lack general maintenance," resulting in a system with "vastly different levels of park services."[187] "Although this is a citywide problem," one park advocate stated, "it is no secret that a disproportionate amount of the most severe issues exist in poor neighborhoods, in areas populated by people of color."[188] The inequity between "pristine" parks supported by private organizations in affluent areas and "poorly maintained" parks in low-income neighborhoods of color became so vast that it was "tantamount to a civil rights issue," one advocacy group declared.[189]

The park system changed in ways even the most adamant early supporters of greater private involvement likely never envisioned. Advocates for greater private involvement sometimes expressed the hope that turning toward greater outside support for individual parks would alleviate pressure on city resources so that it could provide better care for parks throughout the system.[190] But as the park system increasingly moved away from relying principally on government resources and toward casting parks into a market-oriented system in which the private sector chose which parks to support, park disparities in neighborhoods across race and class grew. This was not the desired outcome the affluent and business sectors initially sought, nor was it imposed by municipal leaders who hunted for a solution to declining budgets.[191]

The widespread formation of grassroots park revitalization groups beginning in the late 1960s was the first critical step toward the eventual development of these large-scale park organizations a decade later. Both the community groups that focused on volunteerism and small fundraising and the major, nonprofit initiatives that formed to facilitate major fundraising for and management of parks that followed years later accepted and promoted the idea that the city was no longer capable of caring adequately for its parks. As more and more residents took to community parks, their efforts brought greater attention to the widespread dissatisfaction with city care. As their numbers grew, they received greater support—positive press, encouragement from officials, promotion by groups like the Parks Council and Citizens Committee—all of which reinforced the idea that government support was inadequate but also that there was little those concerned with parks could successfully demand from government. These community initiatives laid critical groundwork for the subsequent large-scale and elite-supported efforts that similarly proposed to use nonstate resources to improve parks.

The fiscal crisis was no doubt central to these grander initiatives gaining ideological and political ground. The extensive across-the-board cuts to public services reinforced the fledgling sentiment that the city was incapable of caring for its public spaces. Even the advocates who came to the aid of parks adopted similar logics about the failures of municipal government and the nonviability of fighting for greater government resources as those promoted by the powerful figures who imposed austerity. The fiscal crisis helped advance proposals to reorient parks toward the private sector that emerged in the early 1970s toward becoming a hallmark of the Koch administration.

Significantly, both before and immediately after the fiscal crisis, the call for greater private involvement did not come primarily from the corporate or business sphere. Instead, the range of advocates included Lindsay's Park Commissioner Richard Clurman, ex-Parks official Donald Simon, long-time park advocates and park scholars as Barlow, major educational and nonprofit institutions like the New York Public Library, and a handful of philanthropists and foundations, without whom initial efforts to foster private support would have faltered. These actors promoted the notion that a much more extensive opening of New York's parks to those outside of government was needed.

Parks required not just volunteers and private donations, but new forms of governance for their survival.

To be sure, the campaigns around Central, Madison Square, and Bryant Parks all encountered significant hurdles. It took years of legwork and many failures before substantive numbers of city elites behind powerful businesses and institutions became convinced to support public parks. The momentum these campaigns built toward a park system less dependent on government eventually quickened not only because of diminished faith in government but also as elites saw an opportunity to exert greater control over a matter that directly affected their economic viability. As these campaigns around individual parks gained widespread support of city officials like Mayor Ed Koch alongside prominent businesses and corporations, major foundations, and cultural institutions, the wellbeing of New York's parks transformed to become contingent on the market and affluent.

4

Patrolling City Streets

IN JANUARY 1971, hundreds of Brooklyn Heights residents braved the cold to attend a community meeting at the St. George Hotel. Attendees crowded into a second-floor salon, but as the room swelled to capacity, the hotel had to shift the group to the grand ballroom. There, for more than two hours, over five hundred residents discussed the neighborhood's rising crime.[1]

"Crime, crime, crime is the greatest problem today in the streets. . . . [and] in your homes," proclaimed Benjamin Rosenberg, vice chairman of the Better Brooklyn Committee, an umbrella group of civic associations. Everyone in the crowd seemed to agree. Indeed, robberies and muggings in the area had increased 73 percent between 1969 and 1970 and then another 79 percent the following year.[2] Neighbor after neighbor declared that "no one was safe" in Brooklyn Heights. Merchants spoke of increased holdups. Residents described women who were "pushed to the ground" and had their purses stolen. "We never had anything like that before," stated a man who lived at 75 Henry Street. Another resident told of a local pharmacist in business for thirty-five years who just a few days earlier had closed his shop after a series of holdups. "He turned the key and locked the door and said he was never coming back."[3]

Heights residents no doubt hoped that representatives from the local precinct would offer solutions. What they heard, however, sounded more like resignation. The police "do not have the cure" for rising crime, Captain Robert Geary of the 84th Precinct told the crowd. Crime was climbing too quickly. Geary likened the police's role to that of a physician treating a terminal illness: "He recognizes the symptoms and he can write a prescription that will help ease the pain, but a complete cure does not seem possible."[4]

With the police overwhelmed, Heights residents increasingly considered what they themselves could do to reduce crime in their neighborhood. "You can't fight a problem by running away from it," Rosenberg told the crowd. "You have to face up to it."[5] Some of those at the St. George that night were likely already involved in efforts to do so. Indeed, the Brooklyn Heights Association—the city's oldest ongoing neighborhood association—had recently launched a series of initiatives to involve residents in reducing crime. The group had organized an "Eyes on the Street" program, which encouraged residents "to be intelligently suspicious about what is going on around them," and distributed "incident-report forms" so residents knew how to accurately record suspicious activities.[6] "Police effort alone is not sufficient to check crime in our community," the Association's Crime Committee proclaimed.[7] By the time of the January meeting, the Association was considering even bolder steps: organizing citizen patrols and hiring private guards to augment the seemingly overwhelmed local police.[8]

Brooklyn Heights was just one of many New York communities whose residents were increasingly concerned about crime in the late 1960s and 1970s. Though official crime statistics from this period vary in their reliability, overwhelming evidence points to significant increases in crime.[9] Nationally, violent crime increased on average by 50 percent during this period; in New York, it rose over 450 percent.[10] Reported robberies jumped from 6,579 in 1960 to 74,102 in 1970, while burglaries leaped from 36,049 to 181,694.[11] While this increase was due in part to Mayor John Lindsay instituting more meticulous crime reporting, homicides—the most reliable crime measurement—nearly tripled to 1,117 from 390 between 1970 and 1960.[12] New York's "crime wave of the 1960s," as historian Eric Schneider wrote, "was neither a reporting artifact nor the result of a media-driven moral panic."[13]

That is not to say that the media did not amplify residents' fears. The city's papers filled with anecdotes about how crime was fundamentally altering urban life. Gothamites, the *New York Times* reported in the late 1960s, were living "ever-larger portions of their lives behind locked doors. Feeling themselves besieged by an army of muggers and thieves, they are changing their habits and styles of life, refusing to go out after dark, peering anxiously through peepholes before opening their doors, sidestepping strangers on the streets. . . . and spending large sums to secure their homes with locks, bolts, alarms, and gates."[14] "Everywhere a person turns," the *New York Post* reported in 1971, "he runs into someone who has been mugged or knows someone who has been. One male victim now carries a bat to and from work. . . . Women are coming to look upon scissors, nail files and hair sprays more as weapons than beauty aids."[15]

Unlike other major problems city officials faced at this time—such as dilapidating parks and decaying housing—Mayor Lindsay initially devoted substantial municipal resources to the problem of crime. Lindsay's pledge to fight rising crime had been central to his 1965 mayoral campaign victory. During his first term his administration declared a "war on crime," deeming law-breaking "the number one issue in New York."[16] It oversaw the addition of more than 5,500 policemen, the expansion of walkie-talkies, and the implementation of the 911 emergency telephone system. Nonetheless, crime continued to spiral, exasperating New Yorkers.[17]

It is difficult to discern the causes of such a complex social phenomenon as crime, but historians typically identify two major factors behind its rise. Heroin usage—which reportedly increased tenfold over the 1960s—was one major cause, especially for street crimes.[18] Another was that the city's industrial economy, which had brought decades of expanding access to jobs and wages and helped crime to decline, was retracting by the 1960s. Coupled with the ongoing exodus of various industries to the suburbs and sunbelt, economic opportunities for residents were contracting significantly, creating conditions for crime to fester.[19]

As in Brooklyn Heights, residents throughout the city typically first turned to the police, but officers were often blunt about the protection they could offer, given how rapidly crime was rising. In the late 1960s, for instance, Captain Richard Di Roma of the "crime-ridden" 24th precinct on the Upper West Side, told angry community members that even though he had been able to increase patrolmen by 12 percent over the past year, he was only able to "play checkers" with muggers. "We increase the patrols on one street and they move to the next."[20]

As New Yorkers grew progressively frustrated by ineffective municipal efforts to combat crime, many began to join Brooklyn Heights residents in considering what they themselves could do. From Harlem to the Far Rockaways, from Midwood to the Bronx, neighborhood groups banded together to patrol their own streets on foot and in cars. Beginning in the late 1960s, these citizen patrols not only grew in number but also began to gain approval from government officials and private organizations whose support helped them to proliferate.

For some communities, however, volunteering to patrol streets was not feasible or was simply unappealing. Nonetheless anxious to increase the surveillance of their neighborhoods, these New Yorkers turned to another innovative solution: hiring a private guard to patrol their block. While private security working a public street was rare in the late 1960s, guards slowly spread throughout residential blocks.

Just as residents started to band together to supplement what they saw as a beleaguered police force, businesses and institutions began to do so as well. Many agreed that there was no substitute for more eyes and ears on the street. Rather than legions of pinstriped businessmen patrolling streets themselves, they turned to private guards. Just like the forces hired by residents, these guards increasingly moved outside their long-established domain—private property and the interiors of buildings—to patrol public streets. Over time, groups of real estate owners, businesses, and institutions worked to expand guards' role from simply deterring crime by their presence to actively policing crime.[21]

While scholars of policing, incarceration, and the carceral state have richly documented how in the latter twentieth century government mechanisms to police and incarcerate expanded at the local, state, and federal level, they have overlooked a profound transformation of this period: the vastly expanding role of private actors in surveilling and policing public streets.[22] Citizen patrols and private security guards shattered what had in the postwar decades been in essence a state monopoly on the official surveillance of public spaces. Both grew out of the shared belief that public streets were under siege, local government was unable to adequately respond, and municipal services needed to be supplemented. These initiatives expanded alongside one another and reinforced a similar logic about the need for private action against crime. Neither initially was intended to replace the police; proponents stressed that they aimed to augment a besieged police department. But both pushed to expand the role of surveilling public space beyond the municipal force.

At first, neither effort was widely accepted. Citizen patrols often started and stopped. Private businesses questioned why they should step in when municipal resources fell short. While both efforts struggled, in the 1970s, citizen patrols had far greater success in gaining public attention and support from government officials and the media. In contrast, private guards were lambasted as unprofessional and as likely be to participants in crime as deterrents to it.

In the 1980s, however, the fortunes of each of these initiatives shifted. Support for citizen patrols peaked early in the decade; however, the number of residents involved in anti-crime initiatives thereafter stagnated. In contrast, private security guards took on a more active role in combatting crime, spread to more and more streets, gained greater support from officials, and established a more formal relationship with the police. In New York, as across the country over the 1970s and 1980s, private guards spread as crime grew and as many cities were constrained by economic decline and reductions in federal support (the cost of a security guard was typically a third of a police officer). But in New York this growth was underpinned by the belief that government was inadequately responding to a major crisis, a sentiment shared by both private sector elites and residents from a variety of socioeconomic and racial backgrounds. Across the city, New Yorkers increasingly took action to broaden the surveillance of public spaces through private security and citizen patrols. These initiatives collectively helped to perpetuate and ultimately normalize the place of private actors patrolling city streets.

"Crime-Fighting . . . is Approaching a Complete Breakdown"

When neighborhoods came together in the late 1960s to form patrols they did so principally out of concerns about crime and the city's inability to curtail it, but several other factors motivated residents. One was anxieties that residents had become apathetic, as was underscored by the 1964 murder of Kitty Genovese. The *Times* reported that the murder had been witnessed or heard by thirty-eight Kew Gardens residents, none of whom contacted the police. The claim led journalists and commentators to condemn New Yorkers' supposed callousness as well as soul searching among residents about the importance of overcoming urban indifference.[23]

The widespread belief that the police were inefficient and corrupt was another. Frustration was strongest among African Americans, who had long been long subject to unwarranted criminalization, police violence, and unresponsive policing in their neighborhoods.[24] While there is no question that whiter and monied areas encountered policing that was far more responsive and respectful, what is also striking is how by the mid-1960s concerns about policing were apparent throughout New York. Mayor Lindsay's Law Enforcement Task Force, for example, in 1966 found a "lack of strong public support for the police in the performance of their duties."[25] The *Times* similarly noted that year how "the belief in police corruption is pervasive, shared alike by the citizen in the ghetto and the citizen in a luxury apartment on the East Side."[26] Several investigations in the early 1970s confirmed what many residents already knew: much of the police department was crooked. Among other infractions, police officers routinely accepted payoffs from narcotics dealers to prevent arrests, destroy evidence, or provide false testimony. It was also "commonplace" for police to sell confiscated narcotics or exchange them for stolen goods.[27] Residents also regularly complained that the police were slow, if not unresponsive. One-third of New Yorkers in late 1973 reported having "no confidence" that they could get hold of a police officer quickly if needed.[28] Corruption and unresponsiveness did not change the fact that residents overwhelmingly believed more—and better—policing was the principal solution to crime, but did contribute to their growing confidence that the police needed additional resources to fight crime.

In many white communities, fears of growing populations of color also heightened the sense that new initiatives against crime were needed. Across the nation, sensationalized media accounts and political campaigns commonly fanned racist beliefs about urban crime and unrest.[29] In New York, as the black population more than doubled to 19 percent and the population of Latinx and Puerto Ricans rose from 3 to 16 percent between 1950 and 1970, whites oftentimes blamed growing populations of color for rising crime.[30] This was the case for some white residents of Crown Heights, where the first citizen patrol of this time, the Maccabees, formed in 1964. The Maccabees launched to serve as escorts for residents and as "crime spotters" for the police. Hundreds of volunteers helped patrol Crown Heights each night in cars equipped with a new technology: civilian two-way radios.[31] "We are trying to protect ourselves because there is not adequate police protection," founder and rabbi Samuel Schrage explained.[32]

While the precipitating acts leading to the formation of the Maccabees were the attempted rape of a rabbi's wife and the robbery of a blind newspaper salesman, the growing population of African American residents alarmed many white residents. "I've lived here for nearly 40 years," one white resident stated, "and now I'm afraid to go out at night. It's the schwarzes. They're not all bad, but there are so many of them here now."[33] As African American Crown Heights residents were quick to point out, the Maccabees started their patrol shortly after the number of black residents in the neighborhood began to increase. The largely African American Business and Professional Men's Club of nearby Bedford-Stuyvesant condemned the patrols, expressing fear that its untrained members were more likely to inflict violence on innocent African Americans than to combat actual crime. Rabbi Schrage's assurance that the group was "fighting crime and criminals, without distinction as to color or creed" brought little comfort, particularly after he "gave the impression he was General Custer surrounded by hostile Indians" in a meeting with black leaders.[34]

Ultimately, the Maccabees' initiative against crime won over portions of the African American community during its first few months; black residents even began to work with the patrol.[35] But in other neighborhoods, white community patrols functioned as little more than terroristic mobs. In the early 1970s, a research team from the Center for Policy Research studying community crime groups identified the Beachview Civilian Radio Motor Patrol operating in an anonymized "largely white, largely working and lower-middle class community."[36] Most of the members articulated explicitly "racist attitudes" and blamed the increase in crime on African Americans and Puerto Ricans who were moving closer to the area.[37] Members often surveyed the neighborhood while armed, illegally detained and even attacked innocent persons of color, impersonated police officers, and committed "countless traffic-law violations."[38] Despite the fact that the patrol was itself engaging in numerous criminal acts, the local police supported the group, exercising "considerable control over" its activities.[39]

While it is likely that many white patrols were motivated at least in part by concerns about the city's shifting racial composition, the explicit racism and vigilantism of the Beachview patrol seems to have been exceptional. Most patrols acted within the law and seemingly without ardent racial animus as they organized to deter crime.

Residents of Manhattan Beach in Brooklyn, for example, a largely white and middle-class area, decided to form a car patrol "to combat [the] growing menace of burglaries and armed robberies" after failing "to get these conditions corrected by the authorities," as resident Bruce Elliott put it.[40] Each night, three teams of two volunteers—whose occupations ranged from doctors to musicians to retirees—took to the streets in improvised patrol cars in shifts between midnight to 5 a.m.[41] Most nights their activities hardly resembled the plots of *The Mod Squad* or *Dragnet*, popular television procedurals of the time. An especially eventful night was one that involved chasing away men who had exited a Volkswagen bus and seemed to be scoping out a home. Another involved the community's cantor, Arnold Schraeter, witnessing a burglar leaving a home and giving chase. Although the intruder got away, he dropped the stolen goods he was carrying in the pursuit.[42] Though stopping a crime in progress was rare, volunteers believed the patrol's presence deterred would-be criminals. Indeed, after four months of patrolling, the group "proudly" stated that there was "not one successfully completed burglary during patrol hours."[43]

Concerns about unbridled crime and an unresponsive police force were especially prominent in African American neighborhoods.[44] In one high-crime

FIGURE 4.1 Shortly after this April 1969 meeting, Manhattan Beach neighbors joined a growing number of communities in forming a resident patrol due to concerns with crime and frustration with the police's inability to contain it.

Manhattan Beach Community Group Papers. Courtesy of Brooklyn College Archives and Special Collections.

African American area, for example, researchers from the Center for Policy Research found that because of rising crime, residents "reported dropping evening church activities, cutting out after-dark shopping, refraining from visiting friends, and quitting late-night jobs."[45] Despite this, residents were often unwilling to report crimes because, as one woman put it, "the police will do nothing."[46] "I tried to stop the drug traffic," another resident added.

"I contacted the precinct captain, gave names, dates, and incidents. *Nothing* happened."

This mounting frustration led to the formation of citizen patrols throughout African Americans neighborhoods. In Harlem, Reverend Oberia Depsey of the Upper Park Avenue Baptist Church led two hundred armed volunteers in escorting women to church and locating and reporting drug dealers.[47] The Black Citizens Patrol also traversed Harlem streets with machetes and made citizen arrests.[48] In Bedford-Stuyvesant, seventy-three community groups came together to form the Community Protection Organization that organized three-man patrols, while black shopkeepers concerned with holdups formed their own patrol.[49] With complaints about police brutality widespread in these communities, residents also demanded better policing—"the failure of the cop to wear the uniform in a manner to build respect," as the cochairman of the United Council of Harlem Organizations put it—as well as for greater educational and job opportunities that would address crime at its roots.[50]

Patrols also spread throughout New York's 161 public housing projects, in which about 72 percent of residents were black or Puerto Rican by the late 1960s.[51] While at the time crime rates were actually lower in public housing than the rest of the city, "major crimes like murder robbery, rape, burglaries, muggings and theft of autos and pocketbooks" were all on the rise.[52] Many of the 150,000 residents believed that the 1,100 patrolmen spread out over 1738 buildings and surrounding properties of the New York City Housing Authority (NYCHA) were simply overwhelmed.[53] Dozens of tenants of St. Nicholas Houses in Harlem started the first tenant patrol in 1966 across seven of the development's buildings.[54] By early 1968, tenant patrols had spread to several other major public housing developments in Queens and Brooklyn.[55]

NYCHA officials quickly saw the value of residents patrolling buildings and grounds. They not only "have provided a significant deterrent to crime and vandalism," but also cost the Authority very little, officials reported.[56] Tenants had long demanded 24-hour guards in lobbies, but the estimated yearly expense—$119 million—was considered prohibitive by the Authority.[57] Instead, NYCHA officials looked to capitalize on residents' growing enthusiasm for patrols as a much cheaper alternative. In 1968, NYCHA authorized the management of each development to spend up to $4,000 each year for training and equipment for patrols and also hired William Byrd, the founder of the St. Nicholas Tenant Patrol, to assist tenants in forming patrols.[58] Tenant patrols spread rapidly, from about twenty-five at the end of 1968 to ninety-three patrols covering 495 buildings and involving an astonishing

8,650 volunteers by the spring of 1970.[59] At Betances Houses in the Bronx, for example, about 150 volunteers screened visitors, patrolled ten buildings during the evenings, and assisted students in getting home safely after school each afternoon.[60]

Mayor Lindsay, in contrast, was slow to support resident-led anti-crime initiatives.[61] Although Lindsay acknowledged that "our police cannot fight the war on crime alone," his response to resident patrols was likely colored by the reservations expressed by the police. "There is no redress for errors that untrained volunteers make," police captain Edward Jinkins proclaimed in response to the Maccabees. He continued: "The Police Department trains a recruit for nine months, in techniques and in the rights of civilians—and even we make mistakes sometimes."[62] Police and officials also worried that patrols would encourage vigilantism. Instead, the Lindsay administration favored public education programs, such as distributing over 10 million leaflets in 1967 on "how to your protect the home."[63] The administration also launched a Community Radio Watch in 1967, which simply asked residents with vehicles equipped with two-way radios to report "any street disturbances or accidents they see or anything that strikes them as unusual or suspicious."[64]

Operating largely without outside support or coordination between groups, citizen patrols often struggled to sustain their efforts. It was not uncommon for a group to exist only for a few months or a year before folding due to a lack of volunteers.[65] The initial zeal for protecting one's neighborhood

FIGURE 4.2 The St. Nicholas Youth Patrol was part of the St. Nicholas Tenant Patrol, which surveilled the St. Nicholas Houses public housing project in Harlem.

New York City Housing Authority Papers. Courtesy of the New York City Housing Authority and the La Guardia and Wagner Archives, La Guardia Community College / The City University of New York.

turned into the uncomfortable reality of volunteering for multihour shifts, often at night and potentially in inclement weather. In some neighborhoods, conditions proved dangerous, in others too boring. "I expected it to be more exciting," said one volunteer for a Brooklyn patrol that was considering ending.[66]

Overwhelmingly, however, citizen patrols spread at a much greater pace than they folded, especially with a new phenomenon that began sweeping the city around the turn of the decade: block associations. Block associations grew both out of frustration with "the tide of deterioration that has blighted so many sections of New York" and with a growing emphasis on local action.[67] Historian Suleiman Osman has categorized the 1970s as "The Decade of the Neighborhood" in which "the spirit of localism" infused urban America, leading to an explosion in groups that formed to improve local conditions and residents' voice in governance.[68] This was most evident in the eruption of block associations.[69]

In the 1970s, block associations—which during the decade reportedly formed on upward of 10,000 blocks, around 30 percent of the city's total— became the principal site through which neighbors came together to address a local concern.[70] This sometimes meant pressuring a local politician or agency, but as municipal resources declined early in the decade, this increasingly meant neighbors coming together to address a problem themselves. As the Federation of Laurelton Block Associations in Queens put it: "Name the problem and we can do more to solve it as part of a group. Concerned with schools? Crime?. . . . This is the way to protect your neighborhood and your home. Together. Block by block."[71] By end of 1970, block associations multiplied to over 3,000, spreading from low-income neighborhoods of color to wealthy white areas of Manhattan.[72]

Crime, of course, was just one among many issues these groups tackled, but as neighbors gathered in living rooms to discuss their block's most pressing issues, it was frequently at or near the top, and they addressed it in various ways. The Laurelton association, for example, focused on demanding "improved police protections" and installing "brighter street lighting."[73] Many groups, however, took the more ambitious step of forming patrols. By the end of 1972, the police estimated that there were 15,000 volunteers in tenant and neighborhood patrols and at least seventy-five car patrols.[74]

With the popularity of patrols growing among residents, the Lindsay administration and the police both warmed to these initiatives. The fact that mayoral and law enforcement officials continued to face criticism for being unable to contain crime likely encouraged them to be receptive to new ideas—especially given the fiscal constraints during Lindsay's second term. In 1971, for example, a Lindsay-appointed committee concluded that "crime-fighting and criminal justice in the city is approaching a complete break-down."[75] Officials were also gradually swayed by the idea that an activate citizenry was effective in combatting crime. "Though dubious at first," the *Sunday News* reported in 1972, "police now concede that the . . . city's tenant and neighborhood patrols have cut street crime significantly in high-crime areas."[76] "In buildings where the tenants have organized," one Upper West Side patrolman stated, "we've found the crime rate down one hundred per cent."[77] Officials also worried about alternative actions an increasingly frustrated populace might take. "Our city leaders . . . should send representatives to every area of the city to help us organize ourselves, neighborhood by neighborhood, block by block into civilian patrols," Claire Howard of Whitestone warned in a letter to the *New York Times*. Otherwise, "we will find citizens taking the law into their own hands—either by carrying guns themselves or organizing vigilante groups."[78]

Grassroots anti-crime initiatives, therefore, increasingly seemed to officials to be worth supporting. In 1973, Lindsay's final year in office, he announced a $5 million Block Security Program, a powerful endorsement of residents' mounting initiatives against crime. Recognizing that "more and more local groups are sponsoring self-help security programs," the administration awarded up to $10,000 in matching funds for block associations to purchase equipment like walkie-talkies, uniforms, radios, and lighting.[79] "Many groups have already joined together in self-help, anti-crime programs for their blocks, forming citizen and tenant patrols, serving as trained block-watchers, buying high-intensity lighting, and hiring private guards," Lindsay explained. "We hope to greatly expand such self-help efforts."[80] "If we can get eyes and ears all over the city," he proclaimed, "we can control crime."[81] Like residents, officials never saw these initiatives as a replacement for more police, but their support lent additional weight to the idea that city government could no longer tackle crime on its own.

Hardly all residents were convinced that the growing problem required *them* to be the ones to patrol their neighborhoods, however. Instead, some neighbors pursued a strategy that was costlier but put themselves at less risk: hiring a private guard. Similarly, associations of businesses and institutions also looked to guards. In both residential and commercial areas, however, the use of private guards to patrol public streets encountered hurdles, from a dubious police department to skepticism from the security industry itself about the very idea of using private guards in public spaces. In the late 1960s and early 1970s, both resident-hired guards and private security forces launched by consortiums of businesses and institutions sought to overcome these obstacles and carve out a place for private guards in public space.

"This Street Patrolled by Uniformed Guard"

Security guards began to spread on residential streets in the late 1960s, especially in areas with large populations of white residents who had the economic means to pay for one. Guards were initially most common on blocks of the affluent Upper East Side and gentrifying Upper West Side, the latter was an area beset by crime but a growing number of residents who could contribute toward the costly $10,000 salary for a nightly guard.[82] After the 90th Street West Park Block Association hired a nightly guard in 1969, President Edward Schwarzer reported that crime fell as "muggers are afraid to come to our street now that it's protected."[83] Over the next three years at least seven more Manhattan blocks hired guards.

Block associations stressed that the point of a guard was less to pursue criminals than to deter crime from happening at all. A guard and an accompanying sign reading "this street patrolled by uniformed guard" were thought to have deterrence value. "Our guard isn't Attila the Hun, but he doesn't have to be," John Applegate of the 102–103 Streets Block Association explained. "Most people are still not brazen enough to commit a crime in full view of anyone who bears any resemblance to a law-enforcement officer."[84] A guard was "not there to search suspicious persons, make arrests or fight off interlopers," the *Times* reported of the growing phenomenon. "Instead, they are supposed to telephone the police."[85]

By the early 1970s, private guards spread to middle-income, typically white areas of the outer boroughs. In 1971, for instance, the Manhattan Beach Community Group (MBCG) had to end its citizen patrols due to lack of volunteers, even though "the entire community has been under severe tension and fear," the MBCG wrote to Police Commissioner Patrick Murphy.[86] Most recently, a physician's wife had been murdered. Despite reaching out to the police department, the MBCG believed that the neighborhood was unlikely to be allocated additional police: "All over the city people are clamoring for more police protection, but there is none to be had for lack of money."[87] After several months of fundraising, four hundred families agreed to commit $100 a month for the MBCG to contract with the Mercury Intelligence Service, a twelve-year-old firm, to provide year-round private patrols. "The security guards have a list of paid-up members," the MBCG told residents, "and only those homes will receive their protection and attention."[88] The policy was designed to encourage residents to contribute to the costly patrols, but the warning highlighted the nature of private security: its goal was to protect those who paid for it, not the general public.

Private guards grew in number not just in New York but across America. Businesses, corporations, and institutions like universities and hospitals increasingly hired guards to patrol their grounds out of concern about crime and civil unrest, including urban uprisings and political violence.[89] There was, as historians have documented, a substantial growth in law enforcement personnel (42 percent) and expenditures (90 percent) during the 1960s, but far less recognized is the equivalent rise in private security personnel (42 percent) and even greater increase in expenditures (150 percent).[90]

Though it might have seemed a panacea, the private security industry—and private guards in particular—suffered from a host of problems, including fraud, corruption, and inefficiency.[91] A major 1971 Justice Department-funded study found that the "typical private guard" was "poorly educated, usually untrained and very poorly paid."[92] What's more, private guards were subject to little regulation or oversight. While the Justice Department study cited New York as being among the states with "better statutes, in terms of standards and scope," this was hardly high praise, given that licensing and regulation of the industry were "at best, minimal and inconsistent, and, at worst, completely absent."[93] Indeed, a study of security guards in New York found that there was "insufficient scrutiny of the backgrounds of guards," the *Times* reported, and that most were "ill-prepared for their jobs in terms of training and personal abilities."[94]

The issue was one that had troubled community groups. Manhattan Beach residents found after hiring their guard that "for the wages paid, the type of individual attracted to the job is not of the highest caliper [*sic*]," Vice President Edward Eisenberg explained in one meeting.[95] The quality of guards led another community member to conclude that "the patrol was a deterrent to the foolish, *but not the professional.*"[96]

Those turning to private security also contended with the mixed reactions to the very idea of private guards patrolling public streets. Even as the number of security guards grew, most continued to patrol privately owned spaces, such as industrial plants, banks, office buildings, and retail stores. Many of the city's security firms simply refused to contract with resident groups who wanted to hire a guard for their block.[97] Police often proved similarly unenthusiastic. In Jamaica Estates, for instance, local police explained that they "would much prefer" for residents to organize volunteer initiatives rather than proceed with private guards.[98]

Despite the caliber of private guards and their uncommon presence on public streets, businesses and institutions also hired more guards to patrol commercial areas. In the early 1970s, for example, one hundred merchants on Madison Avenue joined together to hire unarmed, uniformed guards to patrol between 60th and 72nd Streets. "I never see a policeman," explained one participating merchant who had been robbed six times in six months. "There should be a cop on every block, but they can't do that because there aren't enough of them."[99]

By joining together, merchants, real estate owners, and institutions could share costs as well as address the issues hindering the spread of security guards in public spaces. They could, for example, devote greater funding to hire more qualified guards, train guards to take a more active role in policing streets, and use their influence to ameliorate concerns of residents and police. These solutions were much more difficult for a block association to implement.

The Morningside Area Alliance (MAA), for example, used all of these tactics as they brought private security guards to the streets of Morningside Heights, a largely residential neighborhood of middle-class whites with a smaller African American area in its northern tip. Formed as Morningside Heights, Inc. in 1947, the group—comprised of fifteen area educational, religious, and health service institutions, including Columbia University, Riverside Church, and St. Luke's Home for the elderly—aimed "to promote the improvement of Morningside Heights as an attractive residential, educational and cultural area."[100] By the 1960s, its leaders believed that the very foundation of the work of its member institutions was at risk. Members, the group noted, "cannot fully perform their work of educational, religious, and health services if people are fearful for their own safety and the security of their personal property."[101]

The group first considered forming a security patrol for area streets in the early 1960s but encountered a number of challenges. Several member institutions employed guards, but they overwhelmingly patrolled only institutional buildings and areas. "The present institutional guard staff," the board of directors believed, "cannot patrol the streets without neglecting essential duties on institutional grounds."[102] The group then contacted major security guard companies to hire new guards for public areas, but found that "so far they have operated only on private property."[103] What's more, these companies were hesitant to expand guards' domain to public property. When the group reached out to Burns Security—one of the largest firms in the country—firm manager Paul Fitzpatrick expressed reluctance "about having his men patrol the city streets. His organization is generally used to protect life and property on private premises."[104]

The group ultimately found a willing partner in Interstate Industrial Protection Co. The MAA worked with the firm to improve training and supervision and win acceptance for guards on Morningside Heights streets. After several years, the MAA and Interstate had achieved what the firm called "the modern approach to residential security."[105] The twelve-man unit wore light blue unfirms while donning nightsticks and handcuffs as it patrolled between 109th and 125th and Morningside to Riverside Parks.[106] The force had its own captain, Bertram Rodgers, a former policeman in West New York, New Jersey, and its own headquarters on Morningside Drive, which Interstate proclaimed to be "the next closest thing" to police headquarters "on the private side of law enforcement."[107]

Community members had a mixed response to the patrols, however. At the end of the decade, a MAA report found that residents, store owners, and students believed the patrol to be "rather ineffective in light of the scope and gravity of the problems."[108] What's more, many community members "know little about the Patrol and often confuse it with either institutional security forces or the Police, often giving credit to these groups when it rightly belongs with the Patrol."[109]

The group continued to implement changes in subsequent years to further improve the patrol's standing, professionalization, and purview in

FIGURE 4.3 Captain Bertram Rodgers briefs members of the Morningside Heights Street Patrol in the Squad Room of the patrol headquarters.

Morningside Area Alliance records. Courtesy of Columbia University Archives.

patrolling area streets. MAA added more distinctive identification and name badges to its uniforms, changed the name of the patrol from Morningside Heights Street Patrol to Morningside Community Patrol (MCP), and hired a security director who met with "block associations, tenant organizations, and shopkeepers to discuss security problems."[110] The group also appointed a supervisor charged with providing ongoing trainings and ensured that a sergeant was always on duty for the sixteen hours guards patrolled each day.[111]

The MCP also shifted its fundamental orientation from one whose mere presence was meant to deter crime to one that took an active role in policing. In response to continually rising crime, the MCP believed, residents and workers "demand a different kind of apprehension: they want the criminal caught in the act, prosecuted and deterred from practicing in our community."[112] The patrol therefore became increasingly involved in activities previously the domain of police, such as stopping muggings and car break-ins in progress and chasing down suspected perpetrators.[113] It also established a walkie-talkie network that linked all guards, its new patrol car, headquarters, and any institutional security office that wanted to "be informed of all security problems faced by the Community Patrol."[114]

After over a decade in operation, the Morningside Community Patrol had become something akin to a parallel force to the police: a trained and supervised private security force actively policing Morningside Heights streets on foot and by car. The group found these efforts helped improve its reception among the local precinct—with whom the MCP was in growing contact to coordinate its efforts—as well as the general public, from whom the patrol was receiving an increasing number of "appreciative letters or calls from a person who is grateful for the Patrol's help."[115]

Yet the MAA ran up against the limits of private security in the early 1970s when they encouraged the creation of a broader private security network in Morningside Heights. The group pointed to the Bloomingdale neighborhood just south of Morningside Heights where several adjoining blocks had recently each hired a guard. Why couldn't every other block in Morningside Heights do the same, following the lead of Riverside Drive Tenants' Association, which had hired a guard for their block?[116] The smaller number of low-income blocks in the area could still contribute through resident patrols.[117] "Together with private lobby guards," the group envisioned a "network of security forces in a concentrated area."[118] It was a stunning vision for transforming security and policing: a connected, coordinated private security force spread out on each street and commanded by local institutions and residents. Whether due to limited interest or funds, however, few block associations joined the MAA to create this network. Instead, the growth of private guards in Morningside Heights in the years ahead came principally through the MAA and its member institutions.

About sixty or so blocks south, in the bustling midtown business district, another private consortium—comprised largely of real estate owners—aimed to similarly transform and expand the role of private security in policing city streets. The effort was carried out by the Association for a Better New York (ABNY), which real estate mogul Lewis Rudin and other prominent real estate and business leaders formed in 1971 to ensure New York retain its status as "the prime corporate headquarters in the world."[119] The organization initiated a range of projects to address New York's declining economic health—and keep its commercial buildings occupied—from advertising campaigns championing the benefits of locating businesses and headquarters in New York to lobbying for greater federal funding for the city.

Rudin, however, believed crime to be "the most important, the most serious problem facing the eight million people in New York."[120] In 1972, he announced that the ABNY "decided that an all-out commitment of our resources to stop crime is mandatory if we want to make New York better."[121] The group unsurprisingly focused its efforts on the area of midtown where its members had the greatest economic stake. The ABNY aimed to deter crime "without shifting any police from any other area in the city to a particular area."[122] To do so, the group launched a two-part program. First, it expanded the domain of the guards already patrolling the buildings and lobbies in central midtown to include the streets immediately surrounding these buildings.[123] It also paid for doormen and superintendents to be trained to serve as "block watchers" so that they could properly report crimes and suspicious behaviors to the police.

This program relied on the area owners agreeing to allocate resources toward what had principally been a public service. At a press conference announcing the initiative, a reporter asked ABNY leadership whether they resented "the fact that your membership pays millions of dollars in taxes to a city government that's supposed to do the job, and now you've got to do it yourself." Member Alton Marshall, president of Rockefeller Center, angrily replied: "That's the kind of attitude which ... business and the private sector has wallowed in for many years in this city and in this country—the old Roosevelt theory to let government do it."[124] "There is no reason," he told reporters, "why the 30,000 private security people can't be organized to supplement the police." [125]

Marshall's assertion signaled both what elite initiatives like the ABNY (and the MAA) shared with the neighborhood associations and where they diverged. On the one hand, his statement reflected how a growing range of New Yorkers believed that they needed to be actively involved in affairs previously deemed to be the domain of government. Both neighborhood residents and organizations like the ABNY created a new space for private actors in public spaces. On the other hand, neighborhood groups generally saw forming a patrol or hiring a guard as small-scale and temporary. None articulated these steps as part of a larger vision to permanently shift the nature of policing. To the ABNY, in contrast, the crisis of crime could be an opportunity for sweeping change. This change, to be sure, was not one the powerful actors behind the group had long-ago conceived and been lying in wait to enact. Rather, in the early 1970s, as the economic costs of crime rose and as faith in municipal government declined, they began to imagine a new solution to crime, one they saw could lead to an ongoing, citywide private security force.

The ABNY took further steps toward this ambitious vision the following year. The group announced that it would extend its network of dedicated security guards from fifty to over three hundred—including some who were armed—as well as the number of midtown streets on which they patrolled.[126] The program was rebranded as "Operation Interlock," as its radio network directly connected guards with the police.[127] The result was likely the biggest private security team patrolling public streets at the time.

ABNY's initiative won support from officials, no doubt due to its leadership consisting of an array of prominent real estate and business figures. The Manhattan police commander, for example, told the press that he welcomed the effort because the police "were not able to do the job required," as the *Times* put it.[128] Mayor Lindsay applauded the plan, noting "the war on crime can only be effective if we have the strong involvement of the public in every way."[129] "This program is another important step," Lindsay believed, in the business community applying "its great talent and resources to increase the general security."[130]

ABNY officials hoped the program would expand "from neighborhood to neighborhood and then borough to borough."[131] Indeed, the ABNY's vision was even more extraordinary than the private security network imagined by the MAA. The special antenna the ABNY had installed on the Exxon Building to link the network of midtown security guards was capable of connecting guards over the entire city.[132] In commercial areas, real estate and business owners would hire guards; in residential ones, block associations could do so. The goal, Rudin explained, was for local groups to expand on the framework the ABNY established, creating a citywide network of private security guards that would spread "into the Fordham Road area [in the Bronx], into the Steinway Street area [in Queens], into Brooklyn."[133]

Despite this expansive vision, Operation Interlock never spread beyond midtown. Expense and logistics no doubt played a role, with many real estate owners and businesses—let alone residential communities—lacking the funds to hire large numbers of security guards or the means to coordinate even a local network. There was the additional barrier of businesses and residents needing to support the idea of private guards taking a more active role in policing public streets—still a rare sight. The program also ultimately ran up against the limits of law enforcement's enthusiasm for private security at the time. Police Commissioner Michael Codd proved unwilling to support the network of private guards spreading further even into south midtown.[134]

Nonetheless, along with residential groups hiring private guards, the large-scale projects launched by groups like the ABNY and the Morningside Area Alliance facilitated the beginnings of major shifts in the nature and extent of private policing. These efforts helped to professionalize security guards, increase their presence in public streets, gain greater media attention and political support, and shift the role of private security from a visual deterrence to active policing. Visitors to and residents of Morningside Heights and midtown (as well as those reading news coverage of these developments) would have encountered something that had likely never seen in their lifetime: a coordinated, uniformed private security force patrolling city streets.

Alongside citizen patrols, private guards expanded the coordinated surveillance of public spaces beyond the police to a growing number of private actors. Both derived from the belief that a fundamental municipal service needed to be supplemented. In the years ahead, the crime problem not only remained, but municipal cutbacks that accompanied the fiscal crisis only hardened the resolve that greater involvement by residents and private sector actors was necessary to combat them.

In the aftermath of the fiscal crisis, citizen patrols and private security guards continued to spread, but the former especially captured public attention. The patrols were increasingly applauded by officials and the media as viable and necessary. They also gained support, first from new organizations designed to shore up volunteerism during the fiscal crisis and then, later in the decade, from federal programs. And most importantly, thousands of residents continued to be willing to devote their time to these efforts. The result was citizen patrols gaining a larger presence in the streets and greater political legitimacy.

"You Can't Wait for the City"

Despite the growing prevention efforts of residents, businesses, and institutions, crime continued to rise at mid-decade. In 1974 the number of reported rapes, robberies, assaults, and burglaries all increased over prior years.[135] Between 1970 and 1975, murders climbed from 1,117 to 1,645.[136] The 1975 fiscal crisis then resulted in several thousand officers being laid off, totaling nearly 15 percent of the police force.[137] The following year, nearly every neighborhood experienced significant increases in reported crime; city-wide, the number of felonies reached their highest point in the forty-five years the police had tracked these statistics.[138]

Just as the fiscal crisis boosted grassroots initiatives to improve parks and housing, neighborhood groups worked to offset municipal layoffs around security. "The prospect of losing more policemen and firemen," the *Times* reported in 1975, "is mobilizing many residents who had previously taken no interest in community affairs."[139] As cutbacks were announced late in the spring, for example, representatives from over a hundred block associations in Queens convened to redouble their efforts. "You can't wait for the city," co-organizer Lillian Powell proclaimed. Convention chairman Lon DeLeon explained how local groups had increasingly "been working closely with the Police Departments in many neighborhoods to form security patrols."[140]

The Beame administration and the police pledged greater support for community anti-crime initiatives, a position fostered both by municipal cutbacks and the growing view within law enforcement that resident involvement helped deter crime. The police stepped up the efforts begun during the Lindsay administration to educate and train residents in crime prevention methods through its block watcher program. "In light of the present fiscal and manpower crisis," Police Commissioner Codd noted, "it is imperative that as many civilian volunteers as possible become involved in the Department related programs."[141] By late 1977, for example, more than 32,000 residents had gone through its block watcher training.[142] The police also expanded the Civilian Observation Patrol (COP) program, launched in 1973, which provided training materials and courses specifically for patrol groups "to observe street conditions, incidents and to report crimes and violations to local police."[143] The goal was for these civilian groups to "act as extended eyes and ears of the Police Department"; many had a direct radio connection to their local precinct.[144] By 1977, COP groups were active in nearly 65 percent of precincts.[145] With residential patrols typically oriented toward supplementing police, these programs expanded and made official these relationships.

This shift toward citizen involvement in crime prevention was occurring not just in New York but across the country in the 1970s. Early in the decade, "citizen crime prevention programs were not encouraged by law enforcement agencies; citizen patrols, especially, were often disparaged as 'urban vigilantes,'" a major Justice Department study stated. "By the end of the 1970s, however, law enforcement agencies had embraced the concept of an active citizen role in crime prevention."[146] Perhaps most famously, the National Sheriffs' Association in 1972 launched the Neighborhood Watch program, with a grant from the Justice Department's Law Enforcement Assistance Administration (LEAA). Especially targeting suburban and rural areas, the program initially distributed information about protecting homes against burglaries before shifting to promoting the establishment of neighborhood groups to monitor their homes and streets.[147]

In New York, the most notable effort to boost volunteerism around crime came with the formation of the Citizens Committee for New York City (CCNYC) in the fall of 1975. Just as the group advanced volunteerism in parks and other areas, it encouraged residents to become more actively involved in crime prevention in the wake of municipal cutbacks. "I can envision volunteers out in the streets cleaning up, policing blocks, helping direct traffic, manning senior citizen's centers, staffing the libraries and museums, even feeding the animals at the zoo," explained Osborn Elliott, *Newsweek* editor and CCNYC's leader.[148]

The CCNYC looked especially to the city's 6,000 block associations to foster volunteerism. Block associations had already been spreading rapidly since the late 1960s, but this growth accelerated by the CCNYC's proselytizing about volunteerism and producing resources to assist their formation. The CCNYC, for example, published and distributed tens of thousands of copies of a pamphlet (in English and Spanish) titled "Lend a Hand and Improve Your Block," which detailed how to form and successfully run block associations.[149] It sent Volunteers in Service to America (VISTA) workers into neighborhoods to help organize new associations.[150] The organization also cohosted yearly block association gatherings. The *Times* described the atmosphere at the first gathering in May 1976 as "almost evangelical" as block leaders—many of whom came from communities of color—"told of ways they had successfully dealt with safety problems or had found new techniques of raising money for tree-planting."[151] Over its first two years, the

CCNYC claimed to have helped organize over 2,000 new block associations across all five boroughs.[152]

Crime awareness and prevention were key aspects of this work. The CCNYC produced pamphlets such as "Lend a Hand for a Safer New York," which detailed how residents could respond to police layoffs by organizing foot patrols, car patrols, and block watcher programs and included lengthy sections on patrols and block watchers in other publications, such as its 144-page *New York Self-Help Handbook* (1977).[153] Representatives also appeared alongside police at community meetings. The CCNYC's Mort Berkowitz, for instance, spoke along with the commanding officer of the 68th Precinct to six hundred Sunset Park residents, instructing them on how to form block associations to combat local crime.[154]

In late 1976, the CCNYC began providing grants of up to $400 for community groups involved in anti-crime initiatives. These funds were especially important as block associations spread to more low-income neighborhoods of color. "The cost of essential equipment and materials" such as whistles, flashlights, and walkie-talkies were otherwise "prohibitive" for groups in these neighborhoods.[155] Such funding also helped groups in moderate and middle-income areas to launch costlier projects, such as supplying radio equipment for car patrols to communicate directly with local precincts.[156]

The CCNYC's efforts could not have succeeded without the willingness of thousands of residents to become more involved in anti-crime activities. "In the absence of any services we all have to do a little more—not sit back," Ekins Worrell of Queens Village put it at a meeting devoted to organizing patrols in Queens.[157] In nearby Hollis Hills, forty community members patrolled six nights a week.[158] The Isham Area's Block Observation Patrol between West 207th Street and 218th Street relied on over a hundred volunteers and neighbors organizing raffles to pay for their equipment. In the largely African American areas of Crown Heights and Flatbush, twenty-five community groups came together to form the "Civilian Radio Patrols" in which residents patrolled on foot and by car in uniform with radios connected directly to the local precinct.[159] It was ultimately these thousands of volunteers who sustained anti-crime initiatives.

The enthusiasm for citizen involvement in crime prevention even reached federal officials in the late 1970s. In 1976, Congress created the Office of Community Anti-Crime Programs (OCACP) within the LEAA to provide direct funding for citizen anti-crime efforts.[160] Since its founding in 1968, the LEAA had principally funded law enforcement activities, but the OCACP earmarked $15 million in both fiscal years 1977 and 1978 for roughly 150 community groups involved in a variety of anti-crime activities.[161] This was the first time the federal government provided funding directly to anti-crime community groups. "No longer can law enforcement be viewed as a game of cops and robbers in which the citizens play the trees," LEAA Administrator Henry Dogin proclaimed.[162]

The LEAA funded a relatively small number of groups but it did so in amounts that were substantial. By 1978, it had awarded grants to nearly a dozen community or tenant patrols in New York, mostly in low and moderate-income areas. Bedford-Stuyvesant's Central Brooklyn Coordinating Committee, for example, used its $235,514 grant to support patrols, escorting, and block watching programs as well as youth recreation and victim assistance programs.[163] This level of funding transformed what had typically been small initiatives. In Midwood, Brooklyn, for example, a largely white middle-class neighborhood, residents had already formed successful block associations, citizen patrols, and car patrols before the Midwood Kings Highway Development Corporation (MKDC)—which functioned as a sort of umbrella organization for the area's disparate civic groups and block associations—received almost $275,000 in federal funds over 1978 and 1979.[164] The funding allowed the MKDC to hire a former police detective as its anti-crime project director and a community organizer to assist residents in forming over two hundred new block and tenant associations, creating a neighborhood-wide block watcher program. This funding also paid for new cars and radio equipment, enabling six car patrols with an astonishing 1,500 community volunteers to patrol a 200-block area seven nights a week.[165]

A few years later, the Justice Department launched the Urban Crime Prevention Program to provide smaller grants to "increase the participation of citizens in innovative neighborhood crime prevent efforts" in low and moderate-income areas.[166] For New York, the program awarded $450,000 to the CCNYC, which distributed it to twelve local groups, such as a project between the 90th Street West Block Association and the tenant association of the Wise Towers public housing complex, to collaborate on reducing crime in the area.[167] Additionally, in the early 1980s, the Housing and Urban Development's (HUD) Public Housing Urban Initiatives Anti-Crime Demonstration provided funding in thirty-nine cities to foster resident anti-crime initiatives. Although New York was not awarded funding, its public housing patrols were by then recognized as a national model, with 12,955 volunteers working in 866 buildings across 127 developments in 1980.[168] An extraordinary 70 percent of the patrols organized between 1968 and 1970 remained in operation.[169]

Even as participation in anti-crime activities flourished across New York, the city continued to struggle with crime. In 1979, robbery rates reached the highest in the nation, with "more than 1 percent of the population" being robbed each year—"and that's counting only *reported* robberies," historian Jonathan Soffer has observed.[170] Among large cities, New York's national crime rate rose from fifteenth in 1979 to ninth in mid-1980.[171] Meanwhile, a precarious economy that prevented new hiring meant that the number of police officers continued to fall until 1981, when it bottomed out at 22,170, the lowest since 1954.[172]

Little wonder that the administration of Mayor Ed Koch looked to expand on prior administrations' efforts to foster resident participation against crime. "What we are trying to do, literally, is to organize every block and every building in this city and to give people the tools with which to help themselves," explained Richard Shapiro, director of the NYPD's Civilian Participation Program (CPP), which helped oversee programs such as the city's Blockwatcher program, radio patrols, and Civilian Observation Patrols.[173] Shapiro was well acquainted with community anti-crime initiatives, having previously served as the project director for Midwood's extensive program.

Municipal officials, however, had reason to promote these efforts beyond being a low-cost means to combat crime: they also redirected residents' frustration away from vigilantism. Koch was particularly alarmed by the formation of the Guardian Angels who began patrolling subways in 1979 wearing combat boots, fatigue pants, and red berets, pledging to deter and even physically stop crime. Officials denounced the Angels, claiming the group provoked violence, a perception likely fueled in part by the group being comprised largely of young low-income black and Latinx people.[174] The group's founder, Curtis Sliwa, in turn routinely criticized the police and municipal leadership as ineffective in combatting crime and refused to cooperate with officials.[175]

Koch and police officials therefore promoted official programs that would train and monitor citizen groups. Among the most popular was the Civilian Observation Patrol (COP), which grew to include over 110 neighborhood groups by 1981.[176] In Brooklyn Heights, for example, police trained over fifty residents who used their own cars (equipped with a removable lamination and light) to patrol the neighborhood in teams, using radio transmitters and receivers volunteers purchased.[177] "You just can't go to meetings and ask for more police," Brooklyn Heights Association executive director Judy Standon believed. "You have to do something yourself."[178] "The Patrol's visible presence can be one of the best crime prevention tools for the Heights," explained officer Pat McDermott, the local precinct's liaison to the program.[179]

Citizen anti-crime efforts spread across the city in African American, Latinx, and white neighborhoods. In Prospect Heights, 300 African American residents patrolled the streets, while in northern Manhattan 300 Latinx car service drivers formed a radio motor patrol.[180] In the Bronx, 125 of the 3,000 members of the Morris Park Community Association were "on the streets seven nights a week, reporting suspicious activities, escorting the elderly, defusing potentially dangerous situations, and joining in the search for missing persons," according to a *New York* magazine profile.[181] While many of these volunteers participated in city-sponsored programs like COP, many others functioned without municipal or outside support. This included large operations, such as the Interfaith Civilian Patrol, whose 400 volunteers helped ensure Riverdale was patrolled each day. "The police don't have all the manpower they need anymore," said Alan Stolzer, the group's executive director. "If the citizenry of the city just sits back and complains, there will be more victims."[182]

The persistent resolve of residents to volunteer their time, coupled with growing governmental support and the continued involvement of the CCNYC, resulted in the substantial growth of citizen anti-crime initiatives into the early 1980s. The number of residents actively involved in anti-crime programs doubled between 1978 and 1982 to 150,000.[183] Citizen patrols counted sixty groups and 5,000 participants in 1977, which rose to 135 groups and 15,000 people by 1982.[184] Between 1978 and 1983, the number of block watchers expanded from 30,000 to 81,000.[185] Participants in the civilian radio program grew to 12,000 and those volunteering in car patrols jumped to over 7,000.[186] Many city and law enforcement officials credited citizen involvement in part for the 10 percent drop in crime in the early 1980s.[187]

Even if only a small percentage of New Yorkers directly participated in such activities, they nonetheless became a major presence on city streets. While just a few years earlier, it was uncommon to see anyone but a police officer patrolling the street, a 1980s resident likely lived on or traversed a block patrolled on foot or in cars by community members. Nearly 70 percent of residents in a *Times* poll believed that "citizens' neighborhood patrols" were likely to reduce crime, a higher percentage than those who pointed to "more police on foot."[188] Along with the rising number of security guards, resident patrols signaled the growing place for private actors in policing city streets. Born out of a desire to buttress municipal services, fueled by thousands and thousands of volunteers, and ultimately supported by private and public resources, citizen anti-crime initiatives had won an accepted place in the efforts to combat crime by the early 1980s.

"Our Guards are Beholden Only to Us"

Though citizen patrols received much greater attention from officials and the press, residential groups and, especially, the private sector continued to turn to private guards to combat crime and supplement depleted municipal resources. These guards would ultimately have a pronounced—and lasting—effect on the very nature of private and public policing of New York streets.

Private security guards were rapidly proliferating even before the fiscal crisis. By the mid-1970s, the number of guards in New York reached the high five figures, an exponential increase over the prior decade.[189] For many, the fiscal crisis reinforced the need for private guards to fill the gaps left by declining municipal resources. In Crown Heights, Jewish residents ended the volunteer patrols that had been on the streets since 1964 and hired private security officers, a number of whom were recently laid off police officers.[190] "President Ford says New York should take care of New York," explained Mendel Shemtov, chairman of the Crown Heights Jewish Community Council, "so Crown Heights will take care of Crown Heights."[191]

Earlier in the decade residents often spoke of hiring a guard in order to complement a beleaguered municipal service, but increasingly they identified the principal benefit as gaining employees bound specifically to their needs in a way public services never had. On the Upper East Side, for instance, guards patrolled across 91st and 92nd Streets and on several nearby blocks east of Park Avenue. Asked by a reporter why each block did not instead donate the $25,000 a year they spent on private guards to the city for police protection, one resident replied: "Why should we? We get more protection this way. Our guards are beholden only to us."[192]

Residents of middle-income white areas of the outer boroughs—where more and more guards spread—similarly spoke of the special services private guards afforded. In 1977, for example, Manhattan Beach, Brooklyn families contributed $100 a year for the Manhattan Beach Community Group to hire the Pinkerton Agency to patrol the neighborhood.[193] "The patrol is able to respond within minutes," the group explained, "while the police often take as much as 25 minutes."[194] Robert Miller of the Ditmas Park Association spoke of the same benefit in 1982: "If you report a prowler in your back-yard, there's no certainty the police will respond. They simply have too many other calls. But when we call our [private security] patrol, they always come in minutes."[195] By that time, private patrols appeared in more than fifty new communities in Brooklyn and Queens in areas like Canarsie, Howard Beach, and Sheepshead Bay.[196] As *New York* magazine described the growing phenomenon in 1982: "New Yorkers are hiring their own troops in the war on crime."[197] That year, the liberal periodical published a how-to article for neighborhood groups that wanted to hire a security guard.

Residential groups not only helped to bring private security into a growing number of middle-class and affluent white areas, but also facilitated guards taking on characteristics of the police. Patrols typically wore uniforms that from a short distance looked "almost exactly like a regular police officer" and increasingly carried guns.[198] Guards were also more likely to be tasked not only with surveilling public spaces, but apprehending suspected law-breakers.[199]

Officials also progressively supported real estate owners and businesses in hiring private security guards to patrol public streets. This shift occurred for a variety of reasons: growing demand both by residents and the private sector, the effectiveness of large-scale operations like those in Morningside Heights and midtown, the private security industry expanding trainings for and supervision of guards, and the fact that security firms in New York increasingly hired retired police officials for supervisory positions.[200] In 1976 and 1977, for example, legislators established four special assessment districts in downtown areas of Jamaica (Queens), Brooklyn, and Manhattan. This legislation created an innovative tax scheme that allowed area property owners to form an improvement association, collect funds via a supplemental tax, and use the revenues to hire supplemental services such as security and maintenance. While it was "an unfortunate fact that the City is unable to provide adequate services for its citizens," opined the Queens County Overall Economic Development Corporation, "it is a more fortunate fact that our commercial businesses, encouraged by their local redevelopment organizations, are willing to supplement these services."[201] The legislation encouraged these associations to hire private security to patrol area streets, even allowing such guards to "be appointed 'special patrolmen' by the police commissioner."[202] In the years ahead, these assessment districts did exactly that. The ninety property owners who made up the assessment district in downtown Brooklyn, for example, hired armed private security alongside other supplemental services, such as a five-person cleaning crew.[203] Though technically funded by a tax, these guards served at the direction of the property owners within each business district.

Law enforcement officials also grew more receptive to—and even willing to collaborate with—the security guards patrolling public streets. The 60th precinct, for example, offered their "highest commendation" for Manhattan Beach's Pinkerton Agency guards.[204] The Morningside Area Alliance—whose force consisted of twenty-five guards in 1974—began working closely with the local precinct.[205] MAA Executive Director Eugene McDermott started his position just ten days after he retired from a twenty-six year career with the NYPD. This background undoubtedly enhanced the Alliance's relationship with the 26th precinct's captain and sergeant, with whom McDermott was in "constant contact."[206] McDermott coordinated Alliance patrols with the precinct's roll call officer to avoid duplication of patrolling efforts. The Alliance's area institutions even worked with the police on a new initiative called High Visibility Patrols, which brought together fifteen police officers with twenty-five security guards who received special training to begin patrolling the outside of their institutions.[207] Private security was not only becoming active in policing public streets but also collaborating with the police in doing so, a trend that would become increasingly prominent in the years ahead.

The ABNY's Operation Interlock similarly expanded its collaboration with police. While the program remained centered in midtown, each year it grew to include additional personnel who patrolled a greater portion of the district's streets for longer periods of time. By the early 1980s, Interlock operated twenty-four hours a day, seven days a week, with security personnel affiliated with more than three hundred buildings patrolling streets using high frequency walkie-talkies linked directly to the security guard network and a full-time police officer in the 42nd Street police substation.[208] "The police usually respond in a matter of minutes," reported Peter Terlecky, a Helmsley-Spear vice president.[209] "The success of Operation Interlock is evidence of the progressive steps that can be taken when our City's business community joins hands with the police," proclaimed Lewis Rudin. He continued: "What is perhaps most significant about this project is that it provides an effective means to combat crime without any additional cost to the City."[210] The program resulted in over a thousand calls to police in 1982 alone, "reporting bomb threats, three-card monte games, and crimes such as robbery, burglary, grand larceny, and criminal trespassing," which led to 122 arrests.[211]

Private security likewise grew in scale and influence nationwide in the late 1970s. Owing in part to reductions of federal funds to urban areas and local opposition to tax increases, residents and businesses increasingly turned to private guards.[212] Between the mid-1970s and mid-1980s, the number of private security guards increased 50 percent across the country.[213] As in New York, the relationship between the police and private security was becoming progressively collaborative. While there had been little substantive cooperation early in the 1970s, by the next decade, the International Association of Chiefs of Police, the National Chiefs' Association, and the American Society for

Industrial Security all launched initiatives to increase cooperation between public and private security. The Justice Department's National Institute of Justice (NIJ) established the Joint Council of Law Enforcement and Private Security Associations in 1986.[214] "We are witnessing a fundamental shift in the area of public safety," as James Stewart, director of the NIJ, put it. "It's not a loss of confidence in the police, but a desire to have more police."[215]

Across New York state, the total number of guards between the early 1970s and early 1980s doubled to more than 120,000, mainly in New York City, exceeding the number of law enforcement officers in the state.[216] By the mid-1980s, a *Times* poll indicated one in five city residents lived in a building or block that paid for "additional security," with an additional three out of five expressing a willingness to do so.[217] Combined with citizen-led initiatives, the fledgling but growing network of private guards and resident patrols surveilled a growing portion of New York, with the gradual approval and co-operation of city officials and the police department. In the coming years, this multifaceted network continued to transform, with security guards taking on an increasing share of the private surveillance of public space.

IN THE 1980S, the fervor around resident participation in anti-crime activity plateaued. To be sure, the notion that an informed citizenry had an important role in crime prevention remained, but law enforcement officials were more likely to emphasize being aware about area crime trends and properly securing one's residence.

This shift was evident in the direction of federal and national programs. By the early 1980s, the Justice Department had ended programs that provided direct funding to community groups.[218] Its wildly popular public education campaign featuring McGruff the Crime Dog, which debuted in 1980, initially promoted neighborhood watches and citizen awareness, but soon switched to more general anti-drug and anti-gun violence campaigns that did not rely on citizen participation.[219] Programs like Neighborhood Watch, which had spread rapidly across the country for over a decade, began to level off in the 1980s.[220]

In New York, several factors contributed to this stagnation. Other than the handful of organizations that received major federal grants, most groups were never afforded much in the way of resources or protection. This made patrols difficult to maintain, especially in the lower-income areas of color in which block associations grew significantly in the late 1970s that were disproportionately incumbered by crime. Additionally, in the early 1980s, the city finally began to hire more police officers; the number of officers rose to 28,000 by 1988, with a continuing civilianization program enabling an additional 5,000 officers to move from bureaucratic work to active patrolling.[221] These additions may have temporarily assuaged residents who had repeatedly asked for more police in their neighborhoods and for the police to respond more promptly. What's more, while crime did decline in the early 1980s, rates—especially for murder and other violent crimes—sharply increased at mid-decade, despite the additional officers.[222] Anxiety over violent crime, coupled with panic over crack beginning at mid-decade, likely caused many New Yorkers to lose their enthusiasm for being actively involved in combatting crime. This sense may have been heightened by several high-profile instances of vigilantism, from incidents involving the Guardian Angels to Bernhard Goetz's shooting of four black teenagers on the subway in 1984.[223]

While thousands of residents remained active in anti-crime initiatives, rates of involvement slowed. Over of the 1980s, the number of participants in car patrols stayed consistent from earlier in the decade at about 7,000, but the residents involved in tenant or foot patrols declined from 15,000 to about 10,000 and the number of active block watchers dropped from a high of 81,000 to 15,000.[224]

In stark contrast, private security guards continued their meteoric rise in New York and across the nation. Guards flourished as a cheaper alternative to more police and before the widespread introduction of digital technology for surveillance. Though even supporters believed security guards offered less protection than the police, private security would take direction from their employer. Nationally, the percentage of Americans working as security guards doubled between 1970 and 1989, totaling roughly 900,000 people.[225] By the 1980s, spurred by the growing emphasis on privatization and cost cutting, even government increasingly employed private security. By the mid-1980s "nearly as much money is now paid by governments to private security companies as is spent for public law enforcement by the federal and state governments combined," the NIJ reported.[226] "Private security," a NIJ study concluded in 1990, "is now clearly the nation's primary protective resource."[227]

By the mid-1980s, security guards significantly outnumbered New York police.[228] While most guards remained on private property, they continued to move into new realms, from public housing projects to federal buildings and courthouses.[229] City officials also increasingly turned to guards, partially on grounds of cost effectiveness. At mid-decade, a starting police officer cost the city $45,000 in salary and benefits; a private security guard cost $16,000 a year or less.[230]

Perhaps most striking was the continued acceleration of private security guards in public spaces. This growth was boosted by liberal and Democratic officials' growing encouragement of the private sector gaining greater influence over shaping public spaces, a shift evident in other initiatives, including the simultaneous emergence of private groups that began to fundraise for and manage parks. Indeed, though neighborhood groups remained a prominent employer, most of the growth of private security occurred as larger associations of real estate owners, institutions, and businesses followed the lead of the MAA and the ABNY in hiring and coordinating private security forces. In 1984, for example, a forty-nine member security team began patrolling at South Street Seaport. On Roosevelt Island, former police official Neil Hetherington led a thirty-five member private security force. [231] In Rockefeller Center, former assistant police chief Michael McNulty headed a 285 member force that patrolled both the buildings and streets of the twenty-two acre complex.[232]

Private security also grew through Business Improvement Districts (BIDs), the successors of the special assessment districts the state legislature first enabled in 1976. By the early 1990s, two dozen BIDs formed throughout the city; these allowed area property owners to collect a specially assessed, mandatory tax and use it to fund supplemental services. These districts spent the largest portion of their budgets on security, coordinating teams of private guards throughout the city, from Union Square to the Hub area of the South Bronx to Jamaica, Queens.[233] In wealthier areas, BIDs often managed huge forces, such as the 150 security guards hired by those around Grand Central, Bryant Park, Times Square, and 34th Street.[234] These forces were often commanded by men like Richard Dillon, a thirty-two year police force veteran and former assistant chief who oversaw the guards that patrolled the Grand Central and Bryant Park areas.[235] In many senses, these forces were the realized vision of the large-scale private security teams blanketing entire neighborhoods that both the MAA and ABNY had tried to enact in the early 1970s.

The police department began to treat these forces not as competitors but as collaborators. The reasons were numerous. For one, some of the most influential real estate owners, businesses, and institutions were the ones behind these forces. Other factors gaining momentum since the late 1960s also encouraged this shift: the professionalization of private security, greater regulation of the industry, the police-to-private-security pipeline, and rising popularity of privatization initiatives. The police department explained that it had "no objection to private patrolling if it is closely supervised and coordinated

with the police."[236] Indeed, in the 1980s, the police began offering training for
private security supervisors at the Police Academy and organized a monthly
"Area Police/Private Security Liaison" meeting to coordinate efforts between
private security managers and the police.[237] Large BID forces were often in
even greater contact with local police; individual guards were also commonly
connected to the police radio network, giving these forces greater credibility
and resulting in quicker police response times.

Seen from one angle, the growth of private security brought numerous
advantages. It increased the surveillance of streets and, advocates argued, over
time helped New York to become a safer, cleaner city. With private guards
helping police to enforce the dictates of the law, they were able to discourage
criminal behavior and make the city a more appealing place for residents,
business, and tourists.

Seen from another angle, the growth in private security had troubling
consequences. For one, it allowed certain areas—especially whiter and more
affluent ones—to secure the barriers around their districts and push crime
into less resourced neighborhoods already disproportionately burdened by
crime. While municipal policing was hardly dispersed equitably and justly,
private policing was directed by one overriding criteria: the ability to pay for
it. Private security, in New York and across the country, effectively put "less
emphasis on controlling crime for everyone—the job of publicly employed
police officers—and more emphasis on private police officers who carve out
secure zones for those who pay for such protection," the *Times* observed.[238]
Like other market solutions, private security was inherently more accessible to those with greater resources. In contrast, low-income areas of color
lacked both effective policing and the resources to pay for private security,
while being most likely to grapple with high rates of crime—conditions that
mechanisms like resident patrols were ill equipped to combat.

Second, private security empowered businesses, property owners, and
affluent residents to directly influence the policing and surveillance of peoples, behaviors, and activities within public spaces. Real estate owners and
businesses, for example, would use private security to harass the growing
homeless populations—who were disproportionately African Americans—
out of public space in the 1980s. [239] Indeed, the populations least able to afford private guards—poor people of color—were simultaneously most likely
to be on the receiving end of private forces' enforcement of who and what was
deemed permissible in public space.

Third, private security was an important and overlooked part of the
period's larger shift toward addressing social and economic problems with

policing and incarceration. In growing portions of the city, security guards were increasingly at the front lines of responding to issues—public struggles with mental health and addiction, homelessness, and behavioral issues in schools—with arrests and the criminal justice system, rather than social services and supports.

Whatever the disparate consequences of this growth, the expansion of private security derived from views about crime and the city's seeming inability to curtail it that spread across the city beginning in the late 1960s. Far from simply being the result of a top-down scheme, residents and the private sector fought for a new presence beyond the police as they confronted the failings of a key municipal service. Neighborhood groups—whether turning to citizen patrols or private guards—as well as business and institutions that hired security forces all helped to open up greater and greater space over time for private actors to patrol the streets. Resident initiatives were sustained for years by enthusiastic volunteerism and, subsequently, support from officials and private organizations, but these began to stagnate in the 1980s. In contrast, neighborhood groups that turned to private guards and—especially—private sector associations like the MMA and ABNY worked patiently to gain support for the use of private guards in public spaces from officials and law enforcement. That private sector actors had greater resources and influence to sustain these efforts than did citizen patrols was no doubt crucial to their success. But the various initiatives launched during these years all helped to broaden support for expanding the role of who secured city streets and the tactics with which they were empowered to do so. As a result, by the 1980s, the nature of surveillance and policing city streets had been transformed, resulting in the growing power of the private sector over public space.

5

The Trouble with Development

WHEN MAYOR ABRAHAM Beame took office in January 1974, he faced the unenviable challenge of boosting an economy that was entering its sixth year of fiscal turbulence. New York had never recovered from the national recession of 1969; a subsequent nationwide recession that took hold in late 1973 may very well have dampened Beame's enthusiasm for his new position. One government study assessed the period after Beame took office as the "worst economic downtown since the 1930's" for "the New York-New Jersey Metropolitan Area."[1] New York suffered from job loss, a waning tax base, and stagnant development. In the period between 1970 and 1975, for example, the city experienced substantial declines in nearly all major employment categories, from finance, insurance, and real estate (FIRE) positions falling by 37.5 percent to manufacturing jobs plummeting 238.4 percent.[2]

Making matters worse, city officials found themselves with limited fiscal resources to promote economic development. For much of the twentieth century, officials drew significantly from their own budget or from federal and state funding to spur economic growth. Yet even before the fiscal crisis, Beame administration officials struggled to allocate resources to foster development. "Construction work has come to a virtual standstill in New York city. Builders, developers and bankers are shying away from making further investments," Deputy Mayor Stanley Friedman observed. And the city itself "has no money to provide public sector capital."[3] Friedman and other Beame administration officials faced a difficult problem: how to spur economic growth in a city with a weak economy, a dubious climate for investment, and a constrained municipal budget.

In response, officials turned to tax incentives. Tax exemptions and abatements could kindle development by promoting new construction, renovations, building conversions, and infrastructure improvements. They would, as Friedman put it, "create a climate which is conducive to private capital investment, thereby demonstrating the city's desire to encourage investment and development here."[4] The private sector, unsurprisingly, enthusiastically embraced this idea. Richard J. Glover, executive vice president of the 34th Street-Midtown Association, urged city officials to provide tax incentives to induce development. "The Midtown area is suffering from an increasing amount of vacant, however, sound structures. The renewal and revitalization of these buildings will contribute substantially to the upgrading of deteriorating areas such as Times Square," Glover wrote. Simply put, "at a time when . . . city sources for funding are extremely scarce, an incentive for private investment is necessary."[5] A number of civic associations also supported the idea. The independent Citizens Budget Commission, for example, noted: "Given the need to revitalize the City's economy, tax relief may be the only major source of local government aid available for development because the City is in no position to allocate funds for anything but the most essential government service functions."[6]

During the 1970s, New York's Democratic and liberal municipal leaders turned to tax abatements and exemptions as economic levers to spur development. As scholar Paul Peterson would argue early the next decade, the most important tool urban leaders had in their constrained kit to improve tax revenues, capital investment, and jobs was land use.[7] Tax incentives, New York officials believed, were well-suited to take advantage of this valuable resource.

The potential benefits of tax incentives were numerous. They encouraged investment when the city itself had little money to spare. Because they did not require direct expenditures, they protected other budgetary needs. They boosted the construction industry, which had seen jobs decline from 125,300 in 1960 to 77,900 in 1975.[8] Though exemptions initially diminished or made property taxes stagnant, the improvements they brought to revitalized buildings were likely to increase taxes over the long run. What's more, a new or rehabilitated project could bring revenues through such means as the "real property transfer tax, mortgage tax, alternation permit fees, sales tax, income taxes paid by general contractors, subcontractors, construction workers, suppliers of building materials and appliances, architects, accountants, lawyers, real estate and mortgage brokers, insurance brokers, etc," as the City Club of New York, a civic association, wrote in supporting such policies.[9]

Under both the Lindsay and Beame administrations, liberal and Democratic policymakers pursued a variety of new tax exemptions and abatements to foster development. Some of these policies were similar to the kinds of incentives that had been used for years to lure manufacturers and businesses to the Sunbelt and to suburbs across the country.[10] This chapter focuses especially on two policies officials used to promote economic growth through creating or renovating housing: 421-a and J-51.[11] The Lindsay administration nurtured the creation of 421-a, which enabled new housing projects to receive a 100 percent tax abatement the first year of the benefit, with taxes slowing rising over a ten year period.[12] J-51 was initially instituted in 1955 as a rehabilitation program designed to encourage owners of cold water buildings to upgrade to heat and hot water systems, but officials expanded the program in the 1970s to allow developers to rehabilitate commercial property into housing. The exceedingly generous policy enabled owners to forestall tax assessment increases on improvements for twelve years.[13] The program also allowed owners to receive an abatement of up to 90 percent on the costs of these improvements and on the building's land, potentially covering the expenses of a rehabilitation.

Using tax incentives to promote development in the city was not new. Urban renewal, for example, relied on tax abatements, including deploying them to make the housing produced through the program affordable to middle-class residents. Similarly, New York State's 1955 Limited Profit Housing Companies Law (known as Mitchell-Lama) provided below market interest rate financing to private developers as well as tax exemptions for nonprofit and limited profit corporation developers. Like urban renewal, the government played a major hand in Mitchell-Lama projects, with construction and management costs, rent levels, sponsor profits, and other aspects supervised by governmental agencies at the state and city levels.[14]

What distinguished 421-a and J-51 from these initiatives was that they reflected a shift away from state-led development toward policies that fueled private sector–led development. Under programs like urban renewal and Mitchell-Lama, government officials wrote the checks and the rules. They were government-led initiatives that ultimately expanded state capacity, even as they relied on partnering with and providing tax incentives for private actors.[15] With 421-a and J-51, liberal and Democratic officials reversed this relationship. These incentives were designed to bolster the power and resources of the private sector and market in relation to the state. They used a key government resources—taxes—to subsidize private development with no project-by-project government oversight. Indeed, J-51 and 421-a were granted "as of right," meaning applicants automatically received them if they met basic qualifications.

During the Lindsay and Beame administrations, officials responded to widespread concerns about economic stagnation by developing and promoting tax incentives to spur economic growth. While Lindsay initiated the city's earnest foray into these policies, Beame greatly expanded the programs as the city grappled with worsening economic conditions.

Under Democratic Mayor Ed Koch, tax incentives became the principal development strategy. Koch remained an ardent supporter of these policies even though they had begun to come under criticism toward the end of Beame's term. Critics argued that with the real estate market once again gaining steam in the late 1970s, J-51 and 421-a were needlessly incentivizing development. Not only did this result in lost tax dollars, but rapidly accelerating real estate prices were also directly contributing to evictions, harassment, and displacement for low-income populations, particularly persons of color. To Koch, however, overdevelopment was hardly an issue with which city officials needed to be concerned. His support of tax incentives derived from his unbridled confidence that New York's political and economic governing logics needed to be reimagined, as the fiscal crisis and reduced federal support of cities underscored.

Nonetheless, criticism persisted. Opponents came from a variety of backgrounds and had diverse relationships—as community members, housing activists, and even public officials—to City Hall. Together these voices put forward an alternative vision of the city—one less tied to unchecked development. By some measures, these opponents harkened back to New York's socially democratic history in pushing for government to use its resources to protect and provide opportunities for all residents, particularly the economically vulnerable. But their proposals also reflected how the political and economic landscape had shifted by the 1980s, as they both challenged and reflected dominant post–urban crisis governing philosophies that advocated greater reliance on market solutions to meet the needs of a transforming city.

Development Incentives and the Urban Crisis

When Lindsay first proposed 421-a in the late 1960s, he described it as a "bold, perhaps a radical concept"—enacting a temporary tax exemption for nearly all new residential housing.[16] Indeed, only once before, in 1920, had New York City implemented a similar 100 percent temporary tax exemption. At the time, the city's vacancy rate had fallen to an astonishingly low

.3 percent, as steep increases in construction costs and limited access to capital due to World War I led to a lull in building.[17]

Lindsay turned to this drastic strategy as the city struggled through the aftermath of the 1969 recession. The 421-a program offered hope in at least two respects. Most directly, the incentive would address the virtual end of private housing development, a situation that Lindsay's Housing and Development administrator Albert Walsh described as "desperate" and "frightening."[18] Developers claimed that housing was simply too expensive to build other than at the upper end of the market where demand seemed to be saturated. New private housing had thus dipped from 47,500 to 3,000 units a year between 1962 and 1969, "leaving the city with its most acute housing shortage in 20 years."[19] The bill would also produce several broader economic benefits. The 421-a initiative required that new construction "take place on vacant, predominately vacant or under-utilized land." The law would thus transform stagnant cityscapes into construction jobs and fees for architects, lawyers, and real estate agents; taxes through city filings, housing sales, and—as the abatement eased—property taxes; and homes for new residents who would increase the customer base of local businesses.[20]

Though Lindsay administration officials hoped the bill would foster significant economic growth, they intended it primarily to benefit moderate-income residents, not those at the top.[21] Officials believed that the law would finally make new moderate-income housing financially attractive to developers. City officials and real estate experts agreed that most of the resulting housing would be moderate-income housing in the outer boroughs.[22] As an additional measure to ensure 421-a produced affordable housing, the law required that the rents of resulting housing would be stabilized and would start at 15 percent lower than surrounding new construction.

By some measures, 421-a was an immediate success. While private developers built only 2,000 units in 1970 and 2,400 in 1971, after the law's passage housing production increased nearly tenfold in 1972.[23] Developers, however, shrewdly navigated the law's broad parameters to use the incentive to build middle and upper-income housing in Manhattan.[24] This marked a dramatic change from the intention of officials as well as the long-standing emphasis of government intervention into the housing market. "Once upon a time only low-income people lived in subsidized housing," the *New York Times* commented. "Nowadays even 'luxury' housing gets subsidy."[25]

Yet the unexpected result did not dampen Lindsay's enthusiasm for the program. Indeed, in just the year and a half after the incentive became available, 421-a helped transform over a hundred vacant or near-empty lots into

job and revenue producing sites.[26] Grateful for this bright spot amidst a declining economy, Lindsay praised 421-a as "an added resource to attract the
middle class the city needs."[27] His strong support ensured the law's renewal
in 1973, with no additional measure to redirect it toward its initial goal of
producing moderate-income housing.

A handful of critics—including some low-income housing advocates and
state officials—objected to the program primarily producing units affordable only to those in the middle and upper classes in Manhattan. "Tax breaks
to wealthy landlords or tenants," the New York Urban Coalition protested,
"pursues no valid or recognized public policy or necessity."[28] Critics noted
that 421-a was even being awarded to major luxury developments like Olympic
Tower, where apartments were listed at upward of $650,000, making them
among the most expensive in the city.[29]

But support among officials only grew as the city's fiscal positioning
worsened. Although 421-a had expired at the end of 1974, officials in the
Beame administration fought for its revival the next year in the wake of the
fiscal crisis. Housing Commissioner Roger Starr believed that tax incentives
were vital given that the "City was unable to borrow money from the capital
markets to finance new housing."[30]

Beame administration officials not only did nothing to orient the program back toward its initial goal of creating affordable housing, but they
also championed its creation of middle and luxury housing as a selling point.
Beame even dropped the requirement that rents be lower than comparable
new construction in order to further incentive development.[31] There was a
"need for this program," Mayor Beame wrote to legislators, because it created
"homes that attract middle and upper middle income taxpayers." [32] Indeed,
one researcher found that "the residents of Section 421 buildings are young,
well-educated, and are employed in high-paying jobs. These characteristics
distinguish them from all other renters in New York City pronouncedly."[33]

Officials continued to emphasize the broader economic benefits of the
program. Beame championed how, in its short life, 421-a had produced an
estimated $1.3 billion of private investment in housing, which as the abate-
ment eased would bring increased tax revenues.[34] He also reiterated familiar
arguments that 421-a brought immediate economic boosts through "the
thousands of construction jobs that are created; the taxes on income and the
building materials which are collected" as well as by increasing "the City's
tax base." The real estate industry echoed this sentiment. "Far from causing
a tax loss," Kenneth Patton, president of the Real Estate Board of New York
(REBNY), wrote to legislators, the housing already produced through the

program would ultimately bring net gains of over $250 million over a twenty-year period. Tenants of 421-a apartments also contributed "approximately $3300 per year in state and local sales and income taxes." "In a time of fiscal emergency," Patton affirmed, the program was "an essential step" in building municipal revenues.[35]

Enthused by 421-a's success and grappling with continued economic difficulties, Beame officials sought out additional tax incentives to foster economic development. Following years of lobbying by Lindsay administration officials, in 1974 the state legislature enabled the city to create the Industrial Development Agency (IDA), which aimed to slow the extraordinary decline in manufacturing jobs (between 1970 and 1973 alone, such jobs fell by 169,000).[36] The IDA was empowered to issue bonds to provide tax-exempt financing for building or renovating factories and to grant up to 100 percent tax abatements on real estate taxes and improvements.[37]

Lobbying by Beame officials then led in 1976 to the creation of the Industrial and Commercial Incentive Board (ICIB). The ICIB was empowered to grant tax exemptions to commercial property of up to 95 percent of increased valuation resulting from improvements over twenty years and 50 percent of new construction assessments over ten years. Though the IDA had a slow start, the ICIB proved to be immediately popular due its substantial benefits and generous application. Indeed, the Board's liberal administration meant that essentially every office and commercial project that applied was awarded the exemption.[38] Within its first year, the Board approved tens of millions of dollars in exemptions for projects whose costs totaled nearly $300 million.[39] The ICIB, praised Deputy Mayor Osborn Elliott, showed "that New York, by offering incentives comparable to those made available elsewhere, can stimulate commercial and industrial investments, and thus cause jobs to be created."[40]

New York's expansion of programs designed to retain or lure commerce and industry hardly put the city at the leading edge of tax-based economic development schemes. The use of state, city, and regional incentives to attract industry had been growing for decades; by the mid-1960s *Industrial Development* magazine began to collate and publish an annual list of state incentives so that firms could more easily weigh their plethora of options.[41] Incentives continued to grow into the 1970s as industry and corporations pitted regions against one another with threats of relocation. Over the decade, almost every state increased the tax, financing, and special service incentives they offered. By far the most widely offered—and most popular—were tax reductions and exceptions.[42]

Though IDA and ICIB were similar to programs that existed across the nation, more innovative were liberal and Democratic officials' use of housing-oriented tax incentives as a principal economic development strategy. In 1975, Beame officials looked to revamp J-51, a program initially enacted in 1955 to enable needed upgrades to low-income housing. Officials believed that the program's generous incentives could be used to transform underperforming properties into economic engines through their conversion into housing.

This strategy may have seemed an odd proposition to some. Why would a city in dire economic straits turn to housing for economic development? The answer was that despite financial troubles, the multidecade exodus of middle-class residents, and the recent addition of 421-a housing units, there remained a demand for renovated housing for the middle and upper-middle classes. Critically, there also were several categories of nonresidential properties with which owners were struggling to achieve profitability, that were tax delinquent, and/or that officials simply believed to be blights on the cityscape. Because land values and construction costs remained high, it seemed unlikely that most owners of commercial properties could profitably convert these holdings into residential buildings on their own—or, at the least, unlikely that they would do so quickly enough to add needed revenues. Though owners had new enticements through IDA and ICIB to renovate these holdings as commercial or industrial properties, officials believed that for many of these underperforming properties, housing had the best chance of succeeding on the market and thus ultimately to produce tax revenue. It would, however, take tax incentives to ensure that these conversions happened—and happened as quickly as the city wanted.

Beame administration officials proposed that several kinds of property be included under an expanded J-51 program. The first was industrial buildings and warehouses. Years of a declining industrial economy had left a "huge inventory of obsolete loft and factory space, much of it now abandoned and producing no tax revenues"; despite IDA and ICIB, officials knew that manufacturing would never return in numbers that would fill these spaces.[43] When early in 1975 Beame officials announced their sweeping Agenda for Economic Development, converting these spaces into housing was included as one of the plan's most important components.[44] Indeed, loft conversions in SoHo were one of the few real estate bright spots in the mid-1970s and officials wanted these to continue there and to spread to nearby areas like Greenwich Village and Tribeca.[45] Extending J-51 to these properties conversions, officials believed, provided the mechanism to ensure that this would happen.

Beame officials also proposed the benefit be applied to office space. There was at mid-decade, as Leon Schneider, a former municipal housing official put it, a "staggering" amount of vacant commercial space.[46] Indeed, if not another foot of office space opened and landlords somehow managed to fill 10 percent of existing vacant space each year, it would be well over a decade until more office space was needed.[47] The glut of office and industrial space had become so troubling that some owners had stopped paying property taxes; others went so far as to demolish their buildings rather than pay taxes on unprofitable commercial properties. "Any further demolition of property abandonment within Manhattan's [Central Business district] areas will serve to depress both the market and the tax base," H. Claude Shostal, the director of the Mayor's Office of Lower Manhattan, believed. "The possibility of residential conversion, however, appears to be a real alternative."[48]

The third type of building was hotels. Some hotels in Manhattan were experiencing unsustainable vacancy rates as tourism had declined; officials believed these might be more successful as residential buildings. Officials also hoped that the benefit would be used to convert single room occupancy (SRO) hotels, which provided shelter to many of the city's indigent and had long been considered by officials to be blights on the cityscape. What's more, a large number of SROs were located in the Upper West Side and Brooklyn Heights, two areas that were already experiencing an influx of middle and upper-income residents who desired upgraded housing.[49] In addition to expanding J-51 benefits to these types of buildings, officials eliminated a cap that limited the program's use in high income areas and would have prohibited converting hotels into expensive housing.[50] The targeting of SROs especially reflected how the principal policy goal of J-51 shifted from using a city resource—taxes—to improve housing for existing low-income residents to creating housing for middle and upper-income residents, even at the cost of displacing lower-income ones.

The plan to reorient J-51 received support well beyond the Beame administration. Endorsements for the 1975 proposed legislative change came from banks, the construction trades, business associations (e.g., Avenue of the Americas Association), civic groups (e.g., the City Club), trade associations (e.g., the League of New York Theatres and Producers), and the Landmarks Preservation Commission. The Hotel Association of New York City believed that the legislation would improve areas like Times Square "where hotels have closed, resulting in a blight to the neighborhood and/or use of the building for questionable purposes."[51] The bill "would encourage the investment of large sums of private funds into economically obsolete commercial buildings

and hotels," the New York Society of Architects proclaimed. "Such investment will improve the economic condition of the City by increasing real estate assessments (and future tax receipts) [and] stimulating employment in
the sagging building trades."[52] With debates over the renewal of J-51 principally occurring during the fiscal crisis in the second half of 1975, there was "a
strong feeling of support among my colleagues for the J-51 program," reported
Barry Salman, Democrat and Chairman of the City Council's Committee on
Housing and Buildings. "All the efforts now being made to insure New York's
fiscal solvency in the next years will mean nothing if the tax base continues to
disintegrate."[53]

The measure also gained support from groups already using J-51 in low-
income areas. The Bedford-Stuyvesant Restoration Corporation, for example,
testified that J-51 had helped them to undertake renovations and keep buildings
at prices low-income tenants could afford. The Settlement Housing Fund similarly cited their own work at a 200-unit building in the low-income, African
American neighborhood of Crown Heights, Brooklyn. The group was working
with tenants who wanted to form a cooperative, but the project required new
plumbing, wiring, plaster, and other repairs. Without J-51, the renovation
would increase monthly fees for a two bedroom apartment from $140 to $230,
putting it out of reach for low-income families. "We would be very hesitant to
take on the rehabilitation work, unless J-51 is extended," the group noted.[54]

These groups supported J-51 without commenting on what the expanded
scope of the program might mean for low and moderate-income tenants in
areas with large numbers of SROs or commercial properties. Indeed, few
questioned whether this change might ultimately do more harm than good
for low-income residents.[55] Nor did these groups seem to question the effects
J-51 was already having when used by private landlords. It was only shortly
after the law's passage that a major study documented how during the Lindsay
administration over three-quarters of all major J-51 rehabilitation projects
were in Manhattan, with "the bulk of these buildings being located in the
prospering areas of the Upper East Side, the Upper West Side, and Chelsea."[56]
Rents in rehabilitated buildings rose nearly 250 percent.

It is also unclear whether Lindsay or Beame administration officials knew
the extent to which J-51 was already being employed to retool low and moderate-
income housing into middle and luxury housing in Manhattan—or whether
they cared to know. Indeed, these administrations provided scant oversight for
the program. A later Department of Investigation report on J-51 under Lindsay
and Beame found "serious administrative weaknesses" in the program. The application process, investigators discovered, gives "the appearance, at times, of

being dominated by the applicants for the benefits."[57] The finding reflected how officials aimed to maximize private use of the program and to take advantage of its "as of right" nature that required minimal city oversight.

Though J-51's expansion easily passed the City Council in 1975, tax incentives became the target of growing criticism over the next few years. For one, there was rising concern that a significant portion of the rehabilitation the incentive underwrote would have occurred without it. One study, for example, estimated that up to 60 percent of privately financed J-51 projects and upward of two-thirds of 421-a projects would have been undertaken regardless.[58] Critics objected to the programs potentially sacrificing hundreds of millions of dollars in taxes while subsidizing upper and middle-income households.

But Beame administration officials were hardly alone in defending tax incentives. In 1976, Rutgers University's George Sternlieb, perhaps the era's most recognized New York housing expert, acknowledged the criticisms of the programs, but nonetheless believed these were "investments by the city government that may actually repay themselves through the broad simulative effects of increased assessed values and increased spending on construction and by tenants who would not otherwise reside in the city."[59] That J-51 and 421-a subsides are "largely being limited to households in higher income brackets should not deny their importance to the city as a whole," Sternlieb wrote toward the end of Beame's tenure.[60] Citing the city's broader transition to a "new post industrial economy," Sternlieb stressed that "New York City must successfully compete for those enterprises that" facilitate economic growth. "Key to this are housing programs which attract and keep the relatively affluent individuals who possess the specialized skills and talents which are essential to the city's future role." In short, Sternlieb believed, using tax policy to benefit higher income residents—even at the expense of lower-income residents—was an imperative for overcoming fiscal turmoil and transitioning from an industrial economy.

New York's leading Democratic officials shared this sentiment. Real estate was, in many senses, the axis around which the city's economy turned. Its decline was a principal cause of the city's enduring crisis and its renewal was understood by Lindsay and Beame officials to be foundational to New York's future. Officials saw declining real estate as enmeshed with the city's host of problems, causing landlords to abandon buildings, the middle class to leave, parks to decay, and even—by draining public revenues for police and economic opportunities for residents—crime to fester. Over the early and mid-1970s—with real estate still overwhelmingly depressed—tax incentives swiftly became seen as critical to any potential emergence from the long crisis.

In the years ahead, tax incentives would bring to the forefront debates about economic development and, indeed, the city's very future. Over the Lindsay and Beame administrations, the use of tax incentives to fuel the private market moved from the periphery toward the center of municipal development strategies as the city struggled through years of economic instability. As Ed Koch took office in 1978, however, it was clear that a growing number of low and moderate-income neighborhoods were beginning to experience rising rents, cooperative conversions, and the arrival of middle-class and affluent residents. Increasingly, critics identified the emerging costs of using generous tax incentives policies to underwrite this transition and fuel unbridled development—none more devastating than the harassment and displacement of low and moderate-income residents from their homes. Incentives thus raised a troubling question: What if the most promising area of economic development came at the direct expense of the lives of vulnerable populations?

These debates were particularly heightened because no one could dispute that New York remained economically troubled. Koch officials inherited a city that was shut out of the credit market and encumbered by diminishing federal support, ongoing budget deficits, declining infrastructure, and rising inflation and high construction and renovation costs. Koch believed tax incentives were necessary to set the city on the path to economic stability—a path that was anything but assured.

Though these debates about tax incentives had largely occurred within the narrow confines of policy circles, they moved into the mainstream soon after Koch's election. An accelerating real estate market sparked high levels of development brought newfound attention to the policies helping to fuel such conditions. Detractors continued to claim that these programs subsidized the affluent, displaced the working classes and poor, and wasted precious tax dollars. These opponents opened Koch's governing strategies to public scrutiny, raising fundamental questions about who was benefiting and who was being harmed as the city began to emerge from its long economic crisis. This was especially true for the use of J-51, which, as the *New York Times* observed in 1982, became "the most hotly disputed city housing policy since the urban renewal of the 1950's and 1960's."[61]

"We Need Private Capital, and We Intend to Get it"

"Too often, the City has viewed with suspicion and hostility the efforts of those in the private sector," Koch proclaimed soon after he took office. "As of January 1, those days were gone. Even if I didn't want those days to be gone

(and I do) the City simply has no further time to waste and no further opportunity to bask in the luxury of bureaucratic snobbery.... We need private capital, and we intend to get it." Koch went on to explain that tax incentives were
fundamental to this vision for development. "J-51 and 421," Koch explained,
"make an important contribution not only to the housing stock but also to
our City's economic base."[62]

As Koch implemented this governing agenda, he appeared to many to
believe in the need to spur economic development at seemingly any cost.
Even as condemnation of J-51 spread in the late 1970s, Koch encouraged its
use, defended the program, or simply ignored the growing criticism of its
effects that residents, community activists, and even members of his administration brought to light. These contestations exposed the deep division
between two contrasting visions for the city: one in which the fruits of economic recovery would be spread among various classes and one in which
the precarious state of city finances necessitated the absolute privileging of
economic growth.

Criticism of J-51 came principally from the residents and activists living
and working in the neighborhoods in which low-income housing was being
destroyed. In 1978, the (Upper) West Side Tenant's Union pointed to the
program's effects in reducing "the number of available low and moderate income rental housing," as the program gave a substantial economic incentive
to landlords "to buy sound low and moderate rental buildings with the object
of vacating them by the use of various extra-legal harassment techniques."[63]

Though J-51 could be used to subsidize landlords' conversion of traditional
low and moderate-income housing into higher-end rentals, the program's
effects were most devastating to SRO hotels. The 1975 legislative change fueled the destruction of 15,000 units by mid-1979 and another 15,000 units by
the end of 1980.[64] Though Beame administration officials largely ignored this
decline, by the time Koch took office, J-51's role had become broadly known.
As Lawrence Grosberg, a legal housing advocate who worked with SRO tenants, put it in testimony before the City Council: J-51 was having a "devastating impact" by converting low-income "SRO's with significant percentages
of minority tenants" to middle and upper income "apartments with little or
no minority representation."[65]

Ruth Messinger, a left-wing Councilwoman elected on the Upper West
Side in 1978, was instrumental to bringing greater attention to J-51. Messinger
rightly linked the destruction of SRO housing to the surging homeless population in the late 1970s. "SRO conversions," she noted in 1979, "have left the
residents of these hotels without alternative accommodations.... Many are

now living on the streets of the Upper West Side."[66] The number of homeless people rose into the tens of thousands by the early 1980s, a trend line nearly parallel to the losses of SRO housing.

Critics like Grosberg and Messinger sought a moratorium on J-51 benefits for SRO conversions. In 1979, Laurence Klein, the director of the Mayor's Office of SRO Housing, recommended such a moratorium, because the level of "single unattached individuals had reached crisis proportions." The administration, however, denied the request. To Koch and Nathan Leventhal, the Commissioner of Housing Preservation and Development, there was simply too much to gain from such long-standing blight being transformed into revenue-generating properties. "Any moratorium imposed now will simply become a permanent guarantee that this housing will remain dilapidated," Leventhal stated.[67]

Few critics demanded that J-51 end entirely. They recognized its potential to help upgrade poorly deteriorated housing in low and moderate-income areas, and simply wanted its benefits redirected back to its original purpose: improving lower-income housing for existing residents. "J-51," Messinger proclaimed, "was never intended to finance the country's most exclusive apartment buildings and cooperatives or to make gratuitous contributions to a handful of developers who clearly do not need public assistance to turn a profit."[68]

Opponents also believed that the program's granting millions of dollars in incentives to real estate developers and owners was in fact draining municipal resources. Many advocates understood that the city needed capital but saw policies like J-51 as sacrificing tax revenues. "At a time when the city has reduced its services to the poor to a minimum" and when decent affordable housing was "virtually non-existent," Rita Buland of the 752 West End Avenue Tenants Association charged, such policies are "*indecent*" and reflect elected officials' loyalties to "moneyed interest groups, particularly to the real estate industry."[69]

Critics' greatest weapon was simply to publicize the program's use. At a protest in front of 261 Broadway, a luxury cooperative converted from offices that had been granted a 95 percent tax abatement, Messinger proclaimed that "the City cannot afford to grant large tax breaks to luxury apartments such as these."[70] With the city desperate for capital, how could officials justify tax abatements to luxury developments that seemed not to need them? Messinger displayed a list of seventy-six recently renovated Manhattan apartment buildings below 96th Street that under J-51 had paid no property taxes in 1980. In financial year 1981 alone, Messinger chronicled, the combined abatements from J-51, 421-a, and the Industrial and Commercial Incentive Board would "cost" the city $100 million in revenue.

Koch officials largely dismissed such criticism. The administration's position remained relatively simple: tax incentives were necessary for economic development. J-51 was "ultimately expanding our tax base" and producing "immediate investment in the City," Leventhal proclaimed.[71] He pointed to the extensive private outlay attached to the program, declaring that the city "could never have substituted public resources for this private investment."[72] According to city estimates, in fiscal year 1977 alone, J-51 helped create or improve 56,000 units at a private investment of $100 million, which supported an estimated 3,000 construction jobs.[73] With the economy still precarious and the fiscal crisis prominent in public memory, such statistics held considerable sway. Political supporters also pointed to the litany of taxes—from sales tax on materials to mortgage fees—the city gained. What's more, J-51 was helping to "establish a middle class base in a city of the poor or rich," with 30 percent of J-51 residents coming from outside the city.[74] "The prime virtue of this program . . . is that it permits private monies to be used to achieve public objectives with limited capital expenditures," a City Council report concluded.[75]

But condemnation became more difficult for Koch administration officials to dismiss as it was buttressed by critical studies issued by agencies and other officials. In 1979, for example, a state study found that "80 percent of the City's population cannot afford newly constructed apartments or units rehabilitated under the J-51 tax abatement program."[76] In late 1980, the city comptroller recommended the elimination of "all tax benefits for conversions and gut rehabilitations in prime residential areas south of 96th Street."[77] "J-51 has tended to serve the luxury end of the housing spectrum," the comptroller noted. "It is likely that relatively little of the J-51 benefits passed on to tenants. More likely, a portion of the development costs have simply been transferred to the City."[78] "The city is subsidizing investment in luxury and speculative housing markets," City Council President Carol Bellamy concluded in her 1981 report.[79]

The combination of grassroots opposition and city and state reports led to some alterations of J-51. Two 1979 reforms helped encourage the program's use for moderate rehabilitation of lower-income housing and diminish benefits in parts of Manhattan for converting buildings from commercial or industrial use (but not hotels). With growing media attention on J-51, in 1981, the Koch administration finally bowed to pressure and tacitly supported the elimination of the abatements in much of Manhattan between 34th and

72nd Streets.[80] Changes that year also reduced, but did not eliminate, benefits if a SRO was converted to luxury apartments, and increased benefits for upgrading a SRO.

Opponents struggled to win more sweeping reforms. A number of low-income advocacy groups, including the Association of Neighborhood Housing Developers, the Community Service Society, and the New York State Tenant Neighborhood Coalition, formed a coalition to build community and political support and develop legislative proposals. The organization gained powerful allies such as the Archdiocese of New York and State Assemblyman and Chair of the Committee on Housing, Pete Grannis. The group proposed concrete measures to redirect J-51 toward improving low and moderate-income housing.[81]

But Koch met these proposals with "a continuing statement of inflexibility and unwillingness to compromise," as Grannis described.[82] He refused to concede that the program was needlessly subsidizing development. This was relatively simple to do; indeed, no one could definitively prove whether or not such improvements would have been made without the incentives (except, of course, the project's backers, whose interest was to claim otherwise). Critics documented that J-51 tax incentives had ballooned to $80,000,000 in 1982 alone and claimed that since over two-thirds of projects were in Manhattan, it was highly likely they would have taken place without the abatement (housing experts generally agreed this was the case for much—though not all—of this development). The Koch administration simply responded that such assessments were "fallacious" because they "assume that the rehab would have taken place even if there was no tax incentive."[83] Although Koch occasionally expressed concern about abatements being too generous, he believed that the alternative—going too far in curtailing them and ending development—would create a much worse scenario. If that occurred, Koch believed, "the work will stop and then we will be too late to do anything about it."[84] The *Times* agreed, urging the City Council to be cautious in curtailing abatements because "removing a builder's incentive can stop a housing program much faster than it can be started again."[85]

Similar criticism about needlessly subsidizing development was made about the ICIB. City Comptroller Harrison Goldin claimed that in its first twenty months, the board issued $62 million in unnecessary tax breaks.[86] Critics highlighted particularly egregious examples such as awarding a $20 million abatement to AT&T—a company whose profits reached $5.7 billion in 1979—to construct a new headquarters, despite ICIB staff finding that "denial would not cancel construction."[87] Continued critiques ultimately led

Koch administration officials to support minor revisions to ICIB criteria and geographic availability in the early 1980s.[88]

Critics of housing incentives remained especially animated by the human costs—displacement, harassment, homelessness—that the policy fueled. But these claims also failed to move the Koch administration. Koch was straightforward in his view about displacement: "It has been historically true in this city and in others throughout the nation that neighborhood upgrading has been accompanied by some dislocation." Though he added that the administration was doing "our best to minimize this pain," his statement underscored his belief that displacement was worth the benefits brought by economic growth.[89] As Assistant Director of Operations Carol Felstein articulated in an internal memo to Koch: "The revitalization of aging housing, the upgrading of neighborhoods, the directing of investment dollars into the City's housing stock, are goals of the J-51 program." She continued, "Protection of those in need of it is also an overriding concern," but those who prioritized this goal by advocating for curtailing the program "are suggesting solutions which would have a severe long term impact on the economic health of the City."[90]

After all, Koch believed, even substantial increases in Manhattan sales and rents did not offset the city's continued economic troubles. Nor did they guarantee that economic conditions would not continue to improve. By the end of 1980, the city's projected budget deficit for fiscal year 1982 was down significantly from when Koch took office, but remained over $400 million.[91]

Koch's overriding concern was thus keeping the growth machine churning. Indeed, improved land use was no small consideration in a city that received about 50 percent of its revenues from realty taxes.[92] Koch "would joke with people that the taller the building, the more taxes there are," his former Deputy Mayor Robert Esnard recalled. "He would see in these tall buildings policemen and firemen and parks and schools."[93] If the city used J-51 to absolve developers of millions in taxes, those "losses" would ultimately help ensure long-term economic health. The city, officials maintained, simply did not have the money to otherwise promote economic development or upgrade housing. "Exemptions cost us nothing," Gliedman contended. "We can get it all . . . property taxes, construction jobs, more housing units."[94]

Koch officials also repeatedly pointed to diminished federal assistance and its compounding effects on strained municipal resources each time opponents demanded that the incentive be reined in, a position backed by other J-51 supporters. Several *New York Times* editorials supporting J-51 warned against "cutting the scale and potential of J51 just when Federal and state housing programs are in the doldrums, and the demand for rental housing is rising."[95] With limited government funds, the *Times* noted, "encouraging private investment with programs like J-51 remains the best immediate strategy."[96] The real estate industry similarly maintained that the city had no alternative. "The severe cutback of federal government housing subsidies," the Real Estate Board of New York (REBNY) declared, means that "private sector development is needed more than ever."[97]

For Koch, the real estate industry that benefited from J-51 was not simply driving economic development. It also fueled his campaigns. Though none of Koch's critics could prove that his support for incentive policies derived from the substantial financial support he received from the industry, there was no doubt that the real estate and business sectors devoted considerable capital to ensure that Koch stayed in office. Real estate was Koch's largest source of contributions during his 1977 and 1981 campaigns and a principal source of campaign funds in his failed run for governor in 1982.[98] There was even, Koch's opponents documented, a direct link between his campaign contributors and real estate owners and corporations that had received tax abatements. For example, ten of the major contributors to Koch's 1981 campaign were landlords and corporations who had been awarded $60 million in tax abatements.[99] While accusations of Koch's cozy relationship with real estate would dog him throughout his tenure as mayor, they failed to gain enough traction with the public to significantly derail his career.

The debates over J-51 and the nature of economic development continued amidst rapidly growing real estate prices in the early 1980s. As critics increasingly gained media coverage for connecting J-51 to particularly nefarious actions by landlords, they began to swing the political momentum toward reform—gains that were quickly tested by the perceived imperatives of continued economic development.

Gentrification, Arson, and Reforming J-51

To many residents and housing advocates, swiftly accelerating investment and real estate prices in low-income neighborhoods was hardly the panacea that Koch depicted. Low-income tenants increasingly worried about a new problem—gentrification—that had previously been seen principally in the countercultural and artistic neighborhoods of lower Manhattan. Gentrification threatened to displace existing residents as more affluent and overwhelmingly white residents moved into lower-income neighborhoods with large percentages of people of color.

As real estate prices rapidly increased in the early 1980s, the housing options for lower income residents shrank considerably. Median rent prices went from $171 in 1975 to $330 in 1984.[100] The vacancy rate for rental housing dipped to 2.04 percent in 1984, a fifteen-year low.[101] Low-income residents throughout the city faced increasing instances of evictions, doubling up with friends and relatives, living in unsafe conditions, and homelessness.

In short, New York, one journalist described, suffered from "a famine of affordable housing."[102] Donna Figuera, one resident facing these conditions, wrote to Mayor Koch in 1984 asking for his help to "do something before my children and I get hurt." She lived in a one-bedroom Lower East Side apartment with her two young daughters, and her brother, and his wife. The cramped conditions were "the least of our problems." There were, she wrote, "rats that cross our beds," which cause her daughter to wake "up screaming that the rats are attacking her" and the mother to live "in fear of a rat biting my newborn and my 5 year old."[103] Though Koch, like many urban leaders, portrayed economic growth as beneficial to all residents, the fruits of development were hardly equitably distributed.[104] Low-income residents like the Figueras, especially those of color, were twice burdened: largely neglected by officials when lower income areas were plagued by disinvestment and abandonment and then inflicted with new forms of trauma—fear, displacement, harassment—when the real estate in their neighborhoods appreciated.

As J-51 fueled an accelerating real estate market and as rent protections limited elevating rents in proportion to market rates, some landlords used perverse tactics to empty their buildings. In the early 1980s, housing officials became flooded with thousands of reports of landlord harassment: "Squirting glue into front-door locks, withholding services, refusing to make repairs, [and] charging exorbitant late-rent fees."[105] While not limited to instances in which a landlord sought to use J-51, opponents of the program depicted the phenomena as inseparable. J-51 directly greased the rapid development that contributed to gentrification and provided an economic incentive for emptying and rehabilitating lower income buildings. Though Koch officials claimed that gentrification improved housing, existing low-income residents found that their housing conditions could deteriorate as their neighborhood began to gentrify. A study of housing in the Lower East Side, for example, documented how as real estate values increased, a substantial portion of tenants found that their buildings' conditions—deficient vital services, lapsed maintenance, vermin infestations—worsened, likely as part of efforts to push them out.[106]

Landlords who sought to empty and renovate their buildings through J-51 used particularly egregious methods to do so. In one building, owners did not stop at the common tactics of providing inadequate heat and hot water. "Rubbish accumulated in the public hallways, courtyard and vacant apartments," a federally funded report documenting conditions described. "Dead and decaying dogs and cats in the rear yard and fire passage attracted rats," the *Times* noted.[107] The building also had sixteen fires in a three-month period.

Dolores Fernandez, a resident facing similar conditions, wrote to state officials as a new school year approached in 1984. The Fernandez family lived in a one-bedroom apartment on West 63rd Street on Manhattan's Upper West Side, an area that had experienced rampant real estate investment and speculation over the prior decade. Between 1970 and 1980, overall median family income in the area had increased 14.5 percent during a period in which it went down 9 percent overall in Manhattan. Latinx and Black residents had declined over 20 percent, while their numbers grew overall across the city.[108] Fernandez wrote that her family was suffering at the hands of a landlord who "desires all tenants out to renovate the apartments and charge rent too high for us [to] afford." They faced "trauma" from "terrible, environmental exposure." Services "barely exist" and the building had "become [a] fire hazard." Most recently, someone had tampered with the gas tank, filling the building with dangerous fumes. Empty apartments had been taken over by those struggling with drug addiction, a common tactic by landlords attempting to gut a building. The four Fernandez children everyday traversed the stairways marked by blood and open drug use. Though Fernandez had applied for public housing, the Housing Authority said that since her living circumstances did not constitute an emergency, she would be placed on the waiting list.[109] By 1984 that list had mushroomed to over 160,000 families, most of whom were years ahead of the Fernandez family.[110] "Is there anyway," she asked, "for you [to] help me find better living quarters, without paying sky-high rent for a family of five."

To critics, arson was the most nefarious J-51 byproduct. Though residents and housing advocates had for years claimed that J-51 was contributing to arson, a federally funded Arson Strike Force helped bring widespread attention to the connection. Their preliminary report found that landlords receiving J-51 benefits to convert SROs to luxury housing were more likely to have highly suspicious fires. Of the eight SROs that were converted using J-51 in a study test area of the Upper West Side, six had "suspicious or incendiary fires."[111] The report depicted a pattern of "deliberate arson . . . as a method of removing tenants." When the preliminary findings were released in 1982, Koch officials initially refused to act until the final report was issued, projected to be a year later. However, "minutes" after Ruth Messinger held a press conference bringing to light the initial report's findings—and the city's refusal to release them—Koch officials ordered its release and soon supported putting greater protections for tenants.[112]

Housing advocates used the public attention on these particularly horrendous forms of harassment as leverage for curtailing J-51. They demanded not just protections for tenants against harassment and arson, but also a reduction in the amount of rehabilitation costs that could be eligible for J-51 benefits. Activists reasoned that lowering the cap would prevent J-51 from being used in luxury housing. But the Koch administration proclaimed that such caps would eliminate eligibility for major rehabilitation projects of dilapidated buildings even in low-income neighborhoods. Establishing a cap at $30,000 might mean that a gut renovation of an abandoned building in Brooklyn could not utilize J-51, while a $15,000 per unit renovation in the wealthy Upper East Side area could.[113] While an understandable concern, the Koch administration rejected other creative proposals to curtail the program's use in gentrifying and affluent neighborhoods, such as imposing geographic restrictions or limiting the program's use to not-for-profit and government-assisted developers.

Opponents nonetheless used the swirling attention around tax incentives, gentrification, and landlord harassment to finally win significant J-51 reforms in 1983. The state legislature banned benefits for SRO conversions and made landlords convicted of tenant harassment ineligible.[114] Housing advocates also won a measure designed to limit benefits for luxury buildings.[115]

The Koch administration decried the changes. Claiming that "J-51 is the only way to generate investment in housing today," Koch officials implored the City Council—which had been empowered by the state to create further changes—to remove all restrictions in the fifty-six Neighborhood Preservation Areas (NPAs).[116] NPAs were designated by the Planning Commission as in most need of redevelopment and totaled one-third of the city, including many gentrifying areas, such as Manhattan's Lower East Side and Clinton and Brooklyn's Park Slope.[117]

Housing advocates and sympathetic officials were outraged, especially as the city was already empowered to allow developers to receive the benefit in these areas if their projects would increase low and moderate-income housing. The only point of this sweeping exemption, Bellamy proclaimed, was to "allow luxury developments to obtain tax exemption benefits."[118] "Do not make these areas magnets and targets for those who would use harassment and arson to drive out the poor for their own profit at taxpayer expense," pleaded Assemblyman Richard Gottfried.[119]

The Council, however, voted overwhelmingly to remove limitations in NPAs.[120] "To pass through the Lower East Side is to feel a sense of embarrassment, looking at buildings that are crying out for renovation," Queens Democratic Councilman Thomas Manton believed. "I don't see gentrification as an evil. We're attracting people to the city of New York who would like to live where they're willing to be pioneers."[121] "New York's recent economic resurgence has not been inevitable, but the result of shrewd public policies" like J-51, opined Stuart Christie of the Citizens Housing and Planning Council. Neighborhood Preservation Areas "desperately need more rehabilitation."[122]

Though low-income housing advocates had won important concessions, Koch's insistence that J-51 was necessary for continued development prevailed. Between 1977 and the time the diminished restrictions of J-51 passed the Council, benefits for the program totaled a staggering $730,400,000.[123] Through the three major tax benefit programs—J-51, 421-a, and ICIB—the city had granted $2.3 billion in property tax forgiveness through financial year 1982, with two-thirds of this amount awarded since 1980.[124] The continued deployment of tax incentives to promote private development would change the landscape of much of the city.

The New Era of Luxury Development

Although in the early 1980s it was J-51 that attracted the most controversy, the 421-a program was fueling much of the city's new housing construction. But it also began to face increasingly vocal criticism for needlessly subsidizing luxury housing. "The 421a program," an audit by State Controller Edward Regan found, "has been administered without analysis of whether program beneficiaries are reaping unnecessarily high profits through tax benefits paid for by other taxpayers."[125] The Koch administration, already inundated with complaints about J-51, responded that the Housing Department would provide closer oversight of the program. By claiming to curtail 421-a benefits through greater control over the application process, Koch retained administrative autonomy and deflected proposals for greater legislative restrictions.

Koch's pronouncement nonetheless resulted in officials denying some of the more seemingly outlandish applications for the generous abatement. In 1981, for example, the Housing Department denied developer Donald Trump a $20 million tax abatement for his sixty-story Trump Tower, which was designed to become home to some of the wealthiest people in the world. Trump's application was turned down on the basis that the building it replaced was not "functionally obsolete," as was required by 421-a's enabling legislation.[126] Trump, already well known as an ostentatious developer, was infuriated.[127] He declared that his denial was "purely a political act that occurred because of the pressure against granting tax abatements."[128]

Trump took his case to court. The city justified its denial on the basis that 421-a had been designed to encourage the construction of low, moderate, or middle-income housing and that the prior property was not "underutilized," because it had not met the standard of being obsolete.[129] Those arguments, however, were undermined by the entire administrative history of the program. The court, rejecting both arguments, required the city to reconsider Trump's application. When the city again denied the tax abatement for Trump Tower, the case went before the state's highest court, which in 1984 ordered the city to grant the abatement that had by that time risen in value to over $50 million.[130] Koch publicly bemoaned the decision for entitling "some of the most expensive and luxurious accommodations . . . in the world. . . . to a tax break."[131] But the court's finding was due to the failure of his and prior

FIGURE 5.1 The luxury Trump Tower development would ultimately receive a tax abatement valued at over $50 million. Though Koch administration officials protested, the abatement was in line with the city's long-standing record of liberally granting 421-a abatements since the program's inception.

Courtesy of the NYC Municipal Archives.

administrations to enact legislative changes to curtail 421-a's use and to set a stronger precedent for denying abatements, particularly for luxury buildings.

Activists had pushed for substantive reforms to 421-a for years, but it was not until Koch faced considerable public embarrassment from the Trump decision that he supported sweeping changes to the program. Though Koch had previously denied the program had any ill effects, he backed an end to all 421-a benefits in Manhattan between 14th Street and 96th Street, an area in which rents had tripled over the prior four years.[132] By 1984, 421-a benefits exceeded the combined total budgets for capital commitments and the entire Department of Housing and Preservation.[133] However, strong lobbying by the real estate industry created an exemption in which a developer could set aside 20 percent of units for low and moderate-income families or facilitate the creation of an equivalent amount elsewhere in the city.[134] The change would not begin until late 1985, which gave developers well over a year to begin projects, fueling a rush of luxury condo construction.

Housing advocates applauded the restriction, but protested that areas like the Lower East Side were excluded, just as they were for J-51 reforms. Signs of the neighborhood's gentrification were everywhere—evident even in the speculation of a single building, such as the sixteen-story Christodora on Avenue B. The building was sold in 1975 by the city for $62,500 to the only developer who made an offer. It was sold again in 1982 for $1,300,000 and again the following year for $3,000,000 to a developer intending to turn it into luxury condos, even though the building was in the same condition as in 1975: an essentially bombed out structure.[135] Average rent in the area increased more than fourfold in just the prior few years.[136] The Koch administration had produced "no data . . . which demonstrates a need for tax incentives to encourage development" in these kinds of areas, City Council President Bellamy noted.[137] The New York State Tenant and Neighborhood Coalition observed that the legislation "would in effect 'greenline' these [nonrestricted] areas for gentrifying speculators, using public money for exorbitant gain."[138]

As the 421-a restrictions took effect at mid-decade, it was clear to both supporters and critics that the program had already "changed the face of Manhattan," as the *Times* wrote at the end of 1984.[139] In the two and a half years before the restrictions passed, 84 percent of the total 421-a subsidies and two-thirds of the units created were for developments in Manhattan.[140] Significant tax breaks that went to the wealthiest residents were commonplace. "Over one-quarter of the total value" of 421-a exemptions, one report found, "went to buildings located in the wealthiest urban residential area in the nation: 59th Street to 91st Street east of Fifth Avenue."[141] Indeed, despite the public battle against Trump Tower in the early 1980s, even after the Trump denial, the city regularly granted abatements to ultra luxury buildings. These included buildings like the St. James Tower, where the penthouse listed for $7,500,000, and the Viscaya, a condominium where the average selling price was nearly $850,000.[142] Indeed, "virtually every" 421-a subsidy in Manhattan between 1981 and 1984 went to luxury projects.[143]

Real estate prices—fueled by tax abatements, cooperative conversions, condo construction, the growing influx of moneyed residents, and the revival of the finance sectors—continued to surge across the city, particularly in Manhattan. The results were staggering. Though the first million dollar apartment in New York's history had only sold in 1978, prices at the 263-unit Trump Tower averaged one million dollars upon opening in 1983.[144] The first ten million dollar apartment went on the market the next year.[145] This brisk market growth extended well beyond sales at the ultra luxury end of the market. Sales data from Douglas Elliman, a major real estate firm, revealed an astonishing increase in average sale prices for Manhattan cooperatives: from $57,800 in 1975 to $191,279 in 1979 to $626,977 in 1985. These prices shocked even early supporters of the tax incentive programs. "The folks who can buy co-ops and condos are part of the new [New York] City," reflected housing scholar George Sternlieb in 1984. "This is a new world city, it's not a manufacturing city. It's a city of services. It's a city of fun and games. And they're making out like bandits. They represent the 21st century. Left behind, both in lifestyle and income, are the folks who have either fallen off the train or are in the caboose. And, unfortunately, that's a majority of the city."[146]

Opponents of tax incentives struggled to curtail the detrimental effects of such a rapidly accelerating real estate market. Many housing advocates realized this. "Almost nothing has been done to change the pattern of gentrification itself," scholar and housing activist Peter Marcuse noted at mid-decade, "to control it, redirect it, to insure that its benefits spread to all population groups."[147] Some activists began to develop proposals that would harness the capital produced by development to fund low-income housing, such as through a tax on luxury sales and rentals or revisions to the city's regressive property tax structure.[148] "There is no excuse for claiming that money isn't available for housing," Marcuse wrote, "until such ideas, and others like them, have been tried."[149]

In contrast to earlier critiques of J-51 and 421-a, these activists took aim at the logic behind the new mandates of development and offered an alternative path forward: if the city would not curtail development, then it needed to ensure that its fruits were more equitably distributed and reached vulnerable populations. These demands in some ways came to parallel a growing emphasis among officials to limit direct government expenditures and derive public goods from the private sector and market.

Harnessing Private Development for Public Amenities

Activists in the early 1980s began to push in earnest for policies that would link new affordable housing to the tidal wave of real estate development. These came from long-standing housing advocates, including the Association of Neighborhood Housing Developers, as well as newer groups that had formed in response to the SRO and homelessness emergencies. Most powerfully, they advocated for inclusionary zoning, a concept that required developers of new or substantially rehabilitated housing or new commercial construction to contribute to the creation of low and moderate-income housing. Developers could set aside a percentage of housing in a development for low-income residents, build that housing elsewhere in the neighborhood, or donate to a city-run Housing Trust Fund.[150]

Advocates, such as the coalition of nearly two dozen low-income, homeless, and SRO advocacy groups called New Yorkers for Equitable Development, pointed to the adoption of such polices in other cities. San Francisco, for example, required a low-income housing unit for every 1,100 square feet of new office space. Proponents estimated that had an analogous program been required in New York, it would have produced 19,500 units of affordable housing in just the period between 1981 and 1983.[151] Similar proposals began to gain traction outside of activist circles. The New York chapter of the American Planning Association, for example, recommended a tax on all luxury housing that would be used to fund low-income housing.[152]

These proposals drew not just from other cities, but from a decades-old New York policy that linked development to the creation of public goods. These types of programs dated to the city's 1961 rezoning under liberal Mayor Robert F. Wagner Jr., which introduced the concept of "incentive zoning." This allowed commercial and residential developers to increase the height of developments up to 20 percent above regulations in exchange for an amenity, such as a public plaza. Like tax incentives, these programs expanded during the 1970s, with "city officials so eager for large-scale real-estate projects, that few major projects were disapproved."[153] The program, for example, resulted over the 1970s in hundreds of privately owned public spaces (POPS), nearly all of which were in Manhattan. In exchange for a development being allowed to be built far higher than zoning laws allowed, the building's proprietor would own and care for these spaces, which were typically plazas or arcades on the grounds of the new building. However, scant requirements and oversight resulted in spaces that were very often "accessible to the public" but "completely unusable in any functional sense," one major investigation charged.[154]

Koch nonetheless thoroughly embraced these types of bonus amenity programs as win-win scenarios: they propelled development and directly produced public improvements that the city would not pay for itself. The Koch administration oversaw one of the greatest periods of productions of POPS in the program's history.[155] Koch also expanded another program from the early 1970s that allowed developers to increase a building's size in exchange for creating a new subway entrance. Other bonusable amenity programs grew so amorphous so quickly that by the end of the 1970s developers increasingly negotiated directly with the city Planning Commission, even themselves proposing an infrastructure improvement as a means to skirt existing zoning laws.[156] This patchwork system resulted in a variety of amenities—improving esplanades along the East River, building a playground, and even creating profitable enterprises like medical offices—in exchange for 20 percent more floor space above zoning limits.[157] REBNY admitted in 1983 in their trade publication that zoning "exemptions" in exchange for public improvements "have become the rule."[158]

These programs did little to jeopardize Koch's comfortable relationship with the real estate industry. A developer's costs for creating a public plaza or a subway entrance were less than the increased profits they would garner through the increased square footage they were afforded. What's more, these improvements oftentimes increased the value of the building and the potential rents owners could charge. The ability for workers to exit the subway directly into the building, for example, enhanced the building's value to potential commercial tenants.

Proponents of inclusionary zoning were aware of Koch's troubling embrace of amenity programs. New York, after all, was carefully zoned to allow for desired amounts of light, air, and skyline, all of which were lost when a development was able to achieve substantially higher heights. Additionally, by linking the creation and improvement of public amenities to development—which was most likely to take place in economically resourced areas—the city perpetuated an unequal system of public improvements that neglected lower-income areas. But advocates' proposals sought to redirect these types of programs to ensure greater benefits for lower income populations. They proposed shifting the orientation of these zoning laws to produce perhaps the most needed public amenity—affordable housing—as a condition of new development. If Koch repeatedly claimed that development should not be impeded, then why not harness its power for the populations that were most likely to suffer from its effects? Also, if Koch was so willing to provide generous bonuses to developers in exchange for public improvements like street repairs, what greater public need was there in the midst of a housing crisis than affordable apartments? And if the city consistently claimed that fiscal constraints limited its ability to provide more for vulnerable populations, why not harness the resources of the private sector in order to do so? The proposal was, ultimately, an innovative way to reflect Koch's imperatives for rampant economic development and to force his—and developers'—hands to support low-income populations.

Despite the number of inventive proposals to expand public amenity programs to affordable housing, Koch failed to significantly push any of them. His administration formed a "study commission" for a Housing Trust in 1983, but after eighteen months its report neglected to provide any substantive recommendations or direction. Housing advocates charged that the delay and obfuscations were the very point of the commission.[159] No doubt the real estate industry's overwhelmingly opposition to the idea helped to prevent its advancement. The imposition of a mandatory Housing Trust contribution, REBNY believed, would put New York at a competitive disadvantage, meaning "other localities and their real estate property tax bases will profit at New York's expense."[160]

Under increasing pressure from low-income housing advocates and a public perception that Koch was too cozy with real estate, at mid-decade his administration finally implemented affordable housing bonus programs. However, these programs were considerably different than those proposed by housing advocates. Koch refused to impose any requirements that would directly link the creation of new luxury housing or office space to affordable housing. Instead, his programs allowed developers to bypass other restrictions designed to prevent overdevelopment if they contributed to the creation of affordable housing. As earlier described, when the city curtailed 421-a benefits in Manhattan, officials gave luxury housing developers the ability to continue to receive the benefit if 20 percent of the units in the building were reserved for low or moderate income residents or—a far more attractive option for developers—if an equivalent number were built outside of the area.[161] That same year, Koch housing officials also initiated their own version of a zoning program that granted luxury developments a bonus of up to 20 percent of floor space in high density areas of Manhattan and gentrified Brooklyn if the developer built, renovated, or preserved low-income housing within a half-mile of the development.[162] Officials, knowing that most luxury developers would not want to build affordable housing units themselves, also created a system in which affordable housing builders were issued certificates that they could sell at market prices.[163] This allowed developers to benefit from 421-a or build their development 20 percent higher by simply purchasing these certificates. Despite Koch's stern words against the use of 421-a in Manhattan, it also allowed for the continued use of the program for luxury development in otherwise prohibited areas.

This market-based initiative for low-income housing was further incentivized by 1986 revisions in the federal tax code. These changes allowed low-income housing developers to gain federal tax credits for each low-income unit and to sell these tax credits to individuals or corporations.[164] These tax credits could be combined with the monies accumulated through sales of city certificates, creating a market for for-profit developers of low-income housing.

These programs helped to shift the creation of new low-income housing to the market. General Atlantic Realty Corporation, for example, a private, for-profit Manhattan-based real estate company, began to build and rehabilitate lower-income units. Its 765-unit low-income rental building in East New York, Brooklyn, became the first low-income housing built without any direct government subsidy in decades.[165] General Atlantic sold the city tax credits to developers of luxury apartment buildings being built below 96th Street in Manhattan, which paid for the housing's construction. The federal tax credits covered other costs as well as the developers' handsome profit.[166]

By the late 1980s, the 421-a program—which was more popular than inclusionary zoning—was producing about 900 low-income housing units a year. Hailing this as "a considerable achievement," administration officials praised the program for its ability to produce low-income housing with no direct subsidy.[167] It was, Housing Commissioner Paul Crotty later remembered, "essentially a cost-free way for the city to build housing." He continued, "we'd get the immediate housing without any expenditure of dollars."[168] During these same years, for example, New York State spent about $120 million to build 1,300 low-income apartments through its Turnkey-Enhanced program.[169]

While the city touted its programs as ones that required no direct subsidy, critics charged that they were, in fact, exceedingly expensive. The 421-a program, for example, was essentially forgoing $125,000 in taxes for each low-income unit through the tax credit system. By fiscal year 1987, the 421-a program "cost" the city $88.4 million in abatements, a number that rose to $177 million in 1990.[170] The market had grown so lucrative by the end of the

decade that the ability to combine city and federal tax credits created a windfall for low-income housing developers.

The low-income housing the initiatives produced obscured potentially
insidious elements of these programs. For example, 421-a allowed for ongoing subsidization of luxury developments in prime areas of Manhattan.
By keeping low-income housing requirements for new developments low
and voluntary, officials ignored how continued subsidization of luxury development was likely to create greater need for affordable housing than could
be produced through these programs. The very existence of these programs
also provided cover for criticism. As advocates proposed more expansive
low-income housing programs in the later 1980s, city officials like Crotty
dismissed them by noting that "the city already has several programs that link
tax benefits and zoning bonuses to the creation of affordable housing."[171]

Critics continued to call attention to the shortcomings of other bonus
programs, describing how zoning laws had gone from a ceiling to "become
the floor upon which zoning deals are struck."[172] Several audits by the
state comptroller at decade's end of various ad hoc bonus agreements between City Planning and developers found that amenities were "not being
completed on time or at all," even though "developers have been able to
complete their projects as planned."[173] Another comptroller analysis of ten
disparate agreements the city made with developers to exchange public
amenities for zoning bonuses found that developers paid $5 million for
public improvements, but that the increased floor areas added over $100 mil-
lion dollars of value to their buildings.[174] "The public just isn't getting a good
deal," the comptroller concluded. The amenities produced by these programs
were also often of poor quality or otherwise of little public value. A report
prepared for the MTA, for example, found that the subway improvement
program the agency had come to rely on for capital improvements was
"based on what is expedient for the developer rather than on comprehensive planning."[175] Studies by the Municipal Arts Society and others at end of
the decade found that many of the over two hundred public plazas created
through the POPS program were drab and unwelcoming. When they were
not, "some developers and owners have done everything possible to insure
that public spaces operates as private spaces."[176]

These tax and zoning incentive programs reflected a new vision for development that bypassed direct city expenditures and utilized the private sector
and market for social provisions such as public space, public transportation,
and low-income housing.[177] The Koch administration built on the initiatives
of the Lindsay and Beame administrations to elevate incentive programs to

being central municipal strategies for economic development. Despite a variety of proposals from critics that sought to do more to distribute resources to vulnerable populations, city policies were implemented in ways that produced limited benefits even for the broader public while ensuring luxury development could continue apace.

NEW YORK'S LIBERAL AND Democratic officials oversaw a radical shift in development policies beginning in the 1970s. The long-standing overriding principles that tax incentives would be used in conjunction with state-led development schemes, would be short-term or project specific, and would often benefit lower or moderate-income residents all dissipated. Instead, under Lindsay and, especially, Beame, tax incentives became a leading development strategy. These policies underwrote luxury projects and empowered the private sector to take the dominant role in government-subsidized development projects.

Over several administrations, tax incentives and zoning programs became principal tactics of liberal and Democratic officials for remaking both home and public space in order to appeal to middle-class and affluent residents. Paralleling concurrent initiatives that enhanced the role of the market and private sector in the city's livable spaces, Koch administration officials embraced incentive and zoning policies as reflecting the new imperatives of municipal government, especially in the aftermath of the fiscal crisis and decreases in direct federal assistance. These factors justified why development needed to be assisted by public interventions into the market through tax incentives (which totaled $1.3 billion alone for Koch's final year in office).[178] Over the 1980s, municipal development policies not only increasingly subsidized private development with tax incentives, but also allowed developers to bypass zoning restrictions if they contributed to municipal needs like creating new public spaces that would remain privately owned.

The growing use of these types of policies did even more than directly incentivize private development and rely more the private sector and market to address municipal needs. They also further entrenched the idea that incentives to drive development were needed and necessary to protect and expand. After all, development was not just enhancing the tax base, a long-standing defense, but was increasingly providing public provisions—subway entrances, plazas, affordable housing—an argument that further obscured the potential social and economic costs of rampant development. Even as the crisis of abandonment of the 1970s transformed fully into a crisis of affordability in the 1980s, the Koch administration ensured that both tax incentives and bonus amenities remained principal development strategies.

Just how fundamental these development schemes became was illustrated during the administration of David Dinkins. When Dinkins, the city's first African American mayor, was elected in 1989, he used his inauguration speech to contrast his vision with the twelve preceding years under Koch. The liberal Democrat told his crowd of supporters that "this administration will renew the quest for social justice."[179] Indeed, Dinkins's television commercials in the primary campaign had directly criticized Koch's embrace of the unabated growth of luxury housing and promised a major reorientation if elected mayor. "If you're looking for a $1 million co-op, maybe Ed Koch is your man," one ad stated. "But if you're looking for something a little more reasonable, my name is David Dinkins, and I'm running for mayor."[180] Dinkins directly criticized both housing and commercial tax incentives and claimed that he would curtail these subsidizations. He also pledged to reorient the nature of programs that harnessed development for public benefit by supporting the San Francisco plan (then also adopted by Boston and Hartford) that required builders of commercial property to contribute to a fund for affordable housing.[181]

Almost immediately after Dinkins took office, however, New York suffered serious economic setbacks. The city's economy had already been declining; New York lost more than 100,000 jobs between 1987 and 1990, in part because of the adverse effects of Black Monday, when the Dow Jones dropped 508 points on October 19, 1987, following several months of decline.[182] As a national recession spread in 1990, the year Dinkins took office, conditions in New York worsened. Its job slide continued into the early 1990s, resulting in an additional 300,000 job losses.[183]

Real estate likewise suffered. Sales prices of cooperatives and condominiums began to decline at the end of the decade, leading to price decreases of between 25 and 50 percent in some areas.[184] "There are no new buildings going up in New York City," New York State Director of Housing Angelo Aponte put it. "We are in a real estate depression—not a recession, a depression."[185] By 1991, the *New York Times* wrote of the "legacy" of gentrification. "Gentrification may be remembered," the *Times* reported in exaggerated but revealing language, "along with junk bonds, stretch limousines and television evangelism, as just another grand excess of the 1980s."[186]

With economic fortunes shifting, the political momentum to change development policies subsided. One *Times* staff writer questioned whether the city could "afford to stop" subsidizing development, "thereby dealing a further blow to construction, which grew in the 80s into New York's largest industry, but is now floundering?"[187] The real estate industry framed its position in even starker terms. REBNY harkened back to the days of the fiscal crisis. As bad as things looked in the early 1990s, REBNY noted, it was just over fifteen years ago that New York was "counted out." Tax and zoning incentive programs, along with "fiscal discipline," it claimed, "rescued the city."[188] The city's revival, REBNY admonished, "was propelled by the courage of investors who recognized the town's extraordinary assets. That courage was ignited, however, by public policies that made the risks of building for New York's future a bit less daunting."[189] In the face of new economic troubles, "talks about scaling back" incentives, REBNY president Steven Spinola proclaimed, "says the city does not want growth."[190] Indeed, "it is precisely because New York City is under fiscal constraints that it needs incentives for development," the president of the New York Building Congress claimed.[191]

This logic prevailed among policymakers. Though support for changing tax incentive and low-income housing programs had gained momentum during the mayoral campaign, Dinkins never attempted to require developers to contribute to an affordable housing fund. In addition, in 1990, the City Council loosened J-51 requirements and raised caps, increasing eligibility for middle and upper-income cooperatives and condominiums.[192] 421-a benefits remained essentially as they were under Koch, leaving provisions for creating affordable housing only in a small area of the city and enabling unhindered use of the program in Manhattan south of 14th Street and north of 96th Street and in the outer boroughs. While some bonusable amenity programs—like POPS—began to be phased out, little was done to adhere to existing zoning regulations or to drive amenities programs toward improving conditions for low-income neighborhoods. The overriding reliance on incentive policies remained central to development strategies in New York not just during Dinkins's tenure but in mayoral administrations through the new millennium.

6

The Governance of Homelessness and Public Space

BY THE EARLY 1990s, Nathan Leventhal had garnered decades of experience wrestling with the greatest problems confronting New York City. After serving as chief of staff under Mayor John Lindsay, he held the positions of Commissioner of Housing Preservation and Development and then deputy mayor under Mayor Ed Koch. Leventhal was also active in the city's most influential private associations, including the New York City Partnership, an umbrella organization of corporate and civic groups that aimed to improve the city's business and economic climate. Meeting in 1992, as the city struggled through its worst economic downturn since the mid-1970s, the financial titans and executives behind the Partnership proposed a multimillion dollar advertising campaign to boost economic activity.

Leventhal, however, demurred. He agreed that the group "should focus on the public image of New York," but this needed to "go hand in hand with what the city looks like nowadays."[1] To many residents and visitors, the city—particularly Manhattan, though also many outer borough neighborhoods—looked much improved from the 1970s and 1980s. Building abandonment that had overwhelmed areas like Harlem and the Lower East Side had all but ceased; more common sights over the prior decade were renovations by real estate investors and individual gentrifiers. Cooperatives and condominiums continued to spread, providing homes for "professional families" who, as Mark Whitaker, the co-op president of 325 West 86th Street, wrote to Mayor David Dinkins in 1992, "have been able to live and work together to steadily improve the block and make it a place we can all be proud of."[2] The conditions of many parks, too, had noticeably improved. Bryant Park, for example, reopened in 1992 after an extensive renovation by the Bryant Park

Restoration Corporation. The press trumpeted the upgraded space; as one writer described, it reinscribed "secure middle-class values within the urban center."[3]

But Leventhal was concerned about another matter. A resident of or visitor to Manhattan walking just a few blocks in the late 1980s or early 1990s would have noticed a major change: there were thousands of homeless people on the streets, in transportation hubs and subways, and in parks. Surely, Leventhal believed, this was the problem with which business and civic elites needed to be most concerned. "I mean you can't spend $10 million on an ad campaign if you walk outside a luxury Park Avenue apartment and you're accosted by five people who are homeless living on the streets," Leventhal advised. Or if "you can't go in your bank or your post office without having to give a tip to somebody."[4]

Leventhal was hardly alone in expressing concern about the growing numbers of people who—lacking a home—took up residence in public spaces. By the early 1990s, the sentiment that the city needed to get the homeless out of public areas had become common in newspaper articles, opinion pieces, and remarks by residents. Homelessness was a problem that "plague[s] so much of . . . [the] city and put[s] it at risk," Whitaker, the co-op president, wrote to Mayor Dinkins. A "totally disgruntled New Yorker" wrote that the consistent stream of homeless and "phoney" panhandlers on the subways were "adding greatly to the unquality [*sic*] of life in New York." He continued: "God damnit [*sic*] living in this city is stressful enough without having the few minutes one has on a train to collect ones [*sic*] thoughts and relax a bit before the next appointment etc. ruined by pan-handlers. . . . Keep it up and more and more people will leave New York or won't come here on vacation or business."[5]

Such stances had grown more prominent as the homeless population rapidly expanded and transformed over the prior fifteen years. For decades after the Great Depression, the city's homeless had been comprised principally of middle-aged white men who congregated overwhelmingly in Manhattan's "skid row" district, the Bowery. But in the late 1970s the homeless population began to multiply into the thousands, to appear throughout the city and to include the young and elderly, women and children, and a disproportionately high number of African Americans. That by the late 1980s African American men resided in public spaces in the greatest number was central to the degree of alarm public homelessness provoked.

These changes in homelessness, as historian Ella Howard has remarked, "reflected shifts in the socioeconomic realities of urban life."[6] Some of these shifts were national in scope or derived from federal policy, causing rising homelessness in cities across the country: federal cutbacks to social programs, housing, and direct assistance to urban areas, unemployment, a growing carceral system that limited opportunities for those released, and an overall economy shifting toward service-oriented positions with insufficient wages, particularly for those living in cities with high housing costs.[7]

In addition, many cities struggled with the ramifications of state-level decisions to deinstitutionalize mental hospitals, especially as states typically devoted few resources to replacement services. New York State, for example, had since the late 1960s and 1970s been releasing patients from its mental hospitals; the patient population declined from 80,000 in 1965 to 21,000 in 1984. However, state officials reneged on their promise to fund smaller, community-based treatment facilities in lieu of remote large facilities. These decisions further contributed to the initial boom in the homeless population.[8]

New York City faced the highest levels of homelessness in the country and its crisis was heightened by local circumstances that exacerbated national trends and federal- and state-level policy decisions. The growing homeless population also resulted from major 1970s and 1980s policy tenets, including new tax incentives that fueled a rapidly accelerating real estate market, the conversion of nearly all 127,000 single room occupancy (SRO) hotel units into middle and affluent housing, and diminishing municipal social ser-vice provisions.[9] As a result, New York's homeless population rose into the thousands by 1980—numbers not seen since the Great Depression. As pov-erty and a severe lack of low-income housing became the principal drivers of new cases of homelessness in the 1980s, numbers mushroomed into the tens of thousands by the end of the decade.

The homeless crisis posed one of the greatest challenges of the 1980s to city officials. Koch administration officials repeatedly blamed state- and federal-level decisions and engaged in a protracted struggle with Albany and Washington officials over responsibility for the problem. Though local officials were loath to take on such responsibility, they nonetheless faced considerable public pressure to respond. Koch, however, proved unwilling to back policies that targeted the root causes of or long-term solutions for homelessness. As rates of homelessness continued to grow, city officials, re-luctantly and under court pressure, funneled the homeless population into shelters, an expensive and inadequate solution, but one that at least moved the problem off the streets. Yet shelters increasingly failed to hide the home-less population, as growing numbers of people took up residence in public spaces. Koch responded with hostility, and exacerbated residents' impatience toward the homeless by conflating homelessness entirely with individual pathologies. This reaction undermined the rationale for structural solutions and, in ways both explicit and subtle, encouraged punitive responses to those living in public spaces.

Hostile responses toward the visible homeless population were also shaped by major post–fiscal crisis developments, predominately the increased targeting of the consumption habits of the middle and upper classes and the expanding role of the private sector in the governance of public spaces, especially through Business Improvement Districts (BIDs) and park management groups. As public spaces were simultaneously being infused with public and private capital, in some cases for the first time in decades, homeless bodies represented physical barriers to the economic revitalization of these spaces. By the time public homelessness was deemed a "crisis" in the mid- and late-1980s, the private sector—frustrated by the seeming inability of municipal officials to stem public homelessness—began to take a leading role in doing so. Private sector groups used the collective resources and centralized voice that new tools like BIDs enabled to shape the response to public homelessness. They coordinated their efforts with the quasi-public officials who oversaw the subways and major transportation centers to protect recent

FIGURE 6.1 As the number of people experiencing homelessness rose during the 1980s, municipal officials, real estate owners, transportation facility operators, and affluent residents became increasingly concerned with the potential economic ramifications of public homelessness.

Dan Shefelman for *New York Newsday*. Courtesy of Dan Shefelman.

investments in these spaces aimed at attracting moneyed classes. These actors utilized especially punitive practices that municipal officials had seemed unable to implement, given the constraints of the law and public opinion. Tactics and strategies pioneered by BIDs like the Grand Central Partnership were widely credited with removing the homeless from key public spaces. In the years ahead, similarly aggressive measures were implemented by officials who oversaw the subway system and then, by the 1990s, were administered throughout the city's remaining public spaces.

The Emergence of Modern Homelessness and Homeless Advocacy

New Yorkers had long regarded the homeless as unwelcome intrusions on city life. Throughout much of the twentieth century, the homeless were tolerated only to the extent that they stayed within the skid row district of the Bowery. Police, Howard writes, punished "their behavior more severely when they ventured away from the district."[10]

As homeless individuals began to appear in greater numbers throughout the city in the late 1970s, officials and the police initially responded with a modicum of lenience.[11] But such tolerance quickly reached its limit. When New York hosted the Democratic National Convention at Madison Square Garden in the summer of 1980, officials ordered a "weeding of the Garden," as one newscaster callously put it, by having the police remove the homeless and other undesirable populations from the area as the convention approached.[12] In response, homeless individuals, along with a handful of early advocates emerging from existing anti-poverty and religious organizations, such as the Community Service Society and the Franciscan Friars, held nightly vigils outside the convention. Participants held signs listing the names of dozens of homeless individuals who died on New York's streets during the prior year.[13]

The vigil marked the first time that advocates for the poor organized collectively to bring attention to homelessness. The protests sparked conversations among participants about forming an organization "to promote and protect the welfare of homeless people," leading to the founding of the Coalition for the Homeless in late 1980.[14] The group brought together individuals working within the religious and poverty advocacy communities, two Columbia University graduate students researching the homeless (Ellen Baxter and Kim Hopper), and a young attorney, Robert Hayes, who had filed a lawsuit against the city over its shelter policies. The Coalition offered a comprehensive vision for improving conditions for and reducing the numbers of homeless persons. They aimed to increase and improve city shelters, create new "publicly funded community-based shelters," "halt the decline in available low-cost housing," "develop program[s] for creating additional low-cost housing," expand public mental health services, and "develop a city attitude of acceptance of responsibility for homeless people by means of public education and political lobbying."[15]

The Coalition's early work focused especially on the conditions within city shelters. Until the late 1970s, the city had provided shelter for the homeless by issuing a limited number of tickets for Bowery flophouses or by making space at the single municipal shelter. Those who did not find a spot before space ran out had suffered "frostbite and, in several instances, death from exposure" in winter, in the words of Rev. Edward O'Brien, who directed one of the handful of religiously affiliated Bowery shelters.[16] This changed with Hayes's lawsuit, which the Coalition soon assisted. Hayes practiced trust law at the prestigious firm, Sullivan and Cromwell, but had grown disturbed by the rising number of homeless in the streets. When he met with officials, he was told that the city purposely maintained shelters in dreadful conditions to dissuade anyone from relying on them.[17] In response, he filed the *Callahan v. Carey* lawsuit based on a Great Depression–era article of the New York State constitution that required the state and its subdivisions to provide "adequate shelter" and care for all residents. The State Supreme Court agreed with *Callahan's* argument, finding that great harm was being done both to the men squeezed out of shelters and flophouses as well as to those who suffered their decrepit conditions. The court ordered the city to provide "clean bedding, wholesome food and adequate security and supervision" and to open new shelters as demand warranted.[18] City officials appealed, but in 1981 they signed a consent decree agreeing to these provisions, believing that their appeal was going to fail.[19]

Hayes and the Coalition, however, found that the city continued to maintain such unsafe conditions within shelters that many homeless were unwilling to enter their doors. Though the city repeatedly denied such claims, they were bolstered by Baxter and Hopper's 1981 study, *Private Lives / Public Spaces*. Baxter and Hopper's findings, based on extensive ethnographic research and over two hundred interviews, debunked several prominent claims about the homeless. The study, for example, confirmed that most of those without homes found conditions within shelters inhumane. Baxter and Hopper recorded extensive evidence of vermin-infestations, sexual abuse, violence, and degrading policies, leading many homeless individuals to opt for the streets, subway tunnels, terminals, abandoned buildings, and parks.

Homeless advocates capitalized on the widespread press attention the study received. Lawsuits initiated by the Coalition and the Legal Aid Society extended the right to shelter first to women and then to homeless families with children. Advocates also continued to point to smaller-scale, privately run shelters—most of which were affiliated with churches or religious denominations—as a model for municipal shelters. The Coalition, for example, highlighted the St. Francis Residence on East 24th Street, which provided permanent housing to a hundred formerly homeless people and was funded entirely by existing government benefits. However, they pointed to such examples as models—not replacements—for government support. It was government, Hayes noted, that should be "erecting St. Francis residences."[20] The solutions to homelessness, housing, and shelter, the Coalition noted, "must come from city government."[21]

The Coalition and other homeless advocates also proclaimed that these solutions needed to go far beyond temporary shelter. Advocates in the early 1980s explained that the homeless were growing "increasingly more diverse, with the ranks of those with substance abuse and mental health problems being joined and outnumbered by homeless families, battered women, the unemployed and castaway youth." They emphasized the "need for long-term supportive housing, affordable low-income housing, work programs, community residences for the mentally ill, food, and increased welfare allotments."[22] Going beyond such demands, advocates developed detailed proposals for how to direct policy toward reducing homelessness.

Still, advocates faced an uphill battle. They knew that the linchpin in the struggle against homelessness was greater fiscal support—and that city, state, and federal officials tightly guarded resources. While advocacy groups like the Coalition continued to press state and federal officials, their efforts largely targeted local officials in the Koch administration. Administration officials, however, balked at any proposals that were not court-ordered. Though state and federal officials were equally to blame for shirking responsibilities for the homeless, Koch officials refused to fill the void they left. With all three levels of government negligent, homelessness continued to grow.

The Struggle for Government Resources

Koch administration officials had reason to be frustrated with state and federal responses to homelessness. Many of the resources that could have prevented or ameliorated homelessness had for decades been provided principally by the federal government—such as low-income housing and social

security insurance—or the state—such as mental health and addiction services. But funding in both of these arenas declined dramatically in the 1970s
and 1980s. For example, New York's share of federal assistance for housing
production programs decreased from $1.2 billion in 1981 to $240 million in
1987.[23] Federal community development block grants declined by nearly a
third, from $259 million in 1980 to $177 in 1987.[24] State resources for mental
health and addiction counseling also plunged, with the state transferring savings from deinstitutionalization to other areas.[25]

Koch continuously lambasted federal and state retrenchment. Yet his administration was entirely opposed to filling these budgetary holes. His reasons
were numerous. For one, Koch believed the city's still-recovering economy
prevented him from doing more. But he was equally opposed because he was
weary of repeating what he believed to be one of the principal mistakes of
officials in prior decades: providing overly generous social welfare benefits that
attracted the poor and helped bankrupt the city.[26] With rates of homelessness
rising throughout many urban areas in the early 1980s, Koch believed that
if the city provided too many services, it risked not simply draining dollars
from its budget but incentivizing the region's homeless to come to New York.
This was particularly the case for costly proposals such as providing housing.
In response to demands that the city should prioritize renovated city-owned
housing for the homeless, Tony Gliedman, Commissioner of the Department
of Housing Preservation and Development, responded: "I am concerned
that the solution to the present problem begets a larger problem." He continued, "The more service you provide, the more people see it as an attrac-
tion, and will enter the system voluntarily."[27] Such a solution, the thinking
went, would not only attract the homeless from outside of the city but might
also risk propelling the thousands of New Yorkers in substandard housing
conditions—families living doubled and tripled up, for instance—into homelessness to improve their living conditions.

Limiting benefits thus remained an overriding policy objective, evident
even in Koch administration officials' policies toward shelter conditions.
Koch publicly maintained that no mentally stable individual would avoid
shelters, but his administration purposely maintained their bare bones
conditions, believing that doing otherwise might lure a voluntarily homeless
class of New Yorkers.[28] Make shelters nicer than the dilapidated housing in
which many poor New Yorkers lived and they may actually choose shelters
instead.

Koch knew that he had more leverage to force state officials to devote resources to homelessness than the federal government. He therefore

overwhelmingly placed the blame—and thus the fiscal responsibility for homelessness—on the state for its deinstitutionalization policies. Koch repeatedly asserted that individuals remained in public spaces solely because they were "psychotic," not because of conditions within shelters.[29] "It is time," Koch proclaimed, "for New York State to reassume the burden it so cavalierly dumped on local governments when it stopped providing care for a substantial portion of the mentally ill population."[30] While this political tactic had some truth to it, various studies showed that Koch's continual conflation of homelessness with mental illness overstated the link between the two.[31] What's more, despite his claims about mental health, Koch administration officials also refused to provide resources for mental health and addiction services for which the state had provided funding. Robert Trobe, deputy administrator of the Human Resources Administration, bluntly stated the overall policy: "Our goals are very clear—temporary shelter so no one freezes to death."[32]

In order for Koch's claims about deinstitutionalization to have credibility, he also had to ignore other causes of homelessness, such as his own development policies. Koch administration officials refused to acknowledge the role of J-51 tax abatements in underwriting the destruction of the SROs in which many among the poor had traditionally found shelter. Alongside advocates in SRO and poverty organizations, Laurence Klein, director of the Mayor's Office of SROs, pleaded with Koch as early as in January 1979 that SRO tenants undergoing conversion through J-51 were facing "vicious harassment" and displacement that was increasing homelessness.[33] "Without exaggeration" Klein told the mayor, "we are creating in Manhattan a class of homeless people, who should rival the Vietnamese boat people for our attention and sympathy."[34] But for years Koch, along with his Housing Commissioner Nathan Leventhal, as Klein described, remained "unalterably opposed to any limits imposed on J-51 conversions of SROs."[35]

Koch was so committed to blaming deinstitutionalization that well into the 1980s he refused even to acknowledge the roles of poverty and unaffordable housing in driving homelessness. This was true even though the city's own studies found that a growing number of individuals were arriving at shelter doors due to joblessness or eviction or having been forced to leave overcrowded housing with family or acquaintances.[36] Family homelessness, which exploded in the early and mid-1980s, underscored an even more obvious link between poverty and homelessness. When Koch took office, the city helped to shelter around a thousand families; most only sought shelter in the coldest parts of winter because their apartments or rooming houses had no heat.[37] This number tripled by 1984, fueled by inadequate income, unemployment, lack of affordable housing, and insufficient rental allowances for those on public assistance.[38]

Koch administration officials repeatedly defended their policies by pointing to the consistent opening of new shelters. Koch noted, correctly, that New York was the only major city that provided basic emergency shelter to those who requested it. "No other city in America is doing what we are doing," he stated.[39] Officials, however, failed to acknowledge that the Coalition for the Homeless took the administration to court more than thirty times to enforce even the bare bones conditions outlined by the decree.[40] Advocates also charged that Koch administration officials did little to develop a comprehensive plan to address the causes of homelessness or to help the homeless receive adequate resources to overcome their circumstances, which meant city policy was oriented around a seemingly endless cycle of opening new shelters to keep pace with rising homelessness. The average number of individuals in city shelters each night rose from 1,000 in 1978 to 3,000 in 1982 to over 6,500 in 1984. That year, over 30,000 individuals used the city's eighteen shelters.[41] Shelter expenditures—split between the city and state—rose from $7 million in 1977 to $32 million in 1982 to over $100 million by 1985.[42]

Koch's handling of homelessness increasingly came under fire by the mid-1980s not just from homeless individuals and advocates, but also journalists and prominent figures. Indeed, a commission Koch appointed found in 1985 that "the City has directed almost all of its effort and resources toward providing emergency shelters rather than developing measures to reduce the need for shelter." They also found that the principal cause was the lack of "low-cost housing," which was compounded by the fact that "no city agency has the ability to effectively" provide social services that "would allow individuals to live independently."[43] Homeless persons and advocates leveraged this criticism to win some important victories, such officials in 1986 endorsing a proposal for transitional and permanent housing based on different needs (e.g., the elderly or those with addictions).[44]

City resources, however, remained overwhelmingly targeted toward its shelter system. As the city devoted significant resources toward temporary shelter, Koch's rhetoric remained vitriolic whenever he described those who remained in public spaces. Koch used this position as the city's principal spokesperson on homelessness to blame their growing presence on individual pathology, alternatively depicting them as mentally ill or charlatans. As this strategy continued to fail to address either the underlining causes of homelessness or why so many homeless avoided shelters, the numbers of people residing in public spaces continued to rise.

The Seeming Intractability of Public Homelessness

By the mid-1980s, thousands of homeless individuals lived outside of the shelter system. Why many of these individuals congregated in public spaces instead of shelters was not a mystery. They said so. When Rajah Saunders, a homeless man in his late fifties, entered Fort Washington Men's Shelter, which housed nine hundred men in a single drill hall, he "took one look [and] handed back my meal ticket and left." It was "a sure taste of what hell will be like," Saunders believed.[45] Despite pleas from the homeless and advocates, city officials continued overwhelmingly to open large-scale shelters, instead of small facilities, because officials maintained they were more economical to run. Fort Washington, for example, had "endless rows of iron cots," which made it seem "like an emergency hospital for victims of some terrible natural disaster," the *Times* described.[46]

Many individuals also objected to the treatment they faced by staff, security, and administrators. Harold Hopkins, a homeless man in his fifties who lived in Penn Station, described how in the public shelters "they treat you like you're not a human being. They treat you like you're a dog."[47] Shelter residents "report the experience of being shunted from one bureaucrat to another leaves them feeling drained and passive," one advocate explained. "On the streets, homeless people feel that they have at least some control over their lives and can retain some dignity."[48] Conditions were no better in women's shelters. "City shelters are reprehensible," as Annie Quintano, a woman experiencing homelessness, put it. "The inhumane warehousing . . . The intrusive, unnecessary red tape is foreboding at best."[49] A coalition of female shelter residents and advocates described how residents are "verbally, physically, and at times sexually abused by shelter staff" who used threats of eviction "to silence complaints."[50]

Violence and crime were widespread in shelters. Eric White, a twenty-three-year-old man, preferred sleeping in Grand Central because shelters were "rougher than a jail house."[51] Shelters were "unsafe for both residents and staff," the Human Resources Administration Inspector General noted in 1987.[52] The city's own Shelter Security Task Force concluded that security guards were often part of the problem, finding "a lack of respect towards clients, fraternization between guards and clients, unprofessional behavior . . . and an inability or unwillingness to defuse explosive situations."[53]

A 1989 report on women's shelters found that residents faced physically abusive guards, verbally abusive staff, and punishment if they complained.[54]

Koch administration officials ignored or deflected criticism about shelters. At times, they simply feigned ignorance. "There is no question that there are people who will not and do not come into the shelter system, and I honestly cannot say why," said Suzanne Trazoff, a Human Resources Administration spokesperson, as late as 1988.[55] Koch, however, was most likely to blame the homeless themselves, insisting that they were simply too mentally ill to come into shelters. In a typical exchange, when told by a reporter that some people feared shelters, Koch "reacted with outrage, repeatedly shouting 'baloney, baloney,'" the *Times* reported.[56] People avoided the shelter system because "they are mentally disturbed or it's a scam," Koch maintained.[57] They were on the streets "because they are deranged."[58]

It was true that many homeless individuals who resided in public spaces had mental health difficulties. While poverty was the overall leading cause of homelessness, most estimates found that around one-third of the city's street population had mental health issues. Around one-third struggled with drug or alcohol addiction (these populations could overlap).[59] It was also likely that these individuals attracted greater attention while in public than the sizeable population without mental health or substance abuse issues. But Koch's insistence that essentially the entire public homeless population was simply "disturbed" and "deranged" overlooked the fact that many avoided shelters as dehumanizing, unsafe, or just simply unproductive spaces (shelters provided few notable services).[60] Koch's reductive claims instead sought to diminish the pressure to devote resources to improving shelters, let alone instituting measures to address poverty and housing insecurity. They also deflected attention from the role rampant real estate development played in contributing to homelessness.

Though Koch repeatedly expressed his desire for public spaces to be free of the homeless, he had limited means to force them off the streets. Although he could not send the police to arrest individuals without cause, he slowly expanded policing powers as public homelessness grew. Beginning in 1984, Koch declared that if temperatures dropped to below 5 degrees, including windchill, the police were authorized to remove individuals from public spaces and bring them to shelters or, if they refused, hospitals.[61] Such policies were arguably unnecessary since state law already allowed for involuntary commitment of individuals likely to cause serious harm to themselves or others.[62] Yet each subsequent year, Koch broadened this policy, first to authorize police to act when the temperature dropped below freezing, then to any time they believed an individual was in "imminent danger," and then in 1987 to when an individual was "incapable of taking care of themselves."[63] These policies were almost exclusively enforced in white, affluent areas of Manhattan.

Advocates charged Koch with using such programs to distract the public from ineffective policies. As Doug Lasdon of the Legal Action Center for the Homeless commented in 1987, by sending roundup teams into the streets, the Koch administration can say "'I'm doing everything I can. But the homeless don't want to come off the streets.'"[64] They deflected attention from initiatives to reduce homelessness among both the street population and the thousands more in shelters: affordable housing, social services, increased rental assistance and welfare, and job creation. Koch's removal order "diverts public discussion from the underlying causes of homelessness," wrote Norman Siegel and Robert Levy of the New York Civil Liberties Union, and encourages the public only "to see the homeless as mentally ill."[65] Ultimately, the city could find no more than a few hundred instances over the years in which even the expanded parameters of the law enabled city workers to commit an individual.

Though Koch wanted to take more aggressive steps against the homeless, for much of the 1980s, public opinion largely remained sympathetic toward them. There was little reason to believe that large-scale police sweeps would have endeared him to the public, even if they withstood constitutional challenges. Hayes, for instance, could still remark in late 1985 on the "surprisingly deep-rooted public sympathy for New York's homeless."[66] The prior year, a *Newsday* poll found three-quarters of New Yorkers believed that Koch needed to be doing more to help the homeless.[67]

But over the next few years, public opinion began to shift.[68] With little being done to address root causes, the numbers of homeless rose, and the problem increasingly seemed intractable to casual observers. Public sympathy waned; journalists and scholars would label this "compassion fatigue."[69] As Kim Hopper put it: people are thinking "'it's still going on after all these years and after all this money has been poured into it, maybe it's time to get tough.'"[70] Public homelessness garnered particular hostility because it was not difficult for the public to follow Koch's lead and conflate all of the homeless with mental illness. "Ed Koch is right . . . New York is like '*Night of the Living Dead*' with many of these people walking around in a trance," Roslyn Goldstein of the West Village wrote. "They belong back in the institutions from which they were removed in the 60's."[71]

The widespread emergence of panhandlers between the summers of 1987 and 1988 frayed public sympathy.[72] "Panhandlers," the *Times* described in the summer of 1988, suddenly "are all over town."[73] "I was raised never to pass a beggar by," one New Yorker bemoaned, "but there are too many of them and I'm sick of it."[74] While far from all panhandlers were homeless, they were almost always linked together in media articles and public commentaries about the growing public presence of the destitute. That panhandlers were often black and male no doubt contributed to diminishing public sympathy and augmented the perception that panhandlers were increasingly "aggressive." "It is becoming very dangerous just to go to and return home from work," a New Jersey resident wrote to the manager of the Port Authority, citing the rise of the homeless and panhandlers.[75]

William Young was one homeless panhandler. A former truck driver, he had lost his job and then his apartment. Like many panhandlers, he did not receive Medicaid and was dropped from welfare after a missed appointment. Young avoided shelters because they "are dangerous places, where violence often occurs" and found that social services were "designed to maintain and contain—and are not designed to help [the homeless] get back on their feet."[76] Young often begged at Grand Central or nearby subway stations. He used the money he received on food and transportation, including trips to the Bronx where he could make $20 a day unloading trucks and afford a room for the night, and to pay for his ulcer and blood pressure medications, which together cost over $3 a dose.

Young was not unusual. A major study of soup kitchen users found that 69 percent did not receive government benefits and that, of these, 42 percent resorted to panhandling in order to survive.[77] Often, even "those who are on public assistance are still living below the poverty level," Ed Abrahams of the Coalition for the Homeless observed, pointing to how even the $215 monthly assistance benefits these individuals received made it exceedingly difficult to afford an apartment.[78] In Abrahams's experience, many who panhandle "have sought [social services], only to find them inadequate or unavailable."

As homeless numbers continued to rise, a growing number—like Young—turned to the subways and transportation facilities. New York, after all, was a city with inclement weather, including a cold winter. If shelters proved undesirable, there was only so long that streets might suffice. In some senses, transportation centers proved ideal. They provided protection against the elements and had restrooms, discarded food, and, if desired, a consistent population from which to solicit donations. For many, these spaces also allowed for companionship and camaraderie with other homeless individuals.

The operators of the subway system as well as areas in and around three major transportation cities—Penn Station, Grand Central Station, and the

Port Authority, all within a mile of one another in midtown Manhattan—had no desire for them to become respites for the homeless. They were as equally troubled by the presence of the homeless as they were by the seeming inability of municipal officials to curtail their numbers. Yet these operators were not alone in their desire to combat public homelessness. A stream of powerful private actors—particularly real estate owners and business people, whose economic fortunes intersected with the vitality of these spaces—partnered with transportation facilities operators in responding to the homeless.

These spaces to which the homeless were turning were defended so vigorously in part because they were finally being infused with private and public capital, often for the first time in years. Public authority officials and private actors believed that the momentum for revitalizing these spaces would be reversed by homeless bodies. Combating homelessness was an economic imperative, necessary to ensure that these spaces spurred New York's post–fiscal crisis vibrancy—and did not drag the city back toward economic uncertainty. Private and public actors thus came together to ensure these spaces' continued revitalization and role in luring business, tourism, and middle-class and affluent residents.

"You Can't Call This a Homeless Issue . . . It is an Economic and Survival Issue"

Most visitors to or residents of New York would have spent time traveling its subway system or inside one of its three major transportation terminals. Penn Station was the destination point for hundreds of thousands of commuters from Long Island and New Jersey as well as passengers on Amtrak's northeast corridor. Individuals traversed Grand Central 80 million times a year on its subways and its commuter train lines that extended eighty-five miles north and seventy-five miles east.[79] Port Authority was a hub for bus travelers from across the country, along with suburban commuters. Although each facility was operated by different entities, the Metropolitan Transportation Authority (MTA), a public benefit corporation, had the single greatest reach, as it maintained the Metro-North commuter rails of Grand Central, the Long Island Railroad in Penn Station, and the entire subway system, with multiple lines at these terminals.

The conditions of all these spaces, like many other public areas, suffered during the economic difficulties of the 1970s. The subways had entered a prolonged period of deferred maintenance in the late 1960s, leading to increased delays, breakdowns, and refuse throughout the system. The graffiti that covered subway trains in the 1970s and early 1980s symbolized, to many New Yorkers and tourists alike, the decline and danger that engulfed the transit system during the urban and fiscal crises and their aftermath. With subway conditions and New York's population both declining, ridership fell, dropping in 1975 to levels not seen since the 1910s.[80]

As the economy improved, an influx of city and state funds poured into the subways and transportation centers. In the early 1980s, for example, the MTA won approval for an $8.6 billion capital improvement program to revitalize the entire subway system. By 1987, ridership was back up to 1974 levels.[81] "The MTA's massive subway rebuilding program has achieved much," one MTA official detailed in 1989, "4,300 cars overhauled or replaced, almost two-thirds of the track rebuilt, graffiti on the trains wiped out, and the reversal of a long decline in ridership."[82]

Funds to improve transportation systems and facilities did not come only from public coffers. In the case of Grand Central, private capital also spurred the revitalization. In 1985, several leaders within the real estate and business sectors around Grand Central formed the Grand Central Partnership. The group was tied to and influenced by the recent private revitalization efforts in Bryant Park, which sat just three blocks west of the terminal, and even hired the Bryant Park Restoration Corporation's president, Dan Biederman, to simultaneously serve as their own. The fifty-block area around Grand Central constituted the nation's third-largest business district and the Partnership soon became the city's largest BID.[83] At the time of the Partnership's founding, there was a "renovators' market" in the area, with extensive building renovations underway as demand for office space flourished. Though escalating real estate prices had led to various improvements to commercial buildings, the city's "upgrading of the public spaces has lagged behind what the private owners have done," Biederman explained.[84] Therefore, just as groups were doing for parks, the Partnership aimed to raise its own funds to make improvements throughout the area as well as to pressure the city for better sanitation, maintenance, and security.

The Partnership did not limit their efforts to the streets around Grand Central, however. They proposed a "beautification" plan for the station, which would bring "improved lighting, increased security, [and] a better tourist information center." The group quickly raised $300,000 from nearby corporations, hotels, and real estate owners to launch the first phase of the initiative.[85] Alongside this infusion of private capital, Metro-North announced a multimillion dollar improvement plan, which included upscaling the terminal's commercial offerings to attract higher-end restaurants and luxury retailers.[86] With the city once again attracting affluent residents and tourists in the late 1980s, those invested in Grand Central sought to transform it to better entice these customers.

The ambitious revitalization projects targeting the subways and transportation facilities clashed with the rapidly rising homeless population. As one 1988 Port Authority report put it, since 1983 public agencies in the New York/New Jersey area had spent $23.6 billion to make transportation centers "cleaner," "better lit," and tenanted by new "stores and restaurants." But this "modernization effort" had been met by "a simultaneous . . . movement on a different track": a growing homeless population.[87] By 1987, the *Times* reported, the three "ports of entry" for the city—Grand Central, Penn Station, and the Port Authority—had "become unofficial barracks for the homeless."[88] Similarly, the subways had become home to "colonies of the homeless" throughout its tunnels and stations and, increasingly, on the trains.[89] "I think the T[transit] A[authority] does a fine job with the subways," Jeffrey Wilson of the Upper East Side wrote in a letter to MTA officials about recent improvements. "Now if you could only throw the bums out."[90]

Koch officials continued to struggle to apply meaningful and constitutional methods to remove the homeless from public spaces. Officials at mid-decade began to use a loitering law first enacted before the 1939 World's Fair to justify police removal. Homeless advocates, however, challenged the law and won a series of favorable decisions that immediately discouraged its use before the state's highest court declared the law unconstitutional in early 1988. Koch administration officials lamented how "without an enforceable loitering law, we cannot prevent homeless from remaining" in public areas.[91] This did not, of course, mean that police could not harass the homeless. The treatment of the homeless in Penn Station has "worsened with vulgar, contemptuous and derogatory comments by police becoming more frequent," along with growing instances of "physical brutality," as one woman who lived in the station wrote to its manager at mid-decade.[92]

Nonetheless, with the ability to simply arrest the homeless for loitering curtailed, transportation officials turned to different methods. In Grand Central, where the number of homeless individuals grew to several hundred at mid-decade, Metro North removed all but one set of benches to prevent congregating and sleeping.[93] They then eliminated hundreds of lockers many homeless individuals used to store their belongings.[94] Ammonia replaced ordinary detergent for mopping floors to create a more noxious smell to dissuade sleeping.[95] Port Authority officials replaced wooden seats with flip seats that "require so much concentration to balance that sleeping or even sitting for long is impossible."[96] In warmer months, maintenance workers began hosing the sidewalks outside the terminal eighteen hours a day with water. "We're told to do it because it gets rid of the bums," said Danny Dunn, the contractor in charge. "They don't want to sit down and get wet, so they move. It works."[97]

Advocates argued that sweeping people out of public areas would do little to solve the problem of homelessness. Doing so "is plainly misguided . . . and cruelly immoral," Hayes and the Coalition wrote to Koch. "Poor people seek refuge in public places" because "they have been squeezed out of a devastated housing market and then siphoned away from a dangerous and intimidating municipal shelter system."[98] The Coalition also continued to make concrete proposals for how better to house homeless individuals; Koch administration officials consistently rejected them.[99] As they struggled to promote better policy, homeless advocates asked residents to allow the homeless to stay in public spaces. "Poverty, especially the visible kind that stretches out its hand and looks passersby in the eye, has always made Americans uneasy," Kim Hopper noted. "But the answer is not . . . to render invisible that which would otherwise disturb."[100]

Yet as the numbers of homeless individuals rose each year, tolerating the homeless became an increasingly difficult proposition for many New Yorkers to accept. "We've had 10 years of modern homelessness," Doug Lasdon observed, "and people have been walking past it for so long they're getting frustrated."[101] Indeed, the "tenor" of letters to the Transit Authority about the homeless for much of the 1980s was "please do something to help the homeless," wrote Lynette Thompson, who oversaw the outreach homeless program in the subway. But by mid-1989, "they've been saying 'just get them out' . . . It got worse and people got fed up."[102] These sentiments, however, did not mean users necessarily endorsed carceral measures. The MTA's own surveys, for instance, found that "the vast majority of riders do not want increased police sanctions against beggars, and clearly consider other problems such as loud radios, delays, and dirt as far more serious problems in the subway."[103]

Nonetheless, the homeless and panhandling population remained major concerns to station operators. This alarm was likely amplified because this population was overwhelmingly black and male.[104] Objections to the homeless rarely mentioned race, but media articles on the "problems" of subways and transportation facilities lumped together discussions of crime with the homeless with increasing frequency in the late 1980s. For example, a *Times* article on the Port Authority in 1988 described how a growing police presence was responding "to a steep rise in drug-related crime . . . and to the growing ranks of homeless people living there."[105] Another *Times* article on the subways linked together "brazen acts of turnstile vandals and token thieves," robberies, young gangs, and the homeless.[106] Such articles rarely offered proof that the homeless were behind these crimes, but this did not stop media from conflating the homeless with drug dealing, vandalism, and black males. These depictions both reflected and reinforced anxieties among city-dwellers already concerned with crime and likely to associate poor African American men with criminality. While New York's homeless had historically faced harsh treatment, the shift in the 1980s in the composition of public homelessness to African Americans gave particular urgency to combatting a population increasingly viewed as dangerous and growing.[107]

That the public spaces the homeless were taking residence in were vital to the city's economy was especially alarming. As one advisor to the subway system emphasized, the presence of the homeless and panhandlers "undermines not only the subway but the quality of life and the economic vitality of New York City, which is uniquely dependent among American cities on underground transit."[108] There are "600,000 travelers, commuters, visitors, business people from here and abroad who pass through our portals every day and see the homeless," Stephen Berger, executive director of the Port Authority, estimated. "Who will want to relocate a business here? Try to induce workers to come here, to live and work and move here? You can't call this a homeless issue. It is much broader. It is an economic and survival issue for the region—as much and, in many ways, similar to the fiscal crisis of the last decade."[109]

Koch administration officials, already averse to public homelessness, aimed to buttress efforts to remove the homeless from transportation facilities. He urged transportation officials to "take the necessary measures to compel those who are loitering . . . to leave."[110] If a homeless person were to "go into Macy's department store and lie down on the floor and go to sleep, I would assume Macy's would ask you to leave," Koch stated, ignoring the distinction between public and private property.[111] Koch also ordered the city's legal department to investigate ways public facilities could use vagrancy, loitering, and trespassing laws to prevent the homeless from staying in such facilities without running afoul of constitutionality concerns.[112] Administration officials were particularly impressed with regulations the Port Authority enacted that limited sleeping and living in the terminal and formulated measures to dissuade noncommuter use of the bus terminal.[113] City lawyers believed these provisions skirted constitutional issues by prohibiting specific activities rather than instituting a blanket anti-loitering provision, which was not possible in a public space.[114]

The Koch administration also used other city resources to remove the homeless from these areas. For example, at mid-decade the Penn Station area was undergoing a real estate boom and several empty properties began to attract real estate developers, including the former Gimbels flagship store.[115] At a meeting with Koch, three deputy mayors, and prominent developers who had recently purchased the mammoth Gimbels property, officials promised that they would help "clean up the area and rid the tunnel linking Sixth and Seventh Avenues of its large homeless population."[116] Koch officials worked with the Transit Authority on developing ways of "solving the problem to [the developers'] satisfaction," including various physical improvements— such as brighter lighting and narrowing or gating off passageways—to prevent sleeping or gatherings.[117] The MTA then pledged $5.6 million toward redeveloping the tunnels and station, a six fold increase over renovation plans made in 1980.[118]

But as the efforts by municipal and transportation officials were slow to bear fruit in deterring the homeless, private sector groups began to take a greater role. The Grand Central Partnership, in particular, took the lead in these efforts. To do so, it advocated a more aggressive strategy than the one GCP President Dan Biederman and others had utilized in the early years of their work in Bryant Park. In the early 1980s, the Bryant Park Restoration Corporation had largely been guided by the notion that the way to remove "undesirable" populations was to crowd them out with "desirable" users through campaigns to increase usage by the broader public. By the late 1980s, the GCP turned to policing and security as the means to bring more "desirable" customers to businesses as well as corporate tenants to commercial buildings. The Partnership especially utilized its thirty-person security force, which it funded with the Restoration Corporation at the cost of a million dollars a year in 1989.[119] Each officer had direct radio access to the police and the force had its own headquarters on Lexington Avenue.[120] "It's not that police are doing a bad job," Biederman explained. "It's that we think the private sector can help to make the situation better."[121]

The Grand Central Partnership also continued to target the terminal itself. It collaborated with the MTA to develop and implement more stringent user policies within the terminal, which private and public security could use as a basis for removing the homeless, including measures that banned changing or washing clothes in restrooms, taking up more than one seat, and lying on floors, stairs, or landings.[122] The station also closed off the main waiting room, where as many as two hundred homeless people gathered before the terminal closed at 1:30 AM, for a two year renovation (a small waiting area remained open but was limited to ticketed passengers). The MTA, as Peter Stangle, president of Metro-North Commuter Railroad, stated bluntly, was not undertaking a renovation of "Grand Central Terminal for the purpose of accommodating homeless."[123]

These types of private sector–led initiatives spread to other parts of Manhattan. Just a few years after helping form the GCP, Biederman was hired by several major property owners to help create the 34th Street Partnership, a BID for the twenty-eight block area around Penn Station. The Partnership applied the same strategy as the GCP, quickly employing fifty sanitation workers and a fifty-person security force to help police the homeless and similarly undesirable populations around Penn Station.[124]

These private sector initiatives thus helped to expand the strategies for combating homelessness from physically changing spaces—such as increasing lighting and installing benches on which it was impossible to lay down—to more aggressive regulations that were enforced by private security patrols and the police. While aggressive policing of the homeless was not new, the GCP strategies amplified a strategy of using large-scale private security in a concentrated area to remove the homeless.

The MTA soon adopted a similarly intensified policing strategy throughout the subway system. MTA officials believed that the homeless threatened to reverse the recent progress they had made through their multibillion dollar revitalization campaign. While the MTA had been accelerating their efforts around homelessness and other perceived signs of "disorder" for years, the numbers of homeless individuals in the system had only grown.[125] In response, in October 1989, MTA officials launched a public campaign called Operation Enforcement.[126] The MTA police would enforce a zero tolerance policy against acts like panhandling, begging, lying down, sleeping, littering, and drinking alcohol.[127] Like the Grand Central plan, this strategy ostensibly targeted behaviors—and supposedly not the status of being homeless—which seemed to make the program constitutionally viable. The intent was nonetheless clear. "One does not have to be a mental giant to see where this is intended—to rid the subways of the homeless," observed William McKechnie, president of the 3,800-member Transit Police Benevolent Association.[128]

The MTA justified the campaign by pointing to alarming incidents attributed to the homeless. Station fires, for example, many of which were likely caused by homeless individuals attempting to keep warm in winter months, tripled between 1986 and 1989.[129] But the policy was as much about perceived effects of homelessness as actual ones. This position was not dissimilar to the one Koch had promoted for years: the very presence of the homeless was a blight on public space. As Stephen Berger put it: "The fact is . . . the deterioration of the quality of life, both real and perceived, created by the growing number of homeless, must inevitably erode the vitality and health of commercial enterprises in the region."[130]

This notion was expanded by two academics, George Kelling and James Q. Wilson, who developed the criminology theory of "broken windows."[131] Kelling and Wilson stressed the link between small signs of "disorder"—panhandling, public drinking, vandalism—and crime. They claimed that these minor instances promoted an atmosphere of lawlessness and encouraged the criminally inclined to engage in more significant crime. Just as importantly, they engendered fear, causing law-abiding individuals to use public spaces less frequently, which ceded more ground to criminal elements. MTA officials did not need to look far to find evidence for the theory. Biederman, for example, credited the broken windows strategy with the Restoration Corporation's success in "retaking" Bryant Park as well as in his work with the GCP.[132] Kelling himself pointed glowingly to Biederman's work in Bryant Park as the model representation of his theory for restoring order to a public space.[133]

MTA officials believed that the theory captured their own experience with graffiti over the prior two decades. Graffiti had created an impression of lawlessness in the subways; as the MTA eliminated graffiti, ridership rose. "We know from our experience with removing graffiti from trains and buses that the signs and symbols of disorder communicate to our customers that the transit system is out of control and, therefore, dangerous," MTA Chairman Robert Kiley explained.[134] The MTA believed that the homeless, panhandlers, and other undesirable elements had caused ridership levels to again decline, threatening shortfalls in revenue. In order "to restore our passengers' confidence in the subway environment and to give them a sense of security when they use the transit system," Alan Kiepper, president of the New York City Transit Authority, wrote, "our police officers must address not only serious crime . . . but also the less serious violations of the Transit Authority Rules."[135]

Operation Enforcement was adopted wholesale from the broken windows textbook. MTA officials had even hired Kelling as a consultant to "evaluate the organizational strategies" of the transit police and to develop the program that became Operation Enforcement.[136] Kelling enacted a twofold strategy. First, he proposed the vigorous enforcement of the "theory of crime causation" that underpinned broken windows. Lumping together acts that were actually crimes (e.g., turnstile-hoping and vandalism) with those associated with the homeless and poor (e.g., holding out a cup for spare change and sleeping), Kelling claimed that these acts equally create "in citizens the sense that things are out of control and that nobody cares. These circumstances, in turn, embolden persons so-inclined to be increasingly obstreperous—even aggressive and criminal. As a consequence, such behavior threatened the viability of the subway system by generating high levels of fear in the passengers, thereby discouraging use of the system."[137] Kelling maintained that this environment led to "serious crime as well," though he did not produce evidence to confirm these claims.[138]

Second, Kelling encouraged the conflation of homelessness and poverty with individual pathology, making punitive responses more acceptable. He maintained that "many panhandlers are not homeless or needy persons; they are people who exploit the confines of the system to intimidate others into giving them money."[139] Kelling simultaneously acknowledged that there were many actual homeless and destitute people, but proclaimed that they should not be allowed to stay or beg there "for their own well-being" because they were "males who have a lengthy history of alcohol and drug abuse and mental illness."[140] Kelling thus continued to conflate homelessness and individual pathology to justify removing them through aggressive measures.

Organizations like the Coalition for the Homeless offered the MTA detailed proposals outlining alternatives to punitive measures. "We should recognize that homelessness is a political, social and economic problem and we should not transform the homeless into a law enforcement problem," pleaded several homeless groups including the Coalition and the homeless-led United Homeless Organization.[141] Instead of simply being offered shelters, the Coalition maintained, those experiencing homelessness needed long-term supportive housing and "rescue centers that would be small, decent, community-based facilities that would provide short-term accommodations and assessment."[142] But these proposals were largely ignored.

The MTA, however, soon faced a more powerful opponent with the election of David Dinkins as mayor in the fall of 1989. A liberal Democrat, Dinkins had spent years as Manhattan borough president criticizing Koch's policies, especially the emphasis on a massive shelter system that was neither "humane nor cost-effective."[143] Homelessness had been a major issue in the mayoral campaign, structured by the question, as *Newsday* put it early in the election, of "whether a kinder, gentler policy toward the homeless or a tougher, meaner one will win more votes."[144] Koch's campaign unsurprisingly tilted in the latter direction, with the mayor beginning 1989 by announcing that removing the homeless from public spaces as subways and parks would be a top priority.[145]

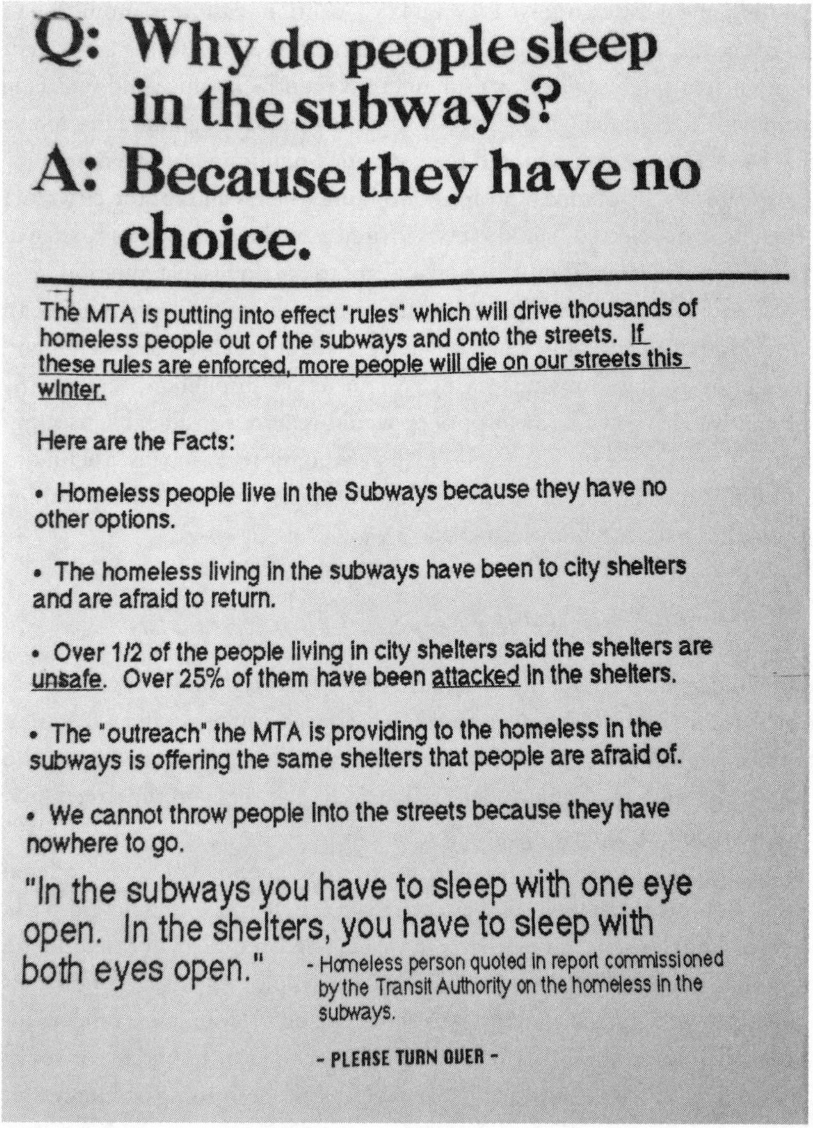

Q: Why do people sleep in the subways?
A: Because they have no choice.

The MTA is putting into effect "rules" which will drive thousands of homeless people out of the subways and onto the streets. If these rules are enforced, more people will die on our streets this winter.

Here are the Facts:

• Homeless people live in the Subways because they have no other options.

• The homeless living in the subways have been to city shelters and are afraid to return.

• Over 1/2 of the people living in city shelters said the shelters are unsafe. Over 25% of them have been attacked in the shelters.

• The "outreach" the MTA is providing to the homeless in the subways is offering the same shelters that people are afraid of.

• We cannot throw people into the streets because they have nowhere to go.

"In the subways you have to sleep with one eye open. In the shelters, you have to sleep with both eyes open." - Homeless person quoted in report commissioned by the Transit Authority on the homeless in the subways.

- PLEASE TURN OVER -

FIGURE 6.2 The Coalition for the Homeless and other homeless advocacy organizations struggled to prevent more punitive policies against those experiencing homelessness from being enacted.

Courtesy of Coalition for the Homeless.

Dinkins, in contrast, endorsed several key Coalition platforms, promising to cut to the heart of the problem of public homelessness by closing 80 percent of municipal single shelters within eighteen months in office and replacing them with transitional and permanent housing as well as community rescue centers.[146] His election reflected the continued public appeal of a more progressive governing platform both toward homelessness and for the city more generally. Once elected, Dinkins even invited homeless individuals Koch had recently evicted from Tompkins Square Park to attend his inauguration.[147]

When Dinkins assumed office in January 1990, his administration faced a population of 35,000 individuals seeking private or public shelter each night, in addition to the thousands trying to find refuge in public spaces.[148] Any substantive change to homeless policy would require considerable fiscal resources. But because the city faced a major economic recession just as Dinkins took office, the new mayor faced significant obstacles in shifting the prevailing approaches to public homelessness.

Dinkins and the Perpetual Homeless Crisis

As Dinkins's mayoral tenure began, he continued to distance himself from Koch's record on homelessness as well as aggressive initiatives like Operation Enforcement. Police sweeps of the estimated 3,000 to 4,000 individuals who lived in the subways, Dinkins declared, merely "put them on the streets, and they just come right back again."[149]

But facing an immediate decline in the city's economy, Dinkins offered scant resources that might help coax the MTA toward a different approach. Indeed, Dinkins told Kiley that even continued resources for a program in which Human Resources Administration employees engaged homeless individuals at "targeted stations" was "not realistic."[150] Municipal officials instead called upon the MTA to devote more of its own resources for social service and volunteer outreach.[151] The MTA had been using Volunteers of America to offer homeless individuals food, medical attention, and transportation to shelters. But "we, as a transportation provider," as Kiley wrote to Dinkins, "are ill equipped to provide the support services these people desperately need."[152] What's more, even this strategy—which relied on directing individuals to the shelter system to which they did not want to return—was not very effective, something Kiley stressed to the mayor. Less than 10 percent of the 54,600 individuals contacted agreed to go to city shelters. Shelter conditions had hardly improved under Dinkins, something administration officials acknowledged. "We agree with you that the City shelters are not the best option for the homeless individuals residing in the subway system," Deputy Mayor Norman Steisel confessed to advocates. "However, it is the only option available at present."[153]

Dinkins administration officials did little to fulfill his campaign promise to provide more permanent housing or create viable options beyond shelters. At the end of his first year, 20,000 individuals entered municipal shelters, but only seventy-two men and women were placed into permanent housing.[154] "Fiscal constraints preclude us from dedicating any new money to our capital budget programs," Deputy Mayor Steisel explained.[155] The administration, however, did find funds for other measures, including a $1.8 billion "safe streets" initiative in the summer of 1990 in response to concerns about crime. Top Dinkins advisors privately told the Coalition for the Homeless that they could not devote similar allocations to homelessness because "people just don't care anymore."[156]

With seemingly no shift in municipal policy or resources, Dinkins offered little to dissuade the MTA from continuing Operation Enforcement alongside regular police sweeps of the homeless. Under new Transit Police Chief William Bratton—a devotee of broken windows who was personally recruited by Kiley and Kelling—these policies broadened.[157] Bratton, for example, instructed transit officers to eject all panhandlers—even those simply extending a cup—without any first warnings and even in subfreezing weather.[158] By early 1991 subway ejections rose thirteen times from what they were in December 1989.[159]

Other station officials soon implemented similarly aggressive policing policies that built on the approaches of the GCP and the MTA. Port Authority officials plastered 250 posters throughout the terminal announcing Operation Alternative, which would evict anyone for loitering, panhandling, drinking, or sleeping, even in subfreezing weather.[160] Officials hired 140 new police officials to enforce the policy. Despite the fact that the bus station did indeed have high rates of crime, combating homelessness was the most prominent feature of the campaign. Just as with broken windows, officials pointed to the need for such an aggressive course because of perceptions of the homeless rather than their actual actions. "There is a feeling of discomfort and lack of security among the commuters because of the presence of the homeless," said Richard Kelly of the Port Authority. "We want our customers to perceive the bus terminal as a clean, safe place to come to."[161]

Unlike the MTA, the Port Authority instituted an on-site assessment center in which a counselor could evaluate and refer individuals "to the appropriate social service agency."[162] The center's opening was cited as justification for the more aggressive measures, as they allowed Port Authority police to offer each person a choice: go to the referral center, leave the terminal, or be arrested. "No matter how cold it is outside, if the person is sitting or lying on the floor—no matter how harmless they are—we have to tell them to leave or lock them up," explained Port Authority Police Officer Mike Defilippis.[163] Within a year, the Port Authority removed nearly 7,000 homeless persons.[164] Not coincidentally, shortly after the enactment of Operation Alternative, Port Authority officials announced a $90 million renovation plan that upscaled the terminal's commercial businesses and brought new "restrooms, brighter lighting and signs, and the elimination of many small open spaces where homeless people gather."[165] A few years later, the *Times* reported that while the station had previously been "filled with homeless people" and "tawdriness," now "nicely dressed crowds patronize clean, well-lighted shops resembling a bustling suburban shopping mall."[166]

The Grand Central Partnership also expanded their work into providing services that accompanied aggressive policing measures. The group entered into a $1 million contract with city officials to operate a drop-in center, following a major lobbying effort by the group.[167] Area businesses supplemented the effort with an additional half-million dollars.[168] Just as in the Port Authority, the ability to offer limited referral services and rides to shelters justified stepped up policing in which homeless individuals were increasingly ticketed, ejected, or arrested.

The GCP soon contracted out its combination of limited social service offerings and private policing. Within just a few years, over one-third of GCP's social service budget came from "businesses wishing to have GCP outreach workers clear their premises of homeless people."[169] Area banks paid the Partnership close to a million dollars each year to prevent the homeless from residing in and around ATM vestibules. Additionally, several residential groups near Grand Central solicited the Partnership's assistance. The Tudor City Association, for example, had grown frustrated by the inability of the police to remove a homeless encampment and paid the GCP several thousand dollars each month to do so.[170] The combination of offering services and security workers physically and verbally abusing individuals ended the encampment.[171] A few years later, the GCP became engulfed in a major scandal and lost a half-million dollars in federal grants when news broke that employees harassed and physically brutalized homeless individuals in order to drive them out of ATM vestibules and public areas.[172]

The increasingly aggressive measures by both public authorities and private sector groups in the subways and terminals led homeless peoples to take refuge outdoors. The Parks Department reported that the number of individuals living in parks jumped from 271 in March 1989 to 1,580 in the summer of 1990. The homeless spanned essentially every park in the system, including several hundred in the newly renovated Central Park and forty in major Manhattan parks like Union Square and Madison Square.[173] "We have nothing to offer people other than our shelters, which they do not seem to want to use," noted Nancy Wackstein, the director of the Mayor's Office on Homelessness.[174]

City officials had first taken aim at the growing homeless presence in parks under Koch. In 1989, Parks Commissioner Henry Stern proposed more aggressive measures than even those Koch had suggested: prohibitions on begging, laying on a bench, and sleeping overnight, along with provisions that limited possessing or accumulating personal belongings.[175] These rules would have effectively outlawed most homeless from the parks. Considerable opposition from homeless and park advocates like the Parks Council prevented the harshest of these provisions from being enacted.[176]

Instead, the Parks Department imposed curfews to prevent the homeless from sleeping in parks overnight. The policy was ultimately successful in its goals, but resulted in heated battles in Tompkins Square Park, located the rapidly gentrifying East Village. The city first tried to impose a curfew in the summer of 1988, leading to a riot involving over 400 police officers.[177] In 1989, 300 officers in riot gear removed over 150 homeless individuals living in a tent city.[178] Finally, under the Dinkins administration in the summer of 1991, the park was closed and sealed for fourteen months for a $4 million renovation. When it was reopened, it had a high metal fence and a strictly enforced midnight curfew. "The park is not going to be a campground [for homeless] again," announced Parks Commissioner Betsy Gotbaum.[179]

Pushing the homeless out of one park often meant they went to another and by the late 1980s, the growing number of private organizations that fundraised and managed parks alongside city government began to confront the homeless presence. In late 1985, Union Square Park, for example, had closed for thirteen months to undergo a $3.6 million renovation funded by the Parks Department and a private development corporation formed by area businesses. After its reopening, the 14th Street Union Square Business Improvement District, which had formed out of the development corporation, took a greater role in park operations. As the homeless population rose in the early 1990s, the group paid for fencing and worked with police to impose a midnight curfew. BID Director Robert Walsh also "emptied all the budget lines out" to devote the BID's resources to security and sanitation.[180]

"When I started seeing tents and a hundred people one night like an outdoor shelter, I became frightened," Walsh explained. "We're just trying to protect our own turf. With the other parks closed, you really have no choice."[181]

In some cases, concerns about the homeless presence even helped spur the formation of new private groups that gained control over parks. In response to the growing number of homeless in Madison Square Park, for example, the city enacted an overnight curfew. The businesses in the rapidly revitalizing area around the park then formed a Conservancy group that helped raise several million dollars to hire a park manager, maintenance workers, and security guards to enforce park policies and curfews.[182]

The Central Park Conservancy also contended with the rising homeless population. In the late 1980s, roughly two hundred homeless individuals were largely allowed to sleep in the park.[183] "Every morning the early maintenance crews do a 'sweep' of the Park in which homeless are moved on," Central Park Administrator Elizabeth Barlow Rogers explained.[184] But the Conservancy faced increasing pressure to do more from users and especially from major donors to the organization. "You are not responsible for curing the addiction, mental illness, etc. of the people who sleep in the park, but you are responsible for seeing that the park is not used as a campground. It closes at night and this rule must be enforced," prominent financier and donor Thomas G. Kahn wrote to the Conservancy. "I have been delighted to support the Conservancy's effort in the past, but I am loathe to do so in the future if Central Park is becoming an illegal campground for street people."[185] With the space too large to fence off, the Conservancy soon began working with police to begin strictly enforcing an overnight curfew and destroying structures used for sleeping.

Dinkins administration officials also continued to face pressure to take action on public homelessness. "Not a single week goes by where my office does not receive a request from an elected official, another City agency or community people to 'do something' about a particular group of homeless people" in public space, lamented Nancy Wackstein, director of the Mayor's Office on Homelessness.[186] The public was largely unaware of the inefficiencies of municipal policies but all too conscious of the growing number of homeless bodies appearing in public spaces. "After a decade of talk and little action, people are just fed up with the sight and smell of homeless people on the street," acknowledged Mary Brosnahan, the executive director of the Coalition for the Homeless.[187]

Such growing frustration was exhibited in and amplified by the media. At the end of Dinkins's first year in the office, the *New York Times* published an editorial series on how to "restore New York City." It described how "the heart of civility and of urban life" was the streets, but that New York's currently "resemble a New Calcutta." The series argued that the city needed to "reclaim the streets" by "fighting three related enemies," urging action against growing crime, trash, and getting "the homeless off the streets."[188] The series marked an astonishing progression in equating homeless people with trash and crime in mainstream discourse over just a few years.

Caught between growing public animosity and an economic downturn that constrained municipal resources, Dinkins administration officials shifted their position. In Dinkins's second year in office, for example, the administration came out in support of Bratton's rigid enforcement of broken windows as a needed effort to "reclaim the subway system."[189] Dinkins also began to target the large homeless encampments in public spaces—doing so with a frequency that outpaced Koch. Officials bemoaned how the homeless in these encampments "reject the City shelters as unsafe and undesirable" even as they acknowledged that shelters were indeed inadequate and unwelcoming.[190] But "maybe if you turn down the comfort level in public places they will come inside," as one official put it.[191] Though these encampments grew throughout the city, Dinkins officials ordered their removal overwhelmingly in wealthy or gentrifying areas of Manhattan like Riverside Park and in Columbus Circle, near the Convention and Visitors Bureau.[192] The Columbus encampment sent "extremely negative signals" to tourists and business travelers, Convention and Visitors Bureau President Marshall Murdaugh believed. "While we're trying to market the city on a worldwide basis, this is a liability."[193] Homeless individuals increasingly moved out of Manhattan and into the outer boroughs, where they typically faced less harassment.[194]

This turnaround in Dinkins's positions, coupled with more aggressive policing of public homelessness, did more than simply disappoint advocates. It transformed their demands. Since the beginning of the crisis in the late 1970s, advocated overwhelmingly emphasized the need for government to lead the response to homelessness. Although they highlighted private and nonprofit initiatives, they overwhelmingly did so as models for government. They had, for example, long pointed to well-run religiously affiliated shelters as ideal small-scale emergency respites in which those sheltered were offered resources and treated with respect. Similarly, they had highlighted nonprofits that combined permanent affordable housing with social services as a model for the kind of facilities government should develop. By and large, advocates believed that pressuring government was preferable to privatizing services. As prominent advocates Steve Banks and Doug Lasdon put it in 1987, nonprofits have "served somewhat as a model for the city's own provision of emergency housing and services. But it would be a mistake to [allow] the city to privatize a governmental obligation." Lasdon continued, "privatization of government functions is actually a very dangerous concept. Rather than being charity, assistance should be your right. When it is charity, [implicit] in that is the ability to take it away at any time."[195]

But by the early 1990s, the position of many advocates changed. As, for example, the Coalition chronicled the continued dangerous and abusive conditions of city shelters in yet another report, the group concluded that the findings "are more than an indictment of the City in its failed attempt to operate safe shelters for the homeless . . . they are proof that after ten years, the City is ill-suited for this responsibility."[196] Increasingly, homeless advocates began to point to private, nonprofit services as replacements—not models— for government initiatives.

This position was also gaining steam beyond the advocates who had long criticized municipal efforts. In January 1991, for example, a *Times* editorial titled "When City Hall Fails, Do It Yourself," praised not just the GCP's policing and sanitation efforts but its homeless service center as a needed private sector–led initiative that should be replicated, as city government was "overwhelmingly preoccupied by fiscal crisis."[197] Later that year Dinkins appointed a Commission on the Homeless, chaired by Andrew Cuomo, the son of Governor Mario Cuomo, who had founded a private nonprofit that developed housing for the homeless. The Commission's report called for a vast overhaul of the entire governmental response to homelessness, which it declared an "indisputable . . . policy failure" that cost the city and state about $400 million a year.[198] "Unsafe and expensive shelters that fail as a housing resource and provide too few services and too little hope of future independence make no sense," the Commission concluded. [199] Public homelessness was further proof of such failures. The current system had led to a "large number of homeless adults in New York City's transportation facilities, parks, street corners and other public places," a situation that was "intolerable."[200]

In place of the municipal shelter system, the Commission recommended "not-for-profitization"—closing or turning over existing shelters to nonprofit operators who would run or develop new small shelters offering services designed for different populations. Transferring responsibility to nonprofits would "accelerate the delivery of badly needed facilities and services" and do so more cheaply and efficiently than "public sector development," Mark Page, the city's General Counsel, contended.[201] Homeless services would join the other areas that in recent years had been offloaded to outside government.

The Commission also recommended that the city essentially repli-
cate the strategy pioneered by the Grand Central Partnership and Port
Authority: increased services coupled with harsher policing. It called for
the city to target the homeless residing in public spaces by contracting with
nonprofits to increase outreach and develop referral centers. Once the homeless were offered these (temporary) alternatives, however, the Commission
recommended strict and consistent "enforcement of existing ordinances related to behavior in public space in its new community policing initiative."[202]

The Commission's report was largely heralded in the press. "The Cuomo
commission," the *Times* wrote, "offers the momentum needed to break the
political paralysis that has left thousands suffering on the streets or in squalid
shelters."[203] Critics, like the editors of the housing advocacy magazine *City
Limits*, lambasted the plan's emphasis on shelters rather than "substantive
plans to end the crisis of homelessness."[204] Alongside other housing and
some homeless advocacy organizations, the editors maintained that "any
attempt to focus on shelters instead of permanent housing is a grave mistake." Nonetheless, Dinkins eventually endorsed most of the Commission's
recommendations, including privatizing homeless services and shifting the
blanket right to shelter toward a model that pressured homeless individuals
and families to go through programs and treatments as a condition of receiving shelter and housing.

Dinkins's remaining years in office were marked by a slow transition to
not-for-profit shelters, while maintaining vigorous police enforcement
against Manhattan homeless encampments. Indeed, during the 1993 mayoral
election, Dinkins's Republican opponent, Rudolph Giuliani, stressed that he
would privatize homeless services and use the police to clamp down on public
homelessness. In response, Dinkins administration officials noted that they
had been working on doing exactly that. "As far as I can see, he's talking about
doing the things that we're already doing," acknowledged First Deputy Mayor
Norman Steisel, reflecting how far Dinkins had drifted away from his stance
in the 1989 campaign.[205]

WHILE THERE WERE profound similarities between the homeless policies
of Dinkins and those proposed by Giuliani, there were also critical differences.
Giuliani's proposals, including undoing the right to shelter provision, were
clearly more hostile to homelessness than were Dinkins's. Giuliani's campaign
relied heavily on a message of confronting various "quality of life" issues—
public homelessness, panhandlers, "squeegee men," litter, and crime—through
an even more aggressive form of broken windows policing.

After Giuliani defeated Dinkins by a narrow margin, he wasted no time following through on this campaign promise. William Bratton, appointed by Giuliani as chief of police, brought broken windows policing out of the subway system and to the entire city. This strategy vastly accelerated punitive and carceral measures against the homeless.[206] Advocates had for years proclaimed that, in formulating a policy response to public homelessness, "until we offer a decent alternative these people aren't going anywhere," as Doug Lasdon put it.[207] But Bratton's broken windows policing—modeled on initiatives carried out in the subways and in the Grand Central business district—did indeed show there was another way: police harassment and incarceration.

Giuliani, for his part, offered no pretense about "solving" the crisis of public homelessness; he instead professed that his aim was to remove the homeless from sight. With Bratton at the helm, the number of homeless individuals in public did indeed decline significantly during Giuliani's two terms. But the overall number of homeless people rose over 20 percent to nearly 30,000.[208] At the same time, Giuliani focused on privatizing existing shelters, while placing little emphasis on closing warehouse-style shelters, creating small scale transitional shelters, or developing permanent affordable housing for the poor.[209]

Nearly fifteen years before Giuliani took office, advocates for the homeless had laid out a blueprint for effectively curtailing homelessness. Although both homeless individuals and advocates consistently pressured officials, there was little political will to devote the resources to do so. At times, homeless bodies, along with the work of homeless and domiciled advocates, served as a spur to force government to address systemic failures; more often, however, public homelessness was depicted as being the sole result of individual pathologies.[210]

Years earlier, advocates had worried openly about what the ramifications of ineffective policy would mean for people experiencing homelessness. "I'm concerned that the city is spending 'bad' money, which will give the homeless a bad reputation," Hayes noted in 1983.[211] He observed how "what happens too frequently is the politicians who preside over the government agencies which fail don't get the blame. The people who are supposed to be receiving the benefits of these tax dollars receive the blame when government fails to execute properly."[212] Hayes's words would prove prophetic.

Indeed, by the late 1980s and early 1990s, the equation of public homelessness and individual failing appeared regularly in mainstream media depictions. "During the last two years," a 1993 *City Limits* editorial described, "nearly every time an article about homelessness has appeared in *The New York Times, New York Magazine, The Wall Street Journal* and many other newspapers and magazines, the reporters have either explicitly or implicitly assumed that most homeless people are in dire circumstances as a result of mental illness, drug addiction or some other character deficiency. . . . Accepting that premise is the easiest way to avoid responsibility for dealing with social and economic inequities in our city."[213]

Rising rates of homelessness and the gaining traction of homelessness-as-pathology narratives created an ideal environment for more punitive measures targeting public homelessness, especially as this population was overwhelming black and male. These punitive responses were driven not just by officials' depictions of the homeless and the perceived inadequacies of public policy to quell public homelessness, but the rising value of public spaces in the 1980s. It was little coincidence that the subway system, which the MTA had recently spent billions reinvigorating, was among the earliest locations in which aggressive policing policies toward public homelessness were enacted. Similarly, the most forceful "public removal" campaigns of the homeless under Koch overwhelmingly targeted capital rich areas of Manhattan. Additionally, the most pointed punitive measures proposed against public homelessness during the Koch administration occurred through the Parks Department, which had in just the prior few years begun to revitalize parks, often with the support of private capital. The new imperatives of the post–fiscal crisis city were not just to protect rising land and real estate values but also to make the city more attractive to middle-class and affluent residents, business, and tourists. Public homelessness became understood as akin to problems like crime and refuse-infested parks: a threat that could reverse the revitalization of public spaces, with all of their importance for the economy.

The growth of and response to public homelessness ultimately reflected the culmination of trends that began during the urban crisis and were hastened by the fiscal crisis. 1980s New York was marked by a growing embrace of private sector governance over public space, vigorous private-public defense of land values, privatization, and initiatives to attract white middle class and affluent consumer spending, all of which shaped the response to public homelessness. These shifts also enabled the private sector to take a major role in the response. As city officials seemed not to be doing enough to quell the rising numbers of homeless peoples in the 1980s, these actors began to take an increasingly influential role in homeless politics and in protecting the increased value of real estate in the post–fiscal crisis city. Their initiatives built on over a decade of growth of the private sector exerting greater influence in and even control over public space. Ultimately, the "successful" efforts of the private sector and public benefit corporations in removing the homeless from the subways, transportation centers, and business districts would underpin the implementation of citywide broken windows policies toward the homeless and other "undesirable elements" in public space under Giuliani. Though this response hardly solved homelessness, it temporarily ended the crisis of public homelessness that threatened the economic progress of the city.

Conclusion

IN THE FALL of 1990, in the midst of the city's worst economic downturn since the fiscal crisis, the magazine *City Journal* first appeared on New York newsstands. Published by the Manhattan Institute, a free-market think tank formed thirteen years earlier, the magazine promised to use its pages to promote "radical solutions to New York's radical problems" in order to make "the city livable once again."[1] Noting that "it would not take much to turn New York around," the editors emphasized the need for improvements to the city's livable spaces, such as having "a reasonable housing market, civility on the streets, [and] faith that there is some law operating here besides the law of the jungle."[2] In its first few years, *City Journal* published an array of articles on accomplishing these goals, highlighting solutions that unleashed the market, enhanced law and order policing, and reduced the "welfare state."[3]

The speed with which the magazine's influence reached City Hall was stunning. Indeed, many of the magazine's positions were adopted nearly wholesale by Mayor Rudolph Giuliani (1994–2001), a vigorous proponent of marketization.[4] "If there was kind of like a charge of plagiarism for political programs," Giuliani would later note, with tongue only slightly in cheek, "I'd probably be in a lot of trouble because I think we plagiarized most of them, if not all of them . . . from the thinking and analysis of the Manhattan Institute."[5]

City Journal's influence came in part because it went beyond theoretical appeals or abstract proposals. Instead, contributors repeatedly pointed to concrete examples of market and private sector–led initiatives implemented in the city. Articles, for instance, detailed recent triumphs of reduced rent regulations, volunteer and nonprofit initiatives in parks, private security on the streets, homeowning enterprises in low-income neighborhoods, Business Improvement Districts, and broken windows-influenced policing in business districts and transportation centers.[6]

Although *City Journal* held up these applications of free-market initiatives as recent phenomena, their portrayal belies a longer and more complicated history chronicled in these pages. As *The Long Crisis* has described, their roots can be traced back to projects launched as the city entered a prolonged period of economic turmoil in the late 1960s. In response, a variety of city-dwellers worked to counteract what they saw as significant threats to their communities and livelihoods. Their actions were spurred by city government's seeming inability to adequately address their concerns—at first, perhaps momentarily, but once economic conditions worsened, indefinitely. Though the residents behind these efforts were not usually driven by an ideological adherence to free-market principles, their actions initiated and expanded the role of private actors and the private sector in addressing concerns that had typically been served by government.

Turbulent economic conditions both outside and particularly within the city shaped New Yorkers' sense of political possibilities. These circumstances tempered demands for greater government resources, especially during the 1970s—a process reinforced by the austerity measures imposed by governmental and financial elites during the fiscal crisis. Residents' expectations had been built over the preceding decades of relatively robust urban liberal policies and it was only as these conditions were no longer met that residents sought solutions that looked beyond government. Even then, they did so principally not to reject liberalism but rather to attempt to maintain the conditions that liberal governance had promised. Indeed, rather than retreat from public life or widely proclaim that government itself was the problem, New Yorkers experimented with new initiatives to improve urban life. The imaginative remedies New Yorkers at different scales of power advanced for the conditions plaguing streets, parks, and homes gained influence, leading not only to specific policies but over time helping to fashion a broader logic that expanding the presence of the market and private sector in governance was necessary. As these projects grew, they helped alter two fundamental ideas: who could—and should—provide key services and what city residents could expect from government.

No doubt those with a greater proclivity for the market were important to the expansion of marketization. But what's striking is how often this path was forged by those with less ideological motivations—say, the homesteaders who emphasized self-help and individual ingenuity or park advocates who pushed volunteerism and private donations. What's more, commonly these efforts coalesced with initiatives launched by market advocates—such as the block associations that expanded private patrolling in residential areas as business associations did the same in commercial ones, or the tenants who came to embrace the conversion processes their landlords supported to reduce rent regulations. Collectively, these projects implemented new mechanisms that looked beyond government and ultimately moved the city away from traditional institutions of mid-century liberal governance for urban problems and toward relying more on private citizens, the private sector, and market.

Alongside the growing adoption of market solutions, this book has chronicled how there was consistent opposition to these shifts. The trajectory of marketization was neither particularly abrupt nor a fait accompli, with residents impeding initiatives to further such policies, especially when they believed they would hurt vulnerable populations, particularly poor and working-class people of color. These New Yorkers ultimately lost more battles than they won, but as the city underwent profound change between the 1960s and 1990s, they successfully curtailed certain pro-market and private sector policies, and helped to preserve or enact socially democratic and even anti-capitalist-inspired visions of city life. The examples in this book— from those who fought for permanent affordable housing to advocates for publicly controlled and equitably resourced public spaces—demonstrate the continued effects of left-wing activism into the late twentieth century. They bely any depiction of the rise of neoliberal policies as unchallenged or unidirectional. Yet they also illustrate the difficulty more socially democratic proposals had in gaining greater traction as neoliberalism ascended.

Among the greatest challenges these opponents to marketization faced was that support came from a series of liberal and Democratic administrations. Lindsay administration officials helped to expand a range of projects city-dwellers launched that looked beyond municipal government as New York encountered economic troubles in the late 1960s. Under Abe Beame, the drive toward private sector and market solutions grew, as officials offered both rhetorical and programmatic support for these efforts and ratcheted up municipal programs with similar aims. Koch believed promoting private sector and market-based policies to be paramount and pursued them vigorously. This trajectory reveals not only the central role of Democratic and liberal officials in ushering in the market turn, but also how Democratic Party politics transformed in the late twentieth century. Over the 1970s marketization moved to the center of Democratic governing agendas in New York, a position would that triumph at the federal level by the 1990s under President Bill Clinton, such as in his support for tax incentive fueled Enterprise Zones to promote urban development, his emphasis on market-solutions for addressing poverty, and his dismantling of Aid to Families with Dependent Children.[7]

Ultimately, by the late 1980s, market forces and private entities in New York gained a dominant presence in the governance of civic life. This transformation has often been associated with the tenure of Mayor Giuliani.[8] As this book has shown, marketization had churned for decades and firmly matured into a central governing strategy well before Giuliani took office in 1994. Giuliani nonetheless brought unbridled enthusiasm for the market and private sector as well as a caustic view of the poor and people of color. Asked, for example, at a 1995 budget briefing whether it was his "unspoken strategy that poor people should move to another city or state," Giuliani responded, "that's not an unspoken strategy. That's the strategy."[9] Giuliani's extensive marketization policies ranged widely. "Instead of cutting here and there," as one author put it, Giuliani "wanted to shrink, sell off, or just eliminate whole areas of city government."[10] He pushed for the public school system to adopt the use of vouchers (commenting at one point that "the whole school system should be blown up").[11] He vowed to privatize municipal hospitals and repeatedly tried to do so before being blocked by the state supreme court.[12] After shifting city policy away from the Koch and Dinkins administrations' practice of seizing and rehabilitating tax-delinquent properties, Giuliani shored up measures to sell these holdings to private investors.[13] He also made official the relationship between the city and the Central Park Conservancy, formalizing the contract with the private organization that had at that point for seventeen years helped operate and fundraise for the park.[14]

The marketization processes chronicled throughout this book have continued into the administrations of Democrat-turned-Republican-turned-Independent Michael Bloomberg (2002–2013) and Democrat Bill De Blasio (2014–2021). Private guards patrol both public and private property; across the state, private guards now outnumber the police by two to one.[15] The city also has continued to allow developers to create and own public spaces as a means of skirting zoning restrictions on new construction. A recent city comptroller audit found that the majority of these "privately owned public spaces" violated city guidelines, such as by having "public access restricted by some type of fence or barricade; signs stating 'For Private Use Only'; [or] a lack of required amenities."[16] "New Yorkers are literally getting cheated out of tens of millions of dollars in public space," the comptroller concluded.[17]

Between 1991 and 2017, the percentage of rent-stabilized or rent-controlled units within New York City's total housing stock declined from nearly 41 to 28 percent.[18] During this same period, the number of owner units grew over

20 percent (this increase has been most notable in Manhattan where home-ownership rates have doubled since 1981).[19] Tax incentive programs have also continued to grant major abatements and exemptions for new development. After the 11,000 square foot penthouse at One57 on West 57th Street sold in 2015 for over $100 million dollars, its new owner received a 95 percent tax exemption thanks to 421-a. The program granted $1.4 billion in exceptions each year, though in 2014 less than 8.5 percent of units produced through the program were "earmarked for low-and moderate-income tenants."[20] In addition, due to loose area median income standards, those families qualifying for "affordable" apartments could earn over $130,000 a year. The program briefly ended in 2015, before being revived by state officials in 2017 under a new name, Affordable New York Housing Program, even though it "does little to actually create affordable housing, with 79 cents of every 421-a dollar spent going to luxury development and only 11 cents going to support affordability," as the Association for Neighborhood and Housing Development noted.[21]

In 2020 more than 62,500 people slept in homeless shelters each night, about 90 percent of whom were black or Latinx and over 70 percent of whom were families.[22] The shelter system, which consumes a yearly budget of nearly $2 billion, has not only expended the energies of a significant portion of the broader homeless advocacy community, but relies on an extensive network of operators, including for-profit ones.[23] Critics have come to refer to the system as the "shelter industrial complex," to call attention both to the immense resources that continue to go into providing temporary shelter instead of long-term housing as well as to how sheltering the homeless has become a lucrative business.[24] Bloomberg in particular expanded the use of for-profit shelters, which came to house the majority of homeless families in 2013.[25]

New York also epitomizes the astonishing inequality of the United States. The city's economic development since the fiscal crisis has been remarkably uneven; the top 1 percent income earners accounted for nearly two-thirds of all income growth during the 1980s and 1990s and 55 percent of income growth since 2000.[26] Overall, the top 1 percent income earners garner over 40 percent of the city's total income, while the entire bottom half of New Yorkers comprise just 5.6 percent of the total.[27] Income disparities are also highly marked by race; median earnings for white New Yorkers are 60 percent higher than Asian and black workers and double a typical Latinx worker.[28] Although nearly one in every twenty New Yorkers is a millionaire, 43.5 percent of residents live at or near the poverty line, with Latinx, African American, and Asian populations experiencing the highest rates of poverty, while also typically being concentrated in neighborhoods with substantially fewer resources than affluent white ones.[29]

New York is hardly alone in the shift toward marketization and privatization. Cities throughout the country have adopted policies that have allowed market forces and private entities to take the helm in major areas of civic life over which government had previously been the dominant force. Just as *The Long Crisis* has explored numerous instances of this phenomenon—from reducing rent regulations and state production and maintenance of low-income housing to the reorientation and explosive growth of generous tax incentives to spur private development—there are an astonishing array of examples from across the country. In Kansas City, Missouri, for example, legislators recently transferred ownership of the sidewalks of an entertainment district to the Westport Improvement District, which screens and polices visitors to the area on weekends.[30] In Chicago, private investors paid $1.16 billion to take over parking meters for seventy-five years (investors are on pace to recoup their investment after just thirteen years).[31] Over half of the nation's major cities now have private park conservancies that manage public parks.[32] These trends are hardly only an urban phenomena, as evidenced by examples ranging from the spread of private prisons to the growth of school vouchers to the increasing use of private public partnerships for infrastructure revitalization projects.

Proponents claim that these processes lead to increased efficiency, government savings, and better service delivery. No doubt sometimes they do, but results are often mixed.[33] Perhaps even more importantly, these shifts raise fundamental questions about whether accountability, public access, and the common good are served well in these processes. As one journalist recently put it: "Is the purpose of municipal parking meters to maximize revenue, or is it to provide a low-cost amenity to citizens and the businesses they patronize?"[34]

Take examples from this book. While reducing rent regulations has led to needed improvements to an aging housing stock, it worsened the city's affordability crisis. Though private coffers renovated major parks, this contributed to a two-tiered park system bifurcated by race and class. While wealthy BIDs have "cleaned up" prominent commercial districts, they refashioned public areas to appeal to the affluent and tourists and signal to lower income people, particularly those of color, that such spaces are not for them. While private security has increased surveillance of public streets, it also contributed to the over policing of poor people and people of color. Indeed, while wealth disparity is perhaps the starkest indication of inequity, the processes traced through *The Long Crisis* similarly raise fundamental questions about how and for whom the city has been remade over the preceding decades.

In the years ahead, cities must continue to reckon both with the successes and the costs of the encroaching market and private sector. But so too must those concerned with the future of cities grapple with how these processes came to be. As much as recent decades have been marked by the expanding presence of the market and private sector, this growth was not inevitable. Nor are the disparities that have been exacerbated by these shifts intractable. In New York, as across the nation, residents are at work on an extraordinary array of creative campaigns that challenge growing inequalities, such as by forming tenant unions, strengthening rent protections, expanding community land trusts for housing and public space, and demanding that public parks be more equitably dispersed and resourced, to name just a few of the initiatives targeting the city's livable environments.[35] By tracing how cities have come to be so reliant on market solutions, *The Long Crisis* will hopefully allow city-dwellers to better position themselves to continue to struggle for a more equitable and just metropolis.

Notes

ABBREVIATIONS

Archives

ABNY   Association for a Better New York Archives, Association for a Better New York, New York

ADB   Abraham D. Beame Mayoral Papers, Municipal Archives, New York

AH   August Heckscher Papers, Municipal Archives, New York

BHA   Brooklyn Heights Association Records, Brooklyn Public Library

BPC   Bryant Park Corporation Files, Bryant Park Corporation, New York

CCNYC   Citizens Committee for New York City Files, Citizens Committee for New York City

CHL   City Hall Library, New York

CSL   Personal Papers of Charles S. Laven (in possession of Charles S. Laven)

CNYCC   Council of New York City Cooperatives Files, Council of New York City Cooperatives, New York

COH   Mayor's Commission on the Homeless (DND Papers), Municipal Archives, New York

CPC   Central Park Conservancy Files, Central Park Conservancy, New York

CTH   Coalition for the Homeless Files, Coalition for the Homeless, New York

DHS   Department of Homeless Services Subject Files (DND Papers), Municipal Archives, New York

DND   David N. Dinkins Mayoral Papers, Municipal Archives, New York

DPR   New York City Department of Parks and Recreation Archives, Department of Parks and Recreation, New York

EH   Elizabeth Holtzman Subject Files (JVL Papers), Municipal Archives, New York

EIK   Edward I. Koch Mayoral Papers, Municipal Archives, New York

FXM	Francis X. McArdle Subject Files (JVL Papers), Municipal Archives, New York
HC	Governor Hugh Carey Papers, New York State Archives, Albany, NY
HPD	Housing Preservation and Development Files (EIK Papers), Municipal Archives, New York
HS	Henry Stern Papers, Municipal Archives, New York
HTA	*Habitat* Archive, *Habitat* Magazine, New York
JG	Judah Gribetz Subject Files (ADB Papers), Municipal Archives, New York
JN	Papers of Jack Newfield, Briscoe Center for American History, The University of Texas at Austin
JVL	John V. Lindsay Mayoral Papers, Municipal Archives, New York
KH	Private Collection of Kim Hopper (in possession of Kim Hopper)
LF	Lewis Feldstein Papers (JVL Papers), Municipal Archives, New York
JS	Jay Steingold Papers, Queens Library, Queens, New York
MAA	Morningside Area Alliance Records, Columbia University
MAS	Municipal Arts Society Archive, Municipal Arts Society, New York
MBCG	Manhattan Beach Community Group Papers, Brooklyn College
MCH	Metropolitan Council on Housing Records, Tamiment Library and Robert F. Wagner Labor Archives, New York University
MM	Marsha Martin Papers (DND Papers), Municipal Archives, New York
MMC	Governor Mario M. Cuomo Papers, New York State Archives, Albany
MW	Governor Malcolm Wilson Papers, New York State Archives, Albany
NL	Nathanial Leventhal Files (EIK Papers), Municipal Archives, New York
NS	Norman Steisel Papers (DND Papers), Municipal Archives, New York
NYBJ	New York Bill Jacket, New York State Archives, Albany
NYCC	New York City Council Records, the LaGuardia and Wagner Archives, Fiorello H. LaGuardia Community College/CUNY
NYCHA	New York City Housing Authority Papers, the LaGuardia and Wagner Archives, Fiorello H. LaGuardia Community College/CUNY
NYSAH	New York State Assembly Hearing Files, the Assembly Standing Committee on Housing (1973_1979), New York State Archives, Albany
NYSL	New York State Library, Albany
OHC	Columbia Center for Oral History Collection, Columbia University
PC	Parks Council Records, Columbia University
RE	Robert Esnard Department Subject Files (EIK Papers), Municipal Archives, New York
RL	Ronald Lawson Research Files for the *Tenant Movement in New York City*, Tamiment Library and Robert F. Wagner Labor Archives, New York University
RS	Robert Sweet Papers (JVL Papers), Municipal Archives, New York
SL	Sally Leonard Subject Files (ADB Papers), Municipal Archives, New York

TCRH	New York State Temporary Commission on Rental Housing, Hearing Transcripts and Office Files, 1977–1980, New York State Archives, Albany
UJC	Urban Justice Center Files, Urban Justice Center, New York
UHAB	Urban Homesteading Assistance Board Files, Urban Homesteading Assistance Board, New York
VAF	Vincent Astor Foundation Records, Manuscripts and Archives Division, The New York Public Library
VCMK	Private Collection of Vicki Chesler and Matt Kovner (in possession of Vicki Chesler and Matt Kovner)

Periodicals

CFC	*The Consumer-Farmer Cooperator*
CJ	*City Journal*
CL	*City Limits*
CPGT	*Central Park Good Times*
CSM	*Christian Science Monitor*
CT	*Chicago Tribune*
ESE	*East Side Express*
HT	*Habitat*
MC	*Manhattan Cooperator*
ND	*Newsday*
NH	*Neighborhood: The Journal of City Preservation*
NY	*New York*
NYAN	*New York Amsterdam News*
NYDN	*New York Daily News*
NYLJ	*New York Law Journal*
NYP	*New York Post*
NYSN	*New York Sunday News*
NYT	*New York Times*
NYTM	*New York Times Magazine*
REN	*Real Estate News*
RER	*Real Estate Reporter*
SR	*Saturday Review*
VV	*Village Voice*
WP	*Washington Post*

Interviews

Winifred Armstrong, August 7, 2013, New York
Roberta Axelrod, January 16, 2013, New York
Ellen Baxter, July 8, 2013, New York

William Beinecke, April 22, 2013, New York
Vicki Chesler and Matt Kovner, November 20, 2012, New York
David Clurman, October 25, 2012, via telephone
Gordon Davis, June 19, 2013, New York
David Goldstick, December 28, 2012, New York
Francis J. Greenburger, January 16, 2013, New York
Robert Hayes, June 17, 2013, White Plains, NY
Ann Henderson, September 6, 2012, New York
Henry Lanier, September 27, 2012, New York
Doug Lasden, June 11, 2013, New York
Charles Laven, September 27, 2012, New York
Marc Luxemburg, January 10, 2013, New York
Ruth Nazario, September 7, 2012, via telephone
Carol J. Ott, December 20, 2012, New York
Andrew Reicher, August 15, 2012, New York
Betsy Barlow Rogers, April 24, 2013, New York
N. Anthony Rolfe, December 11, 2012 and December 13, 2012, via telephone
Daniel Rose, October 17, 2012, New York

INTRODUCTION

1. Barry Gottehrer, "Foreword," in *Herald Tribune* staff, *New York City in Crisis* (New York: David McKay Company, Inc., 1965), vi.
2. *Herald Tribune* staff, "Indictment: Reasons for Outrage and Reasons to Act," in *New York City in Crisis*, 195.
3. Gottehrer, "Foreword," in *New York City in Crisis*, v.
4. Richard J. Whalen, *A City Destroying Itself: An Angry View of New York* (New York: William Morrow, 1965), 7.
5. The most influential historical work on the urban crisis remains Thomas Sugrue, *The Origins of the Urban Crisis: Race and Inequality in Postwar Detroit* (Princeton, NJ: Princeton University Press, 1996).
6. As scholars such as Suleiman Osman have observed, cities' economic fortunes are rarely unidirectional; during this period, for example, "Brownstoners" were gentrifying several Brooklyn neighborhoods. See Suleiman Osman, *The Invention of Brownstone Brooklyn: Gentrification and the Search for Authenticity in Postwar New York* (New York: Oxford University Press, 2011). On a similar but distinct track, signs of hope and resolve were evident throughout this period, from black freedom and queer/trans rights organizing to new musical forms coming out of the Bronx to the various mobilizations chronicled in this book.

7. Joshua B. Freeman, *Working-Class New York: Life and Labor Since World War II* (New York: The New Press, 2000), 256 and Jonathan Soffer, *Ed Koch and the Rebuilding of New York* (New York: Columbia University Press, 2010), 113–120.

8. See Kim Phillips-Fein, *Fear City: New York's Fiscal Crisis and the Rise of Austerity Politics* (New York: Metropolitan Books, 2017).

9. This book joins other recent histories that have looked to the local level to explore the political and economic shifts of the late twentieth century. Recent histories of post-1960s New York City that focus especially on political and economic change include: William W. Buzbee, *Fighting Westway: Environmental Law, Citizen Activism, and the Regulatory War That Transformed New York City* (Ithaca, NY: Cornell University Press, 2014); Tamar Carroll, *Mobilizing New York: AIDs, Antipoverty, and Feminist Activism* (Chapel Hill: University of North Carolina Press, 2015); Themis Chronopoulos, *Spatial Regulation in New York City: From Urban Renewal to Zero Tolerance* (New York: Routledge, 2011); Brian D. Goldstein, *The Roots of Urban Renaissance: Gentrification and the Struggle over Harlem* (Cambridge, MA: Harvard University Press, 2017); Miriam Greenberg, *Branding New York: How a City in Crisis Was Sold to the World* (New York: Routledge, 2008); Sonia Song-Ha Lee, *Building a Latino Civil Rights Movement: Puerto Ricans, African Americans, and the Pursuit of Racial Justice in New York City* (Chapel Hill: University of North Carolina Press, 2016); Frederick Douglass Opie, *Upsetting the Apple Cart: Black-Latino Coalitions in New York City from Protest to Public Office* (New York: Columbia University Press, 2014); Osman, *The Invention of Brownstone Brooklyn*; Lana Dee Povitz, *Stirrings: How Activist New Yorkers Ignited a Movement for Food Justice* (Chapel Hill: University of North Carolina Press, 2019); Phillips-Fein, *Fear City*; Soffer, *Ed Koch and the Rebuilding of New York*; Aaron Shkuda, *The Lofts of SoHo: Gentrification, Art, and Industry in New York, 1950–1980* (Chicago: University of Chicago Press, 2016).

10. See, for example, Jack Newfield, *The Full Rudy: The Man, the Myth, the Mania* (New York: Thunder's Mouth Press, 2002) and Robert Polner, ed., *America's Mayor: The Hidden History of Rudy Giuliani's New York* (New York: Soft Skull Press, 2005).

11. The scholarship on the growth of market-based principles and policies in twentieth-century America is vast. Especially notable recent histories include: Angus Burgin, *The Great Persuasion: Reinventing Free Markets since the Depression* (Cambridge, MA: Harvard University Press, 2012); David Harvey, *A Brief History of Neoliberalism* (New York: Oxford University Press, 2005); Daniel Stedman Jones, *Masters of the Universe: Hayek, Friedman, and the Birth of Neoliberal Politics* (Princeton, NJ: Princeton University Press, 2012); Nancy MacLean, *Democracy in Chains: The Deep History of the Radical Right's Stealth Plan for America* (New York: Viking, 2017); Bethany Moreton, *To Serve God and Wal-Mart: The Making of Christian*

Free Enterprise (Cambridge, MA: Harvard University Press, 2009); Kim Phillips-Fein, *Invisible Hands: The Making of the Conservative Movement from the New Deal to Reagan* (New York: Norton, 2009); Phillips-Fein, *Fear City*; Daniel Rodgers, *Age of Fracture* (Cambridge, MA: Harvard University Press, 2011); Elizabeth Tandy Shermer, *Sunbelt Capitalism: Phoenix and the Transformation of American Politics* (Philadelphia: University of Pennsylvania Press, 2013); and Judith Stein, *Pivotal Decade: How the United States Traded Factories for Finance in the Seventies* (New Haven, CT: Yale University Press, 2010).

12. Recent works by scholars Allen Dieterich-Ward, Tracy Neumann, Elizabeth Shermer, and Timothy P. R. Weaver have also depicted the onset of neoliberalism as a local (and uneven) process that began decades earlier than the 1980s. They focus especially on officials and business elites and their collaborative efforts to spur economic development. See Dieterich-Ward, *Beyond Rust: Metropolitan Pittsburgh and the Fate of Industrial* America (Philadelphia: University of Pennsylvania Press, 2015); Neumann, *Remaking the Rust Belt: The Postindustrial Transformation of North America* (Philadelphia: University of Pennsylvania Press, 2016); Shermer, *Sunbelt Capitalism*; and Weaver, *Blazing the Neoliberal Trail: Urban Political Development in the United States and the United Kingdom* (Philadelphia: University of Pennsylvania Press, 2015). Phillips-Fein's outstanding chronicle of New York's fiscal crisis, *Fear City*, similarly focuses overwhelmingly on political and economic elites. This book, in contrast, demonstrates how shifting conceptions about municipal government and its limits went far beyond officials and elites to a much broader range of New Yorkers and illustrates how their actions proved critical to the expansion of marketization across city life.

13. Historians of this period have also examined the role of local residents and organizations (especially Community Development Corporations) in urban development—including, at times, in facilitating more market-based approaches—with different points of emphasis than mine. For a work that traces the influence of 1960s-era demands for community control and role of local residents and community-based organizations in neighborhood-level gentrification of Harlem, see Goldstein, *The Roots of Urban Renaissance*. For a history that emphasizes both the successes and challenges of African American-led community development in achieving lasting gains for greater civil and economic rights, see Julia Rabig, *The Fixers: Devolution, Development and Civil Society in Newark, 1960–1990* (Chicago: University of Chicago Press, 2016). For an especially sanguine account of community-led redevelopment of inner-city neighborhoods, see Alexander Von Hoffman, *House by House, Block by Block: The Rebirth of America's Urban Neighborhoods* (New York: Oxford University Press, 2003).

14. This work joins Suleiman Osman in depicting neoliberalism as taking form through a process that was local, ideologically diverse, and unsystematic. Osman, "Glocal America: The Politics of Scale in the 1970s," in *Shaped by the State: Toward*

a New Political History of the Twentieth Century, ed. Brent Cebul, Lily Geismer, and Mason B. Williams (Chicago: University of Chicago Press, 2019), 241–260.

15. Soffer, *Ed Koch and the Rebuilding of New York*, 4.

16. This book joins other recent works on the transformation of the Democratic Party and liberalism after the 1960s. For a discussion of modern liberalism's shift toward representing the interests of affluent white suburban knowledge workers, see Lily Geismer, *Don't Blame Us: Suburban Liberals and the Transformation of the Democratic Party* (Princeton, NJ: Princeton University Press, 2014). Other historians have also pointed to New York as a key site of transformation for liberalism and the Democratic Party. Jonathan Soffer has posited that Mayor Ed Koch's emphasis on "government intervention to shape and subsidize private enterprise" and resistance to redistributive social programs pioneered similar shifts in the Democratic Party nationally (*Ed Koch and the Rebuilding of New York*, 4). Phillips-Fein has argued that many of the actors who ushered in austerity during the fiscal crisis were self-identified liberals who believed that "what this meant had undergone a profound change" (*Fear City*, 9). This book charts the reconceptualization of liberalism back to the tenure of Mayor John Lindsay, while also tracing how beliefs about municipal government's constraints became widespread and spurred residents into action.

17. Vincent Cannato, *The Ungovernable City: John Lindsay and His Struggle to Save New York* (New York: Basic Books, 2001), ix.

18. In contrast, historians of the late 1960s and 1970s have commonly emphasized the growing influence of conservative activists and politicians and their abilities to discredit and foment popular opposition to liberal government. Notable recent works with varied points of emphasis include: Meg Jacobs, *Panic at the Pump: The Energy Crisis and the Transformation of American Politics in the 1970s* (New York: Hill and Wang, 2016); Philip Jenkins, *Decade of Nightmares: The End of the Sixties and Making of Eighties America* (New York: Oxford University Press, 2006); Bruce Schulman and Julian E. Zelizer, eds., *Rightward Bound: Making America Conservative in the 1970s* (Cambridge, MA: Harvard University Press, 2008); and Robert Self, *All In the Family: The Realignment of American Democracy Since the 1960s* (New York: Hill and Wang, 2012).

19. John Louis Recchiuti, *Civic Engagement: Social Science and Progressive-Era Reform in New York City* (Philadelphia: University of Pennsylvania Press, 2007), 2.

20. Mason B. Williams, *City of Ambition: FDR, La Guardia, and the Making of Modern New York* (New York: Norton, 2013), 390.

21. Ibid., 193–195.

22. Ibid., xv.

23. See, for example, Martha Biondi, *To Stand and Fight: The Struggle for Civil Rights in Postwar New York* (Cambridge, MA: Harvard University Press, 2003); Lee, *Building a Latino Civil Rights Movement*; Brian Purnell, *Fighting Jim Crow in the County of Kings: The Congress of Racial Equality in Brooklyn* (Lexington: University Press of

Kentucky, 2013); Clarence Taylor, *Fight the Power: African Americans and the Long History of Police Brutality in New York City* (New York: New York University Press, 2019); Walter Thabit, *How East New York Became a Ghetto* (New York: New York University Press, 2003); Craig Steven Wilder, *A Covenant with Color: Race and Social Power in Brooklyn* (New York: Columbia University Press, 2000).

24. Williams, *City of Ambition*, xv.

25. Freeman, *Working-Class New York*, 67–68.

26. Ibid., 66.

27. Samuel Zipp, *Manhattan Projects: The Rise and Fall of Urban Renewal in Cold War New York* (New York: Oxford University Press, 2010), 7.

28. Hilary Ballon, "Robert Moses and Urban Renewal: The Title 1 Program," in *Robert Moses and the Modern City: The Transformation of New York*, ed. Hilary Ballon and Kenneth T. Jackson (New York: Norton, 2007), 97. See also Joel Schwartz, *The New Approach: Robert Moses, Urban Liberals, and Redevelopment of the Inner City* (Columbus: Ohio State University Press, 1993).

29. Historians such as Allen Dieterich-Ward and Tracy Neumann have similarly chronicled how public–private partnerships were a hallmark of urban renewal programs (Dieterich-Ward, *Beyond Rust* and Neumann, *Remaking the Rust Belt*). For more on the continuities between the policies and assumptions associated with the post-1970s period of neoliberalism and earlier decades, see *Shaped by the State*.

30. Barry Gottehrer, "Foreword," in *New York City in Crisis*, vii.

31. *New York City in Crisis*, 201. See also Joseph P. Viteritti, "Times a-Changin'," in *Summer in the City: John Lindsay, New York, and the American Dream*, ed. Joseph P. Viteritti (Baltimore: Johns Hopkins University Press, 2014), 11.

32. Geoffrey Kabaservice, "On Principle: A Progressive Republican," in *Summer in the City*, 38.

33. See, for example, Bruce J. Schulman, *The Seventies: The Great Shift in American Culture, Society, and Politics* (New York: Da Capo Press, 2001), 48–49.

34. Thomas Borstelmann, *The 1970s: A New Global History from Civil Rights to Economic Inequality* (Princeton, NJ: Princeton University Press, 2012), 122.

35. Charles R. Morris, *The Cost of Good Intentions: New York City and the Liberal Experiment, 1960–1975* (New York: Norton, 1980), 141.

36. Though this loss was offset somewhat by increases in service jobs, for each manufacturing job the city traded for one in service it lost close to $1,000 in annual income taxes. Roy W. Bahl, Alan K. Campbell, and David Greytak, *Taxes, Expenditures, and the Economic Base: Case Study of New York City* (New York: Praeger Publishers, 1974), 12, 26.

37. Ibid., 145.

38. Morris, *The Cost of Good Intentions*, 150.

39. Fred Ferretti, *The Year the Big Apple Went Bust* (New York: G. P. Putnam's Sons, 1976), 38.

40. The Parks Council, "Citizens View Their Parks: Citizen Attitudes About New York City's Parks Disclosed by a Survey of Sitting Park Users" (1963), 3. CHL.

41. David K. Shipler, "104th St. Walk-Up Offers Profile of Abandoned Building," *NYT*, January 18, 1969.

42. Jeff Greenfield, "Hail and Farewell: Reading John Lindsay's Face," *NYT*, July 29, 1973.

43. US Bureau of the Census, *City Government Finances in 1973–1974* (Washington, DC: US Government Printing Office, 1975).

44. Freeman, *Working-Class New York*, 256–259.

45. Fein, *Fear City*, 89–202.

46. Ibid., 206–207. Critically, however, these financial leaders proposed "few innovative policy ideas" associated with neoliberalism, such as "privatizing city services" or "load-shedding," as Sulieman Osman has noted. Osman, "Neoliberalism in New York City from Below," *Labor: Studies in Working-Class History* 15, no. 4 (December 2018): 108–109.

47. Freeman, *Working-Class New York*, 272.

48. William K. Tabb, *The Long Default: New York City and the Urban Fiscal Crisis* (New York: Monthly Review Press, 1982), 56.

49. See Morris, *The Cost of Good Intentions*, 189 and Jack Newfield and Paul Du Brul, *The Permanent Government: Who Really Rules New York?* (New York: The Pilgrim Press, 1981), 11–42. Similarly, unlike any other major city outside of New York, the state made the city responsible for a quarter of the costs to hospitals and physicians for those uninsured and on Medicaid. A change in this policy—or the federalization of health-care costs—also would have likely prevented the fiscal crisis. See Soffer, *Ed Koch and the Rebuilding of New York City*, 150–152.

50. Elizabeth Barlow, "32 Ways Your Time or Money Can Rescue Central Park," *NY*, June 14, 1976, 32, 34.

51. Eric C. Schneider, *Vampires, Dragons, and Egyptian Kings: Youth Gangs in Postwar New York* (Princeton, NJ: Princeton University Press, 1999), 49.

52. Freeman, *Working-Class New York*, 172.

53. Wolfgang Quante, *The Exodus of Corporate Headquarters from New York City* (New York: Praeger Publishers, 1976), 44–49.

54. See Michelle Nickerson and Darren Dochuk, eds., *Sunbelt Rising: The Politics of Place, Space, and Region* (Philadelphia: University of Pennsylvania Press, 2011); Shermer, *Sunbelt Capitalism*; Bruce Schulman, *From Cotton Belt to Sunbelt: Federal Policy, Economic Development, and the Transformation of the South, 1938–1980* (New York: Oxford University Press, 1991).

55. New York officials made use of a variety of programs and federal dollars and saw its general revenue from the federal government increase tenfold between the city's 1964 and 1972 budgets. US Bureau of the Census, *City Government Finances in 1963–1964* (Washington, DC: US Government Printing Office, 1965) and US

Bureau of the Census, *City Government Finances in 1972–1973* (Washington, DC: US Government Printing Office, 1974).

56. Roger Biles, *The Fate of Cities: Urban America and the Federal Government, 1945–2000* (Lawrence: University of Kansas, 2011), 112.

57. Ibid., 160–199.

58. Jon C. Teaford, *The Rough Road to Renaissance: Urban Revitalization in America, 1940–1985* (Baltimore: Johns Hopkins University Press, 1990), 262.

59. US Bureau of the Census, *City Government Finances in 1972–1973* (Washington, DC: US Government Printing Office, 1974) and US Bureau of the Census, *City Government Finances in 1987–1988* (Washington, DC: US Government Printing Office, 1990).

60. See Cannato, *The Ungovernable City*, especially chapters 4, 8, 9, 10, and 12.

61. Jonathan Rieder, *Canarsie: The Jews and Italians of Brooklyn against Liberalism* (Cambridge, MA: Harvard University Press, 1985), 6.

62. One important exception was the use of private schools to avoid desegregation.

63. See Mollenkopf, *A Phoenix in the Ashes*, especially chapters 1 and 5. See also Soffer, *Ed Koch and the Rebuilding of New York City*, 105–113.

64. See Soffer, *Ed Koch and the Rebuilding of New York City*, 145–160.

65. "Interview with Ed Koch," *Playboy*, April 1982.

66. See Oliver Cooke, *Rethinking Municipal Privatization* (New York: Routledge, 2008) and Roy Rosenzweig and Elizabeth Blackmar, *The Park and the People: A History of Central Park* (Ithaca, NY: Cornell University Press, 1992).

67. Mollenkopf, *A Phoenix in the Ashes*, 153. While there were 238,383 employees in 1989, this number was higher than in 1961 (200,706), but significantly lower than in 1969 (278,161). Charles Brecher and Raymond D. Horton with Robert A. Cropf and Dean Michael Mead, *Power Failure: New York City Politics and Policy since 1960* (New York: Oxford University Press, 1993), 36.

68. Brecher et al., *Power Failure*, 20.

69. Williams, *City of Ambition*, xv.

70. John Hull Mollenkopf, "The Place of Politics and the Politics of Place," in *Power, Culture, and Place: Essays on New York City*, ed. John Hull Mollenkopf (New York: Russell Sage Foundation, 1988), 278.

71. Steven Lee Myers, "Giuliani Moves on 'Privatization' Pledge," *NYT*, December 26, 1993.

72. See E. S. Savas, *Privatization in the City: Success, Failures, Lessons* (Washington, DC: CQ Press, 2005), 138.

CHAPTER 1

1. Lee Dembart, "Carter Takes 'Sobering' Trip to South Bronx," *NYT*, October 6, 1977 and Michael Sterne, "A Loan and Some 'Sweat Equity' Create an Oasis Amid Desolation," *NYT*, October 7, 1977.

2. Alan S. Oser, "Housing Supply in City Eroding Amid Construction Standstill," *NYT*, February 8, 1970. "In the 1970s," Brian Goldstein notes, "the rate of abandonment reached at least 21,000 units a year and perhaps as many as 40,000 units annually in the first eight years of the decade." Brian Goldstein, *The Roots of Urban Renaissance: Gentrification and the Struggle over Harlem* (Cambridge, MA: Harvard University Press, 2017), 157.

3. Robert Kolodny, *Study of Low-Income Cooperative Housing Conversion in New York City: Interim Report* (August 1972). Sponsored and Published by United Neighborhood Houses, prepared under contract with the Borough Improvement Board of Manhattan.

4. Robert Kolodny (assisted by Marjorie Gellerman), *Self Help in the Inner City: A Study of Lower Income Cooperative Housing Conversion in New York* (September 1973). Prepared under contract with the Borough Improvement Board of Manhattan and with the assistance of The J. M. Kaplan Fund, Inc., 12.

5. Urban Homesteading Assistance Board, *Second Annual Progress Report and Proposal for Funding* (January 1976), 14. UHAB.

6. This support was also aided by changing views about urban policy in the 1970s. As Suleiman Osman has observed, insistences on community control "dovetailed seamlessly with a new conservative skepticism about government bureaucracy and fiscal waste." Ideas like "volunteerism, sweat equity rehabilitation, neighborhood power, cultural heritage, and historic preservation replaced modernization and renewal on the urban agenda." Suleiman Osman, *The Invention of Brownstone Brooklyn: Gentrification and the Search for Authenticity in Postwar New York* (New York: Oxford University Press, 2011), 231.

7. Housing and Development Administration (HDA), "Proposal for a Demonstration Program with Respect to Abandoned Properties," May 14, 1971. Box 4, Folder "HDA, Urban Affairs." LF.

8. The rates of landlord abandonment likely peaked between 1966–1968 when municipal officials encouraged tenants in buildings with code violations to withhold rent.

9. HDA, "Proposal for a Demonstration Program."

10. Kolodny, *Self Help in the Inner City*, 5.

11. Ibid., 61–67.

12. HDA, "Proposal for a Demonstration Program."

13. "Young Gang Turns to Housing Reconstruction," *CFC,* January 1974 and Lawrie Mifflin, "Equity is Sweat but the Reward is Sweet," *NYDN,* January 9, 1975.

14. "Renegades Housing Movement" flier. Undated but likely 1974. Box 20, Folder "Renegades" [*sic*]. RL.

15. Ibid.

16. HDA, "Proposal for a Demonstration Program."

17. Kolodny, *Self Help in the Inner City*, 18–21.

18. This hesitancy came in part from Lindsay's Housing Commissioner, Albert Walsh. See, for example, Nat Leventhal to John V. Lindsay, November 23, 1970. Box 1230, Folder "H.D.A. 1970–1972." JVL.

19. Quoted in Goldstein, *The Roots of Urban Renaissance*, 175.

20. In the early 1970s, several investigations exposed the program as primarily benefitting corrupt private contractors, developers, and housing officials, leading to major shakeups of both the program and the Housing and Development Administration. James Ryan, "A Sorry Story of Cupidity, Stupidity and Sloth," *NYDN*, January 25, 1972.

21. Office of Special Improvements, "Sweat Equity Program" (May 18, 1973), UHAB and The City of New York / Office of Special Improvements, "Returning Housing Control to the People. . . Sweat Equity and You" included as part of *A Proposal for the Urban Homesteading Assistance Board*.

22. Office of Special Improvements, "Sweat Equity Program."

23. Municipal official became more receptive to homesteading after President Richard Nixon imposed a freeze on federal funding for housing subsidy programs in January 1973. With no sign of the crisis of abandonment abetting and little federal support for the creation of new low-income housing, Lindsay announced programs to enable low and moderate-income tenants to rehabilitate and purchase buildings that had come under city control. Press release by Andrew P. Kerr, Administrator, HDA, July 18, 1973. Box: Robert M. Heller—HDA, D-L, 1972–1973, Folder "FDA-Freeze—File III." JVL.

24. Municipal Service Administration Press Release, December 18, 1973. Included as part of *A Proposal for the Urban Homesteading Assistance Board*.

25. See Wayne King, "Homesteaders Combating Urban Blight," *NYT*, September 16, 1973.

26. See Sol Linowitz, "A Modest Plan for Cities," *NYT*, December 22, 1973 and Walter H. Waggoner, "Homestead Project Seeking to Halt Decay in the Cities," *NYT*, March 3, 1974.

27. WCBS editorial, November 30, 1973. Reprinted in *A Proposal for the Urban Homesteading Assistance Board*.

28. Howard Husock, "Sexiest Political Idea of the Year," *Boston Phoenix* 2, no. 40, October 2, 1973.

29. Robert Schur and Virginia Sherry, *The Neighborhood Housing Movement: A Survey of the Activities and Services Provided by Non-Profit Community-Based Organizations to Residents of Low- and Moderate-Income Communities in New York City* (New York: Association of Neighborhood Housing Developers, Inc., 1977).

30. Author interview with Henry Lanier (September 27, 2012).

31. Quoted in *Interfaith Adopt-a-Building: 5 Year Report, 1970–1975* (1975). UHAB.

32. See, for example, Martha Bondi, *To Stand and Fight: The Struggle for Civil Rights in Postwar New York City* (Cambridge, MA: Harvard University Press, 2003) and

Thomas J. Sugrue, *Sweet Land of Liberty: The Forgotten Struggle for Civil Rights in the North* (New York: Random House, 2008).

33. Interfaith Adopt-A-Building newsletter (1973). Box 15, Folder "Adopt a Building 4." RL.

34. Robert Schur, "A Report of the Activities of the Association of Neighborhood Housing Developers, Inc. and a Proposal for its Future Activities and Funding," (April 1975), 8. UHAB.

35. Homefront, *Housing Abandonment in New York City* (1977), 114.

36. These critiques had grown since the inception of urban renewal in the early 1940s. Samuel Zipp, *Manhattan Projects: The Rise and Fall of Urban Renewal in Cold War New York* (New York: Oxford University Press, 2010), 10.

37. "Youth Turns to Housing Reconstruction," *CFF*, January 1974.

38. Ibid.

39. Memo from Albert A. Walsh to John V. Lindsay, August 7, 1972. JVL.

40. *A Proposal for the Urban Homesteading Assistance Board*, iii.

41. Ibid., i.

42. Ibid., 4–5 and 2.

43. Quoted in "How the Sun Came to Shine on 'La Casa del Sol,'" *Morgan Guaranty News*. Reprinted in Urban Homesteading Assistance Board, *Second Annual Progress Report*.

44. *A Proposal for the Urban Homesteading Assistance Board*, 4.

45. Urban Homesteading Assistance Board, *Second Annual Progress Report*, 1 and 13.

46. Ibid., ii.

47. Michael Woodsworth, *Battle for Bed-Stuy: The Long War on Poverty in New York City* (Cambridge, MA: Harvard University Press, 2016), 126.

48. Ibid.

49. "Hope for Housing" *NYT*, November 23, 1973 and "The Housing Wheel," *NYT*, November 29, 1974. See also WCBS-TV Editorial, November 28, 1973; Editorial, "Co-op Housing and Hope in Tenements," *NYP*, June 30, 1973; and Polly Kline, "Brownsville is Building with Hope," *NYDN*, February 22, 1976.

50. New York Urban Coalition, *Housing Rehabilitation Task Force: Report and Proposal* (January 1976), 26 and 23.

51. Jorge Hernandez, "U-Hab Luncheon," *Our Town*, November 29, 1974.

52. Ronald Lawson with Reuben E. Johnson III, "Tenant Responses to the Urban Housing Crisis, 1970–1984," in *The Tenant Movement in New York City, 1904–1984*, ed. Ronald Lawson with the assistance of Mark Naison (New Brunswick, NJ: Rutgers University Press, 1986), 235.

53. Statements by Comptroller Abraham D. Beame requested by WABC Radio, May 22, 1973. Box 7, Folder 165. JG.

54. "The Housing Wheel," *NYT*.

55. Lawson, "Owners of Last Resort," 68.

56. "Sweat Equity 1976: Time for the Banks to Come on Board." UHAB.

57. Schur, "A Report of the Activities of the Association of Neighborhood Housing Developers," 14–16a; Author interview with Henry Lanier (September 27, 2012); and Author interview with Ruth Nazario (September 7, 2012).

58. Michael Freedberg, "Rebuilding the City: 519 East 11th Street, New York," *Communities: Journal of Cooperative Living* 26 (May-June 1977): 8.

59. Testimony of Charles Leven, The Urban Homesteading Assistance Board Before the Assembly Subcommittee on Neighborhood Preservation, November 15, 1976. Box 1. NYSAH.

60. Quoted in *Interfaith Adopt-a-Building: 5 Year Report.*

61. Robert Schur, "Statement to the City Planning Commission on the Proposed Amendment to the First Year Community Development Program," December 10, 1975. UHAB.

62. Philip St. Georges, "Testimony at the Board of Estimate Hearing on Amendments to the First Year Community Development Plan," January 13, 1976. UHAB.

63. UHAB, *Second Annual Progress Report and Proposal for Funding*, 1.

64. Joseph P. Fried, "City Housing Administrator Proposed 'Planned Shrinkage' of Some Slums," *NYT,* February 3, 1976.

65. Robert Schur, "City's Chief Calls for Nationwide Housing/Employment Program Based on New York City Efforts," *CL,* December 1976, 5.

66. Author interview with Charles Laven (September 27, 2012).

67. Robert Schur and Virginia Sherry, *The Neighborhood Housing Movement,* 5.

68. Rita Reif, "Self-Help Housing: Within Limits, It Works," *NYT*, July 11, 1976.

69. Joyce Maynard, "519 East 11th St.: Neighbors Rebuild Hopes," *NYT*, July 8, 1976 and Robert McG. Thomas, "11th St Tenants Tilt with Windmill and Con Edison," *NYT,* November 13, 1976.

70. Reif, "Self-Help Housing."

71. Michael Garrison, "Peoples Development Corporation," *CL,* June–July 1976, 3.

72. People's Development Corporation, "Proposal for a Community Design Center," undated but likely late 1977. UHAB.

73. Quoted in Freedberg, "Rebuilding the City," 14.

74. Jill Jonnes, *South Bronx Rising: The Rise, Fall, and Resurrection of an American City* (New York: Fordham University Press, 2002), 233 and 256.

75. John Mullane, "They Settle in Wilds of the Bronx," *NYP,* Unknown date, but likely late June 1976.

76. Ian Donald Terner, "Will Success Spoil Homesteading in New York City," (undated but likely 1978), 12. UHAB.

77. Ramon Rueda and Joan Allen, "Rebuilding the Bronx through Sweat and Cooperation," *CFF,* January 1977, 3. See also Jones, *South Bronx Rising*, 304.

78. Thomas Glynn, "Something Good is Growing in the South Bronx: People's Development Corporation," *NH,* December 1977, 7. CSL.

79. Quoted in Vernetta Hill, "Receives Grant to Rehab Apartment Building," *NYAN,* June 26, 1976, A9.

80. U-HAB, "Sweat Equity and the Urban Homesteading Assistance Board (U-HAB) in New York City" and U-HAB, "Presentation and Discussion at HUD," September 9, 1976. UHAB.

81. William G. Conway, "'People Fire' in the Ghetto Ashes," *SR*, July 23, 1977, 14.

82. Ibid., 15.

83. People's Development Corporation, "What is a Community Design Center," undated but likely early 1978. UHAB.

84. People's Development Corporation: Washington Avenues / Morrisania Economic Redevelopment, undated but likely 1977. UHAB.

85. People's Development Corporation, "A Position Paper: A Prescription for Curing Our Urban Ills," *NH*, December 1977, 29, CSL and People's Development Corporation, "Planning and Design Unit Description," January 10, 1978. UHAB.

86. Quoted in Beth Fallon, "Carter Kindles Spirit in South Bronx," *NYDN*, October 6, 1977.

87. Peter McLaughlin and Robert Carroll, "A New Kid Strolls Tough Turf," *NYDN*, October 6, 1977.

88. Jonnes, *South Bronx Rising*, 316.

89. Speech given by Vice President Walter F. Mondale at the 'Spirit of City' Award Cathedral of St. John Divine, Americana Hotel, New York City, December 15, 1977. 9, 10. UHAB.

90. Edward Ranzal, "Morrisania Designated by Beame for Urban 'Homesteading' Effort," *NYT*, October 29, 1977.

91. Juan Villanueva, "Banking on Self-Help," *NH*, December 1977, 28. CSL.

92. Glynn, "Something Good is Growing in the South Bronx," 13.

93. Roger M. Williams, "The New Urban Pioneers: Homesteading in the Slums," *SR*, July 23, 1977.

94. This was followed by a $500,000 HUD grant to employ seventy-five youths to work on improvement projects. "Bronx Group Carter Visited Gets Grant," *NYT*, March 14, 1978.

95. Sterne, "A Loan and Some 'Sweat Equity.'"

96. UHAB, "Sweat Equity and the Urban Homesteading Assistance Board (U-HAB) in New York City."

97. Philip St. Georges / UHAB, "The Housing Issue of 1978: City Owned Buildings," Undated, but likely January 1978. UHAB.

98. Mary Breasted, "New York Wins Fight on Tax Foreclosure," *NYT*, December 17, 1977.

99. Michael Goodwin, "City-Owned Houses come Complete with Pandora's Box," *NYT*, January 7, 1979.

100. Ibid.

101. See, for example, Charles Laven, "Testimony of the Urban Homesteading Assistance Board—Public Hearings on Local Law Int. No. 956-A at the Executive Chamber, City Hall, October 6, 1976," UHAB.

102. Activists produced several reports that demonstrated how bureaucratic delays were strangling the program and made suggestions for how it could be improved. See Wendy Faxon, "New Hope for Tenants of City-Owned Buildings (INREM)," *CFF*, January 1979, 5 and The Cathedral Church of St. John the Divine Press Release, "Black Elected Officials and Bishop Moore Call on Next Mayor to Implement Direct Sales Program," September 6, 1977. UHAB.

103. Memorandum from Ed Koch to Nat Leventhal dated January 22, 1979. Box 174, Folder 5. EIK.

104. The Task Force on City Owned Property, "The Report on the Task Force on City Owned Property," March 29, 1978, 3 and 2. UHAB.

105. Geoffrey Stokes, "Shelter Skelter: Abandoned Housing: A Problem Worse than the Fiscal Crisis," *VV*, March 6, 1978.

106. John Kifner, "Tax-Delinquent Realty Groups Buys More Property at Municipal Auction, Though Law Bars the Sales," *NYT*, March 2, 1978.

107. Quoted in Susan Baldwin, "City's Auction Sales: Going, Going, Gone?" *CL*, September 1978, 2.

108. Susan Baldwin, "City's In Rem Program May be a Wayward Bus," *CL,* January 1979, 14. See also "The Reminiscences of Ruth Messinger," 15 (1994). OHC.

109. Susan Baldwin, "City Asks Feds to Fund $100M CD Plan for City-Held Units," *CL,* March 1979, 16–17.

110. See Task Force on City-Owned Property, "Statement on the Proposed Public Auction Policy," August 10, 1979. Box 5, Folder "In Rem-Organiz'l '79." MCH.

111. Nat Leventhal memorandum to Ed Koch, January 30, 1979. Box 174, Folder 5. EIK.

112. Jonathan Steinberg, "How City Tenant Groups Take Steps Toward Ownership," *NYT*, September 9, 1979.

113. Nathan Leventhal memorandum to Edward Koch, "Adoption of a Citywide Sales Policy for Disposition of City-owned (In Rem) Properties to Non-Profit Groups," December 11, 1978. UHAB.

114. Jonathan Soffer, *Ed Koch and the Rebuilding of New York City* (New York: Columbia University Press, 2010), 142.

115. See chapter 5 of this book.

116. Leventhal memorandum to Koch, January 30, 1979.

117. Glenn Fowler, "$55.6 Million by Fall to Help South Bronx is Pledged by U.S.," *NYT*, April 13, 1978.

118. Ibid.

119. Susan Baldwin, "$250 Buys More Sweat Than Equity in City's Low-Cost Housing Sales," *CL*, December 1979, 11.

120. Richard Goldstein, "The Gentry Comes to the East Village," *ND*, May 19, 1980.

121. David Bird, "Mayor Will Seek Agencies to Run Seized Dwellings," *NYT*, April 12, 1979.

122. Task Force on City-Owned Property to Carol Bellamy, May 8, 1979. Box 4, Folder "HPD: POMP." HPD.

123. Susan Baldwin, "Owners Play 'POMP' and Circumstance, Get $1.5M CD Funds for In Rem Units," *CL,* June/July 1979, 2 and 17.

124. Tom Robbins, "Sales Price for Clinton Buildings is Still a Secret," *CL,* August–September 1982, 11.

125. Susan Baldwin, "City Reneges on $250 Sales Policy," *CL*, October 1979, 4.

126. Susan Baldwin, "The City and Clinton Tenants Spar on Leases," *CL*, December 1980, 11.

127. "Mr. Mayor: We Want to Keep Our Homes" Flier. Box 62, Folder "In Rem HPD '81–'80 City Owned Buildings." MCH.

128. Tom Robbins, "City Sales Tag on Clinton Buildings?" *CL,* April 1982, 5.

129. William Eimicke and Valerie Asciutto to Deputy Mayor Leventhal, August 9, 1982. Box 10, Folder "July 82–." NL.

130. Bonnier Brower, "Requiem for a Housing Policy: Selling Alternative Management," *CL,* October 1982, 23 and 24.

131. Bernard Cohen and Susan Baldwin, "Sales Controls Pose Problems for Low Income Ownership," *CL,* January 1980, 16.

132. Susan Baldwin, "Tenants Win $250 Sales Pledge But There's a Catch," *CL,* December 1982, 18.

133. Eimicke and Asciutto to Leventhal, August 9, 1982.

134. These restrictions would last for ten years for TIL buildings and fifteen years for Community Management buildings. See Baldwin, "Tenants Win $250 Sales Pledge," 18.

135. Statement by Council President Carol Bellamy, November 18, 1982. Box 10, Folder "HPD—September 1982." NL.

136. Carol Bellamy, "Letter to Editor," *NYT,* November 6, 1982.

137. See, for example, Julia McDonnell Chang and Tom Robbins, "Keeping the Prices Right on TIL Apartments," *CL*, April 1984, 12.

138. Commissioner Anthony Gliedman to Mayor Edward I. Koch, December 14, 1982. Box 176, Folder 3. EIK.

139. Victor Maldonado, "On a TIL Mission in Park Slope," *CL,* April 1984, 14.

140. Chang and Robbins, "Keeping the Prices Right on TIL Apartments," 12.

141. Ibid.

142. Bernard Cohen, "Growth: An Agenda for the 1980's," *CL*, August–September, 1979, 4.

143. Susan Baldwin, "Community Management Productivity," *CL,* December 1979, 16–17 and Ronald Lawson with Reuben E. Johnson III, "Tenant Responses to the Urban Housing Crisis, 1970–1984," 237.

144. "Memorandum from Housing Conservation Coordinators, Inc. to The Tenants of the Community Management Buildings," October 14, 1977. Reel 104. HC.

145. Housing Conservation Coordinators Newsletter, Undated. Reel 104. HC.

146. Erika Mallin and Lisa Glazer, "The End of an Era," *CL,* October 1992, 14.

147. Memorandum from Carol Felstein to Nathan Leventhal, September 30, 1980. Box 38, Folder "HPD September 1980." NL.

148. Cohen, "Growth: An Agenda for the 1980's," 5.

149. Quoted in David Gonzalez, "In the South Bronx, the Grass Roots Grows Up," *NYT,* January 7, 1993.

150. Harold DeRienzo, "Managing the Crisis," *CL,* December 1994, 25.

151. Lueck, "The Tenant-as-Landlord Movement."

152. Lisa Glazer, "Beyond Bricks and Mortar," *CL,* May 1992, 13.

153. Gonzalez, "In the South Bronx, the Grass Roots Grow Up."

154. Julia McDonnell Change, "Rebuilding Home: Tenants Take a New Lease on City Life," *CL,* April 1984, 8.

155. *Self Help in Our Own Words: UHAB, 1974–1988* (New York: The Urban Homesteading Assistance Board, 1989), 10.

156. Ibid., 7.

157. Susan Saegert, "Survey of Residents of Currently and Previously City-Owned Buildings in the Bronx," in *Housing in the Balance: Seeking a Comprehensive Policy for City-Owned Housing,* ed. M. Cotton (New York City: Task Force on City Owned Property, 1993), 2.

CHAPTER 2

1. Unknown author, letter to Mayor John V. Lindsay, December 17, 1969. Box 17, Folder "Coop/Condo Conversion 1970–1974 #1." MCH.

2. Quoted in "Tompkins Warns on Co-Op Curb," *RER,* August 25, 1969, 1.

3. Joseph P. Fried, "Rent Rises: Exorbitant or Not," *NYT,* July 28, 1968.

4. Kristina Ford, *Housing Policy and the Urban Middle Class* (New Brunswick, NJ: The Center for Urban Policy Research, 1978), xxv.

5. In 1960, only 21 percent of the city's housing was owner-occupied, with much of this stock concentrated in single-family homes in the outer boroughs or in owner-occupied units in small rental buildings. Cooperatives—the principal homeownership structure in the multifamily buildings that dominated much of New York's built environment—accounted for less than 1 percent of the housing stock at that time. Department of Housing and Urban Development, *Condominium/Cooperative Study,* Volume 2 (July 1975), C-9-11.

6. Following the enactment of zoning regulations in the mid-1960s, new construction plunged. Only one privately built cooperative opened in Manhattan between 1966 and 1967, and none were completed in either 1968 or 1969. Franklin Whitehouse, "Co-op Drought Goes on Here for 2d Year," *NYT,* May 11, 1969.

7. Quoted in Alan S. Oser, "Shift to Coops Grows in City," *NYT,* November 23, 1969.

8. "Tompkins Scores Bill On Co-Op Conversions," *RER,* April 12, 1971, 1.

9. Herman B. Glaser, "Letter to the Editor," *NYT*, December 6, 1970.

10. Ford, *Housing Policy and the Urban Middle Class*, 119.

11. George Goodman Jr., "Co-Op Curbs Asked by Tenant Groups," *NYT*, March 26, 1972.

12. Thomas W. Ennis, "More Tenants Seeking 'Landlord' Role," *NYT*, March 16, 1969.

13. W. Dennis Keating, "Rent Regulation in New York City," in *Rent Control: Regulation and the Rental Housing Market*, ed. W. Dennis Keating, Michael B. Teitz, and Andrejs Skaburskis (New Brunswick, NJ: Center for Urban Policy Research, 1998), 156.

14. Memorandum from Joseph Polser, Director of Public Relations to Commissioner Frederic S. Berman, January 20, 1967. Box 5035, No folder. RS.

15. "Seminar on How to Co-op Apts," *RER*, October 6, 1969, 1.

16. Unattributed 1969 newspaper article titled "Rent Bill Hearing Will Draw Debate at City Hall." Included as part of Box 50267, Local Law 50, 1969. NYCC.

17. Quoted in "Tompkins Warns on Co-Op Curb," *RER*, August 25, 1969, 1.

18. See Samuel Zipp, *Manhattan Projects: The Rise and Fall of Urban Renewal in Cold War New York* (New York: Oxford University Press, 2010).

19. Alan S. Oser, "Shift to Co-ops Grows in City," *NYT*, November 23, 1969.

20. See Ira S. Lowry, *Rental Housing in New York City, Volume 1: Confronting the Crisis* (New York: The New York City RAND Institute, 1970).

21. Ronald Lawson with Reuben E. Johnson III, "Tenant Responses to the Urban Housing Crisis, 1970–1984," in *The Tenant Movement in New York City, 1904–1984*, ed. Ronald Lawson with the assistance of Mark Naison (New Brunswick, NJ: Rutgers University Press, 1986), 211. Critics noted that Sternlieb's "data demonstrated no consistent relationship between rent control and either disinvestment or housing deterioration." David Bartelt and Ronald Lawson, "Rent Control and Abandonment: A Second Look at the Evidence," *Journal of Urban Affairs* 4, no. 4 (September 1982): 53.

22. Bartelt and Lawson, "Rent Control and Abandonment," 51.

23. Tony Sanders, "Mayor's Homeownership and Home Improvement Program," July 31, 1969, 2. Box 26, Folder 464. JVL.

24. Ibid.

25. Thomas W. Ennis, "Co-op Conversions Amended by State," *NYT*, June 22, 1969 and Oser, "Shift to Co-ops Grows in City."

26. Matthew Gordon Lasner, *High Life: Condo Living in the Suburban Century* (New Haven, CT: Yale University Press, 2012), 258.

27. Rita Savoy to Honorable Louis J. Lefkowitz, June 2, 1969. Box 5035, Folder "Rent and Rehabilitation." RS.

28. For an excellent overview, see Lasner, *High Life*, 263–265.

29. Attorney General Louis Lefkowitz to Mayor John V. Lindsay, May 12, 1969. Box 5035, Folder "Rent and Rehabilitation." RS.

30. See Thomas W. Ennis, "State Bars Plan to Set Up Co-ops," *NYT*, May 14, 1969.

31. Author interview with David Clurman, October 25, 2012. See also Ennis, "Co-Op Conversions Amended by State."

32. "Report on Meeting of New York City Tenants' Association for Fair Cooperative Practice," March 21, 1970. Box 17, Folder "Coop/Condo Conversion 1970–1974 #1." MCH.

33. "N.Y.C. Tenants Association Against Unfair Cooperative Practices flier," April 15, 1970. Box 17, Folder "Coop/Condo Conversion 1970–1974 #1." MCH.

34. "Stop Cooperative Coercion Now! Flier," Box 17, Folder "Coop/Condo Conversion 1970–1974 #1." MCH.

35. Judith C. Lack, "Apartments Go Co-op 'Outside the Law,'" *NYT*, January 5, 1975.

36. "Park Terrace Gardens Tenants' Association Opinion of the Prospectus for the Co-Operative Plan, 1971," 6. Box 17, Folder "Coop/Condo Conversion 1970–1974 #1." MCH.

37. Ibid., 8.

38. Ibid., 1.

39. Savoy to Lefkowitz, June 2, 1969.

40. Housing and Urban Development, Division of Policy Studies, *The Conversion of Rental Housing to Condominiums and Cooperatives*, Volume 2 (June 1980), 217.

41. Christine E. Samurovich, "Pro," *NYT*, April 22, 1973.

42. Elise Leoni, "Letter to the Editor," *NYT*, December 6, 1970.

43. Vermeer Tenants Organization Bulletin, February 3, 1972. Box 17, Folder "Coop/Condo Conversion 1970–1974 #1." MCH. Emphasis in the original.

44. Vermeer Tenants Organization Flier, January 1972. Box 17, Folder "Coop/Condo Conversion 1970–1974 #1." MCH.

45. Vermeer Tenants Organization Bulletin, February 24, 1972. Box 17, Folder "Coop/Condo Conversion 1970–1974 #1." MCH.

46. Ibid.

47. Henry Miller, "Letter to the Editor," *NYT*, January 9, 1972.

48. Oser, "Shift to Co-ops Grows in City."

49. This was particularly the case in rent-controlled buildings, where tenants might range from lower-income residents holding on to their apartment out of necessity to the affluent keeping tenancy because of its "cheap" rent.

50. David A. Andelman, "In the Excelsior, Bitterness Replaces Tenant Unity," *NYT*, August 2, 1970.

51. Joel Mandelbaum, "Tenants Evaluate Shift to Co-op," *NYT*, April 23, 1972.

52. Steven R. Weisman, "The Excelsior," *NYT*, November 23, 1969; Glenn Fowler, "Excelsior's Owners Ease Terms," *NYT*, April 26, 1970; and Andelman, "In the Excelsior."

53. Leona Mindy Roberts, "Cooperative Apartments—A Important Factor in Housing," *REN*, April 1971, 11.

54. Henry Hart Rice, "Co-ops in New Form Can Save Housing," *NYT*, January 24, 1971.

55. Arnold Witte, Commerce and Industry Association of New York, Inc., "Concerning Cooperative Apartment Restrictive Legislation, Prepared for Presentation before the City Council Committee on Housing, March 22, 1971." Box 50803. Introduction 113. 1970. NYCC.

56. Roberts, "Cooperative Apartments," 11.

57. Quoted in Joel, "Tenants Evaluate Shift to Co-Op."

58. See, for example, "Banking Superintendent Sees Cooperative Apartment Loan Program Expanding Rapidly Soon," *REN*, February 1972, 30 and Lasner, *High Life*, 265–266. With privately developed cooperatives traditionally purchased by the very affluent, financing had typically not been needed. When offered, it was commonly through personal loans, which hardly benefited middle-class purchasers, as without a home they typically had little to provide as collateral.

59. Quoted in Peter Hellman, "The New Way to Buy a Co-Op," *NY*, January 24, 1972, 52.

60. Lasner, *High Life*, 265.

61. Alan S. Oser, "Broad Loan Aid to Buy Co-Ops Found Unlikely," *NYT*, August 1, 1971 and *Condominium / Cooperative Study*, C-21.

62. Hellman, "The New Way to Buy a Co-Op," 52.

63. Lasner, *High Life*, 266.

64. Samuel Boksenbom to Hon. Donald R. Manes, Chairman. Box 50804. Housing Committee, Introduction 113, 1970. NYCC.

65. "Co-Op Conversion," *NYT*, April 16, 1973.

66. *Condominium/Cooperative Study*, Volume 2, C-24.

67. Ibid., C-25.

68. Joseph P. Fried, "Fraud is Charged in Building Co-Op," *NYT*, April 20, 1974.

69. Martin Gansberg, "Pressure is Cited in Co-op Changes," *NYT*, March 23, 1971.

70. Vincent Cannato, *The Ungovernable City: John Lindsay and His Struggle to Save New York* (New York: Basic Books, 2001), 549.

71. *Condominium/Cooperative Study*. Volume 2, C-3.

72. See, for example, "The Case for Conversion to Co-ops: Sulzberger Testifies," *Realty*, May 3, 1977.

73. Tenant Owned Apartment Association, Inc., "Cooperative Apartment Conversions: Their Importance and the Adequacy of Existing Restrictions," April 3, 1970. Box 50804. Housing Committee, Introduction 117. 1970. NYCC.

74. Great American Realty Corporation to Thomas Cuite, March 22, 1971. Box 50804. Housing Committee, Introduction 113. 1970. NYCC.

75. Alfonso A. Narvaez, "Albany Bill to Make Co-op Conversions More Difficult is Bogged Down," *NYT*, April 19, 1973.

76. John R. O'Donoghue, REBNY to Stanley M. Friedman, August 15, 1973. Box 50807. Housing Committee, Introduction 1294. 1973. NYCC.

77. Zipp, *Manhattan Projects*, 78.

78. William G. Connolly, "Helmsley Makes Parkchester a Testing Ground," *NYT*, December 24, 1972 and William G. Connolly, "Parkchester Condominium Authorized," *NYT*, December 15, 1972.

79. Connolly, "Helmsley Makes Parkchester a Testing Ground."

80. "Parkchester Tenants Act to Bar Condominium Conversion Plan," *NYT*, April 4, 1974. Quote from John J. Whalen, President of the Parkchester Defense Fund to Governor Malcolm Wilson, June 3, 1974. L. 1974. ch. 1021. NYBJ.

81. Parkchester Tenants Association Condominium Information Sheet," January 4, 1973. Box 14, Folder "Parkchester Tenants Association Folder." RL.

82. Allan M. Siegal, "In Parkchester, Old Tenants Fear Condominium Plan," *NYT*, June 6, 1974.

83. John Dearie, "The Conversion Game: The Newest Housing Crisis," *VV*, April 11, 1974, 15.

84. *Report on Housing and Rents of the Temporary State Commission on Living Costs and the Economy of the State of New York to the Governor and the Legislature* (January 1974). Reel 27. Subject: Housing General (Misc.). MW.

85. Tenant opposition was also motivated in part by racist concerns that the conversion would disrupt the nearly all-white composition that MetLife had maintained. Rent control meant that there had been little turnover of units even after the sale to Helmsley. But a conversion would likely bring in new residents, whom many residents believed would be moderate-income African American and Latinx residents of the Bronx. Allan M. Siegal, "In Parkchester, Old Tenants Fear Condominium Plan," *NYT*, June 6, 1974.

86. Georgia Dullea, "It's Decision Time at Parkchester," *NYT*, February 4, 1973.

87. Dearie, "The Conversion Game," 14–15, 18.

88. Ibid., 18.

89. If owners proceeded with an eviction plan, they previously were able to hold a percentage of apartments vacant before the conversion and then could count sales of these units in reaching 35 percent. Under the new law, landlords who proceeded with eviction plans for rent-controlled buildings could not count sales to outsiders in reaching 35 percent and had only six months to achieve the requisite number of sales. If the building was predominately rent-stabilized, landlords could count sales to outsiders in reaching 35 percent and typically had eighteen months to do so. See Edward H. Lehner and David J. Sweet, "Goodman-Dearie Expiration Leaves Coop Conversions Radically Altered," *NYLJ*, November 16, 1977.

90. Gerald Goldie to Michael Whiteman, May 24, 1974. L. 1974. ch 1021. NYBJ.

91. Biagio P. Riina to Michael Whiteman, June 4, 1974. L. 1974. ch 1021. NYBJ.

92. Dearie, "The Conversion Game: The Newest Housing Crisis," 18.

93. John J. Whalen, President of the Parkchester Defense Fund to Governor Malcolm Wilson, June 3, 1974. L. 1974. ch 1021. NYBJ.

94. Robert E. Tomasson, "Parkchester's Conversion to Condominium Halted," *NYT*, April 1, 1975 and "New Law Induces Helmsley to Delay Tudor City Change," *NYT*, June 17, 1974.

95. Quoted in Walter Rugaber, "Condominium Trend Cuts Rental Market," *NYT*, September 28, 1974.

96. Department of Housing and Urban Development, *Condominium/Cooperative Study*, Volume 1 (July 1975), V-35.

97. Department of Housing and Urban Development, *Condominium/Cooperative Study*, Volume 3 (July 1975), 1. F-9.

98. Department of Housing and Urban Development, *The Conversion of Rental Housing to Condominiums and Cooperatives: National Study of Scope, Causes and Impacts* (June 1980), XII-4.

99. Testimony of Benjamin Rosenthal in Department of Housing and Urban Development, *Transcript of Hearings on Condominiums and Cooperatives*, February 10, 1975, 19.

100. Ibid., 10.

101. Robert E. Tomasson, "Banks are Easing Co-op Loan Rules," *NYT*, July 2, 1972 and Samurovich, "Pro," *NYT*, April 22, 1973.

102. Alan S. Oser, "Law Hampers the Switch of Rental Housing to Co-ops," *NYT*, April 30, 1976.

103. Ibid.

104. Wendy Schuman, "Co-op Owners Battle Rise in Costs," *NYT*, January 11, 1976.

105. *Condominium/Cooperative Study*, Volume 1, 1.

106. *Condominium/Cooperative Study*, Volume 2, C-11 and Volume 1, 1.

107. "Condo-Cooperative Offers Flexible Financing and Marketing, Meets Instant Success," *The Condominium Report* 3, no. 6 (July 1975).

108. Wendy Schuman, "Luxury Condominiums Attract Corporate Owners," *NYT*, April 11, 1976.

109. Ronald Smothers, "Measure to Let Museum Build Apartment Loses," *NYT*, June 29, 1976.

110. Ronald Smothers, "Assembly Reverses Vote and Approves Plan for Museum," *NYT*, June 30, 1976.

111. See James R. Hudson, *The Unanticipated City: Loft Conversions in Lower Manhattan* (Amherst: University of Massachusetts Press, 1987); Aaron Shkuda, *The Lofts of Soho: Gentrification, Art, and Industry in New York, 1950–1980* (Chicago: University of Chicago Press, 2016); and Sharon Zukin, *Loft Living: Culture and Capital in Urban Change* (Baltimore: Johns Hopkins University Press, 1982).

112. Hudson, *The Unanticipated City*, 66.

113. Ibid., 61.

114. Ford, *Housing Policy and the Urban Middle Class*, 19–22.

115. David Clurman, "Building Conversions a Survival Tactic for Owners, Lenders," *NYLJ*, November 10, 1976.

116. "Lefkowitz Ruling 'Legalizes' Co-Op Apartment Ownership in Soho Area." Press Release of the Office of Attorney General Louis J. Lefkowitz. Box 65, Folder "Coop/Condo Conversion 1975–1977 #2." MCH.

117. Allan Talbot, "Preface" in *Housing Policy and the Urban Middle Class*, xix.

118. Hudson, *The Unanticipated City*, 71.

119. Brewster Ives, "The Douglas Elliman-Gibbons & Ives Index," *Douglas Elliman-Gibbons & Ives, Inc. Newsletter* 2, no. 1 (Winter 1978–1979). Ives's comments originally appeared in the fall 1977 newsletter.

120. Brewster Ives, Tenant-Owned Apartment Association, Inc. "Testimony before the New York State Assembly Standing Committee on Housing, March 11, 1977." Box 1. NYSAH.

121. Though the Democratic-controlled Assembly passed a three-year extension, it failed to pass the Republican-controlled Senate. Lehner and Sweet, "Goodman-Dearie Expiration Leaves Coop Conversions Radically Altered."

122. "A Housing Law Nobody Needs," *NYT*, March 21, 1977.

123. David Clurman, Condominium Committee of the New York State Bar Association, to Counsel of the Governor, July 13, 1976. L. 1976. ch. 504. NYBJ.

124. Dee Wedemeyer, "From Rental to Co-op: A Stormy Passage," *NYT*, August 6, 1978.

125. Alan S. Oser, "A Cooperative Conversion Without Evictions," *NYT*, March 24, 1978.

126. "The CYNC is Born," *HT*, May 2007, 49. HTA.

127. Ibid. and author interview with Marc Luxemburg, January 10, 2013.

128. Marc Luxemburg, President Council of West Side Cooperatives to Manhattan Media Corporation, April 14, 1978. CNYCC.

129. Joseph P. Fried, "Conversion of Rental Apartments Ticklish Concern for Legislature," *NYT*, April 8, 1977.

130. Sam Campbell, "Co-Op Conversion Increase Looming?" *The Westsider*, March 30, 1978.

131. "Calendar of Events," *NYT*, May 4, 1978.

132. Suleiman Osman, *The Invention of Brownstone Brooklyn: Gentrification and the Search for Authenticity in Postwar New York* (New York: Oxford University Press, 2011), 189.

133. Shkuda, *The Lofts of Soho*, 135 and 143.

134. "The Council of New York Cooperatives," *MC*, April 1981. VCMK.

135. "Council of New York Cooperatives Newsletter," 6, no. 2 (April 1981). CNYCC.

136. "Welcoming Remarks by Ray Hoey, President of the Council of New York Cooperatives," October 17, 1981. CNYCC.

137. "Editorial: Integrating the Co-op Community," *MC*, April 1981. VCMK.

138. Author interview with Carol Ott, December 20, 2012.

139. Duffie Cohen, "Co-Op Availability: The Market Today," *MC*, October 1981 and Hank Sopher, "Condominiums: Wave of the Future?" *MC*, December 1981. VCMK.

140. Austin Haldenstein, "The Renaissance of the West Side," *MC*, April 1981. VCMK and Tom Soter, "The Winds of Change," *HT*, May/June 1984. HTA.

141. See, for example, Nelson Boone, "Insider's Rights," *MC*, August 1981. VCMK; Carol Davis, "Don't Lose Your Inside Price," *MC*, July 1983. VCMK; "Getting Co-oped," *HT*, June 1982. HTA; and Stanley B. Dreyer, "Reading a Prospectus," *HT*, May/June 1983. HTA.

142. Boone, "Insider's Rights."

143. David W. Dunplap, "400 Attend a Conference on Running a Co-op," *NYT*, October 18, 1982.

144. Edward I. Koch, "Letter to the Editor," *HT*, May/June 1984. HTA.

145. "Text of Address Delivered by Koch at His Inauguration as Mayor of New York City," *NYT*, January 2, 1978.

146. Robert A. Kandel (Office of the Mayor Ed Koch) to Newton Avrutis, September 24, 1979. Box 67, Folder "Coop/Condo Conversion 1978–79 #3." MCH.

147. This quote is a *Times* summary of a statement by Koch's legislative representative. "Bill to Limit Use of Personal Data by State Gains Bipartisan Support," *NYT*, June 6, 1980.

148. Many of these new homeowners had been already living in the city when they purchased an apartment. *The Conversion of Rental Housing to Condominiums and Cooperatives*, Appendix 1, 218.

149. "The Manhattan Cooperator Reader Survey," *MC*, October 1981. VCMK.

150. Michael A. Stegman with Doug Hillstrom, *Housing in New York: Study of a City, 1984* (Prepared for the City of New York, Department of Housing Preservation and Development, 1985), 216, 230. The owners of units converted during this period were actually more likely to be people of color than the tenants who previously occupied those units. While whites comprised 79.4 percent of the owners of converted apartments, they had accounted for 84.3 percent of the tenants in these units prior to conversion. The percentage of African Americans in converted units increased from 10.1 to 13.3, while the number of Puerto Ricans decreased from 3 to 1.9 percent. Stegman, *Housing in New York*, 215–217.

151. See, for example, Michael McKee, "State Legislators Pass Group Funding, Reject Co-Op Protection Bill," *CL*, June–July 1980, 14.

152. Blake Fleetwood, "The New Elite and an Urban Renaissance," *NYTM*, January 14, 1979.

153. Leonard Sahling and Rona Stein, "Co-op Fever in New York City," *FRBNY Quarterly Review* (Spring 1980): 15.

154. Jeffry H. Gallet, "The Costs of Going Co-op: Can You Afford to Buy," *NY*, March 31, 1980, 51.

155. Vicki Chesler, "The New 51% Co-Op Law: An End to Eviction Conversions," *MC*, October 1982. VCMK.

156. Previously, the 35 percent threshold applied to rent-regulated tenants; the 1982 law raised this amount to 51 applied to all tenants in residence. The bill also

strengthened protections for seniors and handicapped tenants, significantly lengthened occupancy periods for nonpurchasing tenants in eviction plans, and included strong anti-harassment protections.

157. Michael McKee, "How the City Got a New Co-op Law," *CL*, August–September 1982, 26–28.

158. The most significant change during this time was the Emergency Tenant Protection Act (1974), which declared that any rent-controlled apartment vacated by its current tenant would become rent-stabilized. The law also made all apartments built after 1969—which had previously been unregulated—rent-stabilized.

159. Stegman, *Housing in New York*, 208.

160. Mary Keefe, "The Rise of the Counterfeit Co-op," *CL*, February 1990, 14–15, 17.

161. Alan S. Oser, "Rest of Parkchester's Tenants Get Conversion Plan," *NYT*, September 16, 1983.

162. Ibid.

163. "A Conversation with Robert Abrams," *RER*, April 1983, 9.

164. "The Real Estate Reporter Essay: Cooperative and Condominium Housing," *RER*, April 1983, 15.

165. Laurie Johnston, "Co-Ops Leading Latest Renaissance in Brooklyn," *NYT*, October 16, 1979.

166. Dee Wedemeyer, "Q & A with the Real Estate Board's President," *NYT*, October 3, 1982.

167. Thomas J. Lueck, "Homeownership at Record Level for New Yorkers," *NYT*, June 10, 1991.

168. Quoted in James Barron, "Tenants in Luxury Buildings Uniting to Press Their Complaints," *NYT*, January 20, 1980.

169. Carty B. Horsley, "Cashing in on Co-op Fever," *NYT*, December 3, 1978 and William G. Blair, "Co-op Prices in Manhattan at High in '79; Activity Dips," *NYT*, March 2, 1980.

170. Carter B. Horsley, "Study Shows Co-op Prices Nearly Quintupled," *NYT*, August 30, 1981.

171. Vicki Chesler, "The $3 Million Condo," *MC*, March 1984. VCMK.

172. Stegman, *Housing in New York*, 98.

173. For condominiums outpacing other forms of housing in the early 1980s, see Lee A. Daniels, "Condominiums Take the Lead," *NYT*, November 28, 1982.

174. Diane Henry, "Abrams Would Tighten Co-op Conversion Laws," *NYT*, May 23, 1981.

175. Walter H. Waggoner, "Brewster Ives is Dead at 81," *NYT*, May 7, 1985.

176. Clyde Haberman, "Study for City Calls Realty Tax 'Hideously Inequitable,'" *NYT*, April 24, 1981. See also E. J. Dionne Jr., "Legislature Overrides Carey, Property Tax Bill is Now Law," *NYT*, December 4, 1981 and "Council Helps Secure Fair Tax Treatment for Coopers," *Council of New York Cooperatives Newsletter* 7, no. 2 (April 1982): 5. CNYCC. Tax assessments remained severely

unequal in subsequent decades. Independent Budget Office, *Twenty-Five Years after S700A: How Property Tax Burdens have Shifted in New York City* (December 5, 2006).

177. Vicki Chesler, "The Growing Co-op Lobby," *MC*, September 1982. VCMK.

CHAPTER 3

1. Quoted in "Clurman Threatens to Shut Bryant Park," *NYT*, September 13, 1973.

2. Joseph B. Treaster, "Bryant Park: An Oasis Plagued by Crime," *NYT*, June 26, 1976.

3. Fred Ferretti, "Loss of a Headquarters: Why Union Carbide Corp. Opted to Leave New York," *Barron's National Business and Financial Weekly*, August 2, 1976.

4. "Civic Leader Wants Bryant Park Closed, Police Oppose Move," *NYT*, June 24, 1976.

5. John V. Lindsay, "White Paper: Parks and Recreation," October 8, 1965, 5. Box 66, Folder 831. JVL.

6. The Parks Council, "Citizens View Their Parks: Citizen Attitudes About New York City's Parks Disclosed by a Survey of Sitting Park Users" (1963). CHL.

7. "Park Travesty," *NYT*, May 5, 1976.

8. "Clurman Threatens to Shut Bryant Park," *NYT*, September 13, 1973.

9. New York's growing reliance on the private sphere for its parks was not simply the result of the policies of Mayor Rudolph Giuliani in the 1990s, nor did they originate with Mayor Ed Koch in the 1980s, as some scholars have argued. See Oliver D. Cooke, *Rethinking Municipal Privatization* (New York: Routledge, 2008) and Jonathan Soffer, *Ed Koch and the Rebuilding of New York* (New York: Columbia University Press, 2010).

10. Fred Siegel, "Reclaiming Our Public Spaces" *CJ*, Spring 1992; Jennifer Steinhauer, "For Parks, It's Not Easy Getting Green," *NYT*, May 21, 2004; and Citizens Budget Commission, *Making the Most of Our Parks*, June 2007, 2.

11. Danid Schuyler, *The New Urban Landscape: The Redefinition of City Form in Nineteenth-Century America* (Baltimore: Johns Hopkins University Press, 1986), 7.

12. Galen Cranz, *The Politics of Park Design: A History of Urban Parks in America* (Cambridge, MA: MIT Press, 1982).

13. Mason Williams, *City of Ambition: FDR, La Guardia, and the Making of Modern New York* (New York: Norton, 2013), 195.

14. Ibid., 194.

15. Robert A. Caro, *The Power Broker: Robert Moses and the Fall of New York* (New York: Random House, 1974), 331–332.

16. To be sure, there is a long history of elite involvement in New York parks. During the nineteenth century especially, wealthy individuals were not infrequently involved in influencing the development of new parkland and, at times, were involved in their administration. Central Park, for example, was governed from its initial

opening in 1857 to 1870 by a board of commissioners comprised of government-appointed Republican elites. Though calls for a nonpartisan board of guardians for Central Park continued into the early twentieth century, they were rarely made for other parks. Rare too in the late nineteenth and twentieth centuries was the explicit involvement in parks by the business or corporate spheres. Elites' influence never disappeared, but in the twentieth century their involvement in park administration disappeared and even their financial assistance diminished. Additionally, while there was a substantial history of resident involvement in parks, citizen movements in the late nineteenth and earlier twentieth centuries most commonly focused on developing new parks and playgrounds, rather than becoming involved directly in helping to administrate or care for parks (except one off-clean ups). See Roy Rosenzweig and Elizabeth Blackmar, *The Park and the People: A History of Central Park* (Ithaca, NY: Cornell University Press, 1992).

17. Rosenzweig and Blackmar, *The Park and the People*, 439–489. This included not just parkland, but all land under the domain of Parks and Recreation. New York Department of Parks and Recreation, "A Timeline of New York City Department of Parks & Recreation History." http://www.nycgovparks.org/about/history/timeline/robert-moses-modern-parks, accessed June 1, 2018.

18. The Parks Council, "Citizens View Their Parks," 2.

19. Ibid. 2.

20. Ibid. 6.

21. Lindsay, "White Paper," 13.

22. Department of Parks, "Press Release, June 29, 1967." Box 1, Folder "City Cultural Council." AH.

23. August Heckscher, "Recreation and the Urban Crisis," December 4, 1967. Box 64, Folder 808. JVL.

24. Quoted in Lester Abelman, "Park Boss: Be-Ins Are Too Far Out," *NYDN*, April 14, 1969.

25. The Parks Service Research Team of the State Charter Revision Commission, *Decentralizing Parks Services in New York City* (April 1975), 30. CPC and Deirdre Carmody, "A Rise in Deterioration of City's Parks is Feared Because of Budget Cutbacks," *NYT*, August 11, 1975. The Department's troubles went well beyond its budget. It continued to be ridden with patronage appointments and lacked even basic supervisory controls into the 1970s. Jack Newfield and Paul Du Brul, *The Permanent Government: Who Really Rules New York?* (New York: The Pilgrim Press, 1981), 112–113.

26. "Minutes of the 46th Annual Meeting of the Members of the Parks Council, Inc," June 8, 1972. Box 10, No folder. PC.

27. Herschel Post, "The Prospect for Parks" (likely mid-1972). Box 10, No folder. PC.

28. Park Association of New York City, Inc and Council for Parks and Playgrounds, Inc., "Park and Recreation White Paper—1969," October 17, 1969. Box 7391, Folder "Parks Dept." EH.

29. Joan Altman, "How to Adopt a Park," *The Livable City*, April 1979, 5.

30. George Murphy / Asphalt Green testimony at the Speak Out for the Future of Central Park, November 11, 1978. CPC.

31. George Murphy, "The Building and Recycling of a Landmark in a Model of Urban Partnership of Community Residents with Foundations, Business, and Government." Box 50026, Folder #8. Series: Local Laws. 1987. NYCC. Emphasis in original.

32. The Neighborhood Committee for the Asphalt Green, "Asphalt Green," April 15, 1976. Box 55, Folder "Grant Files, 1976. The Neighborhood Committee for the Asphalt Green." VAF.

33. Remarks of Mayor Abraham D. Beame, April 25, 1975. Box 55, Folder "Grant Files, 1976. The Neighborhood Committee for the Asphalt Green." VAF.

34. Dick Brass, "Volunteers Clean Up Parks All Over City," *NYSN*, August 15, 1976.

35. Ibid.

36. Fred Ferretti, "Citizen Group Suggests Volunteers be Used to Fill Gaps in City Services," *NYT*, December 2, 1975 and Howard E. Kane, "Queens Housewives Fill $1,000 Gap in Park Plan," *NYT*, March 25, 1973.

37. See Joseph P. Fried, "Queens Park Rises in Ruins of Wasteland," *NYT*, August 3, 1985 and N. R. Kleinfield, "Noisily Nurturing the Grass Roots," *NYT*, November 7, 1993.

38. Author interview with Gordon Davis, June 19, 2013.

39. Brass, "Volunteers Clean Up Parks All Over City."

40. Suleiman Osman, "We're Doing it Ourselves': The Unexpected Origins of New York City's Public–Private Parks during the 1970s Fiscal Crisis," *Journal of Planning History* 16, no. 2 (2017): 163.

41. In 1968, August Heckscher started a small Volunteers in Parks program, but the program remained "understaffed" and "virtually lost" within city bureaucracy. Park Association and Council for Parks and Playground, "Park and Recreation White Paper—1969."

42. Herschel Post to Jane Kosloff, March 29, 1973. Box 13, Folder 160. JVL.

43. Gordon Davis to Edward I. Koch, December 2, 1978. Box 225, Folder 6. EIK.

44. Martin King, "Call for More Volunteers to Clean Parks," *NYDN*, March 20, 1977.

45. Fred Ferretti, "New Yorkers Volunteer to Maintain Parks," *NYT*, June 7, 1977.

46. Ferretti, "Citizen Group Suggests Volunteers."

47. "Tooling up for Park Volunteers," *CPGT*, Spring 1977, 3. CPC and CCNYC, "Park Applications (Grants Made 3/30/1977)." Box 52, Folder "Grants Files, 1976 (Citizens Committee for New York City, Inc)." VAF.

48. The Parks Council, "Press Release: Mary Beame Opens the Season for Volunteers in Parks," June 14, 1977. Box 13, Folder 17. PC.

49. Jeannette Bamford to Linda Gillies, Director, December 26, 1978. Box 77, Folder "Grants Files, 1979 Parks Council." VAF.

50. John Hamill, "Vols Tend Parks in Face of Dried-up City Budget," *NYDN*, July 3, 1977.

51. Tom Buckley, "Central Park's New Era: Fun for Everyone," *NYT*, September 23, 1968.

52. "Pollution of the Park," *NYT*, May 5, 1971.

53. Lee Dembart, "Nearly All of Central Park's Trees Suffer from Neglect and Poor Care," *NYT*, June 4, 1973; Edward Hudson, "Central Park Condition Decried," *NYT*, June 8, 1973; Lucinda Franks, "An Oasis of Green in Need of Rescue," *NYT*, March 22, 1974.

54. The most prominent citizens group focused on Central Park in the late 1960s and early 1970s was the Friends of Central Park, which was devoted to protecting what they understood as the original Frederick Law Olmsted and Calvert Vaux vision for the park. As such, they opposed potential encroachments and raised money for hiring skilled horticulturists.

55. Betsy Haggerty, "The Park is for Playing," *ESE*, March 24, 1977.

56. Ferretti, "New Yorkers Volunteer to Maintain Parks."

57. Linda Gillies to Commissioner Martin Lang, February 11, 1976. Box 46, Folder "Grant Files, 1975. Central Park Task Force." VAF.

58. Interview with Betsy Rogers [Barlow], Summer 2009, CPC and Author interview with Betsy Barlow Rogers, April 24, 2013.

59. "Abandon Central Park?" Central Park Task Force pamphlet. Likely mid/late 1970s. CPC and "Toward a Zero Litter Park," *CPGT*, April/May 1976, 3. CPC.

60. "Toward a Zero Litter Park."

61. Lee Dembart, "Parks Agency Plight Epitomizes the City's," *NYT*, October 23, 1975.

62. "Helping to Keep the City's Longest Running Show, Central Park, Alive and Well," *CPGT*, Spring 1977, 3. CPC.

63. "Task Force Wins NEH Grant," *CPGT*, Summer 1978, 1. CPC.

64. Karen Shashowa, "A Brighter Future for Belvedere Castle," *CPGT*, Spring 1979, 2. CPC.

65. "Central Park Task Force Grant Application to Develop an Environmental Education Program using Central Park as a Curriculum Resource." Box 52, Folder "Grants File, 1976, Central Park Task Force." VAF.

66. Quoted in Myron Magnet, "The Growth Investor," *Philanthropy Magazine* (Summer 2010).

67. Richard Gilder Jr. and George Soros, "A Progress Report on the Program to Rehabilitate Central Park," undated, but likely mid-1973. CPC.

68. The City of New York Parks, Recreation and Cultural Affairs Administration, "Central Park Project," Box 36, Folder "Grant Files 1973. New York City Department of Parks and Recreation." VAF.

69. E. S. Savas, *Managing Central Park* (June 1974), 33. CHL.

70. Ibid., 25.

71. Ibid., 1.

72. Ibid., 55.

73. Anna Levin, Executive Vice President to Joseph Davidson, Commissioner of Recreation, March 16, 1976. Box 46, Folder "Grant Files, 1975. Central Park Task Force." VAF.

74. Central Park Community Fund fundraising letter, September 15, 1975. CPC.

75. Interview with Richard Gilder, Summer 2009, CPC.

76. Quoted in Jill Gerston, "Central Park Called Badly Managed; Report Urges a Board of Guardians," *NYT*, November 20, 1974.

77. Interview with Gilder.

78. Alexander W. Allport, Central Park Community Fund, "Letter to the Editor," *NYT*, May 26, 1976.

79. Quoted in Grassroots: Central Park Community Fund Newsletter, Winter 1977–78. CPC.

80. Elizabeth Barlow, "32 Ways Your Time or Money Can Rescue Central Park," *NY*, June 14, 1976, 32.

81. Ibid.

82. "In Gratitude," *CPGT*. August/September 1976. CPC.

83. Ibid.

84. Elizabeth Barlow, "Aftermath," *NY*, August 2, 1976.

85. Ward Morehouse III, "Rescuing New York's Central Park from Urban Blight," *CSM*, November 11, 1977.

86. Edward I. Koch, *The Mayor's Management Report*, August 18, 1978, 36. Included as part of New York Interface Development Project, "An Evaluation of Alternative Governance Proposals for Central Park." 1978. CPC.

87. Commissioner Gordon J. Davis, "Statement Before the Subcommittee on National Parks and Insular Affairs of the United States House of Representatives Committee on Interior and Insular Affairs," August 21, 1978. Included as part of "An Evaluation of Alternative Governance Proposals for Central Park."

88. "Toward a Zero Litter Park," *CPGT*.

89. David Noonan, "Central Park: The Way it Is," *ESE*, March 24, 1977.

90. Senator Patrick Moynihan Testimony at the Speak Out for the Future of Central Park, November 11, 1978. CPC.

91. The idea was not preposterous. The Department of Interior already operated Ellis Island and the Statue of Liberty and the Gateway National Recreation Area had been created in 1972 through the federalization of parts of Brooklyn, Queens, and Staten Island.

92. Leslie Maitland, "Special Management Plan Urged to Combat Central Park's Decay," *NYT*, November 12, 1978.

93. Gordon J. Davis to Clare Beckhardt, General Manager, New York State Parks Commission—New York City, March 19, 1981. Box 23, Folder "May 1981." NL.

94. Ibid.

95. Author interview with Davis.

96. Gordon J. Davis, "Proposal Summary: Central Park Administrator's Office Within the Department of Parks and Recreation," November 1978. CPC.

97. "Elizabeth Barlow, Author and Task Force Director, Appointed to Oversee Central Park," *Grassroots: Central Park Community Fund Newsletter* (Winter–Spring 1979): 1. CPC and Gordon J. Davis to Central Park Community Fund, December 26, 1978. CPC.

98. David Bird, "Now, a Better View Up in Central Park," *NYT*, September 27, 1979; "Doubled 'Green' Yields Greenery," *NYT*, May 18, 1979; and Grace Glueck, "A Conservancy Will Seek Private Central Park Aid," *NYT*, August 16, 1980.

99. *Grassroots: Central Park Community Fund Newsletter* (Winter–Spring 1979), 4. CPC.

100. Michael Goodwin and Anna Quindien, "New York City Park System Stands as a Tattered Remnant of its Past," *NYT*, October 13, 1980.

101. Michael Goodwin and Anna Quindien, "Parks Plagued by a Shortage of Good Help," *NYT*, October 14, 1980.

102. "Losing Ground in the Parks," *NYT*, October 15, 1980.

103. Gordon J. Davis to Edward I. Koch, September 22, 1980. Box 225, Folder 6. EIK.

104. Goodwin and Quindien, "New York City Park System Stands as a Tattered Remnant of its Past."

105. Deirdre Carmody, "Davis Quits Parks Post," *NYT*, January 27, 1983.

106. William Beinecke, "Letter from the Chairman," Central Park Conservancy Annual Report: 1981, 3. CPC.

107. Office of the Mayor Edward I. Koch, Press Release: December 1980. CPC.

108. Quoted in Glueck, "A Conservancy will Seek Private Central Park Aid."

109. *The Central Park Conservancy* (Undated, but likely early 1981). CPC

110. Author interview with Barlow Rogers. The proposal for a nonpartisan governing board of trustees was more than a century old, but faded in the early twentieth century. Rosenzweig and Blackmar, *The Park and the People*, 507.

111. Author Interview with Davis.

112. William S. Beinecke, *Through Mem'ry's Haze: A Personal Memoir* (New York: Prospect Hill Press, 2000), 478.

113. Quoted in "Conservancy's Beinecke Steps Down as Chairman," *CPGT*, Summer 1985, 10. CPC.

114. *The Central Park Conservancy*, 12.

115. William Beinecke, "Letter from the Chairman," Central Park Conservancy Annual Report: 1982 and Central Park Conservancy Annual Reports, 1981 and 1982. CPC.

116. Fred Ferretti, "Private Funds Help Park to Get More Loving Care," *NYT*, November 1, 1979.

117. This dynamic was described in several newspaper articles about Madison Square Park and Bryant Park. See, for example, Robert McG. Thomas Jr.,

"Clean-Up-or-Close Order is Driving 'Undesirables' Out of Bryant Park," *NYT*, October 29, 1973.

118. Historians have chronicled how throughout northern areas in the twentieth century, whites fought to keep public spaces like beaches and swimming pools segregated and even abandoned recreational spaces as they integrated. See, for example, Andrew W. Kahrl, *Free the Beaches: The Story of Ned Coll and the Battle for America's Most Exclusive Shoreline* (New Haven, CT: Yale University Press, 2018); Bryant Simon, *Boardwalk of Dreams: Atlantic City and the Fate of Urban America* (New York: Oxford University Press, 2004); and Thomas Sugrue, *Sweet Land of Liberty: The Forgotten Struggle for Civil Rights in the North* (New York: Random House, 2008), especially chapter 5.

119. Urban Park Plazas, "A Proposal to Provide Management, Supervision, and Supplemental Maintenance Services at Bryant Park," October 16, 1979, 2. Folder "Urban Park Plazas '80, '81, + '82." BPC.

120. Urban Park Plazas, "Madison Square Park Revitalization Program. Pilot Project. Final Report," January 16, 1980, 2. Folder "Urban Park Plazas '80, '81, + '82." BPC.

121. Quoted in Ferretti, "Private Fund Help Park to Get More Loving Care."

122. John Lewis, "A Broom and Bloom Effort for Parks," *NYDN*, December 18, 1979.

123. Urban Park Plazas, "A Proposal to Provide Management," 1.

124. "With Company's Help, a 'New' Park," *New York Life News* (likely late 1979 or early 1980). Folder "Urban Park Plazas '80, '81, + '82." BPC.

125. Urban Park Plazas, "A Proposal to Provide Management," 2.

126. Richard M. Clurman to Richard R. Shinn, President, Metropolitan Life Insurance Company, July 10, 1979. Folder "Bryant Park Restoration Corporation, 1979–1981." BPC.

127. Ferretti, "Private Funds Help Park to Get More Loving Care."

128. Clurman to Shinn, July 10, 1979.

129. Ibid.

130. Urban Park Plazas, "Madison Square Park Revitalization Program. Pilot Project. Final Report," January 16, 1980, 2. Folder "Urban Park Plazas '80, '81, + '82." BPC.

131. William Sweeney, "Cleaning Up the Yard," *Metrolines* 1, no. 6 (December 14, 1979). Folder "Urban Park Plazas '80, '81, + '82." BPC.

132. Robert W. Poole Jr., "Adopting City Parks," *Dollars & Sense*, July 1980, 3.

133. Ferretti, "Private Funds Help Park to Get More Loving Care."

134. Urban Park Plazas, "Madison Square Park Revitalization Program: Annual Report, January 1–December 31, 1981 and 1982 Proposal," January 1982, 1. BPC.

135. Ferretti, "Private Funds Help Park to Get More Loving Care."

136. Mary Breasted, "Fair to Help Fix Up Bryant Park Dampened by Rain," *NYT*, May 10, 1977.

137. Martin Lang to Jerome Gartner, The Bryant Park Steering Committee, April 15, 1977. Box 14, Folder "Bryant Park." HS.

138. Lang to Gartner, April 15, 1977.

139. Quoted in Claire Spiegel, "Bryant Park Cleanup Fouled Up," *NYDN*, September 7, 1977.

140. Leslie Maitland, "Bryant Park is Showing Improvement, but It Still Has Its Ups and Downs," *NYT*, July 1, 1978.

141. Andrew Heiskell, Doctorate Commencement Address, City University of New York, May 31, 1984. Folder "BPRC Chron April, May, June '84." BPC.

142. Quoted in Stan Pinkwas, "Taming Bryant Park," *ESE*, May 27–June 2, 1982.

143. Bryant Park Restoration Corporation, "A Plan for the Restoration of Bryant Park," April 1980, 2. BPC.

144. Ibid. The group did encourage the city to provide as much maintenance as possible and called for increased policing.

145. Walter H. Weiner to J. R. Mulhearn, February 11, 1980. BPC.

146. Minutes of a Meeting of the Board of Director of the Bryant Park Restoration Corporation, October 24, 1983. Folder "BPRC Bd. Meeting and Minutes, 10/24/83." BPC.

147. "A Plan for the Restoration of Bryant Park," 21. BPC.

148. Bryant Park Restoration Corporation, "Annual Report: 1980," March 1981, 4. BPC.

149. Editorial, "Counterattack in Bryant Park," *NYT*, November 13, 1981.

150. "Bryant Park Restoration Corporation, Major Grants, 1980–1986," Folder "Bryant Park Restoration Corporation, 1982–1986." BPC.

151. Dan Biederman, "Memorandum to Supporters of the Bryant Park Restoration Corporation," May 24, 1982. Folder "BPRC Chron Jan-Dec 1982." BPC.

152. Bryant Park Restoration Corporation Board of Directors Meeting Minutes, April 26, 1982. Folder "BPBD Bd. Mtg. and Minutes 11/12/82." BPC.

153. By the end of 1982, reported robberies were down 72 percent from 1979 and grand larcenies, 23 percent. Larry Sutton, "Hope Peddlers of Bryant Park," *NYDN*, March 30, 1983.

154. Bryant Park Restoration Corporation, "A Plan for Bryant Park," February 1983. Folder "BP Drafts of Lease and Blueprints of Lighting 82–84." BPC.

155. Andrew Heiskell with Ralph Graves, "Struggling to Save Bryant Park," *NYT*, September 13, 1998.

156. WNEW-TV, "Transcript: Off the Set," March 3, 1985. Folder "BPRC Radio/TV Reports 83–85." BPC.

157. Bryant Park Restoration Corporation Minutes of Board of Directors Meetings, November 12, 1982. Folder "BPBD Bd. Mtg. and Minutes 11/12/82." BPC.

158. Daniel Biederman, to Peter Solomon, Lehman Brothers Kuhn Loeb, August 13,1981. Folder "BPRC Chron Jan—Dec 1981." BPC.

159. BIDs are discussed in greater detail in chapter 5.

160. Dan Biederman to Andrew Heiskell and Marshall Rose, May 27, 1982. Folder "BPRC Chron Jan-Dec 1982." BPC.

161. Bryant Park Restoration Corporation, "A Plan for Bryant Park," February 1983. Folder "BP Drafts of Lease and Blueprints of Lighting 82–84." BPC.

162. Vartan Gregorian to Diane Coffey / Office of the Mayor, April 21, 1983. Folder "Le Roy Plans." BPC.

163. Dan Biederman to Ann Haskel / Bankers Trust, August 1, 1983. Folder "BPRC Chron July, Aug, Sept 83." BPC.

164. Parks Council, "Bryant Park: The Issues and the Precedent," March 1984. Folder "Parks—Manhattan—Bryant Park—1974–1986." MAS.

165. Emily Melo Marks, President, the Parks Council, "Letter to the Editor," *NYT*, August 7, 1985.

166. Quoted in Deirdre Carmody, "Proposal for Restaurant in Bryant Park Disputed," *NYT*, May 16, 1983.

167. Quoted in "Another Merry Go-Round in Bryant Park," *Metropolis*, June 1984, 9.

168. Quoted in T.J. Collins, "$18-Million Dream to Fix Bryant Park," *ND*, December 4, 1983.

169. Quoted in Peter Breilberg, "Privatizing Bryant Park," *Metropolis*, October 1983.

170. Deirdre Carmody, "Vast Rebuilding of Bryant Park Planned," *NYT*, December 1, 1983.

171. "Restoring Bryant Park," *NYDN*, December 3, 1983.

172. WQXR, "Transcript of New York at 6," December 13, 1983. Folder "BPRC Radio/TV Reports 83–85." BPC.

173. WCBS-TV, "Transcript of Newsmakers," July 7, 1985, 12. Folder "BPRC Radio/TV Reports 83–85." BPC.

174. By the early 2000s, community groups helped care for fully half of the city's parks.

175. City of New York Parks and Recreation, *Seven Years of Progress, 1983–1990* (1990), 24. DPR.

176. For a business-led revitalization initiative, see Sharon Zukin's discussion of the Union Square Partnership in *Naked City: The Death and Life of Authentic Urban Places* (New York: Oxford University Press, 2010), chapter 4.

177. Quoted in Laura Vanderkam, "How Private Citizens Saved New York's Public Spaces," *CJ*, Summer 2011. See also Susan Heler Anderson, "An Oasis Turning to Seed, Riverside Park Wins Friends," *NYT*, October 2, 1987.

178. *Seven Years of Progress, 1983–1990*, 23.

179. Peter Harnik and Abby Martin, *Public Spaces/Private Money: The Triumphs and Pitfalls of Urban Park Conservancies* (San Francisco: The Trust for Public Land, 2015), 7.

180. Ibid., 5.

181. See, for example, sales materials from Helmsley-Spears for 14 West 40th Street. Folder "BPRC Chron July, Aug, Sept 83." BPC.

182. "Minutes of Meeting of the Board of Directors," June 7, 1985. Folder "BPRC Bd. Mtg. and Minutes, 12/20/85." BPC and "The Central Park Conservancy," *The Douglas Elliman Newsletter*, Winter 1983–1984.

183. In the late 1960s, the Parks department's percentage of the city budget was 1.5. This declined to .82 percent in 1986 and .38 by 2004. Its staff was cut 57 percent between 1988 and 2003. "New York City Adopts 'Adopt-a-Park," *Ecopolitics,* Fall 2003; Leonard Post, "Balancing 'Duty,' Resources," *ND,* August 4, 2002; Sam Roberts, "For Parks Chief, Offbeat Charm is His Signature," *NYT,* October 2, 1988. Timothy Williams, "Report Assails Poor Upkeep in City Parks," *NYT,* June 16, 2006.

184. Citizens Budget Commission, *Making the Most of Our Parks,* June 2007. Inspired by the models in Central and Riverside Parks, the city created the City Parks Foundation in 1989 to raise funds for the park system from the private sector. The Foundation would raise tens of millions of dollars in subsequent decades, but did not offset the growing disparities throughout the system.

185. James Bradley, "Faded Glory," *CL,* August–September 1994, 30–32.

186. Ibid.

187. Yael Kohen, "City Gets 'C' on Parks Report Card," *New York Sun,* June 23, 2004. MAS.

188. Frankie Edozien, "'Putrid' Parks," *NYP,* June 16, 2006.

189. Williams, "Report Assails Poor Upkeep in City Parks."

190. George Murphy / Asphalt Green testimony at the Speak Out for the Future of Central Park, November 11, 1978. CPC and Carter Wiseman, "Public Parks, Private Cash," *NY,* October 27, 1980, 21.

191. As Suleiman Osman has noted, the financial leaders, elites, and state officials charged with managing city finances during the fiscal crisis "spoke little of either devolving park management to volunteers and self-help groups, contracting out park maintenance to private companies or load-shedding parks by selling them to corporations or nonprofits." Osman, "We're Doing it Ourselves," 166.

CHAPTER 4

1. Martin Gansberg, "Overflow Brooklyn Heights Meeting Protests Rising Crime and Asks Aid," *NYT,* February 1, 1971.

2. "Minutes of the Board of Governors Meeting of the Brooklyn Heights Association April 13, 1971." Box 4, Folder "B.H.A. Minutes of Board Meetings-1971–73." BHA.

3. Gansberg, "Overflow Brooklyn Heights Meeting Protests Rising Crime and Asks Aid."

4. Ibid.

5. Ibid.

6. "BHA Bulletin," Number 69, April 1969. Box 15, Folder "Brooklyn Heights Association 1967–70." BHA.

7. Brooklyn Heights Association, Letter to Members, January 31, 1972. Box 15, Folder "Brooklyn Heights Association 1967–70." BHA.

8. Ibid.

9. Jonathan Soffer, *Ed Koch and the Rebuilding of New York City* (New York: Columbia University Press, 2010), 321 and Julilly Kohler-Hausmann, *Getting Tough: Welfare and Imprisonment in 1970s America* (Princeton, NJ: Princeton University Press, 2017), 37.

10. Michael Fortner, *Black Silent Majority: The Rockefeller Drug Laws and the Politics of Punishment* (Cambridge, MA: Harvard University Press, 2015), 222–223.

11. Eric C. Schneider, *Smack: Heroin and the American City* (Philadelphia: University of Pennsylvania Press, 2011), 117 and Kohler-Hausmann, *Getting Tough*, 37.

12. Schneider, *Smack*, 117.

13. Ibid.

14. Michael Stern, "Fear Soars with Rate of Crime," *NYT*, December 11, 1968.

15. Hope Macleod, "A Cop's Advice on Muggings," *NYP*, February 18, 1971.

16. Jay Kriegel to Robert Sweet, July 5, 1967. Box 5036, Folder "Crime Commission." RS.

17. Ralph Mahoney, "Mayor Opens All-Out War on N.Y. Crime," *NYP*, March 9, 1967 and Martin Tolchin, "Lindsay Declares Crime is Key Problem Here and Says Fight Against it is Given Priority," *NYT*, May 16, 1969.

18. Kohler-Hausmann, *Getting Tough*, 35 and Schneider, *Smack*, 116.

19. Schneider, *Smack*, 123–124.

20. Stern, "Fear Soars with Rate of Crime."

21. Investigating suspected crime was largely the province of private actors before municipal police forces began to form in the 1840s. Although private security firms offered guard services to patrol public streets, as municipal forces grew, security guards increasingly moved onto private property, especially in the twentieth century. Frank Morn, *"The Eye That Never Sleeps": A History of the Pinkerton National Detective Agency* (Bloomington: Indiana University Press, 1982), 26–34.

22. Notable and recent examples include: Michelle Alexander, *The New Jim Crow: Mass Incarceration in the Age of Colorblindness* (New York: The New Press, 2010); James Forman Jr., *Locking Up Our Own: Crime and Punishment in Black America* (New York: FSG, 2017); Fortner, *Black Silent Majority*; Ruth Wilson Gilmore, *Golden Gulag: Prisons, Surplus, Crisis, and Opposition in Globalizing California* (Berkeley: University of California Press, 2007); Elizabeth Hinton, *From the War on Poverty to the War on Crime: The Making of Mass Incarceration in America* (Cambridge, MA: Harvard University Press, 2016); Kohler-Hausmann, *Getting Tough*; and Naomi Murakawa, *The First Civil Right: How Liberals Built Prison America* (New York: Oxford University Press, 2014).

23. In recent years, the number of witnesses was proven to be vastly overstated; several also had called the police. See Kevin Cook, *Kitty Genovese: The Murder, the Bystanders, the Crime That Changed America* (New York: Norton, 2014) and Marcia M. Gallo, *"No One Helped": Kitty Genovese, New York City, and the Myth of Urban Apathy* (Ithaca, NY: Cornell University Press, 2015).

24. See, for example, Martha Biondi, *To Stand and Fight: The Struggle for Civil Rights in Postwar New York* (Cambridge, MA: Harvard University Press, 2003); Cheryl

D. Hicks, *Talk with You Like a Woman: African American Women, Justice, and Reform in New York, 1890–1935* (Chapel Hill: University of North Carolina Press, 2010); and Clarence Taylor, *Fight the Power: African Americans and the Long History of Police Brutality in New York City* (New York: New York University Press, 2019).

25. Thomas R. Brooks, "The Finest Could be Finer," *NYT*, April 3, 1966.

26. Ibid.

27. *The Knapp Commission Report on Police Corruption* (New York: George Braziller, 1972), 105.

28. David Burnham, "Most Call Crime City's Worst Ill," *NYT*, January 16, 1974.

29. See, for example, Michael W. Flamm, *Law and Order: Street Crime, Civil Unrest, and the Crisis of Liberalism in the 1960s* (New York: Columbia University Press, 2005) and Hinton, *From the War on Poverty to the War on Crime*.

30. Joseph P. Viteritti, "Times a-Changin': A Mayor for the Great Society," in *Summer in the City: John Lindsay, New York, and the American Dream*, ed. Joseph P. Viteritti (Baltimore: Johns Hopkins University Press, 2014), 9.

31. Emanuel Perlmutter, "Teacher is Slain in Crown Heights," *NYT*, May 31, 1964 and Charles Grutzner, "Negroes Deplore Hasidic Patrols," *NYT*, May 28, 1964.

32. Grutzner, "Negroes Deplore Hasidic Patrols."

33. Ibid.

34. Ibid.

35. David Halberstam, "Negro Ministers to Aid Crime Fight," *NYT*, June 12, 1964.

36. Center for Policy Research, *Community Crime Control: An Exploratory Study* (December 1973), 177.

37. Ibid., 181.

38. Ibid., 178.

39. Ibid., 183.

40. Flier for April 23, 1969 Meeting. Box 3, Folder "Security and Police." MBCG and "Minutes of the Meeting of the Board of Directors of the Manhattan Beach Community Group April 30, 1969." Box 2, Folder "Minutes 60s." MBCG.

41. "Manhattan Beach Community Group Newsletter," Volume 69, Number 1, September 1969. Box 3, Folder "Old Bulletins." MBCG.

42. Daniel Link, Chairman, Anti-Crime Committee, "Letter to Neighbors, June 25, 1969." Box 4, Folder "Voluntary Car Patrol—General." MBCG.

43. "Manhattan Beach Community Group Newsletter," Volume 69, Number 1, September 1969. Box 3, Folder "Old Bulletins." MBCG.

44. Fortner, *Black Silent Majority*, 138–139.

45. *Community Crime Control*, 71.

46. Ibid., 74–77.

47. Fortner, *Black Silent Majority*, 184–185.

48. Homer Bigart, "Middle-Class Leaders in Harlem Ask Crackdown on Crime," *NYT*, December 24, 1968.

49. "Claim Hard Drugs Killing Bed-Stuy," *NYAN*, May 7, 1970 and Rudy Johnson, "Officer Opposes Citizen Patrols," *NYT*, April 18, 1971.

50. Earl Caldwell, "Group in Harlem Asks More Police," *NYT*, December 4, 1967.

51. Nicholas Dagen Bloom, *Public Housing That Worked: New York in the Twentieth Century* (Philadelphia: University of Pennsylvania Press, 2008), 174.

52. Mary O'Flaherty, "Tenants Form Patrols to Combat Criminals," *NYSN*, December 1, 1968.

53. Michael Stern, "Fear Soars with Rate of Crime," *NYT*, December 11, 1968.

54. "Draft Press Release, Tenant Patrols Program, June 19, 1968." Box 76B2, Folder 5. NYCHA.

55. Ibid.

56. Irving Wise to Housing Managers and Superintendents, August 1, 1968. Box 64B2, Folder 10. NYCHA.

57. Stern, "Fear Soars with Rate of Crime."

58. Irving Wise, Director of Management to Housing Managers and Superintendents, August 1, 1968. Box 64E2, Folder 10. NYCHA and "Statement on Tenant Patrol Program June 5, 1968." Box 76B2, Folder 5. NYCHA.

59. Samuel Granville to Irving Wise and Samuel Granville, November 18, 1968. Box 67B6, Folder 1. NYCHA and Samuel Granville to Irving Wise, April 13, 1970. Box 67A4, Folder 16. NYCHA.

60. Charles Owens, Tenant Patrol Unit to Sidney Schackman, Director of Management, October 1, 1974. Box 88A2, Folder 2. NYCHA.

61. Thomas Poster, "Lindsay Urges Citizens to Help Reduce Burglaries," *NYDN*, January 7, 1969.

62. Quoted in Grutzner, "Negroes Deplore Hasidic Patrols."

63. Poster, "Lindsay Urges Citizens to Help Reduce Burglaries."

64. Office of the Mayor Press Release, May 27, 1967. Box 70, Folder 866. JVL.

65. *Community Crime Control*, 211.

66. Ibid., 151.

67. Glenn Flowler, "The Block Association, Boon to City Activists," *NYT*, October 19, 1969.

68. Sulieman Osman, "The Decade of the Neighborhood," in *Rightward Bound: Making America Conservative in the 1970s*, ed. Bruce J. Schulman and Julian E. Zelizer (Cambridge, MA: Harvard University Press, 2008), 110.

69. Though neighborhood associations had existed for decades in New York, the widespread formation of groups focused on a single block was new. While community resolve was the principal factor behind the explosion in block associations, a grant program initiated by Bristol-Myers in 1968 that offered $400 to new block associations accelerated their spread. See Kenneth P. Nolan, "Block Fetes Overcome Park Slope Solitude," *NYT*, December 12, 1971.

70. John Goldman, "New Yorkers Chip in for the Old Block," *Chicago Daily News*, November 1977 (exact date unknown). Copy available in CCNYC.

71. "Laurelton Block Association News," February 1972. Box 560, Folder 8. JS.

72. The exact number of block associations in the 1960s is unknown, but multiple observers in the 1970s remarked that they grew significantly beginning at the end of the 1960s. See, for example, Nolan, "Block Fetes Overcome Park Slope Solitude."

73. "Laurelton Block Association News," February 1972.

74. Abe Pevowitz, "Sentinels of the Streets," *NYSN*, December 31, 1972 and Kenneth P. Nolan, "Volunteers Seek to Cut Crime," *NYT*, August 13, 1972.

75. Clyde Haberman, "Panel Says Crime Control is Crumbling," *NYP*, March 16, 1971.

76. Pevowitz, "Sentinels of the Streets."

77. Bryan Taubman, "A Cop Gives Tips to Tenant Patrols," *NYP*, April 1971. Exact date unknown. Copy in Box 28, Folder 487. JVL.

78. Claire Howard, "Letter to the Editor," *NYT*, September 1, 1971.

79. Edward Ranzal, "Block-Security Program is Detailed by Lindsay," *NYT*, March 23, 1973.

80. "Press Release, Office of Mayor John V. Lindsay, March 22, 1973." Box 2, Folder "Block Associations—1980." BHA.

81. Max H. Seigel, "Lindsay Plans Task Force to Cut Single-Room Crime," *NYT*, January 19, 1973.

82. Neighbors had employed guards in the past—such as when the upper-middle-class residents of West 85th Street hired a guard to patrol overnight in the 1930s—but not in the numbers that occurred in the 1970s and 1980s. John Corry, "City Block: Where Fear is a Part of Life," *NYT*, October 5, 1972. Ralph Blumenthal, "Use of Private Patrolmen on City Streets Increasing," *NYT*, July 8, 1971.

83. Martin Arnold, "Private Guards are Enlisted by Tenants to Combat Crime," *NYT*, March 3, 1969.

84. Blumenthal, "Use of Private Patrolmen on City Streets Increasing."

85. Ibid.

86. "Manhattan Beach Community Group to Commissioner Patrick V. Murphy, May 28, 1972." Box 3. Folder "Security and Police." MBCG.

87. Manhattan Beach Community Group Letter to Residents, 1971 (only year is given). Box 4, Folder "Voluntary Car Patrol—General." MBCG.

88. "Beachside Civil League, Letter to Neighbors, July 9, 1971." Box 4, Folder "Voluntary Car Patrol—General." MBCG.

89. Jerry Flint, "Rising Fear of Crime Brings More Jobs for Private Guards," *NYT*, July 20, 1969 and Frank Prial, "Amid Crime, Guard Industry Thrives," *NYT*, January 24, 1972.

90. James S. Kakalik and Sorrel Wildhorn, *Private Police in the United States: Findings and Recommendations* (Santa Monica, CA: RAND Corporation, prepared for the Department of Justice, 1971), 12.

91. David Burnham, "Some Private Guards Found Ill Trained and Corrupt," *NYT*, April 9, 1972.

92. Kakalik and Wildhorn, *Private Police in the United States*, 30.

93. James S. Kakalik and Sorrel Wildhorn, *Current Regulation of Private Police: Regulatory Agency Experience and Views, Volume 3* (Santa Monica, CA: RAND Corporation, prepared for the Department of Justice, 1972), 2 and Kakalik and Wildhorn, *Private Police in the United States*, viii.

94. Reginal Stuart, "Private Guards on the Rise, but Their Service Varies," *NYT*, January 11, 1976.

95. "Meeting of the Police Committee and Beachside Civic League, February 2, 1972." Box 2, Folder "Beachside." MBCG.

96. Ibid. Emphasis in original.

97. Martin Arnold, "Private Guards are Enlisted by Tenants to Combat Crime," *NYT*, March 3, 1969.

98. Laurie Johnston, "Queens Residents Hire a Private Security Patrol," *NYT*, December 5, 1971.

99. "Private Guards Patrol the East Side," *NYT*, August 6, 1970.

100. Quoted in Morningside Heights, Inc. "Proposal, State of New York Office of Crime Control Planning (March 13, 1972), Second Draft Proposal." Box 11, Folder 25. MAA.

101. Morningside Heights, Inc., "Morningside Street Patrol," June 1, 1964. Box 36, Folder 2. MAA.

102. Morningside Heights, Inc. "Memorandum to the Board of Directors Concerning a Private Street Patrol Supervised by Morningside Heights, Inc.," 6. December 1, 1961. Box 36, Folder 2. MAA.

103. Ibid.

104. Stephen R. Wiener to Gilbert Lazerus, Memorandum, January 4, 1962. Box 36, Folder 9. MAA.

105. "Our Morningside Patrol: The Modern Approach to Residential Security," *Interstate Security Services Intercom* 3, no. 9 (December 1964). Box 36, Folder 12. MAA.

106. Morningside Heights, Inc., "Morningside Street Patrol," June 1, 1964. Box 36, Folder 2. MAA.

107. "Our Morningside Patrol," MAA.

108. Interstate Security Services, Inc., *Morningside Street Patrol: A Critical Self-Evaluation*, November 13, 1968. Box 36, Folder 5. MAA.

109. Ibid.

110. *Security: Notes from the Morningside Security Council*, June 25, 1969. Box 11, Folder 1. MAA and *Security: Notes from the Morningside Security Council*, May 2, 1969. Box 36, Folder 7. MAA.

111. *Security: Notes from the Morningside Security Council*, May 2, 1969. Box 36, Folder 7. MAA.

112. *Security: Notes from the Morningside Security Council*, April 15, 1971. Box 11, Folder 1. MAA.

113. Ibid.

114. Alfred I. Dailey, Chief, Morningside Community Patrol to Edward C. Solomon, February 11, 1971. Box 11, Folder 25. MAA.

115. *Security: Notes from the Morningside Security Council*, April 15, 1971. Box 11, Folder 1. MAA.

116. Morningside Heights, Inc. Proposal: State of New York Office of Crime Control Planning, March 13, 1972, 14. Second Draft. Box 11, Folder 25. MAA.

117. Ibid.

118. Ibid.

119. The Association for a Better New York, Inc. Press Release, June 2, 1971. Folder "ABNY: The Very Beginning." ABNY.

120. WMCA Wrap Up transcript, December 22, 1972. Folder "70's Radio Transcripts." ABNY.

121. Murray Schumach, "City-Backed Private Drive on Midtown Crime Opens," *NYT*, December 22, 1972.

122. WMCA Wrap Up transcript, December 22, 1972.

123. Schumach, "City-Backed Private Drive on Midtown Crime Opens."

124. WMCA Wrap Up transcript, December 22, 1972.

125. Schumach, "City-Backed Private Drive on Midtown Crime Open."

126. Murray Schumach, "Private Security Guards to Join Midtown Patrols," *NYT*, June 8, 1973.

127. ABNY, Press Release, June 5, 1973. Folder "Press Releases 1971–1973." ABNY.

128. Schumach, "City-Backed Private Drive on Midtown Crime Opens."

129. Schumach, "Private Security Guards to Join Midtown Patrols."

130. "ABNY Sponsors Area Security," *REN*, June 1973, 22.

131. ABNY, Press Release, June 5, 1973. Folder "Press Releases 1971–1973." ABNY.

132. Will Lissner, "Guards in Manhattan Buildings are Linked to Police by Radio," *NYT*, June 6, 1974.

133. WRFM transcript, June 8. 1973. Folder "Press Releases 1971–1973." ABNY.

134. ABNY Minutes of the Executive Committee Meeting, December 4, 1974. ABNY.

135. Phillips-Fein, *Fear City,* 55.

136. Schneider, *Smack,* 117.

137. "Brooklyn Precinct 'Cut to the Bone' By Police Layoffs," *NYT*, August 2, 1976. See also Phillips-Fein, *Fear City*, 129–137.

138. Selwyn Raab, "Sharp Rise Reported for Serious Crimes in All Five Boroughs," *NYT*, April 10, 1977.

139. "Queens Block Associations Press Patrol Plan," *NYT*, May 18, 1975.

140. Ibid.

141. CCNYC, "The Self-Help Crime Prevention Fund: A Proposal," December 7, 1976. Box 11, Folder "Police Department." FXM.

142. Goldman, "New Yorkers Chip in for the Old Block."

143. Ibid.

144. New York Police Department, *Civilian Observation Patrol: Rules and Regulations* (likely mid-1970s). Box 40, Folder "BHA - Training - COP & Blockwatchers." BHA.

145. "Civilian Patrol Cars to Use Amber Lights," *NYT*, October 9, 1977.

146. William C. Cunningham and Todd Taylor, *Crime and Protection in America: A Study of Private Security and Law Enforcement Resources and Relationships— Executive Summary* (Washington, DC: US Department of Justice, 1985), 2.

147. National Sheriffs' Association, *Neighborhood Watch Manual: USAonWatch— National Neighborhood Watch Program* (National Sheriffs' Association, 2005), https://www.bja.gov/Publications/NSA_NW_Manual.pdf.

148. John F. Burns, "Unit Set Up to Muster Volunteer City Aid," *NYT*, November 2, 1975.

149. CCNYC, "Summary of Current and Future Projects," June 1976, 3. CCNYC.

150. Ibid., 4.

151. Glenn Fowler, "1,300 Neighborhood Activists Attend First Citywide Convention of New York City Block Associations," *NYT*, May 16, 1976.

152. "Citizens Group Handbook Urges New Yorkers to Help Themselves," *NYT*, December 11, 1977.

153. CCNYC, *Lend a Hand for a Safer New York* (undated, but likely 1977), 3. CCNYC.

154. Sara Otey, "Captain to Residents: 'Crime on Decrease,'" *Home Reporter and Sunset News*, September 23, 1977.

155. CCNYC, "The Self-Help Crime Prevention Fund: A Proposal," December 7, 1976. Box 11, Folder "Police Department." FXM.

156. Ibid.

157. "Queens Block Associations Press Patrol Plan," *NYT*, May 18, 1975.

158. Citizens Committee for New York, Inc. *Lend a Hand for a Safer New York*, 3.

159. "How They Protect Themselves Downtown," *NYAN*, December 20, 1975.

160. Samuel L. Myers Jr., W. Victor Rouse, and Edward C. Baldwin, "Federally Subsidized Programs for Fighting Crime in Minority Communities," *Review of Black Political Economy* 11, no. 1 (Winter 1980): 140.

161. Diane Henry, "New Yorkers Patrolling Streets to Watch for Crime," *NYT*, May 4, 1981.

162. Office of Community Anti-Crime Programs of the Law Enforcement Assistance Administration, *We Can Prevent Crime* (Dept. of Justice, Law Enforcement Assistance Administration, 1979).

163. Herb Sturz to Edward Koch, September 11, 1978. Box 114, Folder 12. EIK and "Federal Grant to Fight Against Crime," *NYAN*, July 29, 1978.

164. William DeJong and Gail A. Goolkasian, *The Neighborhood Fight Against Crime: The Midwood Kings Highway Development Corporation* (Washington, DC: US Department of Justice, 1983), 9–10.

165. Ibid., 19 and Diana Shaman, "Neighborhood Security Patrols Double," *NYT*, January 24, 1982.

166. Janice A. Roehl and Royer F. Cook, *Evaluation of the Urban Crime Prevention Program: Executive Summary* (Washington, DC: US Department of Justice, 1984). iii.

167. *The Citizens Report*, Volume 5, Number 3, Fall 1981. Box 82, Folder "Grants Files 1980: Citizens Committee for New York City, Inc." VAF.

168. Charles J. Owens, Chief, Tenant Patrol Division to Bernard Moses, Director of Management, April 1, 1980. Box 3, Folder 95A4. NYCHA.

169. Charles J. Owens, Tenant Patrol Division to Bernard Moses, Director of Management, April 6, 1979. Box 3, Folder 95A4. NYCHA.

170. Soffer, *Ed Koch*, 322. Emphasis in original.

171. Ibid.

172. Diane Henry, "New Yorkers Patrolling Streets to Watch for Crime," *NYT*, May 4, 1981 and Michael Goodwin, "Koch Considers Drive to Recruit Public on Crime," *NYT*, December 11, 1981.

173. Shaman, "Neighborhood Security Patrols Double" and Henry, "New Yorkers Patrolling Streets to Watch for Crime."

174. Nicolas Pileggi, "The Guardian Angels: Help—or Hype?" *NY*, November 24, 1980.

175. Reiko Hillyer, "The Guardian Angels: Law and Order and Citizen Policing in New York City," *Journal of Urban History* 43, no. 6 (2017): 7.

176. Henry, "New Yorkers Patrolling Streets to Watch for Crime."

177. Jane C. McConnell, President Brooklyn Heights Association to Police Commissioner Robert J. McGuire, December 8, 1982. Box 36, Folder "COP Correspondence III." BHA.

178. Joanne Furio, "COP Helps Cops Keep the Heights Safe," *ND*, February 24, 1989.

179. Brooklyn Heights Association, Press Release, March 7, 1984. Box 36, Folder "Press Clippings, Publicity, and Releases." BHA.

180. William Neugebauer, "Citizen Watchdogs Cutting into Crime," *NYDN*, April 1, 1984.

181. Randy Young, "The City's Safest Neighborhoods," *NY*, October 19, 1981, 35.

182. Henry, "New Yorkers Patrolling Streets to Watch for Crime."

183. Shaman, "Neighborhood Security Patrols Double."

184. Randy Young, "Do It Yourself Patrols," *NY*, February 8, 1982, 37.

185. Andree Brooks, "Forming Volunteer Patrols," *NYT*, September 25, 1983.

186. William Neugebaeur, "Citizen Watchdogs Cutting into Crime," *NYDN*, April 1, 1984.

187. Ibid.

188. Robert D. McFadden, "Poll Indicate Half of New Yorkers See Crime as City's Chief Problem," *NYT*, January 14, 1985.

189. Clark Whelton, "In Guards We Trust," *NYT*, September 19, 1976.

190. The Maccabees ended their patrol in 1971, satisfied that "there are enough po-lice in the neighborhood" as Rabbi Schrage explained. But other community patrols continued in Crown Heights. Harry Zlokower, "Job Done, Maccabees of Brooklyn Break Up," *NYT*, October 31, 1971.

191. Leslie Maitland, "Jews in Crown Heights Hire Special Guard," *NYT*, November 16, 1975.

192. Whelton, "In Guards We Trust."

193. Manhattan Beach Community Group, Inc. Bulletin, November 1977. Box 3, Folder "Old Bulletins." MBCG.

194. "Minutes of the Manhattan Beach Community Group," November 30, 1977. Box 2, Folder "Minutes 71–73." MBCG.

195. Randy Young, "Putting a Guard on the Block," *NY*, February 8, 1982, 37.

196. "Private Security Patrols on Rise in City's Middle-Class Areas," *NYT*, September 18, 1983.

197. Young, "Putting a Guard on the Block," 36.

198. Whelton, "In Guards We Trust" and "Private Security Patrols on Rise in City's Middle-Class Areas."

199. Whelton, "In Guards We Trust."

200. Grace Lichtensetein, "Police Moonlighting in Uniform Widespread in Many Big Cities," *NYT*, October 4, 1976.

201. Elise Maiorana Wager, Commercial Development Director, QOEDC, October 16, 1981. Testimony before the NY City Council. Box 50354. Local Law 2. 1981. NYCC.

202. L. 1976. ch. 910. NYBJ.

203. Sam Roberts, "Merchants Taxing Themselves to Offer More Services in Special Districts," *NYT*, October 11, 1983.

204. Manhattan Beach Community Group Bulletin, July 1978. Box 3, Folder "Old Bulletins." MBCG.

205. Reginald Stuart, "Private Guards on the Rise but Their Service Varies," *NYT*, January 11, 1975.

206. Eugene McDermott to Captain Robert Harris, Commanding Officer, 26th Precinct, August 22, 1974. Box 11, Folder 28. MAA and Eugene McDermott, "Memo" August 28, 1974. Box 11, Folder 28. MAA.

207. Ray Bradley, Peter Cross, Roby Ditz, and Betty Sheets, "Collective Gains and Individual Interests: Formal Security Arrangements in Morningside Heights," 1974. Box 11, Folder 28. MAA.

208. Leonard Buder, "Coping with Crime in Office Buildings," *NYT*, June 26, 1983.

209. Ibid.

210. Association for a Better New York Press Release, May 23, 1978. Folder "ABNY Special Events 1978, 1979, 1980." ABNY.

211. "News for a Better New York," 1982. Folder "ABNY Special Events 1978, 1979, 1980." ABNY.

212. Martin Tolchin, "Private Guards Get New Role in Public Law Enforcement," *NYT*, November 29, 1985.

213. Ibid.

214. William C. Cunningham, John J. Strauchs, and Clifford W. Van Meter, "Private Security: Patterns and Trends," *National Institute of Justice Research in Brief* (August 1991), 2.

215. Tolchin, "Private Guards Get New Role in Public Law Enforcement."

216. Robert R. J. Gallati, *Introduction to Private Security* (Englewood Cliffs, Prentice Hall, 1983), 23 and Tolchin, "Private Guards Get New Role in Public Law Enforcement."

217. Robert McFadden, "Poll Indicates Half of New Yorkers See Crime as City's Chief Problem," *NYT*, January 14, 1985.

218. Paul J. Lavrakas, "Community-Based Crime Prevention: Citizens, Community Organizations, and the Police," in *Crime, Communities, and Public Policy*, ed. Lawrence B. Joseph (Chicago: Center for Urban Research and Policy Studies, 1995), 99.

219. Wendy Melillo, *How McGruff and the Crying Indian Changed America: A History of Iconic Ad Council Campaigns* (Washington, DC: Smithsonian Books, 2013), 164–165.

220. James Garofalo and Maureen McLeod, "Improving the Use and Effectiveness of Neighborhood Watch Programs," *National Institute of Justice: Research in Action* (April 1988), 1. Additionally, a number of academic studies published in the first half of the decade questioned how effective community anti-crime initiates were. Paul J. Lavrakas and Susan F. Bennett, "Thinking about the Implementation of Citizen and Community Anti-Crime Measures," in *Communities and Crime Reduction*, ed. Tim Hope and Margaret Shaw (London: Her Majesty's Stationery Office, 1988), 222.

221. Todd Purdum, "Politics of Police Strength," *NYT*, September 13, 1990.

222. Soffer, *Ed Koch*, 322, 347–348. Todd S. Purdum, "After a 4-Year Drop, Crime in City is Rising, Leaving Experts Puzzled," *NYT*, May 24, 1986.

223. See, for example, George P. Fletcher, *A Crime of Self-Defense: Bernhard Goetz and the Law on Trial* (Chicago: University of Chicago Press, 1990) and Mark Uhlig, "3 'Angels' Are Stabbed in Fight in Manhattan," *NYT*, June 12, 1988.

224. Felicia R. Lee, "On Dark Streets, 'Eyes and Ears' for the Law," *NYT*, October 1, 1990.

225. Louis Uchitelle, "Sharp Rise of Private Guard Jobs," *NYT*, October 14, 1989 and Kevin Strom, Marcus Berzofsky, Bonnie Shook-Sa, Kelle Barrick, Crystal Daye, Nicole Horstmann, and Susan Kinsey, *The Private Security Industry: A Review of the Definitions, Available Data Sources, and Paths Moving Forward* (2010), https://www.ncjrs.gov/pdffiles1/bjs/grants/232781.pdf.

226. James K. Stewart, "Foreword," in *Public Policing—Privately Provided*, ed. Marcia Chaiken and Jan Chaiken (National Institute of Justice, June 1987), iii.

227. Quoted in Ralph Blumenthal, "Private Guards Cooperate in Public Policing," *NYT*, July 13, 1993.

228. Tolchin, "Private Guards Get New Role in Public Law Enforcement."

229. Ibid.

230. Ibid.

231. Ralph Blumenthal, "And Now a Private Midtown 'Police Force,'" *NYT*, August 22, 1989.

232. Ibid.

233. New York City Economic Policy and Marketing Group, *New York City's Business Improvement Districts: An Evaluation* (1994), 22.

234. George James, "Midtown Crime Reported Down Sharply," *NYT*, June 2, 1992.

235. Blumenthal, "And Now a Private Midtown 'Police Force.'"

236. Ibid.

237. Blumenthal, "Private Guards Cooperate in Public Policing."

238. Louis Uchitelle, "Sharp Rise of Private Guard Jobs," *NYT*, October 14, 1989.

239. See chapter 6.

CHAPTER 5

1. Quoted in Joshua B. Freeman, *Working Class New York: Life and Labor Since World War II* (New York: The New Press, 2000), 272–273.

2. The Temporary Commission on City Finances, *The City in Transition: Prospects and Policies for New York* (New York: Arno Press, 1978), 23.

3. "Statement by Deputy Mayor Stanley M. Friedman on Intro. No. 859—J-51 Tax Abatement Program Expansion before the City Council Housing and Buildings Committee, November 5, 1975." Box 50309. Local Law 60. 1975. NYCC.

4. Ibid.

5. "Richard J. Glover to Members of the Housing and Buildings Committee of the City Council, 24 November 1975." Box 50309. Local Law 60. 1975. NYCC.

6. Cited in Citizens Budget Commission, *A Review of Real Estate Tax Incentive Programs in New York City* (March 1977), vi. CHL.

7. Paul E. Peterson, *City Limits* (Chicago: University of Chicago Press, 1981).

8. The Temporary Commission on City Finances, *The City in Transition*, 23.

9. "City Club of New York, Memorandum re: Section J51.25 of the Administration, October 23, 1975." Box 050309. Local Law 60. 1975. NYCC.

10. See, for example, Elizabeth Tandy Shermer, "Sunbelt Boosterism: Industrial Recruitment, Economic Development, and Growth Politics in the Developing Sunbelt," in *Sunbelt Rising: The Politics of Place, Space, and Region*, ed. Michelle Nickerson and Darren Dochuk (Philadelphia: University of Pennsylvania Press, 2011), 31–57.

11. The law was initially implemented as 421, before changing to 421-a in 1977. For consistency, I refer to the law as 421-a throughout.

12. Edward C. Burks, "Tax-Abatement Plan Seeks to Stimulate City Housing," *NYT*, October 31, 1971.

13. This could extend up to thirty-two years for moderate rehabilitations.

14. George Sternlieb, Elizabeth Roistacher, and James W. Hughes, *Tax Subsidies and Housing Investment: A Fiscal Cost-Benefit Analysis* (New Brunswick, NJ: The Center for Urban Policy Research, 1978), 15.

15. John Hull Mollenkopf, "The Place of Politics and the Politics of Place," in *Power, Culture, and Place: Essays on New York City*, ed. John Hull Mollenkopf (New York: Russell Sage Foundation, 1988), 278.

16. Quoted in Homer Bigart, "Lindsay Urges Incentives to Spur Private Housing," *NYT*, October 24, 1969.

17. Robert M. Fogelson, *The Great Rent Wars: New York, 1917–1929* (New Haven, CT: Yale University Press, 2013), 357.

18. Quoted in Francis X. Clines, "Landlords Assail Plans to Spur Housing in City," *NYT*, August 11, 1970 and "City Urges Tax Plan to Aid Construction," *NYT*, April 13, 1970.

19. David K. Shipler, "Tax Aid is Proposed to Spur Building in the City," *NYT*, March 29, 1970.

20. Edward C. Burks, "Tax Abatement Plan Seeks to Stimulate City Housing," *NYT*, October 31, 1971.

21. John V. Lindsay to Nelson A. Rockefeller, May 17, 1971. L. 1971. Ch. 1207. NYBJ.

22. See Bigart, "Lindsay Urges Incentives to Spur Private Housing" and Shipler, "Tax Aid is Proposed to Spur Building in the City."

23. Robert C. Rosenberg to Lester Shulklapper, Extension of the 421 Partial Tax Exemption Law, January 16, 1973. L. 1973. Ch. 480. NYBJ.

24. A city-supported 1975 study found that 63 percent of completed 421-a units were built for higher income residents in Manhattan. Cited in Citizens Budget Commission, *A Review of Real Estate Tax Incentive Programs*, 15.

25. Alan S. Oser, "City Housing Details Offered in Directory," *NYT*, September 27, 1974.

26. Robert C. Rosenberg to Lester Shulklapper, re: Extension of the 421 Partial Tax Exemption Law, January 16, 1973. L. 1973. Ch. 480. NYBJ.

27. John V. Lindsay to Honorable Nelson A. Rockefeller, May 7, 1973. L. 1973. Ch. 480. NYBJ.

28. New York Urban Coalition, Comments on Assembly Bill 466-A. L. 1973. Ch 480. NYBJ.

29. Thomas F. McGrath to the Honorable Judah Gribetz, August 6, 1975. L. 1975. Ch. 857. NYBJ.

30. Roger Starr, "A Report on Activities at the Housing and Development Administration: January 1, 1974–October 1, 1976," 24. Box 7, Folder 101. SL.

31. Carter B. Horsley, "City Seeks to Revise Incentives for Housing," *NYT*, June 8, 1975.

32. Abraham Beame to Honorable Hugh L. Carey, July 17, 1975. L. 1973. Ch. 480. NYBJ.

33. Kristina Ford, *Housing Policy and the Urban Middle Class* (New Brunswick, NJ: Center for Urban Policy Research, 1978), 65.

34. Beame to Carey, July 17, 1975.

35. D.K. Patton, Real Estate Board of New York to Hugh L. Carey, July 17, 1975. Reel 101. Section: Housing—Legislation. HC.

36. Michael Stern, "Continued Job Declines Threatened City Economy," *NYT*, July 21, 1974.

37. John Darnton, "11 are Appointed to Industry Unit," *NYT*, September 3, 1974.

38. Only industrial projects were supposed to receive the incentive "as of right." Alan S. Oser, "Developer Recycles Film House into a Successful Store Group," *NYT*, February 8, 1978.

39. Ibid.

40. "Industrial Incentive Board Gives Some Exemptions on Realty Taxes," *NYT*, February 25, 1977.

41. Steven R. Kale, "U.S. Industrial Development Incentives and Manufacturing Growth during the 1970s," *Growth and Change: A Journal of Urban and Regional Policy* 15, no. 1 (January 1984): 27.

42. Ibid., 27–28.

43. Michael Stern, "City Offers Ambitious Plan for an Economic Revival," *NYT*, February 16, 1975.

44. Ibid.

45. Carter B. Horsley, "City to Seek Extension of Tax Aid for Housing," *NYT*, June 29, 1975.

46. Leon D. Schneider, "Statement Before the Committee on Housing of New York City Council, Re: Int. No. 859," November 5, 1975. L. 1975. Ch. 857. NYBJ.

47. Citizens Budget Commission, *A Review of Real Estate Tax Incentive Programs*, 24.

48. H. Claude Shostal to Barry Salman, Chairman, Housing Committee, City Council. November 21, 1975. Box 50309. Local Law 60. 1975. NYCC.

49. Carter B. Horsley, "City to Seek Extension of Tax Aid for Housing," *NYT*, June 29, 1975.

50. Janice C. Griffith, "Revitalizing of Inner City Housing Through Property Tax Exemption and Abatement: New York City's J-51 to the Rescue," *Urban Law Annual* 18 (1980): 163–165.

51. "Albert A. Formicola to Barry Salman, Chairman Housing & Buildings Committee, City Council. 21 November 1975." Box 50309. Local Law 60. 1975. NYCC.

52. "Milton Glass to Honorable Thomas J. Cuite [*sic*], November 20, 1975." Box 50309. Local Law 60. 1975. NYCC.

53. "New York City Council Press Release, November 4, 1975." Box 50309. Local Law 60. 1975. NYCC.

54. "Testimony of Carol Bernstein, Assistant Director, SHF Housing Development, Statement Before New York City Council Favoring Retention of J-51 Tax Exemption, November 5, 1975." Box 50309. Local Law 60. 1975. NYCC.

55. Some affordable housing advocates criticized how the change did little to encourage using the program to improve housing for poor and low-income residents. See Robert Schur, "Government Housing Programs J-51 Tax Exemption and Tax Abatement," *CL*, August–September 1976.

56. George Sternlieb, Elizabeth Roistacher, and James W. Hughes, *Tax Subsidies and Housing Investment: A Fiscal Cost-Benefit Analysis* (New Brunswick, NJ: The Center for Urban Policy Research, 1976), 15.

57. Joseph P. Fried, "Tax-Break Program is Found Poorly Run," *NYT*, April 7, 1978.

58. Sternlieb, Roistacher, and Hughes, *Tax Subsidies and Housing Investment*, 25 and 69.

59. Ibid., 3.

60. George Sternlieb, "Introduction," in Ford, *Housing Policy and the Urban Middle Class*, xxxii.

61. Lee A. Daniels, "Debate Continues to Rage on City's J-51 Tax Policy," *NYT*, December 3, 1982.

62. Mayor Edward I. Koch, "Statement on Housing Policy, the Citizens Housing and Planning Council, May 10, 1978." Box 5, Folder "Housing Policy." TCRH.

63. Quoted in "The West Side Tenant's Union Opposes the Extension of the J-51 Tax Abatement and Exemption Program," April 1978. Box 65, Folder "Tax Prop." MCH.

64. Susan Baldwin, "Council Eyes Renewed J-51 Plan for Even Bigger Tax Giveaway," *CL*, October 1979, 9.

65. "Statement of Lawrence M. Grosberg to the Committee on Housing and Building of the New York City Council, September 25, 1979." Box 50336. Local Law 77. 1979. NYCC.

66. Ruth Messinger, "Statement on the Proposed Extension of the J-51 Tax Program," August 15, 1979. Box 65, Folder "Tax Prop." MCH.

67. Nat Leventhal to Laurence A. Klein, September 5, 1979. Box 175, Folder 1. EIK.

68. Sharon McDonnell, "Tax-Break Reform Brought to the Council," *CL*, October 1981, 6.

69. Rita Buland, representing the 752 West End Avenue Tenants Association, "Address to the Housing and Buildings Committee of the New York City Council," August 15, 1979. Box 65, Folder "Tax Prop." MCH. Emphasis in original.

70. Office of City Council Member Ruth W. Messinger, "Press Release: Where the Money Is." Box 37, Folder "HPD June 80." NL.

71. Nat Leventhal to Ed Koch, January 15, 1979. Box 174, Folder 5. EIK.

72. Nat Leventhal to Harry Tichelman, October 17, 1980. Box 146, Folder 7. EIK.

73. "Office of the Mayor, City of New York: Press Release, March 6, 1978." Page 469. Box 50327. Local Law 12. 1978. NYCC.

74. "Report of the Committee on Housing and Buildings, May 5, 1978." Page 96. Box 50326. Local Law 12. 1978. NYCC.

75. "Report of Legal Services Division, City Council." Page 285. Box 50327. Local Law 12. 1978. NYCC.

76. Remarks by Victor Marrero, Commissioner of the New York State Division of Housing and Community Renewal before the Metropolitan Council of the American Jewish Congress, May 3, 1979. Box 65, Folder "Tax Prop." MCH.

77. City of New York Office of the Comptroller, *J-51 Tax Abatement and Tax Exemption Housing Benefits: Emerging Policy Issues, with a Focus on Conversions*, October 20, 1980, 6. CHL.

78. Ibid., 37.

79. Quoted in Frank Domurad, "It's 1985. Do You Know Where Your Tax Dollars Are?" *CL*, August–September 1985, 26.

80. Edward A. Gargan, "Koch Seeking Curbs on Tax Abatements," *NYT*, April 7, 1981 and Michael Goodwin, "Recasting Incentives," *NYT*, April 29, 1981.

81. These included eliminating J-51 for SRO conversions and limiting benefits overall, except for nonprofit groups.

82. Pete Grannis to Edward Koch, November 9, 1982. Box 10, Folder "HPD— September 1982." NL.

83. Carol Felstein to Nat Leventhal, November 18, 1982. Box 10, Folder "HPD— September 1982." NL.

84. Quoted in Ronald Smothers, "Tax Relief Plan is Said to Benefit Luxury Housing," *NYT*, December 1, 1980.

85. Koch officials maintained that the program's "as of right" nature was necessary, not just to keep administrative expenses low, but also to ensured financing. Banks, officials noted, would be more hesitant to commit financing for rehabilitation projects without "as of right" status.

86. "3 Proposed Midtown Towers to Get Nearly $30 Million in Abatements," *NYT*, December 20, 1978.

87. Ann Crittenden, "City Panel Toughens Terms of Tax Breaks for Builders," *NYT*, December 19, 1980.

88. Joyce Purnick, "Abatements Persist," *NYT*, January 22, 1982.

89. "Statement by Mayor Edward I. Koch," Press release issued July 21, 1982. Box 10, Folder "HPD July 82–." NL.

90. Carol Felstein to Nat Leventhal, November 18, 1982. Box 10, Folder "HPD September 1982–." NL.

91. Jonathan Soffer, *Ed Koch and the Rebuilding of New York City* (New York: Columbia University Press, 2010), 208.

92. "A Defense Against the Trump Tax," *NYT*, July 10, 1984.

93. Quoted in Soffer, *Ed Koch and the Rebuilding of New York City*, 259.

94. "The Real Estate Reporter Essay: Housing Maintenance," *RER*, January 1983, 6.

95. "Housing Still Need Tax Help," *NYT*, March 4, 1983.

96. "Housing's Best Hope," *NYT*, October 24, 1983.

97. Real Estate Board of New York, *Housing in Crisis: 1985* (New York: Real Estate Board of New York, 1985), 9. CHL.

98. "Barbaro Charges 10 Koch Real Estate Pals Gave Campaign $175,000, Got $60 Million in City Tax Breaks," Press Release, August 27, 1981. Box 135, Folder "Koch $ (Money), 1980–1986." JN and Martin Shefter, *Political Crisis / Fiscal Crisis: The Collapse and Revival of New York City* (New York: Columbia University Press, 1992 [1982]), 177.

99. "Barbaro Charges 10 Koch Real Estate Pals Gave Campaign $175,000."

100. Chester Hartman and Tom Robbins, "No Vacancy: The Disappearance of Affordable Housing," *VV*, April 1, 1986.

101. Commissioner Anthony Gliedman to Deputy Mayor Bob Esnard, December 10, 1984. Box 51, Folder 22. EIK.

102. Jack Newfield, "The Dirty Dozen: New York's Worst Landlords," *VV*, April 9, 1985, 11.

103. Letter from Donna Figuera to Honorable Edward Koch, November 1, 1984. Reel 38, Section: Community Development, Housing, New York City. MMC.

104. John R. Logan and Harvey L. Molotch, *Urban Fortunes: The Political Economy of Place* (Berkeley: University of California Press, 2007 [1987]), 13.

105. Michael deCourcy Hinds, "The Bitter Battles Over Harassment," *NYT*, May 27, 1984.

106. Frank F. DeGiovanni, *Displacement Pressures in the Lower East Side* (New York: Community Service Society of New York, 1987), 32–37.

107. Quoted in Maurice Carroll, "A Pattern of Fires Cited in Subsidized Buildings," *NYT*, September 3, 1983.

108. Department of City Planning, *Private Reinvestment and Neighborhood Change* (New York City Department of City Planning, March 1984), 64–65.

109. Dolores Fernandez to Governor Mario Cuomo, September 14, 1984. Reel 37. Section: Community Development, Housing, Low Income. MMC.

110. Harriet Achtentuch, Frank Domurad, Ruth Messinger, and James Silvers, *The Rich Get Richer Part II: 421a Tax Breaks in New York City, 1981–1983* (New York: New York Public Interest Research Group Report, 1984), 3.

111. Quoted in Sydney H. Schanberg, "Arson and J-51," *NYT*, July 20, 1982.

112. Michael Goodwin, "City Housing Programs Tied to Arson in Report," *NYT*, July 21, 1982. The final report concluded that J-51 buildings were more likely to suffer suspicious fires, though at lower rates than the preliminary report found. See The New York City Arson Strike Force, *A Study of Government Subsided Housing Rehabilitation Programs and Arson: Analysis of Programs Administered in New York City, 1978–1981* (September 2, 1983).

113. Anthony Gliedman to Nathan Leventhal, December 11, 1982. Box 10, Folder "HPD—September 1982." NL.

114. Koch finally agreed to such a ban, but only because it became clear that the entire program might have been allowed to expire without one. These reforms occurred in the state legislature, which was required to pass legislation for the program's continuation.

115. This measure prevented buildings with postconversion assessments of over $38,000 from receiving exemptions, though these projects remained eligible for abatements. Edward A. Gargan, "Pact Reached in Legislature on Tax Abatements by City," *NYT*, June 23, 1983.

116. Edward A. Gargan, "Housing Tax Incentive Opposed at City Hearing," *NYT*, October 19, 1983.

117. Tom Robbins, "Look Out for the New J-51 Law," *CL*, November 1983, 3.

118. Carol Bellamy memo to Council members, October 25, 1983. Box 12, Folder "HPD-October 83." RE.

119. Statement by Assemblyman Richard N. Gottfried, October 18, 1983. Box 12, Folder "HPD—8/83." RE.

120. David W. Dunlap, "Council Votes to Limit Tax Incentives for Buildings," *NYT*, October 26, 1983.

121. Ibid.

122. "Stuart Christie, Citizens Housing and Planning Council, Testimony on the Proposed J-51 Legislation before the City Council, October 21, 1983." Box 50368. Local Law 56. 1983. NYCC.

123. Deloitte Haskins & Sells, *Review of the J-51 Program* (Report for the New York City Department of Housing Preservation and Development, 1984), C-5 and C-11. CHL.

124. Michael Altman, Frank Domurad, Dan Kaplan, Ruth Messinger, Martin Rosenblatt, and James Silver, *How am I Doing? Business and Real Estate Tax Breaks in New York City* (New York: New York Public Interest Research Group, 1982), i.

125. Quoted in Achtentuch, Domurad, Messinger, and Silvers, *The Rich Get Richer Part II*, 11.

126. Lee A. Danile, "Trump Denied Tax Abatement for Fifth Ave. Tower," *NYT*, March 29, 1981.

127. Anthony Gliedman to Edward Koch, Confidential Memo, March 27, 1981. Box 175, Folder 7. EIK.

128. Danile, "Trump Denied Tax Abatement for Fifth Ave. Tower."

129. E.R. Shipp, "City's Denial of a Tax Break to Trump is Ruled Improper," *NYT*, December 15, 1982.

130. David Margolick, "Top State Court Rules Trump is Entitled to Tax Break for Midtown Tower," *NYT*, July 6, 1984.

131. Quoted in ibid.

132. Edward I. Koch, "Letter to the Editor," *NYT*, October 9, 1984 and Jesus Rangel, "Koch Moves to Limit Breaks for New Midtown Housing," *NYT*, October 16, 1984.

133. "Testimony of City Council President Carol Bellamy, Before the City Council Housing and Buildings Committee Regarding 421a Tax Exemption Bill, Intro 815-A, November 7, 1984." Box 50259, Folder 1 (2). 1984. NYCC.

134. Anthony Gliedman to Edward I. Koch, July 25, 1984. Box 178, Folder 2. EIK. See also "Limiting Builders' Tax Breaks," *ND*, November 28, 1984.

135. "The Real Estate Reporter Essay: Here Comes the Neighborhood Gentrification's Mixed Blessings," *RER*, June 1985, 23.

136. Ibid.

137. Carol Bellamy to Ed Koch, September 28, 1984. Box 69, Folder 14. EIK.

138. New York State Tenant and Neighborhood Coalition, September 13, 1984. Box 50258, Folder 9. 1984. NYCC.

139. "The Controversy Over Apartment Tax Breaks," *NYT*, October 21, 1984.

140. Achtentuch, Domurad, Messinger, and Silvers, *The Rich Get Richer Part II*, 1.

141. Ibid.

142. Ibid., 21.

143. Ibid., 16.

144. Dee Wedemeyer, "A Turn in the Market for New Apartments," *NYT*, July 3, 1983.

145. "No End to the Spiral," *MC*, September 1984, 2.

146. Quoted in Achtentuch, Domurad, Messinger, and Silvers, *The Rich Get Richer Part II*, i.

147. Hartman and Robbins, "No Vacancy."

148. Peter Marcuse, "A Luxury Housing Tax," *CL*, December 1983, 15 and "Building a Housing Trust Fund," *CL*, December 1983, 13–14.

149. Marcuse, "A Luxury Housing Tax," 17.

150. "Building a Housing Trust Fund," 13–14 and Sam Howe Verhhover, "Board Approves Zoning Bonus for Luxury Towers," *NYT*, May 23, 1987.

151. Testimony of Brian T. Sullivan to the Mayor's Development Commitment Study Commission, September 22, 1983. Box 110, Folder "Housing Trust Fund (1981–1983)." JN and "Building a Housing Trust Fund," 14.

152. See Martin Gottlieb, "'Tax' on Developers," *NYT*, July 14, 1983.

153. Paul Goldberger, "Shaping the Face of New York," in *New York Unbound: The City and the Politics of the Future*, ed. Peter D. Salins (New York: Basil Blackwell, 1988), 133.

154. Jerold S. Kayden, *Privately Owned Public Space: The New York City Experience* (New York: Wiley, 2000), 16.

155. Ibid., 44.

156. Goldberger, "Shaping the Face of New York," 132.

157. Martin Gottlieb, "A Citywide Fund to Aid Housing is Being Studied," *NYT*, July 11, 1983.

158. "Zoning Policy's New Frontiers," *RER*, October 1983, 20.

159. Brian Sullivan, "Missing Out on Housing Trust Funds," *CL*, August/September, 1985, 29.

160. "Zoning Policy's New Frontiers," *RER*, October 1983, 30.

161. For condominium and cooperatives, the percentage increased to 30 percent. Anthony DePalma, "New Rules on 421a Tax Incentives," *NYT*, January 11, 1987.

162. Just as for the 421-a program, developers could escape building or renovating such housing themselves through the market-based certificate program. Sam Howe Verhhover, "Board Approves Zoning Bonus for Luxury Towers," *NYT*, May 23, 1987.

163. DePalma, "New Rules on 421a Tax Incentives."

164. Alan Finder, "Swapping Tax Credits for Housing," *NYT*, June 21, 1988.

165. Ibid.

166. Ibid.

167. Alan S. Oser, "Perspectives: 421a Certificates; An Innovative Program's Clouded Future," *NYT*, December 9, 1990.

168. The Reminiscences of Paul Crotty, interviews conducted in 1992, page 87. OHC.

169. Oser, "Perspectives: 421a Certificates."

170. Iver Peterson, "Linking 421a to Low-Income Housing," *NYT*, December 17, 1989.

171. Sam Roberts, "Dinkins Offers a Housing Plan to Lower Costs," *NYT*, August 22, 1989.

172. Thomas J. Lueck, "The Bulk-for Benefits Deal in Zoning," *NYT*, July 23, 1989.

173. Office of the State Comptroller, *Follow-Up on Granting Special Permits for Bonus Floor Area. Report A-14-92* (November 12, 1992), 2.

174. Lueck, "The Bulk-for Benefits Deal in Zoning."

175. Jennifer Stern, *The Subway Vs. The Sky: Awarding Private Developers Zoning Bonuses for Improvements to the New York City Subway System* (July 1989), vii.

176. Lueck, "The Bulk-for Benefits Deal in Zoning."

177. To be sure, the Koch administration did initiate a ten-year, $4.2 billion Housing Plan, which would rehabilitate or build around 140,000, principally moderate-income housing units. It was a tremendous commitment of municipal resources. But it was a temporary measure that would not ensure the continued creation of affordable housing in the future. In contrast, the complex tax credits system was designed to do just that. The two programs did share the goal of not relying on substantive ongoing municipal resources. Indeed, the Housing Plan, historian Jonathan Soffer has described, was "primarily an economic development program, not a welfare program. Koch aimed to rebuild areas devastated by abandonment and neglect into neighborhoods that were viable and self-sustaining without continuing cash subsidies or maintenance expenses that would have to be paid from the expense budget." Soffer, *Ed Koch and the Rebuilding of New York City*, 295. See also Gregg G. Van Ryzin and Andrew Genn, "Neighborhood Change and the City of New York's Ten-Year Housing Plan," *Housing Policy Debate* 10, no. 4 (1999): 799–838.

178. Kim Moody, *From Welfare State to Real Estate: Regime Change in New York City, 1974 to the Present* (New York: The New Press, 2007), 123.

179. "Text of Dinkins Speech," *NYT*, January 2, 1990.

180. Celestine Bohlen, "Dinkins TV Ad Criticizes Koch on High-Rises," *NYT*, August 12, 1989.

181. Sam Roberts, "Dinkins Offers a Housing Plan to Lower Costs," *NYT*, August 22, 1989.

182. Richard Levine, "Middle-Class Flight Feared by New York City Experts," *NYT*, April 1, 1991.

183. Moody, *From Welfare State to Real Estate*, 121.

184. Thomas J. Lueck, "Prices Decline as Gentrification Ebbs," *NYT*, September 29, 1991 and Alan Finder, "Tax Value Off for Property in New York," *NYT*, January 15, 1991.

185. Quoted in Nick Ravo, "New Housing at Lowest Since '85," *NYT*, August 30, 1992.

186. Thomas J. Lueck, "Prices Decline as Gentrification Ebbs."

187. Thomas J. Lueck, "Time for a Change in Builder Incentives," *NYT*, December 8, 1991.

188. "Who Can Talk About Development Incentives at a Time Like This?" *RER*, Spring 1990, 19.

189. Ibid., 29.

190. Lueck, "Time for a Change in Builder Incentives."

191. Ibid.

192. Office of the Speaker (Peter Vallone 1990–2001). Box 52432. Local Laws 49. 1992. CCNY.

CHAPTER 6

1. The Reminiscences of Nathan Leventhal. Interviews conducted in 1992. Page 103. OHC.

2. Mark Whitaker to David Dinkins, November 24, 1992. Box 178, Folder 1572. NS.

3. Herbert Muschamp, "Remodeling New York for the Bourgeoisie," *NYT*, September 24, 1995.

4. Reminiscences of Nathan Leventhal, 103.

5. A Totally Disgruntled New Yorker to Douglas Lasdon, May 22 [likely 1990]. Box "Archie/Kessler," Folder "Hate Mail." UJC.

6. Ella Howard, *Homeless: Poverty and Place in Urban America* (Philadelphia: University of Pennsylvania Press, 2013), 184.

7. See Joel Blau, *The Visible Poor: Homelessness in the United States* (New York: Oxford University Press, 1992) and Martha R. Burt, *Over the Edge: The Growth of Homelessness in the 1980s* (New York: Russell Sage Foundation, 1992).

8. Jonathan Soffer, *Ed Koch and the Rebuilding of New York City* (New York: Columbia University Press, 2010), 276–281 and Deirdre Carmody, "The City Sees No Solution for Homeless," *NYT*, October 10, 1984.

9. SRO units fell to less than 14,000 in 1984. Peter Rihss, "Influx of Former Mental Patients Burdening City, Albany is Told," *NYT*, November 23, 1980; Carmody,

"The City Sees No Solution for Homeless"; Alexander B. Grannis, "Letter to the Editor," *NYT*, December 8, 1984.

10. Howard, *Homeless*, 5.

11. Ellen Baxter and Kim Hopper, *Private Lives / Public Spaces: Homeless Adults on the Streets of New York City* (New York: The Community Service Society, 1981), 97.

12. Ibid., 95 and Author Interview Ellen Baxter, July 8, 2013.

13. Robin Herman, "Some of City's Homeless Gather in Convention's Shadow," *NYT*, August 14, 1980.

14. "Minutes of the First Organizational Meeting of the Coalition for the Homeless," December 11, 1980. Box 95. CTH.

15. "Proposed Objectives of the Coalition," May 14, 1981. Box 95. CTH.

16. Quoted in Charles Kaiser, "A State Justice Orders Creation of 750 Beds for Bowery Homeless," *NYT*, December 9, 1979.

17. Kim Hopper and L. Stuart Cox, "Litigation in Advocacy for the Homeless: The Case of New York City," *Development: Seeds of Change* 2 (1982): 58.

18. Kaiser, "A State Justice Orders Creation of 750 Beds."

19. The Reminiscences of Robert Esnard. Interviews conducted in 1994. Page 56. OHC.

20. Robert M. Hayes to Honorable Mario Cuomo, November 2, 1984. Reel 37. Section: Social Services, General: Homeless, 11/1/83–. MCC.

21. Sheila Rule, "Study Calls City Indifferent to Growing Crisis of Hunger," *NYT*, November 17, 1983.

22. "The First Report of the Governor's Task Force on Housing the Homeless," July 20, 1983. Folder "NYC Hearings and Summaries." KH.

23. "Edward Koch before the Ad Hoc Task Force on the Homeless and Housing," January 21, 1988. Box 35, Folder 1. EIK.

24. Ibid.

25. Carol Bellamy, "Letter to the Editor," *NYT*, October 22, 1982.

26. See, for example, Michael Goodwin, "Koch Shifts on Shelters," *NYT*, January 22, 1983.

27. Bella English, "For Homeless, it's Bleak," Undated *NYDN* article (most likely from November 1983). CTH.

28. See, for example, Michael Goodwin, "Costs to Shelter Homeless in City Climbing Sharply," *NYT*, October 2, 1983.

29. Edward A. Gargan, "Ducking for Cover Over the Homeless," *NYT*, November 27, 1983.

30. A. O. Sulzberger Jr., "Mayor Defends City's Handling of its Homeless," *NYT*, November 20, 1981.

31. See, for example, Baxter and Hopper, *Private Lives / Public Spaces*.

32. Quoted in Sara Rimer, "The Other City: New York's Homeless," *NYT*, January 30, 1984.

33. Laurence Klein to Mayor Edward Koch and Ronald Gault, "Bi-Weekly Summary—March 1–March 15, 1979." Box 256, Folder 7. EIK.

34. Laurence Klein to Edward Koch, July 3, 1979, "Bi-Weekly Summary—June 15–July 1, 1979." Box 63, Folder 11. EIK.

35. Laurence Klein to Edward Koch, "SRO Issues at West Side Town Hall on February 22nd." Box 63, Folder 11. EIK.

36. Deirdre Carmody, "Study Blames Poverty for Most Homelessness," *NYT*, November 2, 1984. See also Human Resources Administration of the City of New York, "Chronic and Situational Decency: Long-Term Residents in a Shelter for Men," May 1982. Box 189, Folder 2. EIK.

37. Goodwin, "Costs to Shelter Homeless in City Climbing Sharply."

38. Ibid. and Deirdre Carmody, "The City Sees No Solutions for Homeless," *NYT*, October 10, 1984.

39. Carmody, "The City Sees No Solutions for Homeless."

40. Blau, *The Visible Poor*, 100.

41. Sydney H. Schanberg, "Reagan's Homeless (Cont'd)," *NYT*, April 3, 1984; Carmody, "The City Sees No Solutions for Homeless."

42. "The Homeless in New York: The City's Program," early 1982, Box 189, Folder 2. EIK.

43. Quoted in Schanberg, "Fingers in the Dike."

44. Quoted in Crystal Nix, "City Proposes Separate Housing of Homeless with Special Needs," *NYT*, May 30, 1986.

45. Quoted in Barbara Basler, "2 Shelters for Homeless Offer Stark Contrasts," *NYT*, November 16, 1985.

46. Ibid.

47. Statement by Harold Hopkins, November 26, 1984. No box, Folder "Q." CFH.

48. Jordan Milsstein (Legal Action Center for the Homeless), "Hospitalization, Shelters Won't Get Homeless Off Streets," *The West Side Spirit*, February 21, 1988.

49. Annie Quintano to Joe Arcuri, District Managers Office, Penn Station, August 15, 1984. No box, Folder "Q." CFH.

50. Homeless Women's Rights Networks, "Press Release: Victims Again: A Report on the Conditions of Women in the City's Shelter System," January 17, 1989. Box 1, Folder 19. MM.

51. Quoted in Lydia Chavez, "Despite Bitter Cold, Many of Homeless Shun Shelters," *NYT*, January 7, 1988.

52. Quoted in Robert Hayes to Ed Koch, March 13, 1987. No box, Folder "Grand Central." CFH.

53. Quoted in Coalition for the Homeless, *A False Sense: A Study of Safety and Security Issues in New York City's Municipal Shelters for Men* (October 1989), 19. Box: Doe (armory Shelter) / Tolle. UJC.

54. Homeless Women's Rights Network, *Victims Again: Homeless Women in the New York City Shelter System* (January 1989). Box: Doe (armory Shelter) / Tolle. UJC.

55. Quoted in Chavez, "Despite Bitter Cold."

56. Josh Barbanel, "Homeless in City Facing Koch Edict," *NYT*, November 14, 1985.

57. Quoted in Sharman Stein, "Bypass Beggars, Koch Plan Urges," *ND*, August 19, 1988.

58. Quoted in Ronald Sullivan, "Mayor Offers Aid and Hand to Homeless," *NYT*, March 25, 1983.

59. The Council of the City of New York, *Report of the Select Committee on the Homeless* (January 22, 1987), 15. Box 59, Folder "Brooklyn Arms (1973–1988)." JN.

60. As late as 1985, only three shelters had even part time on-site mental health workers. Sara Kellerman and Katharine Legg to Stanley Brezenoff, August 9, 1985. Box 217, Folder 5. EIK.

61. Suzanne Golubski and James Harney, "Cold Day in Hell of Homeless," *NYDN*, December 3, 1985.

62. "Forced Shelter," *NYT*, February 19, 1982 and Ronald Sulliver, "Mayor Offers Aid and Hand to Homeless," *NYT*, March 25, 1983.

63. Suzanne Daley, "New York Expands Treatment Policy for Homeless," *NYT*, August 29, 1987.

64. "Interview with Steven Banks and Douglas Lasdon," *ND*, December 9, 1987.

65. Norman Siegel and Robert Levy, "The Real Problem is Housing," *NYT*, December 17, 1985.

66. Robert Hayes, "The Mayor and the Homeless Poor," *CL*, August–September 1985, 6.

67. Ibid., 7.

68. Public opinion also suffered due to a few prominent cases, most notably that of Joyce Brown. Living on the streets of the Upper East Side, Brown would at times run into traffic, rip up unsolicited money given by passersby, and use the streets as a bathroom. After she was involuntarily committed by city workers in 1987, the New York Civil Liberties Union took up her case, which attracted extensive national media attention; her attorneys repeatedly proclaimed her to be mentally stable. After her release in 1988, Brown appeared on various television shows and was even discussed in a meeting between Ronald Reagan and Mikhail Gorbachev, before she again suffered severe mental health difficulties and reemerged on the streets. Koch and many commentators pounced on Brown's turmoil as proof that the homeless street population was all mentally ill. See, for example, Eric Breindel, "Billie Boggs Proves a Point," *NYP*, February 2, 1989.

69. See, for example, David Wagner with Jennifer Barton Gilman, *Confronting Homelessness: Poverty, Politics, and the Failure of Social Policy* (Boulder, CO: Lynne Rienner, 2012), 121–145.

70. Sara Rimer, "Doors Closing as Mood on the Homeless Sours," *NYT*, November 18, 1989.

71. Roslyn Goldstein to Norman Seigel / American Civil Liberties Union, September 1, 1987. No box or folder. CFH.

72. Fox Butterfield, "New Yorkers Growing Angry over Aggressive Panhandlers," *NYT*, July 29, 1988.

73. "Varieties of Begging," *NYT*, August 3, 1988.

74. Butterfield, "New Yorkers Growing Angry."

75. Lorraine Mishkin to Susan Baer, Manager, Port Authority, March 13, 1987. Box 95, Folder "Grand Central." CFH.

76. "Affidavit of William B. Young, Jr." William B. Young Jr. and Joseph Walley against the New York City Transit Authority, Metropolitan Transportation Authority of the State of New York, Metro-North Commuter Railroad Company, and Robert R. Kiley, November 22, 1989. Box "Young," Folder "Affidavits (and Supplemental Aff.) of Walley, Young, and Lasdon." UJC.

77. Quoted in Sharman Stein, "Bypass Beggars, Koch Plan Urges," *ND*, August 19, 1988.

78. Ed Abrahams, "Letter to the Editor," *NYT*, August 10, 1988.

79. Richard Levine, "Plan Urges New Look at Terminal," *NYT*, January 11, 1988.

80. Michael W. Brooks, *Subway City: Riding the Trains, Reading New York* (New Brunswick, NJ: Rutgers University Press, 1997), 195.

81. Joe Austin, *Taking the Train: How Graffiti Art Became an Urban Crisis in New York City* (New York: Columbia University Press, 2001), 222.

82. Andrew C. Hyde to Robin Jacobson, November 21, 1989. Box 32, Folder "Subway Monitoring." CFH.

83. Shawn G. Kennedy, "Grand Central Area Gains," *NYT*, September 10, 1986.

84. Ibid.

85. Josh Barbanel, "Plan Seeks to Reduce Homeless at Terminal," *NYT*, July 25, 1986.

86. Richard Levine, "Plan Urges New Look at Terminal," *NYT*, January 11, 1988.

87. Rita Schwartz, *The Homeless: The Impact on the Transportation Industry* (New York: Port Authority of New York and New Jersey, 1988), 1. NYSL.

88. Jane Gross, "A First Look at Homeless is Raw Sight for Tourists," *NYT*, November 9, 1987.

89. Jim Dwyer, "On Trains, in Tunnels, Homeless Toss and Turn," *ND*, January 29, 1987.

90. Jeffrey Wilson to Tito Davila, June 17, 1990. Box "Archie/Kessler," Folder "Hate Mail." UJC.

91. Jack Lusk to Stanley Brezenoff, "34th Street Subway Complex: Homeless Issues," June 25, 1986. Box 71, Folder 13. EIK.

92. Quintano to Arcuri, August 15, 1984.

93. Council of the City of New York, *Report of the Select Committee on the Homeless*.

94. Barbara Basler, "Citing Safety Issue, Two Depots Begin Removing Lockers," *NYT*, April 3, 1986.

95. The Council of the City of New York, *Report of the Select Committee on the Homeless*.

96. Rimer, "Doors Closing as Mood on the Homeless Sours."

97. Quoted in Jim Nolan, "Wet Side Story," *NYP*, likely June 1990. CFH.

98. Robert Hayes to Edward Koch, March 13, 1987. No box, Folder "Grand Central." CFH.

99. See, for example, Robert Hayes to Edward Koch, March 16, 1987 and Edward Koch to Robert Hayes, March 19, 1987. No box, Folder "Grand Central." CFH.

100. Kim Hopper, Supplemental Affidavit, Wally and Gates against New York City Transit Authority et al. February 1991. Box: "Young / Bacon." UJC.

101. Jorge Casuso, "Compassion for Homeless Turns to Fear," *CT*, July 22, 1990.

102. Rimer, "Doors Closing as Mood on the Homeless Sours."

103. Affidavit of Robert N. Bontempo, Young et al. against New York City Transit Authority et al. January 18, 1990. Box "Young / Bacon," Folder "Affidavit of Robert N Bontempo (critique of MTA survey)." UJC.

104. Nearly 80 percent of the homeless living in the subways were black or Latinx and nearly 85 percent were male. David E. Pitt, "New Strategy for Homeless in Subways," *NYT*, July 22, 1989.

105. Jennifer A. Kingson, "Bus Terminal Adding Police as Crime Rises," *NYT*, April 6, 1988.

106. Kirk Johnson, "Battling Subway Crime, Both Real and Perceived," *NYT*, October 2, 1989.

107. For example, a study conducted in the 1990s found that the more white people associated homelessness with African Americans, the more likely they were to view the homeless population as dangerous. Wagner, *Confronting Homelessness*, 144.

108. George Kelling, "Reclaiming the Subway," *CJ*, Winter 1991.

109. Stephen Berger, "The Homeless—a Regional Crisis," Keynote Address at "Action Day '88," January 30, 1988.

110. Quoted in Bob Herbert, "Dodging the Homeless Issue," *NYDN*, March 19, 1987.

111. Quoted in Joyce Purnick, "Grand Central Bars 'Loitering' by Homeless during Day," *NYT*, February 14, 1985.

112. David Karnovosky, Assistant Corporation Counsel to Peter Zmiroth and Paul Rephen, "The Impact of People V. Clark and the Port Authority's Enforcement Response," May 5, 1988. Box 71, Folder 13. EIK.

113. Jack Lusk to Edward Koch, May 8, 1988. Box 71, Folder 13. EIK.

114. Karnovosky, "The Impact of People V. Clark and the Port Authority's Enforcement Response."

115. Philip Lentz, "Gimbels Throws in The Discount Towel At Herald Square," *CT*, July 24, 1986 and Alan S. Oser, "Perspectives: Vertical Shopping Malls," *NYT*, June 7, 1987.

116. Jim Dwyer, "Clearance Sale on the Homeless," *ND*, May 26, 1987.

117. Lusk to Brezenoff, "34th Street Subway Complex: Homeless Issues."

118. Dwyer, "Clearance Sale on the Homeless."

119. "Minutes of the Joint Meeting of the Boards of the Bryant Park Restoration Corporation and Bryant Park Management Corporation," November 10, 1988. Folder "BPRC/BPMC Bd. Mtg 2/1/89." BPC.

120. "Minutes of the Joint Meeting of the Boards of the Bryant Park Restoration Corporation and Bryant Park Management Corporation," February 1, 1989. Folder "BPRC / BPMC Bd. Mtg. 6/1/89." BPC.

121. Quoted in Sonya Reyes and Leo Standora, "Midtown Bizmen Bring in Own Cops," *NYP*, September 14, 1988.

122. Alex Vitale, *City of Disorder: How the Quality of Life Campaign Transformed New York Politics* (New York: New York University Press, 2008), 129 and Michael Freitag, "New Barriers to Homeless at Station," *NYT*, September 17, 1989.

123. David Dunlap, "Grand Central at 75: Beauty and Misery," *NYT*, February 1, 1988.

124. Rachelle Garbarine, "A Special Tax Will Help Spruce Up Around 34th Street," *NYT*, September 11, 1991.

125. The MTA had conducted periodic police sweets of dozens of stations with large homeless populations and had banned panhandling on trains and in stations. Richard Levine, "Subway Musicians Told to Keep Distance," *NYT*, October 17, 1987.

126. Memorandum of Law in Support of Plaintiffs' Application for a Preliminary Injunction. William B. Young Jr. and Joseph Walley against the New York City Transit Authority, Metropolitan Transportation Authority of the State of New York, Metro-North Commuter Railroad Company, and Robert R. Kiley. November 1989, 10–12. Box: "Young." UJC.

127. Affidavit of Douglas H. Lasdon, November 28, 1989. William B. Young Jr. and Joseph Walley against the New York City Transit Authority, Metropolitan Transportation Authority of the State of New York, Metro-North Commuter Railroad Company, and Robert R. Kiley, November 22, 1989. Box "Young," Folder "Affidavits (and Supplemental Aff.) of Walley, Young, and Lasdon." UJC.

128. Quoted in Sara Rimer, "Pressed on the Homeless, Subways impose Rules," *NYT*, October 25, 1989.

129. Officials also pointed to the high number of non-natural deaths of homeless individuals in the subway, which rose to an average of six per month in 1989. George L. Kelling and Catherine M. Coles, *Fixing Broken Windows: Restoring Order and Reducing Crime in Our Communities* (New York: The Free Press, 1996), 119.

130. Berger, "The Homeless—a Regional Crisis."

131. George Kelling and James Q. Wilson, "Broken Windows: The Police and Neighborhood Safety," *Atlantic Monthly* (March 1982), 29–38.

132. Michael Tomasky, "Quality of Life," *NY*, December 23–30, 1996, 26.

133. Kelling, *Fixing Broken Windows*, 112–114.

134. Robert R. Kiley, Chairman to The Honorable David Dinkins, June 15, 1990. Box 32, Folder "MTA." CFH.

135. Alan Kiepper, President of the New York City Transit Authority to Mary Brosnahan, Coalition for the Homeless, June 27, 1990. Box 32, Folder "MTA." CFH.

136. Affidavit of George L. Kelling, December 11, 1989. William B. Young Jr. and Joseph Walley against the New York City Transit Authority, Metropolitan Transportation Authority of the State of New York, Metro-North Commuter Railroad Company, and Robert R. Kiley, Page 13. Box "Young," Folder "D's memo in further opposition to P's motion for P.I. with Affid of Geo. Kelling." UJC.

137. Ibid., 3.

138. Affidavit of George Kelling, February 26, 1991. Joseph Walley and Glenn Gates et al. against New York City Transit Authority et al., Box: "Young / Bacon." UJC.

139. Affidavit of George Kelling, December 11, 1989, 5.

140. Ibid., 6.

141. Coalition for the Homeless, Inc., Doe Fund, Inc., New York Civil Liberties Union, The Partnership for the Homeless, and United Homeless Organization to Mary Ann Crotty and Michael J. Dowling, November 17, 1989. Box 32, Folder "Subway Monitoring" (3). CFH.

142. Safety Network / NY: The Newsletter for the Coalition for the Homeless (November 1989). CFH.

143. Quoted in Ronald Smothers, "Dinkins Rejects Koch Shelter Proposal," *NYT*, November 21, 1986.

144. Clara Hemphill, "Policies Seek an Answer," *ND*, February 23, 1989.

145. Lucette Lagnado, "Parks Boss is Coy on Evicting Homeless," *NYP*, March 21, 1989.

146. Rimer, "Doors Closing as Mood on the Homeless Sours." See also Coalition for the Homeless, "Ending Homelessness in New York City: A Mayoral Program," May 1989. Box 3, Folder 71. MM.

147. Sarah Ferguson, "Fire and Ice," *VV*, December 26, 1989.

148. Coalition for the Homeless, "Ending Homelessness in New York City."

149. Quoted in Calvin Sims, "IND Vagrants to be Ejected Tonight," *NYT*, July 15, 1990.

150. David Dinkins to Robert Kiley, August 14, 1990. Box 8, Folder "Metropolitan Transportation Authority (1)." DHS.

151. Sims, "IND Vagrants to be Ejected Tonight."

152. Robert Kiley to David Dinkins, June 15, 1990. Box 8, Folder "Metropolitan Transportation Authority (1)." DHS.

153. Norman Steisel to Ad Hoc Alliance on MTA Homeless, December 10, 1991. Box 8, Folder "Metropolitan Transportation Authority (1)." DHS.

154. Mary Brosnahan, "Testimony of the Coalition for the Homeless before the New York City Council Committee on General Welfare," January 18, 1991. Box 28. CFH.

155. Norman Steisel to Mary Brosnahan, December 31, 1992. Box 179, Folder 1580. NS.

156. Mary Brosnahan, Testimony before the Mayor's Commission on Homelessness, January 14, 1992. Box 3, Folder "Public Meeting 1992." COH.

157. William Bratton with Peter Knobler, *Turnaround: How America's Top Cop Reversed the Crime Epidemic* (New York: Random House, 1998), 141.

158. Calvin Sims, "Some Police Skeptical of Any Plans to Roust Beggars," *NYT*, May 12, 1990 and Seth Faison Jr., "Tough Campaign is Vowed against Homeless in Subway," *NYT*, October 19, 1991.

159. Affidavit of William J. Bratton, Walley and Gates et al. against New York City Transit Authority et al. February 1991. Box: "Young / Bacon." UJC.

160. Thomas Morgan, "Port Authority to Evict the Homeless from Bus Terminal," *NYT*, November 7, 1991 and Jacques Steinberg, "Crackdown on Homeless is Begun at Bus Terminal," *NYT*, December 2, 1991.

161. Quoted it Morgan, "Port Authority to Evict the Homeless from Bus Terminal."

162. Bruce Lambert, "Croissants? A Clam Bar? Is This the Port Authority Terminal?" *NYT*, August 6, 1995 and Marcus Felson, Mathieu E. Belanger, Gisela M. Bichler, Chris D. Bruzinski, Glenna S. Campbell, Cheryl L. Fried, Kathleen C. Grofik, Irene S. Mazur, Amy B. O'Regan, Patricia J. Sweeney, Andrew L. Ullman, and LaQuanda M. Williams, "Redesigning Hell: Preventing Crime and Disorder at the Port Authority Bus Terminal," in *Preventing Mass Transit Crime*, ed. Ronald V. Clarke (Monsey, NY: Criminal Justice Press, 1996), 22.

163. Mitch Gelman, "Rousting Homeless a Thankless Task," *ND*, December 23, 1989.

164. Joseph Deitch, "On Homeless Beat at the Bus Terminal," *NYT*, January 10, 1993.

165. "Plan for Bus Terminal," *NYT*, October 22, 1992.

166. Lambert, "Croissants? A Clam Bar?"

167. Vitale, *City of Disorder*, 130.

168. Margo Schneidman, "For Some of the Homeless, Membership Has its Privileges," *CL*, April 1990, 10.

169. Quoted in Christian Parenti, "Sidewalk Mercenaries vs. Homeless," *Z Magazine*, November 1994, 19.

170. Vitale, *City of Disorder*, 131.

171. Parenti, "Sidewalk Mercenaries vs. Homeless," 18–21.

172. Bruce Lambert, "Group Bullied the Homeless, Agency Finds," *NYT*, July 6, 1995.

173. Nancy Wackstein to Norman Steisel and Barbara Fife, August 9, 1990. Box 40, Folder 336. NS.

174. Ibid.

175. See David W. Dunlap, "Stern Seeks Expanded Rules to Curb Abuse of Parks in New York," *NYT*, March 15, 1989.

176. Parks Council, "Comment in Response to Proposed New Rules of the Department of Parks and Recreation," April 24, 1989. CPC.

177. "52 Hurt as Cops Clear E. Village Park," *NYDN*, August 8, 1988.

178. Rheka Basu, Mark Mooney and Andrea Peyser, "Riot Cops Clear Out Tompkins Sq. Again," *NYP*, July 7, 1989.

179. Jessie Mangaliman, "Tompkins Sq. Park Reopens," *ND*, August 26, 1992.

180. David Hochman, "Turning Around a Square," *Our Town*, June 15, 1994.

181. Bruce Lambert, "Confronted by the Homeless Domino Effect, Another Park Cracks Down," *NYT*, June 12, 1994.

182. See Monte Williams, "Giving Madison Square Park a Face (and a Facelift)," *NYT*, June 25, 1995; Monte Williams, "Madison Square Park to Regain Its 19th-Century Luster," *NYT*, November 8, 1998; and Barbara Stewart, "Partnerships Restore City Parks, Within Limits," *NYT*, June 12, 2001.

183. Sasha Nyary, "Home in the Parks," *The West Side Spirit*, October 31, 1988.

184. Elizabeth Barlow Rogers to Michael Peskoff, November 15, 1993. CPC.

185. Thomas G. Kahn to Betsy Barlow Rogers, September 16, 1991. CPC.

186. Nancy Wackstein to Ruth Messinger, June 24, 1991. Box 115, Folder 955. NS.

187. Quoted in Douglas Martin, "A Squatter's Colony Called Home," *NYT*, November 29, 1993.

188. "First, Reclaim the Streets," *NYT*, December 30, 1990.

189. Sharon Landers to Norman Steisel, April 30, 1991. Box 8, Folder "Metropolitan Transportation Authority (1)." DHS.

190. Nancy Wackstein and Michael Kharfen to David Dinkins, September 12, 1991. Box 115, Folder 956. NS.

191. Quoted in Sam Roberts, "Evicting the Homeless," *NYT*, June 22, 1991.

192. Roberts, "Evicting the Homeless," *NYT*, June 22, 1991.

193. Tony Brown, "City Cleans up for Visitors," *ND*, March 29, 1991.

194. Quoted in Ian Fisher, "The Coliseum's Nocturnal Homeless," *NYT*, September 2, 1993.

195. "Interview with Steven Banks and Douglas Lasdon."

196. Coalition for the Homeless, *A False Sense: A Study of Safety and Security Issues in New York City's Municipal Shelters for Men*, October 1989, (3). Box "Doe (armory Shelter) / Tolle." UJC.

197. "When City Hall Fails, Do it Yourself," *NYT*, January 13, 1991.

198. Commission on the Homeless, *The Way Home: A New Direction in Social Policy* (February 1992), 11.

199. Ibid., 10.

200. Ibid., 29.

201. Mark Page to Norman Steisel, August 14, 1992. Box 1, Folder "Development of Homeless Housing 1993." DHS.

202. Commission on the Homeless, *The Way Home*, 13.

203. "For the Homeless, Practicality," *NYT*, February 24, 1992.

204. "Shelters Versus Housing," *CL*, February 1992, 2.

205. Celia W. Dugger, "Giuliani to Call for Curtailing Services for Some Homeless," *NYT*, September 17, 1993. See also "Response to Giuliani Position Paper on Homelessness." Box 235, Folder 2188. NS.

206. See Vitale, *City of Disorder*.

207. Quoted in Sam Roberts, "Evicting the Homeless," *NYT*, June 22, 1991.

208. Coalition for the Homeless, "Number of Homeless People Each Night in the New York Shelter System, 1983–2015." http://www.coalitionforthehomeless.org/wp-content/uploads/2014/04/NYCHomelessShelterPopulationCharts01-2015.pdf

209. See, for example, The Coalition for the Homeless, "Losing the Way Home: Privatization and the Municipal Shelter System," (October 1997). Box 28, Folder "Homeless [Coalition for the Homeless Report]." JN.

210. For more on the organizing by those experiencing homelessness during this period, see Ben Holtzman, "When the Homeless Took Over." *Shelterforce.* October 11, 2019. https://shelterforce.org/2019/10/11/when-the-homeless-took-over/

211. Goodwin, "Costs to Shelter Homeless in City Climbing Sharply."

212. *Newsmakers* transcript, October 14, 1984. Box 36, Folder 11. EIK.

213. "One in 12 Children!" *CL*, December 1993, 2.

CONCLUSION

1. The Editors, "Welcome to NY," *CJ*, Autumn 1990.

2. Ibid.

3. Stephen G. Craig, "Where the Money Goes," *CJ*, Autumn 1991.

4. See Jason Horowitz, "The Rudy Giuliani Conservatives," *The Observer*, December 12, 2007 and Janny Scott, "Promoting Its Ideas, the Manhattan Institute Has Nudged New York Rightward," *NYT*, May 12, 1997.

5. Quoted in Horowitz, "The Rudy Giuliani Conservatives."

6. See, for example, George L. Kelling, "Reclaiming the Subway," *CJ*, Winter 1991; Editors, "Unbearable Obligations," *CJ*, Summer 1991; Editors, "Handle with Care," *CJ*, Spring 1991; George Kelling, "The Contagion of Public Disorder," *CJ*, Spring 1991; Richard Vigilante, "How to Save the City," *CJ*, Autumn 1991; George L. Kelling, "Crime and Metaphor: Toward a New Concept of Policing," *CJ*, August 1991; James Taranto, "Terminal Illness," *CJ*, Winter 1992; Editors, "Comforting Thoughts," *CJ*, Spring 1992; Fred Siegel, "Reclaiming Our Public Spaces," *CJ*, Spring 1992; Editors, "The Trouble With Tenancy," *CJ*, Summer 1992; and Howard Husock, "New Frontiers in Affordable Housing," *CJ*, Spring 1993.

7. For example, see Timothy P. R. Weaver, *Blazing the Neoliberal Trail: Urban Political Development in the United States and the United Kingdom* (Philadelphia: University of Pennsylvania Press, 2016) and Lily Geismer, "The Places Left Behind," *Jacobin*, May 2016, https://jacobinmag.com/2016/11/bill-clinton-poverty-tour-hillary-new-markets.

8. Critics have commonly heralded the Giuliani administration as embodying the neoliberal turn of the late twentieth century, describing his administration as a "neoliberal juggernaut," "a neoliberal state" and as "staunchly neoliberal." See Vijay Prashad, *The Karma of Brown Folk* (Minneapolis: University of Minnesota Press, 2001), 200; Laam Hae, *The Gentrification of Nightlife and the Right to the*

City: Regulating Spaces of Social Dancing in New York (New York: Routledge, 2012), 126; and Themis Chronopoulos, *Spatial Regulation in New York City: From Urban Renewal to Zero Tolerance* (New York: Routledge, 2013), 169.

9. Roger Sanjek, *The Future of Us All: Race and Neighborhood Politics in New York City* (Ithaca, NY: Cornell University Press, 1998), 184.

10. Andrew Kirtzman, *Rudy Giuliani: Emperor of the City* (New York: William Morrow, 2000), 74.

11. Quoted in Jack Newfield, *The Full Rudy: The Man, the Myth, the Mania* (New York: Thunder's Mouth Press, 2002), 56.

12. Sanjek, *The Future of Us All*, 180–182.

13. Ibid., 183.

14. Douglas Martin, "City Offers Private Group Contract to Maintain Central Park," *NYT*, September 6, 1997.

15. Adam Wisnieski, "NY's Security-Guard Industry Grows Amid Lax Oversight," *CL*, May 3, 2016, https://citylimits.org/2016/05/03/as-security-guard-industry-grows-with-little-oversight-problems-persist/.

16. Kelsey Thomas, "NYC Official: Time to Review City's Not-So-Public Public Spaces," *Next City*, April 21, 2017, https://nextcity.org/daily/entry/nyc-privately-owned-public-spaces-access-audit-POPS-report.

17. Tanay Warerkar, "Many of NYC's Privately-Owned Public Spaces Still Flout Rules: Report," *Curbed New York*, November 22, 2017, https://ny.curbed.com/2017/11/22/16690978/nyc-privately-owned-public-spaces-stringer-audit.

18. Furman Center for Real Estate and Urban Policy, *Fact Brief: Rent Stabilization in New York City*, April 2012, http://furmancenter.org/files/publications/HVS_Rent_Stabilization_fact_sheet_FINAL_4.pdf and New York City Department of Housing Preservation and Development and the US Census Bureau, "Selected Initial Findings of the 2017 New York City Housing and Vacancy Survey," February 9, 2018, https://www1.nyc.gov/assets/hpd/downloads/pdf/about/2017-hvs-initial-findings.pdf.

19. Furman Center for Real Estate and Urban Policy, *Fact Brief* and Department of Housing Preservation and Development and the US Census Bureau, "Selected Initial Findings." Ownership rates in Manhattan increased from 11.4 in 1981 to 24.6 percent in 2017. See Michael A. Stegman for the Department of Housing Preservation and Development, *Housing in New York: Study of a City, 1984* (February 1984), 45 and "Selected Initial Findings."

20. Charles V. Baglio, "In Program to Spur Affordable Housing, $100 Million Penthouse Gets 95% Tax Cut," *NYT*, February 1, 2015.

21. Charles V. Baglio, "Affordable Housing Program Gives City Tax Break to Developers," *NYT*, April 10, 2017.

22. Giselle Routhier / Coalition for the Homeless, *State of the Homeless 2020: Governor and Mayor to Blame as New York Enters Fifth Decade of Homelessness Crisis*, March 2020. https://www.coalitionforthehomeless.org/wp-content/uploads/2020/03/

StateofTheHomeless2020.pdf and "Facts about Homelessness," https://www. coalitionforthehomeless.org/facts-about-homelessness/, accessed March 17, 2020.

23. Nikita Stewart, "Homeless Shelters Name Their Own Rates in New York, Audit Finds," *NYT*, Oct 15, 2017 and Citizens Budget Commission, "A $3 Billion Problem," May 24, 2018, https://cbcny.org/research/3-billion-problem.

24. Picture the Homeless Research Committee, *The Business of Homelessness: Financial & Human Costs of the Shelter-Industrial Complex*, March 2018, http:// picturethehomeless.org/wp-content/uploads/2018/03/PtH_White_paper5.pdf.

25. Coalition for the Homeless, *State of the Homeless: 2014*, March 12, 2014, http:// www.coalitionforthehomeless.org/state-of-the-homeless-2014. Mayor De Blasio pulled back on the use of run-down, privately owned apartments for homeless families, but private developers and landlords (and hotel operators) continue to make large profits from sheltering the homeless. See Rich Bockmann, "Raising the Stakes on Homeless Space," *The Real Deal*, January 1, 2019, https://therealdeal. com/issues_articles/homeless-housing-development-nyc. See also David Brand, "NYC's Homeless Hotel Population Surges as City Grapples with Housing Crisis," *City Limits*, January 29, 2020, https://citylimits.org/2020/01/29/nycs-homeless-hotel-population-surges-as-city-grapples-with-housing-crisis/.

26. James A. Parrott, "Inequality and New York City Economic Structure," June 2017, https://www.gc.cuny.edu/CUNY_GC/media/LISCenter/Parrott-Stone-Center-June-2017-Inequality-NYC-econ-structure-FINAL3.pdf.

27. Parrott, "Inequality and New York City Economic Structure" and New York City Independent Budget Office, "How Has the Distribution of Income in New York City Changed Since 2006?," April 2017, ibo.nyc.ny.us/cgi-park2/2017/04/how-has-the-distribution-of-income-in-new-york-city-changed-since-2006/.

28. Measure of America of the Social Science Research Council, *A Portrait of New York City 2018: Well-Being in the Five Boroughs and the Greater Metro Area*, 2018. https://ssrc-static.s3.amazonaws.com/moa/pony.full.pdf.

29. Rob Wile, "1 Out of Every 21 New Yorkers is a Millionaire," *Business Insider*, July 22, 2014, https://www.businessinsider.com/one-out-of-every-21-new-yorkers-is-a-millionaire-2014-7; Mayor's Office of Operations, *New York City Government Poverty Measure 2005–2016*, April 2018, https://www1.nyc.gov/assets/opportu-nity/pdf/18_poverty_measure_report.pdf; and New York University Furham Center, *2016 Focus: Poverty in New York City*, furmancenter.org/files/sotc/SOC_2016_FOCUS_Poverty_in_NYC.pdf.

30. Mark Dent, "Kansas City Privatizes Sidewalk in Rowsey Entertainment District," *Next City*, January 17, 2018, https://nextcity.org/daily/entry/kansas-city-privatizes-sidewalks-in-rowdy-entertainment-district.

31. Fran Spielman, "Parking Meter Deal Keeps Getting Worse for City as Meter Revenues Rise," *Chicago Sun Times*, May 14, 2018.

32. The Trust for Public Land, *Public Spaces/Private Money: The Triumphs and Pitfalls of Urban Park Conservancies*, February 2015, https://www.tpl.org/sites/default/files/files_upload/ccpe-Parks-Conservancy-Report.pdf, 13.

33. The scholarly and popular literature on these issues is vast, but for a snapshot of recent debates see Molly Ball, "The Privatization Backlash," *The Atlantic*, April 23, 2014. See also Hunter Blair, *No Free Bridge: Why Public–Private Partnerships or Other 'Innovative' Financing of Infrastructure Will Not Save Taxpayers Money*, Economic Policy Institute, March 21, 2017, https://www.epi.org/files/pdf/121302.pdf.

34. Ball, "The Privatization Backlash."

35. For a small sampling of these campaigns, see the work of: Equality for Flatbush (equalityforflatbush.org), the Crown Heights Tenant Union (crownheightstenantunion.org), Picture the Homeless (picturethehomeless.org), Make the Road New York (maketheroadny.org), Community Voices Heard (cvhaction.org), New Yorkers for Parks (www.ny4p.org), and NYC Community Land Initiative (nyccli.org).

Index

For the benefit of digital users, indexed terms that span two pages (e.g., 52–53) may, on occasion, appear on only one of those pages.

"Abandon Central Park?" (poster and pamphlet cover), 108*f*
abandoned buildings
  declining real estate enmeshed in city's problems, 177
  homesteading as local response to, 20–22, 24–27
  impact on lower income areas, 21*f*
  landlord desertion, 10–11, 23–24
  no tax revenue from, 32, 174–75
  150,000 units in 10,000 buildings, 38
ABNY. *See* Association for a Better New York (ABNY)
Abrahams, Ed, 213
Adopt a Building, 36, 39, 40, 42
affordable housing. *See also* cooperative ownership; rent control; urban homesteading of low-income housing
  construction shifted to market, 48, 50–52, 173–74, 194–97, 199
  funding by developer incentives, 192–96
  homelessness driven by poverty and lack of, 208–9
  J-51 tax incentives and, 186, 187

private market's inability to provide rental, 23–24, 180, 185, 191–92, 193–95
Affordable New York Housing Program, 238–39
African Americans. *See also* homelessness; race/racial politics
  Business and Professional Men's Club, 139
  "Civilian Radio Patrols," 155
  concerns about policing, 137–41, 158
  fears regarding park use by, 118, 121
  homeless men in public spaces, 165–66, 201
  as owners of converted units, 267n150
Agenda for Economic Development (1975), 174
"Alternative Governance Proposals for Central Park," 114
amenities, and private development for public, 192–97, 233–34. *See also* bonus amenities
American Standard, 123
ANHD. *See* Association of Neighborhood Housing Developers (ANHD)

Aponte, Angelo, 198
Applegate, John, 145
arson and fires, 186–87, 220–21
Arson Strike Force, 186–87
as of right, 169–70, 176–77, 293n85
Asphalt Green project, 101–2
Association for a Better New York
    (ABNY), 150–52, 161, 164, 166
Association of Neighborhood Housing
    Developers (ANHD), 36,
    37–38, 39–40
AT&T tax abatement, 182–83
ATM vestibules, driving homeless
    from, 226
auctions of buildings, 44, 45–46

Badillo, Herman, 47–48
Ballon, Hilary, 8
Bamford, Jeanette, 126–27
Banana Kelly, 54
Banks, Steven, 229–30
Barlow, Elizabeth "Betsy," 107, 111–12,
    114–15, 117, 123, 131–32, 228
Baxter, Ellen, 204–6
Beachview Civilian Radio Motor Patrol,
    racist group supported by local
    police, 139
Beame, Abraham
    blamed for poor fiscal management, 14
    housing issues and, 35, 37–38, 42, 44,
        45–46, 80
    open to role of private sector in
        governance, 4–5, 55–56, 237–38
    public park issues and, 95, 101–2,
        103–4, 110
    support for community anti-crime
        initiatives, 153–54
    tax incentives as principal
        development strategy, 167, 168–69,
        170, 172–78, 196–97
Bedford-Stuyvesant Restoration
    Corporation, 176

Beinecke, William, 116–17
Bellamy, Carol, 50–52, 181, 187–88, 190
Berger, Stephen, 218, 220–21
Better Brooklyn Committee, 133
Biederman, Daniel
    broken windows strategy and, 221
    Bryant Park restoration and, 122–23,
        124–25, 126
    Grand Central Partnership and,
        215, 219
    134th Street Partnership and, 220
Biles, Roger, 13
Black Citizens Patrol (Harlem), 141
block associations. *See also* citizen patrols
    CCNYC and, 154–55, 156
    cost of private guards and, 146–47
    grants to, 155, 156
    growth and decline, 145,
        162–63, 281n69
    MAA network and, 149–50, 151–52
    meetings, 143–44, 153
block watcher programs, 144, 150,
    153–54, 155, 156, 158, 163
Bloomberg, Michael, 238, 239
Board of Guardians (Central Park),
    109–10, 114, 118, 269–70n16
bonus amenities, 192–95, 196, 197, 199
BPRC (Bryant Park Restoration
    Corporation). *See* Bryant Park
Bratton, William J., 225, 229, 232
Bristo-Myers grants, 281n69
broken windows theory and policy, 220,
    221–22, 225, 229, 231–32, 233–34
Bronx. *See also* South Bronx
    community park improvements, 102
    park conditions impacted by
        economic disparities, 130
Brooklyn brownstones, 84
Brooklyn Heights, 133–34, 135, 157
Brosnahan, Mary, 228
Brown, Joyce, 301n68
Brown Harris Stevens, 58–59, 71

Bryant Park
  BPRC establishment and
    initiatives, 122–26
  BPRC renovation, 200–1, 215,
    219, 221
  Bryant Park Community
    Fund, 121–22
  Bryant Park Steering
    Committee, 121–22
  in business district, 95, 121–23
  controversy over BPRC management
    of, 121, 126–28
  property values and ". . . Bryant Park
    plans," 129
  restaurant as part of plan, 125, 126
Buland, Rita, 180
Burns Security, 147–48
Business and Professional Men's
  Club, 139
Business Improvement Districts (BIDs),
  125–26, 164–65, 203–4, 215,
  220, 240
businesses and corporations.
    See also private sector
  exodus to suburbs and sunbelt,
    12–13, 135
  overlooking Bryant Park, 121–22,
    123, 124
  overlooking Madison Square
    Park, 118–19
  parks in business districts subject to
    crime and neglect, 95, 118
  support for Central Park, 110–11, 117
  support for parks, 120
  use of private guards with neighboring
    institutions, 136, 147–52
Byrd, William, 141–42

Callahan v. Carey, 204–5
Carl Schurz Park Association, 100–1
Carnegie House, 82
Caro, Robert, 98–99

Carter, Jimmy
  sunbelt favored over inner cities, 13, 47
  visit to South Bronx (1977), 20, 40–42
Castle Hill, 102
CCNYC. *See* Citizens Committee for
  New York City (CCNYC)
Central Brooklyn Coordinating
  Committee, 156
Central Park, 105–13. *See also* Board of
  Guardians (Central Park)
  business and corporation support for,
    110–11, 117
  elite governance of, 269–70n16
  federalization proposal, 113
  fiscal crisis impact on, 110–11, 112–13
  tax incentives for supporters, 118
  volunteers, 107–9, 110, 111–12
Central Park Community Fund
  (CPCF), 105, 106, 108–13, 114,
  115, 116
Central Park Conservancy, 113–18,
  127–28, 129, 228, 238
Central Park Task Force (CPTF)
  "Abandon Central Park?"
    (poster and pamphlet cover),
    106–9, 108f
  Barlow built on its work in Central
    Park Conservancy, 115
  complementarity with Community
    Fund, 112–13, 114
  merged into Central Park
    Conservancy, 116
  organized to promote volunteerism
    and public awareness, 105
  tag for trash bags, 108f
  "32 Ways Your Time or Money
    Can Rescue Central
    Park," 111–12
Chemical Bank, 42
Chesler, Vicki, 85
Chicago parking meters, 240
Christie, Stuart, 188

Christodora, 190

citizen patrols. *See also* Queens
  considered in Brooklyn Heights,
    134, 135
  fluctuation of support for, 136–37,
    142–43, 158, 162–63, 166
  normalization of private guards and,
    17, 152–58
  NYCHA tenant patrols, 141–42
  St. Nicholas Tenant Patrol (Harlem),
    140*f*, 141–42

Citizens Committee for New York City
  (CCNYC), 104, 154–55, 156, 158

Citizens Housing and Planning
  Council, 188

City Club of New York, 168

City Journal, on radical solutions to New
  York's radical problems, 235–36

City Limits, 51*f*, 53–54, 231, 232–33

City Parks Foundation, 278n184

city-dwellers. *See also* citizen patrols;
    volunteers
  actions to improve conditions for
    themselves, 2–6, 15, 93–94
  forged pathways for private actors and
    private sector, 4, 5, 6, 236–37

city-owned housing. *See* in rem
    properties

civic services. *See also* government; law
    enforcement; local officials; parks
  belief in local government as ideal
    provider of, 6–9
  city inability to provide, 4, 68–69,
    166, 209, 213–14, 230
  marketization emerged from residents
    helping provide, 5, 236–37
  solutions beyond government needed,
    9, 10–11, 14–15, 16

Civilian Observation Patrol (COP),
    153–54, 157–58

Civilian Participation Program (NYPD's
    CPP), 157

civilian radio programs, 139, 142, 155, 158

Clinton, Bill, 237–38

Clurman, David, 65, 67, 72–73, 82

Clurman, Richard M., 95, 96, 103–4,
    108–9, 119, 120, 131–32

CNYC. *See* Council of New York
  Cooperatives (CNYC)

Coalition for the Homeless, 204–6, 209,
    217, 222–24, 223*f*, 225, 230

Codd, Michael, 152, 153–54

Cohen, Norman, 104–5

color, people of. *See* African Americans;
    Latinx; race/racial politics

Commerce and Industry
  Association, 71–72

Commission on the Homeless, 230–31

Community Consultant Contracts
  program, 52

Community Development Block Grant
  (CDBG) program, 36–37, 48–49

community housing movement
  challenges at end of 1970s, 47
  divided by resale price issue, 50
  establishment of DAMP, 46
  groups became part of government
    programs, 52–55
  neighborhood housing movement,
    29–31, 35–40

Community Management program
  contracts toward cooperative
    ownership, 38, 44–45, 46–47
  criticism of community housing
    groups, 53–54
  emphasis on private ownership, 30–31
  resources to buildings in TIL and, 48
  state law required sales to low-income
    people, 49

Community Protection Organization
  (Bedford-Stuyvesant), 141

Community Radio Watch, 142

Community Volunteers for Yellowstone
  Park, 102

Community-Volunteers-in-Parks, 104–5
compassion fatigue, 212, 301n68
Comprehensive Employment and
    Training Act (CETA), 37–38, 116
condominiums
    cooperatives vs., 79–80
    emergence of luxury, 79–80, 82
    loft conversions during fiscal crisis,
        79–82, 88–89
cooperative conversions. *See also* Dearie-
    Goodman law; real estate industry
    growth and regulated tenants, 61–63
    growth in conversions, prices, and
        rents, 91–93
    middle-class exodus and, 59–60
    supported by Koch, 86–89
    tenant protections against
        displacement by, 78–79
cooperative ownership. *See also* renters
        becoming owners
    financing, 72
    legislation to encourage, 72–74
    by low-income tenants, 38, 44,
        48–52, 54–55
    use of J-51 by low income
        families, 176
Council of New York Cooperatives
    (CNYC), 83–85, 93–94
Council of West Side Cooperatives
    (CWSC). *See* Council of New York
    Cooperatives (CNYC)
CPCF. *See* Central Park Community
    Fund (CPCF)
CPTF. *See* Central Park Task
    Force (CPTF)
crime/crime prevention. *See also* broken
    windows theory and policy; citizen
    patrols; law enforcement; police;
    private security guards
    action by city-dwellers, 17,
        135–37, 153–58
    apathy and indifference, 137

association of homeless with, 217–18,
    220–21, 225, 228–29
"crime fighting . . .approaching
    complete breakdown," 137–45
increases in crime, 133–35, 157
Port Authority used as excuse for
    crackdown on homeless, 225
criminal justice system vs. social
    services, 165–66
Cronkite, Walter, 34–35
Crotty, Paul, 195, 196
Crown Heights, 138–39, 159, 176
cultural institutions, supporting
    parks as, 97–98, 107, 112, 113,
    116, 117
Cuomo, Andrew, 230
CWSC. *See* Council of West Side
    Cooperatives (CWSC)

Davis, Gordon J., 114–17, 124, 126
De Blasio, Bill, 238, 239, 310n25
Dearie, John, 75–78, 91–92
Dearie-Goodman law, 77–78, 79, 82,
    84, 264n89
Defilippis, Mike, 225–26
DeLeon, Lon, 153
Democrats
    Democratic National Convention
        (1980), police removal of
        homeless, 204
    liberals fundamental to market
        turn, 4–5
Department of Alternative Management
    Program (DAMP), 46–47,
    48–49, 52
Department of Housing Preservation
    and Development (HPD),
    45–47, 49, 50
Depsey, Oberia, and Baptist
    volunteers, 141
deterrence value, of neighborhood
    action, 139, 145, 149, 153–54, 158

development. *See also* tax incentives
  gentrification, arson, and reforming
    J-51 tax incentives, 184–88
  harnessing private sector for public
    amenities, 192–97, 198
  incentives and urban crisis, 17, 170–78
  new era of luxury housing, 188–92
  policies reducing low-income
    housing, 211
Di Roma, Richard, 135
Dillon, Richard, 164
Dinkins, David, 198–99, 222–25, 227,
  228–30, 231–32
Direct Sales program, 44–45
Ditmas Park Association, 159–60
Dogin, Henry, 155–56
Douglas Elliman (real estate firm), 81,
  92–93, 191
drug abuse, crime and homelessness, 135,
  162–63, 186
Dunn, Danny, 216–17

Eddy, Norman, 36
Eisenberg, Edward, 146
Elliott, Bruce, 139
Elliott, Osborn, 154, 173
Esnard, Robert, 183
eviction/noneviction plans, 73, 74, 75–76,
  82, 88, 90, 91–92
"Eyes on the Street" program, 134

Federation of Laurelton Block
  Associations in Queens, 143
Felstein, Carol, 183
Fernandez, Dolores, 186
Figuera, Donna, 185
fires. *See* arson and fires
fiscal crisis
  as catalyst for market turn,
    10–12, 14–15
  debates over renewal of J-51 tax
    incentives, 175–76

homelessness trend hastened
    by, 233–34
  impact on Central Park, 110–11,
    112–13
  impact on New York policing, 1–2,
    153, 159
  impact on public parks, 95–96, 100,
    102–5, 115, 131–32, 278n191
  impacts on housing and development,
    35–40, 79, 167, 172, 198–99
Fitzpatrick, Paul, 147–48
Ford, Gerald, 11, 13, 37–38, 47, 159
Ford Foundation, support for Urban
  Park Plazas, 119, 120–21
Fort Tryon Park, 128
Fort Washington Men's Shelter, 210
foundations. *See also specific foundations*
  Bryant Park business donations
    outpaced by, 124
  involvement in parks needed, 96,
    112, 128–29
  solicited for homesteading financing,
    38, 101–2
  Task Force funded by Brooke
    Astor's, 106–7
421-a tax incentives. *See also* affordable
  housing
  criticized for increasing real estate
    prices, 170
  incentivized real estate
    conversions, 174
  subsidized luxury housing, 177, 180–81,
    188–91, 196, 238–39
  tax abatement for new housing
    projects, 168–73
14th Street Union Square BID, 227–28
Freeman, Joshua B., 8
Friedman, Stanley M., 167–68
Friends of Central Park, 272n54

Galleria condominiums, 80
Gartner, Jerome, 95

GCP. *See* Grand Central
      Partnership (GCP)
Geary, Robert, 133
General Atlantic Realty Corporation, 195
gentrification, 48–49, 93, 184–88, 190,
      191, 198
Gilder, Richard, 108–9, 115, 127–28. *See
      also* Central Park Community
      Fund (CPCF)
Gimbels property renovation, 219
Giuliani, Rudolph
   adopted positions of Manhattan
      Institute, 235
   credited with ushering in privatization
      policies, 2, 238
   homeless policies, 231–34
Glaser, Herman, 59–60
Gliedman, Anthony, 51–52, 183, 207
Glover, Richard J., 167–68
Goetz, Bernhard, 162–63
Goldin, Harrison, 182–83
Goldstein, Roslyn, 212
Gotbaum, Betsy, 227
Gottehrer, Barry, 1
Gottfried, Richard N., 187–88
government. *See also* civic services;
      local officials; US Department of
      Housing and Urban Development
      (HUD); US Department
      of Justice
   blaming victims for failures, 232
   changing expectations from, 236–38
   federal and state cutbacks in
      social programs, 162, 183–84,
      201–2, 206–8
   federal urban policy changes as
      catalyst for market turn, 12–13
   homesteaders looked for funding from
      federal, 37–38
   oversight and housing policy,
      169–70, 188
graffiti removal, 124, 126, 214–15, 221

Grand Central Partnership (GCP), 203–
      4, 215–16, 219–20, 221, 226, 230, 231
Grand Central Terminal, 214
Grannis, Pete, 182
Great American Realty Corporation, 74
Great Society initiatives, 13
Gregorian, Vartan, 125, 126
Grosberg, Lawrence M., 179, 180
Guardian Angels, 157

Hayes, Robert M., 204–6, 212, 217, 232
HDA. *See* Housing and Development
      Administration, New York (HDA)
Heckscher, August, 99–100
Heintz, Jeffrey, 48
Heiskell, Andrew, 122, 123, 124–25
Helmsley, Harry, 71, 75–78, 91–92, 94
Henry Luce Foundation, 124
Herald Tribune, four-month series, 1, 9
Hetherington, Neil, 164
High Visibility Patrol, 160–61
Hoey, Ray, 84–85
Holmes, Edward "Moose," 42
homeless shelters
   building vs. helping homeless, 208–10,
      229–30, 231
   homeless referred to, 224–27
   lawsuit regarding city policies, 204–5
   "not-for-profitization," 230, 232
   for-profit, 239, 310n25
   unsafe conditions, 205–6, 207, 210–11,
      213, 217, 224–25, 230
homelessness
   curfews to prevent sleeping in
      parks, 227–28
   Dinkins and perpetual homeless
      crisis, 222–31
   emergence of homeless
      advocacy, 204–6
   Giuliani's policies, 231–34
   increased services with harsher
      policing, 165–66, 230, 232

homelessness (*cont.*)
    revitalized public space and, 17–18,
        200–4, 214–24
    seeming intractability, 210–14, 233
    struggle for government
        resources, 206–10
homeownership. *See also* cooperative
        ownership; renters becoming
        owners; urban homesteading of
        low-income housing
    appeal to housing advocates, 30–31
    doubled in Manhattan, 238–39
    foreign purchasers of New York
        condominiums and cooperatives, 81
    by middle class, 59, 260n5
    promotion, 12, 16, 82–83
    seen as more beneficial than renting,
        85–86, 89–90, 91–92, 93
homesteading. *See* urban homesteading
        of low-income housing
Hopkins, Harold, 210
Hopper, Kim, 204–6, 212, 217
Hotel Association of New York
        City, 175–76
hotels, single-room occupancy (SROs)
    impact of upgrading on low-income
        tenants, 176, 179–80, 192
    J-51 reforms and, 187, 295n114
    targeted for upgraded housing, 173,
        175, 181–82
    tenant harassment, 186–87, 208
housing. *See also* affordable housing;
        development; in rem properties;
        renters becoming owners; urban
        homesteading of low-income
        housing
    during 1980s, 47–55
    federal policies helped drain city's tax
        base, 12–13
Housing and Community Development
        Act (1974), 36
Housing and Development
        Administration, New York (HDA),
        39–40, 63–64, 171

Housing Conservation Coordinators
        (HCC), 53
Housing Trust Fund, 192, 194
Hoving, Thomas, 99
Howard, Claire, 143–44
Howard, Ella, 201–2, 204
HPD. *See* Department of
        Housing Preservation and
        Development (HPD)
HUD. *See* US Department of Housing
        and Urban Development (HUD)

ICIB. *See* Industrial and Commercial
        Incentive Board (ICIB)
IDA. *See* Industrial Development
        Agency (IDA)
improvement associations, 160
in rem properties, 27, 35, 43–47, 48–49,
        52, 56–57, 97–98
incentive zoning, 192–93
inclusionary zoning, 192, 193–94, 195
Industrial and Commercial Incentive
        Board (ICIB), 173, 174,
        180–81, 182–83
Industrial Development Agency (IDA),
        173, 174
Industrial Development, lists of state
        incentives, 173
inequality, New York epitomizes
        US, 239–41
insider pricing, 82, 89–90, 91
Interfaith Civilian Patrol, Riverdale, 158
Interstate Highway Act (1956), 12
Interstate Industrial Protection
        Co., 148
Ives, Brewster, 81, 92–93

James Felt & Co., 71
Jethwani, Mohan, 104
J-51 tax incentives. *See also* affordable
        housing; hotels, single-room
        occupancy (SROs)
    ban on benefits for SRO conversions,
        187, 295n114

debates and calls for reform, 175–82, 183–87

impact on low-income populations, 170, 176–77, 179–80, 199

incentivized real estate conversions, 174

originally designed to upgrade cold water buildings, 168–70

subsidized luxury housing, 177, 180–81, 188–91

Jinkins, Edward, 142

jobs loss (1960–1970), 10

Johnson, Lyndon B., 13

Kahn, Thomas G., 228

Kansas City sidewalk ownership, 240

Kelling, George L., 221–22, 225

Kennedy, Ethel, 34–35

Kiepper, Alan, 196, 221

Kiley, Robert R., 221, 224–25

Klein, Laurence, 180, 208

Koch, Ed. *See also* J-51 tax incentives

fostering resident participation against crime, 157

housing policy under, 45–49, 52, 56–57, 86–89

market turn and pursuit of private enterprise, 4–5, 9–10, 14–15, 237–38

public park issues and, 114–17, 124, 126, 227, 233

removal of homeless from public spaces, 224, 229, 233

root causes and solutions for homelessness ignored, 202–3, 206–10, 211–12, 216–17, 218–19, 220–21, 222–24

tax incentives as principal development strategy, 170, 178–79, 180, 181–84, 186–91, 193–98, 293n85, 295n114

ten-year Housing Plan, 297n177

Kovner, Matt, 85

La Guardia, Fiorello, 7

land use and urban planners, 168

landlords. *See also* real estate industry; rent control

conversion of housing into higher-end rentals, 179

found guilty of forced conversion deals, 73

harassment of low-income tenants, 178, 179, 185–88, 208

incentives for tenants to convert, 82, 89–90, 91

landlord desertion, 23–25, 43–46, 63

use of J-51 tax provisions, 176, 184

Lang, Martin, 104, 121–22

Lasdon, Douglas H., 212, 217, 229–30, 232

Latinx. *See also* race/racial politics

involved in urban homesteading, 29

as owners of converted units, 267n150

Puerto Ricans, loan approved after protest, 36

radio motor patrol in Manhattan, 158

Laven, Charles S., 31–32, 36

law enforcement. *See also* crime/crime prevention; police; private security guards; security services

government hiring of private security guards, 163

growth in public and private personnel across US, 146

lack of support for Operation Interlock, 152

private guards outnumbered police officers, 162, 163, 238

private sector's effect on policing of New York streets, 159–66

Law Enforcement Assistance Administration (LEAA), 154, 155–56

Law Enforcement Task Force, 137–38

Lefkowitz, Louis J., 65, 67, 74, 78

Legal Action Center for the Homeless, 212

"Lend a Hand and Improve Your Block," 154–55

Leventhal, Nathan, 46–47, 49, 50, 180, 181, 200–1, 208
Levy, Robert, 212
Limited Profit Housing Companies Law (Mitchell-Lama/1955), 169–70
Lindsay, John V.
  crime reduction measures under, 134, 135, 137–38, 142, 143–44, 151, 153–54
  housing issues and, 26–27, 32, 35, 58, 62, 63–66
  maintenance of resources, 10, 14, 177–78, 196–97
  open to role of private sector in governance, 4–5, 9, 237–38
  public park issues and, 95–96, 99–100, 103–4, 108–9
  tax incentives pursued, 168–69, 170–72, 173, 176–77
litter
  litter brigade refuse bags, 107, 108*f*
  vandalism and park maintenance, 100, 101*f*
local officials. *See also* civic services; police; transportation facilities
  accepting expanded role in governance for private actors, 2–3, 4–5, 8, 15, 93, 103–5
  concerns about losing autonomy over parks, 110
  growing support for cooperatives, 26–27, 59–60
  growing support for private guards patrolling streets, 151, 160
loft conversions, 81, 82, 84, 174
loitering laws, constitutional concerns, 216–17, 218–19
Los Angeles Times, ad for owner-occupied building, 71
low-income housing. *See* affordable housing; public housing; urban homesteading of low-income housing

Luxemburg, Marc, 83–84
luxury housing
  condominiums, 79–80, 82
  subsidized by 421-a and J-51 tax incentives, 177, 180–81, 188–91, 196

MAA. *See* Morningside Area Alliance (MAA)
Maccabees citizen patrol, 138–39
Madison Square Park, 118–21, 228
Manhattan Beach Community Group (MBCG), 145–46, 159–61
Manhattan Beach, resident patrol, 139, 140*f*
Manhattan Cooperator, The, 85–86, 88, 90, 92
Manhattan Institute, 235
Manton, Thomas, 188
market turn, catalysts for
  federal urban policy agendas, 9–10, 12–13
  Koch's tenure as mayor, 9–10, 14–15
  racial politics, 9–10, 13–14
  worsening economic conditions, 9–12
marketization. *See also* neoliberal marketization; private sector
  across United States, 240
  cannot be separated from racial politics, 13–14
  experiments facilitation of, 3–4, 6
  government resources deployed to facilitate, 18–19
  homeownership aided shift to, 61, 94
  opposition to reliance on market solutions, 170, 237–38, 241
  processes continued under Bloomberg and De Blasio, 238
  as result of local actors, 3–6, 131–32
Marshall, Alton, 150–51
MBCG. *See* Manhattan Beach Community Group (MBCG)
McDermott, Eugene, 160–61

McDermott, Pat, 157

McKechnie, William, 220

mentally ill
  character deficiencies blamed for
    homelessness, 232–33
  deinstitutionalization of hospitals for,
    202, 207–8, 212
  Kelling's conflation of homeless
    with, 222
  Koch's depiction of homeless as, 202–
    3, 209–10, 212, 301n68
  one-third of homeless as, 211

Mercury Intelligence Service, 145–46

Messinger, Ruth, 179–81, 186–87

Metro-North Commuter Railroad, 214,
  215–17, 219–20

Metropolitan Life Insurance Company
  (MetLife), 74–75, 118, 120

Metropolitan Transportation Authority
  (MTA). *See also* Operation
  Enforcement; subways
  aggressive policing against homeless,
    220–26, 233
  renovation, 214–15, 219–20
  rider comments, 216, 217

middle class
  cooperative ownership growth,
    82–89, 92
  exodus to suburbs, 8–9, 12, 59–60,
    63–64, 69
  lofts converted to cooperatives, 81
  opposition to cooperative conversions,
    58, 60–61, 65–71, 66f, 264n85
  success contrasted with low-income
    residents' experience, 93–94

Midtown area, vacant structures
  increasing, 167–68

Midwood Kings Highway Development
  Corporation (MKDC), 156, 157

Miller, Robert, 159–60

minorities. *See* African Americans;
  Latinx; race/racial politics

Mitchell-Lama law. *See* Limited
  Profit Housing Companies Law
  (Mitchell-Lama/1955)

MKDC. *See* Midwood Kings
  Highway Development
  Corporation (MKDC)

MoMA. *See* Museum of Modern
  Art (MoMA)

Mondale, Walter, 42, 55–56

Morningside Area Alliance (MAA),
  147–50, 160, 164, 166

Morningside Community Patrol (MCP),
  148f, 148–49

Morris Park Community Association, 158

Morton, James P., 31–32

Moses, Robert, 98–99

Mosque of Islamic Brotherhood, 38

Mount Eden Park, 102–3

Moynihan, Patrick, 113

MTA. *See* Metropolitan Transportation
  Authority (MTA)

Mulhearn, J. R., 123

Murdaugh, Marshall, 229

Murphy, George, 101–2

Murphy, Patrick V., 145–46

Museum of Modern Art (MoMA), 80

Nathan, Jason, 63–64

National Institute of Justice
  (NIJ), 161–62

National Sheriffs' Association, 154

nationwide developments
  in crime prevention, 154, 161–62
  housing-oriented tax incentives as
    development strategy, 173–74
  loss of faith in government, 9
  urban homesteading, 28, 35–43

Nazario, Rabbit, 39

neighborhood housing movement. *See*
  community housing movement

Neighborhood Preservation Areas
  (NPAs), 187–88

Neighborhood Watch, 154, 162
neoliberal marketization, 4–5, 6,
    93–94, 237–41
New Deal, 7–8, 12, 98–99
New York Building Congress, 198–99
New York City Housing Authority
    (NYCHA), 141–42
"New York City in Crisis"
    (Gottehrer), 1, 9
New York City Partnership, 200–1
New York Civil Liberties Union
    (NYCLU), 212
New York Community Trust, 124
New York Council for Civic
    Affairs, 59–60
New York Habitat, 85–88, 87*f*
New York Public Library (NYPL), 121,
    122, 123–24, 131–32
New York Realty Owners Association
    (NYROA), 62
New York Self-Help Handbook (1977), 155
New York Society of Architects, 175–76
New York State Tenant and
    Neighborhood Coalition, 190
New York Telephone, 123
New York Tenants Legislative
    Coalition, 77
New York Times series on how to "restore
    New York City," 228–29
New York Urban Coalition, 172
New York Zoological Society, 114
New Yorkers for Equitable
    Development, 192
NIJ. *See* National Institute of
    Justice (NIJ)
90th Street West Park Block Association,
    145, 156
Nixon, Richard M., 13, 36, 47
noneviction plans. *See* eviction/
    noneviction plans
NPAs. *See* Neighborhood Preservation
    Areas (NPAs)

NYCHA. *See* New York City Housing
    Authority (NYCHA)
NYCLU. *See* New York Civil Liberties
    Union (NYCLU)
NYPL. *See* New York Public
    Library (NYPL)
NYROA. *See* New York Realty Owners
    Association (NYROA)

O'Brien, Edward, 205
O'Donoghue, John R., 74
Office of Community Anti-Crime
    Programs (OCACP), 155–56
Office of Parks Partnership, 103–4
Office of Special Improvement (OSI), 27
134th Street Partnership, 220
Operation Alternative, 225–26
Operation Enforcement, 220–22,
    224, 225
Operation Interlock, 151–52, 161
Orsid Realty, 79
OSI. *See* Office of Special
    Improvement (OSI)
Osman, Suleiman, 84, 143, 253n6,
    278n191
Ott, Carol J., 85
Our Town, CWSC response to
    article, 83–84

Page, Mark, 230
panhandling, 201, 212–13, 217–18, 221, 225
Park Terrace Gardens, 67–69
Parkchester, 74–78, 91–92, 94
parking meters, privatization of, 240
parks. *See also* Bryant Park; Central
    Park; Central Park Conservancy;
    litter; Madison Square Park; public-
    private partnerships; volunteers
city inability to manage, 96–105,
    114, 131–32
deterioration, 10–11, 12, 95–99, 115–16
homeless in, 226–28

1970s as transformative decade for New York's, 128–32

private funding and community disparities, 126–27, 129–31, 240, 269–70n16, 278n184

success of non-traditional programs, 99–100

Parks Council, 100, 104–5, 107, 123–24, 126–27

Parks Department. *See also* Urban Park Plazas (UPP)

budget and personnel crises, 104, 129–30

Central Park Task Force established within, 106–7

corporations as fiscal benefactors of, 120

history of New York's urban parks and, 98–99

reliance on federal programs, 116

systematic study under Davis, 114

volunteer numbers compared to employees, 104–5

patrol of city streets. *See* citizen patrols; crime/crime prevention; police

Patton, Kenneth, 172–73

PDC. *See* People's Development Corporation (PDC)

Pelham Bay Park, 130

Penn Station, 210, 213–14, 216, 219, 220

People's Development Corporation (PDC)

"Homesteading in the Slums" (*Saturday Review* cover), 41f

HUD and other grants, 39–40, 41–42

self-help initiatives, 40, 42–43

South Bronx homesteading project, 20, 39–42

Peterson, Paul, 168

philanthropic community. *See* foundations

Phoenix Cooperative in Central Harlem, 24–25

Pinkerton Agency, 159–61

planned shrinkage, 37, 38–39

playgrounds, maintained by parents near Central Park, 106

police. *See also* broken windows theory and policy; crime/crime prevention; law enforcement; private security guards

civilianization of, 162–63

cooperation with private guards, 145, 149, 160–62, 164–65, 219

expanded powers to act against homeless, 211–12, 225

inability to deal with rising crime, 133–34, 135, 136, 137–41, 145

patrols and guards as supplemental to, 136, 152

reduced numbers due to economic downturns, 153, 157

resident patrols and, 142, 146–47, 153–54, 157

retired personnel as private guards, 160, 164

POPS. *See* privately owned public spaces (POPS)

Port Authority, 213–14, 216–19, 225–26, 231

Post, Herschel, Jr., 100

Powell, Lillian, 153

Private Lives/Public Spaces (Baxter and Hopper), 205–6

private sector. *See also* affordable housing; businesses and corporations; city-dwellers; foundations; marketization; parks; public-private partnerships; real estate industry

actors enabled by residents and officials, 5–6

care and management of parks by, 96, 97–98, 110–11, 122–28

homeless services as replacements rather than models, 229–31, 232, 239

private sector (*cont.*)
 impact on policing of New York
  streets, 159–66
 as New York's principal economic
  engine, 8
 pursuit of private enterprise, 4–5,
  14–15, 175–84, 235–36
 support for parks and other public
  spaces, 164
private security guards. *See also* crime/
  crime prevention; law enforcement;
  Operation Alternative; Operation
  Enforcement; police; security
  services
 acceptance of private actors patrolling
  streets, 136–37, 144–53
 advantages and drawbacks,
  165–66, 240
 as alternative to citizen patrols, 135–36
 beholden only to employers,
  159–62, 163–65
 considered in Brooklyn Heights, 134
 policing of homeless, 210–11,
  219–20
privately owned public spaces (POPS),
  192–93, 196, 199
private-public partnerships. *See* public-
  private partnerships
privatization. *See* marketization;
  private sector
property values
 concern over higher, 92–93
 cooperative conversions and,
  68–69, 71
 fluctuations during fiscal crisis, 13–14,
  17–18, 79–80
 homeless (cartoon) and, 203*f*
 park revitalization and, 97–98, 118,
  120, 128–29
 in rem property, 45, 49
public housing
 eschewed by homesteaders, 31, 32

patrols spread throughout
  projects, 141–42
public space. *See also* crime/crime
  prevention; development;
  homelessness; parks; privately
  owned public spaces (POPS);
  transportation facilities
 citizens pushed for solutions for home
  and, 3, 15–18
 protecting enhanced value, 17–18, 116,
  120, 200–4, 233–34
 removal of homeless in wealthier
  areas, 229
public-private partnerships. *See also*
  volunteers
 parks, 16–17, 114–21, 128–30
 urban renewal, 8, 19, 41–42

Queens
 community crime prevention efforts,
  143, 151–52, 153, 155
 park improvements, 102, 104–5
Queens County Overall Economic
  Development Corporation, 160
Quintano, Annie, 210

race/racial politics. *See also* African
  Americans; citizen patrols;
  homelessness; Latinx; People's
  Development Corporation (PDC)
 catalysts for market turn, 9–10, 13–14
 citizen anti-crime efforts,
  138–39, 157–58
 discrimination based on income
  and, 23–24, 27, 93–94, 162–63,
  165, 166
 growth of homesteading in poor
  communities, 16, 20–22, 24, 29–30
 impacts of development, 44, 170, 186,
  233–34, 239–40
 park disparities due to class and, 99,
  126–27, 129–31

perceptions of homeless influenced by,
201, 212–13, 217–18, 233, 239
Rangel, Charles, 113
Reagan, Ronald, 116
real estate. *See also* property values
depression following 1987
crash, 198–99
rising prices/rents impacting low-
income people, 170, 176
Real Estate Board of New York
(REBNY), 63, 74, 183–84, 186, 193,
194, 198–99. *See also* Tompkins,
Rexford E.
real estate industry. *See also* Dearie-
Goodman law; development; rent
control
conversion benefits questioned by
tenants, 67, 68–70, 93
enthusiasm for conversions, 58–60,
61–63, 64–65, 71–74
fueled Koch's campaigns, 184
lobbying for developer
exemptions, 190
support for tax incentives, 172–73
REBNY. *See* Real Estate Board of New
York (REBNY)
Recchiuti, John Louis, 7
Regan, Edward, 188
Renigades of East Harlem
formerly incarcerated young men of
color, 25–26
inspiration for other groups, 39, 54
rehabilitation of abandoned buildings,
26f, 27, 31, 33–35
rent control
affordability vs., 240
blamed for landlord desertion,
23–24, 63
landlords and real estate industry goal
to escape, 58–59, 60–61, 62, 94
opposition to conversion in buildings
under, 70, 76

policies diminished apartments under,
90–91, 92, 238–39
political impasses and, 63–64
rent stabilization laws, 64–66, 82,
90–91, 268n158
renters. *See* tenants
renters becoming owners. *See also*
Parkchester
growth of middle-class cooperative
owners, 83–89, 92
homeownership and the fiscal
crisis, 78–83
middle-class opposition to cooperative
conversions, 58, 60–61, 65–71
overcoming middle-class opposition,
61, 70–74, 82–83, 89–91
owning a piece of New York, 89–94
promoting homeownership in city of
renters, 61–67, 71–74
Republicans
noneviction plans, 90
elite involvement in parks, 269–70n16
Republic National Bank, 123
resale price of $250 per unit, 46, 49–50,
52
residents. *See* city-dwellers
Reyes, Paul, 43
Rice, Henry Hart, 71
Riverside Drive Tenants'
Associations, 149–50
Riverside Park Fund, 128–29
Roberts, Leona, 71–72
Rockefeller, Nelson, 62, 72
Rockefeller Brothers Fund, 123–24
Rockefeller Center, 150, 164
Rodgers, Bertram, 148f, 148
Rogers, Elizabeth Barlow. *See* Barlow,
Elizabeth "Betsy"
Roosevelt, Franklin. *See* New Deal
Rose, Marshall, 124, 125
Rosenberg, Benjamin, 133, 134
Rosenthal, Benjamin, 78–79, 92–93

Rudin, Lewis, 150, 151–52, 161
Rueda, Ramon, 39–41

Salman, Barry, 175–76
San Francisco low-income housing
    policy, 192, 198
Saunders, Rajah, 210
Savas, E. S., 109–10
Savoy, Rita, 64–65
Schmertz, Herbert, 128
Schneider, Eric C., 134
Schneider, Leon D., 175
Schraeter, Arnold, 139
Schrage, Samuel, 138
Schur, Robert, 27
Schwarzer, Edward, 145
Second Century Fund for Central
    Park, 112
security services
    mixed response to hiring private
        guards, 148–50
    preferred to focus on private
        premises, 147–48
    private guards for benefit of those who
        paid, not general public, 145–46
    problems with fraud, corruption, and
        inefficiency, 146–47
    professionalization and regulation
        improved, 164–65
self-help initiatives. *See also* block
    associations; South Bronx; sweat
    equity; urban homesteading of low-
    income housing
    homesteading as, 16, 28, 34–35
    need for government support
        minimized, 22–23, 31, 34, 37–38,
        42–43, 253n6
    PDC support, 40, 42–43
    self-help initiatives, 55–56
Settlement Housing Fund, 176
752 West End Avenue Tenants
    Association, 180

Shapiro, Richard, 157
Shelter Security Task Force, 210–11
shelters. *See* homeless shelters
Shemtov, Mendel, 159
Shkuda, Aaron, 84
Shostal, H. Claude, 175
Siegel, Norman, 212
Simon, Donald, 118–20, 121,
    122–23, 131–32
skid row (Bowery), 201
Sliwa, Curtis, 157, 162–63
Smadbeck, Louis, 60
social democracy
    austerity measures altered city's, 11–12
    contradictions of postwar
        liberalism, 12–13
    New York's version unlike anyplace
        else, 8
social services. *See* civic services
Soffer, Jonathan, 4–5, 47, 157, 297n177
SoHo, 81, 84, 174
Soros, George, 108–9, 115, 127–28. *See
    also* Central Park Community
    Fund (CPCF)
Soto, Danny, 42
South Bronx
    Koch's preference for private
        sector, 47–48
    "self-help" initiatives, 2–3
    Washington Avenue project,
        20, 39–42
South Street Seaport security team, 164
Southern Queens Park Association
    (SQPA), 102
special assessment districts, 160
speculators, activists worked to keep in
    rem property away from, 45
Spinola, Steven, 198–99
SROs. *See* hotels, single-room
    occupancy (SROs)
St. Francis Residence, 206
St. Georges, Philip, 26–27, 31–32, 44

St. John the Divine, 31–32
St. Nicholas Tenant Patrol (Harlem), 140*f*, 141–42
Standon, Judy, 157
Starr, Roger, 35, 37, 39–40, 172
State Comptroller audits of zoning bonuses, 196
Stein, Andrew, 113
Steisel, Norman, 224–25
Stern, Henry, 128, 227
Sternlieb, George, 63, 177, 191
Stewart, James K., 161–62
stock market crash of 1987, 198
Stolzer, Alan, 158
"Stop Cooperative Coercion Now!" 67, 68*f*
Stuhlbarg, William, 95, 96, 121
suburbanization
    exodus of white, middle-class residents, 8–9, 59–60, 63–64, 69
    promotion by federal housing policies, 12–13
subways
    crime in, 157, 162–63
    Dinkins enforcement of broken windows policy, 229
    entrances as bonus amenities, 193, 196
    poster on why people sleep in, 223*f*
    rebuilding after deferred maintenance, 214–15, 233
sweat equity, 31, 33*f*, 33–35, 41*f*, 43. *See also* self-help initiatives
Sweat Equity Program, 27

TACC. *See* Tenants Against Cooperative Conversion (TACC)
Tammany Hall, patronage appointments for park commissioners, 98–99
Task Force on City-Owned Property, 45, 48–49
tax incentives. *See also* Beame, Abraham; 421-a tax incentives; J-51 tax incentives; Koch, Ed; Lindsay, John

affordable housing intention abandoned, 171–72
    as benefit for all population groups, 191–92
    builder resale of certificates and credits, 194–97
    Clinton's use of, 237–38
    importance to city's economic base, 178–79
    for middle- and upper-income residents, 47–48
    as principal development strategy, 167–70, 197–99
    public criticism of tax breaks, 170, 172, 178, 179–81, 182–83, 187–88
    tax deductions for Central Park supporters, 118
tax policy
    foreclosure policy and landlord desertion, 43–46
    political influence of cooperative owners, 93–94
    tax revenue lost (1970–1974), 10
Tenant Interim Lease (TIL) program, 46–49, 52, 54–55
tenant ownership
    HPD refusal to sell apartments to TIL residents, 48–49
    keeping in rem buildings in hands of tenants, 44–45
    problems with institutionalization, 53
tenants. *See also* citizen patrols; hotels, single-room occupancy (SROs); Parkchester; rent control
    acceptance of conversions, 93
    displaced by conversions, 78
    organization of, 28–31, 69–70, 77, 179
    protections enacted in multiple cities, 78–79
    tenant organizations vs. landlords and real estate industry, 60–61, 62, 65–70

Tenants Against Cooperative Conversion
  (TACC), 67–70, 76–77
Terlecky, Peter, 161
Terner, Donald, 31–32, 33–34
"32 Ways Your Time or Money Can
  Rescue Central Park," 111
Thompson, Lynette, 217
325 West 86th Street co-op, 200–1
TIL. *See* Tenant Interim Lease (TIL)
  program
Tompkins, Rexford E., 58–59, 61–62
Tompkins Square Park, 128, 227
transportation facilities. *See also*
  Metropolitan Transportation
  Authority (MTA); police; subways
  aggressive policing against
    homeless, 220–27
  homelessness and, 17–18,
    203–4, 213–24
  measures to discourage
    homeless, 216–20
  Operation Alternative, 225–26
  Operation Enforcement, 220–22,
    224, 225
  referral to shelters services for
    homeless, 224–27
Trazoff, Suzanne, 211
Trobe, Robert, 207–8
Trump Tower tax abatement, 188–90,
  189*f*, 191
Tudor City Association, 226

UHAB. *See* Urban Homesteading
  Assistance Board (UHAB)
Union Carbide move due to park
  crime, 95
Union Square Park, 227–28
United Council of Harlem
  Organizations, 141
United Homeless Organization, 222
UPP. *See* Urban Park Plazas (UPP)
Urban Crime Prevention Program, 156

urban crisis
  development incentives and, 170–78
  homelessness trend begun by, 233–34
  responses by New York locals, 2–6
  signs of New York's, 8–9
  term especially used in late 1960s, 1–2
Urban Homesteading Assistance
  Board (UHAB)
  homesteading's most influential
    proponent, 31–35, 38
  securing federal funds, 36–38
  support for cooperatives, 44, 46
  sweat equity and self-help forums, 33*f*
  work with PDC, 39–40
urban homesteading of low-income
  housing. *See also* "self-help"
  initiatives; sweat equity
  definition, 20–21
  homesteaders imaged as inept or
    lazy, 26–27
  left and right positions brought
    together by, 22–23, 43
  as local response to low-income
    housing crisis, 20–23
  on the national stage, 28, 35–43
  as private-led rejuvenation
    initiative, 55–57
  ripple effect of projects, 38
  urban crisis and, 23–31
Urban Park Plazas (UPP), 119–21
urban renewal. *See also* public housing
  distinguished from 421-a and J-51 by
    government oversight, 169–70
  public-private partnerships, 8, 19, 41–42
US Department of Housing and Urban
  Development (HUD)
  Community Management
    contracts, 38
  first sweat equity homesteading
    project, 40
  housing units sold to cities for
    homesteading, 28

Public Housing Urban Initiatives
Anti-Crime Demonstration, 156
US Department of Justice. *See also*
Law Enforcement Assistance
Administration (LEAA)
National Institute of Justice
(NIJ), 161–62
study on private security guards, 146
Urban Crime Prevention Program, 156

Van Cortland Park, 130
Vermeer Tenants Organization
(VeTO), 69–70
vigilantism
citizen patrols disparaged as, 154
fear regarding citizen patrols and, 142,
143–44, 157, 162–63
high-profile instances, 162–63
Villanueva, Juan, 42
VISTA. *See* Volunteers in Service to
America (VISTA)
volunteers. *See also* citizen patrols
Central Park, 107–9, 110, 111–12
city-dwellers caring for parks, 15, 16–17,
96, 103*f*, 128, 130
involvement in public services, 154–55
Mount Eden Park, 102–3
support of local officials for
park, 103–5
Yorkville park space, 100–2
Volunteers in Service to America
(VISTA), 154–55
Volunteers of America, 224–25

Wackstein, Nancy, 226–27, 228
Wagner, Robert F., Jr., 9, 192–93
Wallace, Lila, 115

Walsh, Albert A., 171
Walsh, Pauline, 102–3
Walsh, Robert, 227–28
War on Poverty, 34
Washington, DC, loss of rental units, 78
Weiner, Walter, 123
West Side Tenant's Union, 179
Whalen, John J., 77
Whalen, Richard, 1
"When City Hall Fails, Do It
Yourself," 230
Whitaker, Mark, 200–1
White, Kevin, 28
Williams, Mason B., 7–8
Wilson, James Q. *See* broken windows
theory and policy
Wilson, Jeffrey, 216
Wilson, Malcolm, 77
windfall profits, 89–90
Witte, Arnold, 71–72
women's shelters, unsafe
conditions, 210
Woodsworth, Michael, 34
World War II, support for government
programs, 7–8
Worrell, Ekins, 155

Yorkville, park cleanups by
volunteers, 100–2
Young, William B., Jr., 213
Youth Legal Services, 30

zoning laws
during mid-1960s, 260n6
shifting orientation of, 192–95,
196–97, 238
in SoHo, 84